THE JEKYLL ISLAND COTTAGE COLONY

JUNE HALL McCASH

THE UNIVERSITY OF GEORGIA PRESS
ATHENS AND LONDON

Published by the University of Georgia Press
Athens, Georgia 30602
© 1998 by June Hall McCash
All rights reserved

Printed in the United States of America

02 01 00 99 98 C 5 4 3 2 1

Library of Congress Cataloging in Publication Data

McCash, June Hall.
The Jekyll Island cottage colony / June Hall McCash.
p. cm.
Includes bibliographical references and index.
ISBN 0-8203-1928-7 (alk. paper)
1. Historic buildings—Georgia—Jekyll Island.
2. Dwellings—Georgia—Jekyll Island.   3. Jekyll Island (Ga.)—
Social life and customs.   4. Jekyll Island (Ga.)—Biography.
5. Architecture, Domestic—Georgia—Jekyll Island.   I. Title.
F292.G58M38   1998
975.8′742—dc21   96-54871

British Library Cataloging in Publication Data available

TO BART

in loving memory

⸬

CONTENTS

PREFACE

This book could never have been written without the loving and productive partnership I enjoyed with my late husband, William Barton McCash, whose influence may be seen in the finished volume and whose presence I felt throughout its writing. Research for the book was begun in 1989 shortly after the completion of our earlier co-authored volume *The Jekyll Island Club: Southern Haven for America's Millionaires* (University of Georgia Press, 1989) and during joint noninstructional assignments that freed us from our teaching and administrative duties at Middle Tennessee State University in order to do the necessary research. Bart, who chaired the History Department at Middle Tennessee State University, was a careful and well-organized research partner, an excellent scholar, and a thinker who was at the same time both impassioned and analytical. We worked well together in a synergistic relationship and with a continued sense of intellectual excitement as we pored over documents in private collections and archives throughout the country. A good portion of the research for the present volume had been completed by the date of his untimely death on February 8, 1991, and we had just begun to write. In fact, he drafted an original version of the Horton section of the first chapter as well as early renderings of the Rockefeller section of the chapter on Indian Mound and the Crane Cottage chapter. His death put an end to the project for five years.

Although I made an effort to continue working on the book in those early years after his death, I was unable to do so productively. Working without him on this project that had been such an important part of our life together was simply impossible for a time. However, by 1995, I felt ready to take up the project again. Coming back to it after such a long hiatus seemed surprisingly natural, and its completion has given me a great sense of satisfaction. No doubt it would have been a better work had Bart had a continued hand in writing it, for well do I remember, as we worked together on the earlier book, the constant revising of drafts back and forth as we read each other's work with a critical eye. And I have longed for that other mind to help me stretch my own. Despite his absence throughout most of the writing of this volume, much of the credit for its completion belongs to him. He left me the legacy of his vision, his diligence, his orderly research, and his persistent belief that the good can always be better, a legacy I have tried to bring to the writing of this book. And I have felt his presence encouraging me throughout the process. Needless to say, it is with continued love and admiration that I dedicate this book to his memory.

Certain matters should be clarified at the outset. The spelling of Jekyll Island was legally changed by the Georgia State Legislature in 1929; thus all sources cited before that date spelled it with a single

l. In order to avoid confusion on the part of the reader, I have opted in this volume, which is not chronologically organized, for the contemporary spelling except in instances when I was quoting a source that used the original spelling. One further documentary consideration: In order to avoid excessive footnoting, I have omitted pointing out in each instance that the dates of arrival for Jekyll members and guests are based on the club's guest register, which was for the most part scrupulously kept throughout the club era. Fortunately, it has survived and is part of the collection of the Jekyll Island Museum.

Needless to say, the writing of this book necessitated trips to many museums, archives, and libraries, and I would like to thank the many people associated with these various institutions who have given generously of their time and assistance. Foremost among them are all the able staff members, past and present, at the Jekyll Island Museum, especially its executive director, Warren Murphey, its recent and present curators, Martha Teall and Karen McInnis, as well as James Bradley, who was at the time I was working with Authority records executive director of the Jekyll Island Authority. They have always stood ready to help, whatever my request. Others who have aided significantly in my task include staff members of the American Institute of Architects in New York; the AT&T Company Historical Archive; the Archives des Côtes-du-Nord in Saint-Brieuc, France; the Art Institute of Chicago; Baker Library at Harvard University and the Harvard University Archives; Barnard College Archives; Brown University Archives; the Carnegie Library of Pittsburgh; the Chicago Historical Society; the Crane Company; the Rare Book and Manuscripts Library of Columbia University; the Georgia Department of Archives and History in Atlanta; the Edwin Gould Foundation for Children; the James J. Hill Library in Saint Paul, Minnesota; the Library of Congress; Lyndhurst in Tarrytown, New York, which is held by the National Trust for His-

toric Preservation; the Middle Georgia Historical Society (with special thanks to Katherine Oliver); the New York Historical Society; the New York State Library; the Pierpont Morgan Library in New York; the Rockefeller Archive Center in North Tarrytown, New York; the Rogers Memorial Library in Southampton, Long Island; the Sea Island Company, especially Alfred Jones; the Smith College Archives; the State Historical Society of Wisconsin; Charles L. Lucy of the Tioga Point Museum in Athens, Pennsylvania; the University of North Carolina's Southern Historical Collection; the University of Pittsburgh's Archives of Industrial Society; and Yale University Library.

I would like to express an enormous debt of gratitude for the cooperation of the families and descendants of many Jekyll cottage owners whose assistance has been essential in the writing of this book, particularly the late Susan Albright Reed, whose reminiscences about her life at Jekyll were vivid and passionate. I am also immensely grateful to Jean O'Donnell, Wirt Thompson Jr., and the late Thomas Maurice, who welcomed us into their homes and shared generously their family papers and photographs, and to Day Ravenscroft, who sent to me the diaries of her grandmother Jean Brown Jennings. Other descendants and relatives of Jekyll Island cottage owners who provided photographs or valuable information include John J. Albright, Tatiana Bezamat, Nathalie Bell Brown, Lois R. Dater, Lady Helen de Frietas, Robert Macy Finn, George F. Goodyear, the family of the late Edwin Jay Gould and his secretary Elsie Orgill, Mrs. Ridgeway Macy Hall, Florence H. Hughes, Amy McKay Kahler, William Kingsland Macy Jr., Helen Mead Platt, Joseph Pulitzer Jr., John Sears, Frederick Shrady, Carol Stevens, and Cynthia Weir.

Still others who do not fall into either of the categories mentioned above have provided valuable assistance to the production of this work, none more so than Liesel Boettcher, the widow of Richard Everett, who allowed us the unrestricted use of her husband's photograph collection, now in the possession of the Coastal Georgia Historical Society at the Museum of Coastal History in Saint Simons, Georgia. Memories, photographs, or important information have also been shared by Peter Asher, B. W. Caples, Howard Etter, Ann Corn Felton, Mrs. Alex Gallion, Prosser Gifford, Doris Liebrecht, Katharine G. Owens, Lee and Elsie Schwarz, and Tallu Fish Scott.

I would also like to thank the Research Committee of Middle Tennessee State University for the noninstructional assignment in the spring of 1996 that freed me from teaching duties and provided an opportunity to complete this book. To C. Brenden Martin and David Rowe, who read and commented on various parts of the manuscript, Lorne McWatters, who assisted with some of the architectural identifications, and the University of Georgia's anonymous readers for their helpful suggestions, I owe still another debt of thanks. Certainly they should in no way be held accountable for the book's weaknesses, though they clearly contributed to its strengths.

A special word of appreciation goes to my wonderful friends and colleagues Suma Clark and Jack Ross, to whom I am indebted beyond measure both for the professional support that they and their creative staffs have provided in terms of graphics and photographs and especially for their friendship and moral support and their trips with me to Jekyll Island at critical moments in the book's creation. The helpful editing suggestions that Suma offered, the cottage floor plans and maps that her staff, particularly Judy Hall, worked on diligently, the myriad family photographs that Jack's staff patiently copied, and especially those that he himself took for me during his visits to Jekyll have added immeasurably to the book.

I would also like to thank Betty McFall in the Interlibrary Loan office at Middle Tennessee State University's Todd Library for her cheerful willingness to help me track down any publication, however obscure, in an effort to uncover all possible sources of information. Only she and I know how much effort it has taken, and I am immensely grateful for both her diligence and her competence at her work.

No book would be complete without its editors. First of all, to Karen Orchard, executive editor at the University of Georgia Press for her support and encouragement during the production of this book and to her able staff, and especially to Jane Powers Weldon, my editor, for her always welcome suggestions and attention to detail, I offer my thanks. All of these, and still others too numerous to mention, have made possible the completion of this book and have turned what could have been merely a difficult task into a labor of joy.

INTRODUCTION

In the years following the Civil War the coastal South witnessed the arrival in the region of the fledgling industry of tourism. The railroads that were beginning to snake their way across the country made the comfortable winter climes of the deep South more accessible, particularly to the new industrial class of wealthy men and women who had the leisure for winter vacations and who sought salubrious climates away from their snowbound northern homes.[1]

Two men with connections to the coastal area were quick to see the opportunities that such a situation presented—John Eugene du Bignon from Brunswick, Georgia, whose family had once owned all of nearby Jekyll Island, and his brother-in-law, Newton S. Finney. In 1886 the two men conceived the scheme of reacquiring Jekyll Island and founding there a hunting club for wealthy northerners. Finney, who was living in New York at the time and was a northerner by birth, took charge of the actual founding of the club and recruiting members predominantly among the New York elite, particularly from the rosters of the exclusive Union Club, with only a few coming from other cities like Chicago and Philadelphia. Du Bignon, on the other hand, handled affairs in Georgia, purchasing the various parcels of the island and reselling it as a whole (at considerable profit to himself) to the newly incorporated Jekyll Island Club. Together they established what would become the most elite and inaccessible social club in the United States—a club associated throughout its history with such names as Vanderbilt, Rockefeller, Astor, and Gould.[2]

The Jekyll Island Club was, in many respects, different from such lavish northern summer resorts as Newport and Bar Harbor and even from other southern resorts like the posh White Sulphur Springs in West Virginia, one of the mineral spring spas that had grown up in the South by the early 1800s. Nor was it like the camps in the Adirondacks where many among the nation's wealthy sought to get away from it all. Certainly it had little in common with social clubs associated with urban areas, like the Union Club in New York or the Chicago Club, which were nonresidential and had memberships of men only.

Although Jekyll Island, like other southern resorts, appealed to the northern industrial elite who sought to escape the hard winters of the North by virtue of its healthy climate, its natural beauty, and its abundant wildlife, there the similarity ended. In other respects the club was unique. First of all, its island location, where strict control of arrivals and departures was possible, made it virtually inaccessible to any who were not authorized to be there. Second, because it was a club it was not open to all comers, even though they might have the wherewithal to afford it. Further, unlike many city clubs in the Northeast, it was open to both men and women members. Though at the outset its membership was exclusively male, the Jekyll Island Club quickly opened its doors to women members, who played an increasingly significant role in its evolution, rising in the club's last decades to such positions as vice president and member of the sacrosanct executive committee. Its organization as a family residential resort, where from the outset women were permitted to participate in all activities in which the men were involved and where accommodations were adequate to serve not only club members but also tutors, governesses, and a full array of servants, reflected in certain respects the structure of Newport and Bar Harbor. However, the similarity was slight, for Jekyll was much smaller and more controlled in terms of the overall environment. And, finally, it was utterly unlike these northern resorts in that it consciously embraced a clearly delineated philosophy of simplicity. It was not, to be sure, the rusticity of the Adirondack camps, but rather a simplicity that allowed for a limited control of nature sufficient to provide the necessary amenities for comfort, without ostentation, reflecting what Stephen Hornsby has called "the ideological influence of the romantic movement and its celebration of nature."[3]

Many among the nation's wealthy seemed bent upon displaying their wealth as they did at Newport, a resort William James condemned as "repulsive" and built on the "moral flabbiness born of the exclusive worship of the bitch-goddess SUCCESS!"[4] Stories spread of wasteful extravagance, of dinner parties at Delmonico's where men allegedly smoked cigars wrapped in hundred-dollar bills, while women gave fancy dress balls that cost as much as $250,000. At Jekyll, however, club members embraced the philosophy of the simple life, a theme that runs as a constant thread not only through the fabric of American society but also through every stage of the club's development.

Although men like Marshall Field and William K. Vanderbilt, whose tastes ran to the extravagant and whose wives were known for their lavish parties, were members of the club, they seldom visited the island and quickly became inactive in the affairs of Jekyll Island, where they evidently felt uncomfortable.

The landscape architect Horace William Shaler Cleveland, hired to lay out the club grounds, assured the members that his design would reflect a "style of severe simplicity," an idea that he repeatedly reiterated in his report. But, he underscored, "its simplicity is the result of careful study," the aims of which were to turn the island into "a natural Paradise." With this idea in mind, he laid out lots and planned roads that would not disturb "the favored haunts of deer or wild fowl."[5] Similarly the club house architect, Charles A. Alexander, designed a Queen Anne structure that was boasted by members to be "homelike" and pronounced to be "constructed for comfort," but with "no attempt at display."[6] The subsequent cottages constructed at Jekyll, which might seem quite grand to the average American of today, were nevertheless simple in design and modest in size when compared to many of the members' summer residences in the North and especially to the so-called cottages at Newport.

Food served at the club table, though elegantly prepared in succulent dishes such as crab Newburg and oysters Rockefeller, nonetheless stressed the natural bounties of the island with its fish and game, all of which, according to club rules, were to "be turned over to the club," unless members and guests elected "to buy a portion of their own shooting, at prices . . . fixed by the Club."[7] Thus the success of the hunt would often control the club menu. Similarly the island's activities were not elaborate; the hunting, riding, and carriage driving that prevailed in the early years grew to include bicycling, golf, and tennis, as these sports gained popularity throughout America. Fancy dress balls were rare,

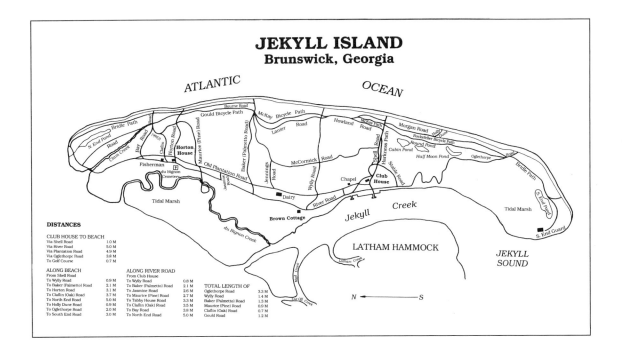

JEKYLL ISLAND
Brunswick, Georgia

ATLANTIC   OCEAN

DISTANCES

CLUB HOUSE TO BEACH
Via Shell Road   1.0 M
Via River Road   5.0 M
Via Plantation Road   4.9 M
Via Oglethorpe Road   3.8 M
To Golf Course   0.7 M

ALONG BEACH   ALONG RIVER ROAD
From Shell Road   From Club House
To Wylly Road   0.9 M   To Wylly Road   0.8 M
To Baker (Palmetto) Road 2.1 M   To Baker (Palmetto) Road 2.1 M   TOTAL LENGTH OF
To Horton Road   3.1 M   To Jasmine Road   2.6 M   Oglethorpe Road   3.3 M
To Claflin (Oak) Road 3.7 M   To Maurice (Pine) Road 2.7 M   Wylly Road   1.4 M
To North End Road   5.0 M   To Tabby House Road   3.3 M   Baker (Palmetto) Road 1.3 M
To Holly Dune Road   0.9 M   To Claflin (Oak) Road   3.5 M   Maurice (Pine) Road   0.9 M
To Oglethorpe Road   2.0 M   To Bay Road   3.8 M   Claflin (Oak) Road   0.7 M
To South End Road   3.0 M   To North End Road   5.0 M   Gould Road   1.2 M

N ←————→ S

though there were frequently dancing and music in the club house after dinner to augment the nightly games of whist and bridge.

Definitions of simplicity are clearly relative, and such a club philosophy did not prevent members from arriving with their butlers, maids, valets, secretaries, grooms, carriage drivers, and, in later years, chauffeurs. However, though they lived well while on the island, they did not, by comparison with other resorts, live lavishly. The Macy governess, Kate Brown, who had not found the Jekyll life style so simple by comparison to that of her own Choate Island where guests waded ashore, nevertheless discovered what simplicity meant to the wealthy when the Macy family left Jekyll to go to the Greenbrier Hotel at White Sulphur Springs. There, she noted, "I begin to see that life at Jekyl Island was simple— positively rural compared to this! This is the sort of thing I don't care for, an enormous hotel, quantities of people, all trying to outdress and outshine the others, and money, money everywhere." [8]

Susan Albright Reed, the daughter of John J. Albright, whose family purchased the Pulitzer cottage in 1914, summed it up from the perspective of the club families: "Jekyll tradition emphasized simple living, and members chose it for that . . . in order to avoid the high life that characterized Palm Beach, Saratoga, and Newport." [9]

Despite such insistence upon the simple life, legends of lavish living grew up around the Jekyll Island Club, fanned by those who had never been there. Not long after the club closed in 1942, rumors about its extravagant life style and activities found their way into print. In 1946 the *Atlanta Constitution* reported on the fanciful tales of Jekyll, one of them claiming that its "streets are paved with gold and its houses studded with pearls and on the doors of the houses are swung huge hunks of diamonds used as knockers. And the people take their baths in warm milk that runs in pipes just like water." [10] Nothing could have been further from the truth, even though many of the names associated with the new club were well known as virtual synonyms for wealth, names like J. P. Morgan, William Rockefeller, and Joseph Pulitzer. On the contrary, frugality was the watchword for all club undertakings. Club officers never wanted to pay excessively for services rendered and deliberated at length, sometimes for years, even before adding modern conveniences such as electricity. The citizens of Brunswick on the mainland, for example, enjoyed electric lights a full decade before the Jekyll Islanders finally replaced the club house's ill-smelling gas fixtures, about which members complained constantly, with electric lights. It was not until the 1903 season that the lights finally came on at Jekyll, even though club members had debated the issue since 1892.

In many respects, Jekyll's clinging to its Victorian traditions was one of the factors that would bring the club era to an end. Most of the early cottages on the island were built in popular styles of the Victorian era, especially Queen Anne and shingle. By the turn of the century, however, tastes had begun to shift toward more European styles such as Italian Renaissance. Efforts were made, especially during the 1920s, to modernize many aspects of the club and appeal to a younger crowd. For example, a swimming pool was added and a new golf course built. Even the two cottages constructed during the 1920s reflected the taste for more modern Spanish eclectic styles of the resorts being built in Florida by Addison Mizner. But it was too little, too late. An air of Victoriana clung to Jekyll long after it was stylish, and even before World War II and especially during the Great Depression, many members began to drift away. Despite its philosophy of simplicity, Jekyll Island was expensive. A new category of associate membership, less costly than the original founders' memberships, was introduced out of

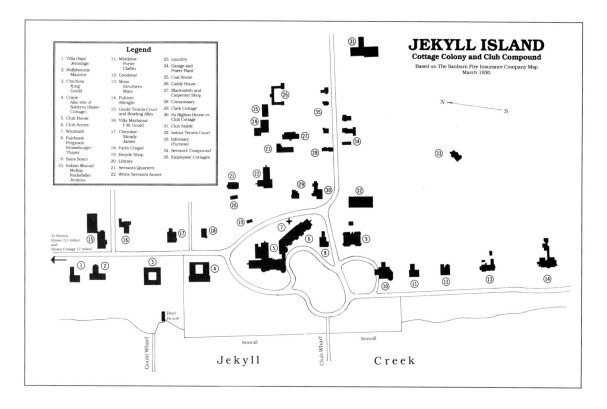

necessity, but the new associate members tended to come and go, treating Jekyll more like an ordinary resort than a residential club. If the depression had weakened the club, World War II would prove to be its coup de grâce.

When the war came to an end, discussions were already under way between Bernon Prentice, then president of the club, and a few other members as to what should be done with Jekyll Island. As things stood by 1945, the Jekyll Island Club had no revenues and fewer than a dozen members to bear the expense of paying the taxes and making repairs to the structures that had fallen into serious disrepair during the war when they stood, for the most part, empty and ignored. And only a few of these members were contributing to the expense. Something had to be done quickly, and the options seemed limited. They could either sell the island to investors, a possibility that was, in fact, seriously considered, or they could reopen the club, though not on its prewar basis. Discussions of reopening centered not on continuing Jekyll as a private club, but rather on refashioning it as a resort styled after the Cloister on Sea Island. However, the death of Frank Miller Gould, one of the backers and an important financial linchpin in the resort scheme, put an end to these plans. (See the chapter on Villa Marianna.) In the end, the state of Georgia stepped in unexpectedly to determine the future of Jekyll Island.

Initial discussions with state officials, who were interested in procuring the island for use as a public park, began in 1946, but it was not until October 1947, after the election of Gov. M. E. Thompson, that the state finally acquired the island through condemnation proceedings. The state of Georgia paid the Jekyll Island Club and the various members who still owned their cottages a total of $675,000 in compensation and took over the island for conversion to a state park.

Unfortunately the acquisition of the island had proved to be a political hot potato and a highly debated campaign issue in one of the most controver-sial gubernatorial elections Georgia has ever witnessed. Because the purchase had been proposed by M. E. Thompson, his opponent Herman Talmadge, then acting governor, staunchly opposed the island's purchase, indicating that the state was paying too much for it, that the island was sinking, and that it would be a hideaway for rich politicians.[11] Inevitably, the rhetoric that surrounded the election had an unfortunate impact on Jekyll Island, creating subsequent problems for those who wished to preserve its history.

From the outset, the Jekyll Island Authority, established in 1950 to oversee the island's resources, was under constant pressure to make money.[12] Although the authority received some state funds in the start-up years, it was soon required to be self-sufficient and, until a modest appropriation was made in Gov. Zell Miller's 1998 budget, has received no additional revenues from the state of Georgia. As a consequence, funds for historic preservation have been relatively limited. In the early years, prior to the current surge of enthusiasm throughout the country for the restoration and preservation of historic structures, little interest was shown in such activities. Thus when a small fire occurred in the Pulitzer-Albright house in 1951, there was no discussion of restoring the cottage. Rather it was targeted for demolition.

Labor in the late 1940s and early 1950s was provided by convicts rather than hired workers. Their task was to clean up the island and the club house and make them habitable for tourists. From this period apocryphal stories abound of bonfires built from "old papers," some of which were undoubtedly club records, and the medical "junk" that was discarded from the island's infirmary. Fortunately, some items were spared, among them the club register, which has been invaluable in reconstructing the records of visits to the club by cottage owners, and the share book, which allows an accurate reconstruction of club membership. Little by little awareness has grown concerning the historical value of the documents and architectural structures that had fallen into the hands of the state, but the mistakes of the early years could not be undone.

There can be no question that many of the early decisions were unfortunate and would ultimately deprive the state of important historical resources; however, given the political pressures and the context of the times, when historic preservation had little value in the public eye, they were understandable. And despite the losses of records, cottages, and furnishings (some of which were sold for a fraction of their value, others of which, according to persistent local stories, were surreptitiously removed from many of the cottages), the state's stewardship of the island has been of significant value. Given the options that were available at the end of the war, the state takeover and subsequent stewardship seems, with the benefit of hindsight, to have been the best choice. Had the island been sold to private investors, it would in all probability have meant the loss of many of the natural areas of the island that have been preserved today and most likely of the historic district as well.

Fortunately, as time went on, state officials learned from their early mistakes, and increasing attention has been paid to the historic district that essentially constitutes a museum of Victorian and post-Victorian architecture in America, containing cottages designed by some of the nation's best-known architects, among them John Russell Pope and Carrère and Hastings. One may regret the loss of some of the structures but rejoice in those that have survived and to which much careful attention is being given today as the Jekyll Island Museum's executive director, Warren Murphey, and his able preservation crew painstakingly seek to restore and maintain the buildings within the Jekyll Island cottage colony. Theirs was not the first restoration effort in the historic district. Earlier attempts were made in the 1970s under the supervision of Roger Beedle, whose work was important in stabilizing the houses and preventing further deterioration. But theirs is the most sustained restoration the island has seen. The current effort is an ongoing process that has thus far and at the time of this writing resulted in the restoration of the du Bignon Cottage, Faith Chapel, Mistletoe, Indian Mound, and Moss Cottage, and the work continues. Clearly, in the final analysis, as one of those involved in Jekyll's final days put it, "it all worked out as a good solution to a difficult problem."[13]

Those who visit the island today find a thriving historic district, with the magnificent club house running successfully as a commercial hotel and beautifully restored under the supervision of Brunswick architect Larry Evans. Taking advantage of a small window of opportunity between 1984, when he first became interested in the project, and 1986, when the tax incentives and grants that made the project possible were eliminated by the federal government, Evans and a friend, Vance Hughes, with the additional support of a group of investors, completed the project. The restored club house was opened as a hotel in December 1986 and has continued to thrive, bringing renewed life and vigor to the island's historic district.

What remains today at Jekyll Island is a unique treasure of architectural history. It is the only place of its type in the South that brings together in such limited space so many building styles that typify resort architecture from New England to Florida during the heyday of Victorian resorts from 1880 to 1930.

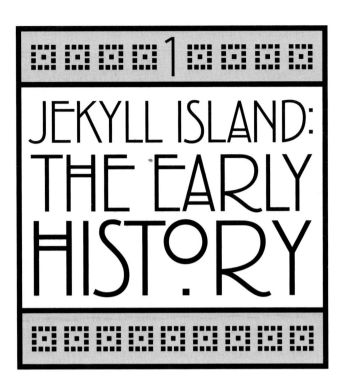

1

JEKYLL ISLAND: THE EARLY HISTORY

THE HORTON HOUSE

Owners: William Horton and heirs, 1736–68; Clement Martin and heirs, 1768–84; Richard Leake, 1784–92; Christophe Poulain du Bignon and heirs, 1792–1886; Jekyll Island Club, 1886–1947

Constructed: 1736; rebuilt, 1742–43

Architecture: Plantation Plain style (tabby variation)

Architect: Unknown

The Horton Years

The ruins of the Horton House stand on Jekyll Island today as a reminder of Georgia's colonial history and as one of only two surviving examples of a two-story colonial plantation house in Georgia.[1] Its builder, the colorful William Horton, served as the right-hand man to Georgia's founder, Gen. James Edward Oglethorpe, and for a time as Georgia's military commander during Oglethorpe's absence. Horton's initial voyage to Georgia was aboard the *Symond,* one of a tiny fleet of only two ships that sailed from Gravesend, England, packed with provisions and passengers, bound for the colony on

The Horton House on the north end of Jekyll Island was rebuilt in 1742–43 after the Spaniards destroyed the original house following the battle of Bloody Marsh. The house would become the home of Christophe Poulain du Bignon, who moved his family to Jekyll Island in the 1790s to escape the dangers of the French Revolution. (Courtesy of Jekyll Island Museum)

October 20, 1735. It was Oglethorpe's second trip to Georgia. Less than three years earlier he had made a similar voyage under the auspices of the Board of Trustees, which had been granted a charter in June 1732 by King George II to establish and administer the colony of Georgia.

In addition to the so-called charity colonists on board the *Symond,* the passenger list included two clergymen, John and Charles Wesley, motivated by "a pious design to convert the Indians" and later renowned as founders of Methodism, and a group of adventurous gentlemen who funded their own passage but were granted five hundred acres of land (the maximum permitted under the trustees' regulations) on the condition that they would transport no fewer than six servants to Georgia and cultivate one-fifth of their grant within ten years.[2] Among these young adventurers who dined at Oglethorpe's table aboard ship, indeed the most important among them, was William Horton, formerly the subsheriff of Herefordshire.[3] He had presented himself to the trustees for approval on September 17, 1735, and, finding him to be a man of good character "worth 3000 pounds," they awarded him a grant of five hundred acres a week later. On October 14 he was aboard the *Symond* with ten servants ready for the voyage.[4]

Prior to the ship's departure, however, one of Horton's female servants was put ashore "for Drinking and indecent behaviour."[5] Horton blamed the Wesley brothers for her banishment, and to show his displeasure, according to John Wesley, late one night he "waked us by dancing [on the deck] over our heads."[6] Though Horton later apologized for his conduct, a residue of ill will between them would remain.

The ship did not reach the Georgia coast until February 6, 1736, when it dropped anchor near Savannah. The ultimate destination of the colonists was Saint Simons Island, situated below the Altamaha River on the southern reaches of the Georgia frontier, where General Oglethorpe planned to establish a town and forts to serve as a military bastion against the Spanish in Saint Augustine, Florida. The *Symond* proved too large for navigation around Saint Simons, and Horton continued his voyage on February 14 on the sloop *Midnight,* accompanied by thirty of the men under his command on February 15, with the other colonists to follow later.[7] From this beginning, the new town of Frederica would spring.

Barely a day after the last of the colonists arrived, General Oglethorpe, accompanied by Horton, launched an expedition to the Saint Johns River on the very doorstep of Spanish-held Saint Augustine "to see where His Majesty's dominions and the Spaniard's join."[8] Oglethorpe later noted that "Mr. Horton who has not undressed himself since he came here, though he has a tent and bed standing, which he has given to the sick[,] has been with me in an open boat all the Southward expedition."[9] Clearly the general viewed Horton as a valuable aide and relied upon him more and more for important and often dangerous assignments.

Not until the end of April did Horton have an opportunity to visit the five-hundred-acre grant that had been set aside for him on Jekyll Island, just south of Saint Simons, which Oglethorpe had named for his benefactor Sir Joseph Jekyll. A scout boat was provided to take him across Jekyll Sound. Upon landing, a swivel gun was fired "by way of signal" to indicate "how the lands bore from the town." The young gunner, apparently in an exuberant mood, opened fire and reloaded with increasing amounts of powder until on the third round the cannon burst and mortally wounded him. Horton rushed the injured soldier back to Saint Simons where he was attended by a surgeon, but he could not be saved. His death the following day made him the first casualty at Frederica.[10]

Although his initial exploration of Jekyll had been cut short by this tragedy, Horton had seen enough to report that "the land was exceedingly rich." He may have left servants on the island to begin cultivating the grant but, if so, there is no record of it. Horton personally had no time to oversee any work that might have been initiated, for on May 2 he was ordered to escort a boatload of ammunition, cannon, and supplies to the Highlanders at Fort Saint Andrews.[11]

That same month Horton and a Major Richards were entrusted with a delicate diplomatic mission, to deliver letters from Oglethorpe to the Spanish authorities in Saint Augustine disclaiming any hostile intent in the recent military buildup and explaining away the presence of patrol boats on the Saint Johns River as a peaceful measure. When they reached the Saint Johns, they found the Spanish outposts abandoned and no way to make contact with the Spanish governor. Horton, ever ready to serve the colony, volunteered to walk the forty miles to Saint Augustine to make their presence known. Though at first the governor received them "very civilly,"[12] suddenly one morning they were placed under house arrest and accused of spying; however, they were soon released with a request on the part of the Spaniards that Horton and Richards arrange for them to negotiate directly with General Oglethorpe.

When the Spanish negotiators arrived shortly thereafter in Georgia, Oglethorpe made provisions for them to sleep on Jekyll Island in "two handsome tents lined with Chinese, with marquises [marquisette] and walls of canvas" so "that they might not go up to the town [Frederica], nor make any discovery of our strength."[13] Unfortunately, little came of the meeting, nor did it guarantee future peace.

The general departed for England in November 1736 to raise another regiment of troops for the defense of the colony, leaving Horton in charge of Frederica.[14] During the general's absence, frequent alarms of a possible Spanish invasion swept Georgia and were reported in South Carolina and as far away as London. Horton informed the Earl of Egmont in March 1737 that the "people resolv'd to defend themselves against the Spaniards if attack'd."[15] However, Horton's greatest problems during Oglethorpe's absence came not from the Spaniards but from infighting among the disgruntled colonists.

In spite of his official duties, Horton managed by the end of 1736 to erect a spacious two-story house on Jekyll Island on an Indian site dating back perhaps a thousand years.[16] The house was a wooden structure with a parlor and a hall on the main floor, at each end of which were substantial fireplaces used for heating and cooking. Upstairs were the sleeping quarters. A front porch and an upstairs balcony adorned the north face of the house. Nearby were servants' quarters, a barn, and various other outbuildings.[17] By January 1738 his servants had fenced in more than twenty acres of land, and cultivation was well underway.[18] His main crop was corn, and a stock of cattle grazed in the brush.

Horton had traveled to Savannah in December 1737 for an extended series of conversations with William Stephens, the newly appointed secretary of the trustees, who had recently arrived in the colony. They struck up a "frank and easy" relationship,[19] and in late January 1738 Stephens made an inspection tour of the southern part of the Georgia colony. Upon his arrival on January 28, Horton was summoned from Jekyll Island by a signal gun about three in the afternoon and met him in Frederica.[20] During the next several days Stephens, accompanied by Horton, visited various forts and settlements as far south as Fort Saint Andrews on Cumberland Island. Among the places he visited was Horton's plantation on Jekyll, which according to Stephens's account was flourishing "with a good Number of Servants, and considerable Improvements made."[21] He spent two nights on the island as Horton's guest and was joined there on February 2, 1738, by Lieutenant Delegal. "Mr. Horton . . . would not allow us to part without dining with him, which I perceived he had made some Provision for, and we fared well."[22]

If Horton's plantation was doing reasonably well, the same could not be said for many others under his jurisdiction on Saint Simons. Drought for a second year in a row was taking its toll, and Horton

Portrait of Sir Joseph Jekyll, for whom General Oglethorpe named Jekyll Island. (Courtesy of Jekyll Island Museum)

informed the trustees in August 1738: "The crops of corn . . . are very bad. The seed was far from being good, and, the season proving very dry, it is generally parched up."[23] Equally devastating were the constant alarms of possible Spanish invasion, causing men to lose valuable time in the fields rushing to arms. It must have been with a sense of relief that Horton began to anticipate the return to Georgia of General Oglethorpe. Nonetheless, he proclaimed to the trustees that "If I can in any shape be serviceable to this colony I shall ever think it my duty to be so and shall esteem it the greatest honour to receive your commands and will to the utmost of my abilities execute them."[24]

In early May 1738 advanced units of the new regiment that Oglethorpe had recruited in England arrived in Savannah. One company was forwarded to Frederica to be commanded by Horton, who had been commissioned an ensign in the regiment. As usual, Horton bent to the task of receiving the troops and preparing for those still on their way to America. Oglethorpe and the rest of his regiment aboard five transports reached Jekyll Island on September 18, 1738, and the following day the general wrote to his friend and supporter, Sir Joseph Jekyll, of his safe arrival. "I am now got to an anchor in a harbour and near an island that bears your name. God has given us the greatest marks of his visible protection to this colony. The Spaniards, though they had 1500 men at Augustine and there was nothing in Georgia but the militia of the country, delayed attacking them 'till the regular troops arrived."[25]

In spite of Oglethorpe's return, Horton continued to exercise important responsibilities. He was sent on various official errands including a trip up the Savannah River to contact Mary Musgrove Matthews, who served as Indian interpreter, and summon her to Frederica and on another excursion to South Carolina to procure supplies for the soldiers.[26] But his most significant mission by far was to England to carry dispatches for Oglethorpe, render an accounting to the trustees, and gather reinforcements for Oglethorpe's regiment. Reinforcements were considered crucial, for the anticipated hostilities with Spain had finally broken out in October 1739 in a conflict known as the War of Jenkins' Ear, and clashes along the Georgia-Florida border began in November.[27]

Horton's reputation for honesty, practicality, devotion to duty, courage, and efficiency was indeed by now thoroughly established, and before his departure for England he had been promoted to the rank of lieutenant.[28] He sailed for England on March 22, 1740.[29] By early May he had landed and was hard at work seeking to fulfill his obligations. Dining with John Percival, the Earl of Egmont, on May 9, he gave him a favorable picture of affairs in Georgia.[30] Before the month was out he had made successful rounds of several royal officials, including the Duke of Newcastle and Sir Robert Walpole, pleading for funds for scout boats and explaining the necessity for a new grenadier company and extra officers to augment Oglethorpe's regiment.[31]

Horton gathered recruits from London as well as from the countryside. Promoted to captain in December 1740 and given command of the grenadiers, he had the company ready for the voyage to Georgia by February 1742. He also received permission to transport women and children with the soldiers free of charge as an inducement for the latter to remain permanently as settlers in Georgia.[32]

Horton and his grenadier company reached Georgia about June 17, 1742.[33] They arrived in the nick of time, for on June 21 a Spanish squadron bombarded Fort William on the southern tip of Cumberland Island, thus precipitating the initial stages of the long-feared Spanish invasion. Cumberland Island, however, was not the main target of the Spanish armada, and on July 5, 1742, the fleet commanded by Gen. Don Manuel de Montiano sailed into Saint Simons Sound and landed troops at Gascoigne's Bluff. On July 7 a Spanish advanced guard marched toward Frederica but was checked by Oglethorpe in two engagements, the second of which is known as the battle of Bloody Marsh. The defeats were not decisive, however, for Montiano's losses were slight, and his main force was still on the island in full possession of Fort Saint Simons.[34] Oglethorpe withdrew to the protection of Frederica where he was joined by Horton and the garrison from Fort William. Horton and his men had boldly crossed Saint Simons Sound in broad daylight and in plain view of the Spaniards.[35] Although Horton had missed the battle of Bloody Marsh, he now became an integral part of the Frederica defensive force.

There was to be no further Spanish attack, however. On July 12 General Montiano began withdrawing his army, razing Fort Saint Simons before their departure. In a final gesture of retaliation, Spanish troops were ferried to Jekyll Island where they burned Horton's house and outbuildings before continuing their long retreat back to Florida.[36]

Oglethorpe conducted a punitive raid on Saint Augustine in March 1743. It would prove to be the final skirmish of his military career in Georgia, for in July he departed for England never to return. Once again, Horton was appointed military commander at Frederica.[37] One of his first tasks was the rebuilding of his house on Jekyll to provide a comfortable, permanent residence for his family, which had probably sought refuge in Frederica during the Spanish invasion. One of his sons, in all likelihood Thomas, the youngest, who was considered "promising," was sent off in August 1743 to be educated under the tutelage of a "French Minister" in Purrysburg, South Carolina.[38]

The new house, completed by late 1743 and erected over the foundations of his burned home, was, like the original structure, a two-story building with chimneys at either end. Unlike the first building, however, it was constructed of tabby, a local mixture of lime, sand, and shells, rather than wood. The downstairs had a tabby floor and was divided into two rooms by a tabby wall.[39] A few hundred yards to the southwest on the bank of a navigable stream (subsequently called du Bignon creek) were located one or two other tabby structures, a dock, and a well. Since 1887 the site has been referred to as Georgia's first brewery, although later archeological findings suggest that the structures probably were not used for that purpose but rather as a dwelling, for wine storage, and as a loading platform.[40] However, the fact that Horton intended to brew beer on Jekyll Island cannot be doubted, for in 1747 he ordered a "Great Copper" pot for that purpose. Whether any beer was actually brewed or, if so, whether it was the first or was for more than home consumption is unknown.[41]

In any case, Horton apparently had grand designs for his Jekyll estate and wrote enthusiastically to William Stephens "on the Subject of Improving land." Stephens had few doubts about Horton's ability to succeed: "I well know he is a gentleman that wants neither a Genius to attempt, nor a

Resolution to carry on, any purpose that he takes in hand." His only concern was that the captain might lack sufficient servants "to accomplish his good Intent."[42]

For a few years Horton's plantation appeared to be in flourishing condition. In August 1746 he entertained a man named John Pye who reported to the trustees that "While I was at ye Southward I had ye Pleasure to see Major Hortons Improvements on the Island of Jeykill. He has a very Large Barnfull of Barley not inferior to ye Barley in England, about 20 Ton of Hay in one stack, a Spacious House & fine Garden, a plow was going wth Eight Horses, And above all I saw Eight Acres of Indigo of which he has made a good Quantity & two Men are now at Work (a Spaniard & English Man) they told me the Indigo was as good as that made in the Spanish West India's."[43] Two years earlier Horton had received three-thousand grape vine cuttings from William Stephens, but there is no indication that they were cultivated with any degree of success, and if his experience was anything like that of Stephens himself, the experiment in vineyards and wine making was a miserable failure.[44]

In fact, Horton's plantation was doing less well than appeared on the surface. One report, written while he was in England, noted that he had become so discouraged at prospects on Jekyll that he declared "the labour was vain" and "set his servants to hire."[45] Despite his earlier enthusiasm and seeming prosperity, in June 1748 he announced that Jekyll Island was "at length found totally unfit for cultivation," and for that reason, he requested that his son Thomas be granted five hundred acres of land on the Great Ogeechee River.[46] The petition on behalf of the younger Horton was ultimately approved, and upon the death of his father he would inherit the Jekyll property as well.[47]

As commander of the southern division of Georgia with headquarters at Frederica, William Horton, who had been promoted to major in the summer of 1745, had not been able to afford the luxury of concentrating his entire attention on farm and family. The War of Jenkins' Ear had merged in 1744

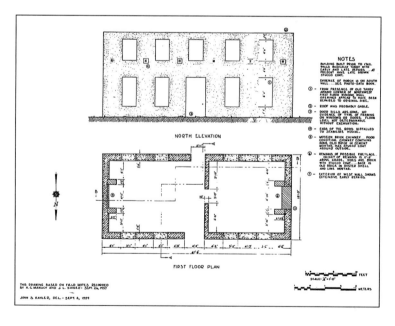

Historic American Buildings Survey drawing of the remains of the Horton House. (From John Linley, *The Georgia Catalog: Historic American Buildings Survey* [Athens: University of Georgia Press, 1982], 23.)

into a much broader conflict, King George's War (1744–48), which would involve the French as antagonists as well as the Spanish. Expecting an attack from Saint Augustine daily, Horton had published the official declaration of war in Frederica in July and begun taking aggressive action against the Florida frontier.[48] His public responsibilities were immense. In any given month in 1744 and 1745, he could be found along the Savannah River attempting to intercept illegal South Carolina trade with the enemy, or in the upcountry parleying with Indians to retain their friendship, or in Savannah consulting about colonial affairs with William Stephens, who had been appointed president in overall charge of Georgia.[49]

Considering the tensions of the time, the ambiguous line between civil and military authority in Frederica, and Horton's occasional disagreements with the town magistrates, it was inevitable that conflicts over jurisdiction and political power would occasionally surface.[50] Nevertheless, Major Horton was held in high esteem by the leading citizens of Georgia. James Habersham, a merchant, planter, and subsequently a secretary to the Royal Council during most of the royal period of Georgia (1752–65), wrote on December 29, 1748, "I have the greatest regard for Major Horton as every Honest Man must and especially every well wisher to this colony."[51]

In October 1747, an epidemic swept Frederica, and Horton was among those who fell ill.[52] Although he recovered this time, the incident evidently left him weakened, for in early 1749, in the midst of a campaign to convince the trustees to alter, under carefully controlled conditions, the prohibition against slavery in Georgia, Horton died "to the universal sorrow of all his acquaintance."[53]

After his death, Horton's Jekyll estate was occupied by a small garrison of troops commanded by Lt. Paul Demere from June 1749 until September 1750 and afterwards by his brother, Capt. Raymond Demere.[54] Thus for the first time Jekyll became a military outpost. Raymond Demere lived in the Horton house, treating the plantation as his own. He renamed Jekyll Creek "Demere Creek" and at his own expense repaired buildings and added new ones. On July 1, 1765, having invested much of his own time and money in the property, he petitioned the council in Savannah for Horton's five hundred acres "for the term of his Life and then the same to descend to the heirs of the said Major Horton." He also requested an additional six hundred acres for use as a range for his cattle. The council granted the six hundred acres but denied him the acreage belonging to the Horton estate.[55]

Nevertheless, Demere remained on Jekyll until his death in 1766. That same year Clement Martin received from the council, on which he served, Demere's six hundred acres, and in early 1768 in a strangely worded petition he asked for the entire island. The petition claimed that "he was lately come into the Province with his family in Order to settle and take up lands Therefore praying for an Island called Jekyl lying to the Southward of the Province he having one hundred Negroes." The petition was approved on the condition that Martin "obtain five hundred acres of land to be laid out and granted unto Thomas Horton in lieu of a settlement long since made on the said Island by his father the late Major Horton deceased or the matter otherwise adjusted."[56] Evidently Martin was able to make a satisfactory settlement with Thomas Horton, because the entire island was officially granted to him on April 5, 1768.

The Martin-Leake Years

Although Clement Martin cultivated Jekyll Island, it is unlikely that he ever lived there on any regular basis. He had become an important man in the colony since his arrival from Saint Christopher's (St. Kitts) in 1754, and he held many important

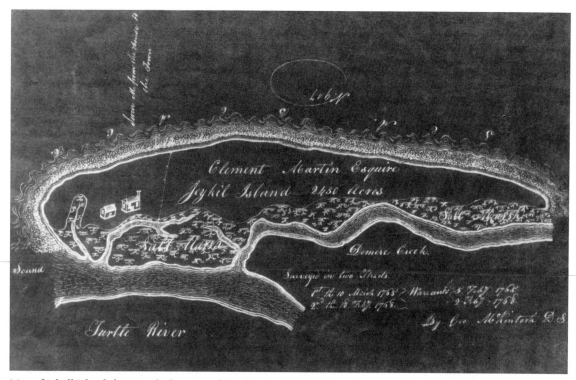

Map of Jekyll Island showing the location of the Horton House during the ownership of Clement Martin. (Courtesy of Jekyll Island Museum)

posts that required him to be often in Savannah, where he had owned property since at least 1756. Within a year after his arrival he was appointed to the King's Council and elected to the General Assembly. Even though he was briefly suspended from the council on September 30, 1755, for unspecified reasons which the governor indicated he would share only with the king, his post was restored sometime after the council itself petitioned the governor on December 10, 1759, to have him reinstated.[57] From that time on until the American Revolution, either Martin or his son, Clement Martin Jr., continued to sit on the King's Council, an honor enjoyed by only twelve men in the colony at any given time. Reflecting the esteem he evidently held on the council, he was authorized on April 11, 1768, six days after all Jekyll Island was granted to him, "to correspond with . . . Benjamin Franklin [who

had been appointed an agent for the colony in Great Britain] and give him such Orders and instructions from time to time as they shall judge to be for the service of this Province." [58]

When Clement Martin died on March 11, 1775, on the eve of the American Revolution, he bequeathed Jekyll not to his eldest son Clement Jr., to whom he left only "six dunhill fowls for having cheated me of six thousand pounds" but in equal shares to his younger son, John, and his daughters, Jane and Ann.[59] It is doubtful whether John or any of the other heirs enjoyed much, if any, benefit from their inheritance. The estate was heavily indebted and as late as 1784 was still being proceeded against by creditors. In any event, with the outbreak of the American Revolution, John sided with the English and soon found himself branded as a traitor. His property was confiscated, and he was banished from

Georgia. He escaped to Saint Kitts while his sisters sought refuge in East Florida.[60]

In 1784 Jekyll Island, still part of the Martin estate, was seized by the sheriff to settle a debt of thirty-four pounds and sixteen shillings and sold at auction. It was purchased for five hundred pounds by Richard Leake, a native of Ireland, who had married Jane, the daughter of Clement Martin, in 1771. (One source that claims to take it from the Spalding family Bible says 1775.) Leake was a surgeon, planter, and himself a former Tory who had only recently returned from exile in Florida.[61]

Although he apparently grazed livestock on Jekyll, Leake may not have lived there, preferring the more lively life of Savannah. Although in June 1785 he moved to his Little Ogeechia Plantation and began experimenting with various types of cotton, he decided in 1791 to sell both the Ogeechia Plantation and Jekyll Island.[62] On February 15 of that year he entered into an agreement with a man by the name of Francis Marie Loys Dumoussay de la Vauve to sell him Jekyll Island for two thousand pounds to found a small colony for a group of French émigrés.[63] This agreement ended more than half a century of British domination at Jekyll and would lead to nearly a century of ownership by the French du Bignon family.

The du Bignon Years

Christophe Anne Poulain du Bignon was the oldest surviving son of a noble but poor Breton named Ange-Paul Poulain and his wife, Jeanne Louise Le Franc.[64] Born in 1739, Christophe went to sea at the age of ten as a cabin boy aboard *L'Hercule*, a vessel of the French East India Company (Compagnie des Indes).[65] He rose rapidly in the company, working his way up to ensign by 1749. When the company was abolished by King Louis XV in 1769, twenty-one-year-old Christophe was pensioned at one hundred pounds a year.[66] He entered the merchant marine, passing the examination to become a

captain in 1775. During the next ten years he was, in essence, his own master, sailing to Portugal, India, South America, and the Isle de France (present-day Mauritius), voyages that, though often risky, turned a handsome profit. In 1778 when France signed an alliance with the United States and officially entered the American Revolutionary War against the British, du Bignon became a privateer in the service of Louis XVI, and in 1779 he could be found carrying dispatches and evacuating wounded sailors.

During a layover on the Isle de France, he met Marguerite Anne Lossieux, daughter of a sea captain, Guillaume Lossieux, and a widow with three children.[67] The two were married in France on August 29, 1778, and enjoyed only four months together before he set off for another voyage. His life at sea was both exciting and arduous, involving long voyages to the coasts of India, Africa, and the Americas, and nearly costing him his life when ships twice sank beneath him. Now married, he was eager to put his seafaring career behind him. Thus in 1784, in the wake of increased hostilities between France and England, Christophe, at the age of forty-five, renounced the sea. Nine months after his return to France, his first son, Joseph, was born.

Christophe, a member of the merchant nobility with high economic aspirations, settled his family in his native Lamballe, France, and began to cast about for ways to invest the profits of his thirty years at sea. Among his ventures was the purchase of a china factory in Nantes. His timing could not have been worse. Rising inflation brought about increasing discontent in France and began to eat away at his financial resources. When revolution broke out in 1789, his thoughts began to turn toward a more secure haven for his family and fortune.

That same year an acquaintance of du Bignon by the name of Francis Marie Loys Dumoussay de la Vauve made an agreement in America with John McQueen, known to many as Don Juan McQueen, to purchase the islands of Sapelo, Blackbeard,

Caberreta, and Little Sapelo off the coast of Georgia. Meeting with a group of potential investors, du Bignon among them, in Saint-Malo, France, Dumoussay told them of Sapelo's beauty and promise as a plantation site. So persuasive was he that Christophe, who had been particularly taken with the description of the massive oaks that would be good for building ships, decided to invest in one-fifth of the island, signing a purchase agreement on November 8, 1790.[68]

Du Bignon wasted no time in planning a voyage to Georgia to look over the property and make certain it would be a suitable home for his family, which now included a second son, Henri Charles, born on August 3, 1787. He departed on the *Silvain* before the month's end, taking with him his five year-old son, Joseph, and leaving behind a pregnant wife and a small boy. His intentions to emigrate were clear and showed keen foresight, for not only was France's rising inflation a threat to his fortune, but the increasingly volatile and violent political situation also posed serious dangers.[69] Châteaux of noblemen in the area had already been burned, and violence and unrest were heating up in Paris and spreading to other parts of France. Upon his departure, du Bignon, in recognition of his status as a property owner in Georgia and perhaps for protection in leaving France without trouble from the revolutionary government, signed himself on the ship's passenger list as a "citoyen des états-unis" (citizen of the United States). Dumoussay and Julien Joseph Hyacinth de Chappedelaine, who accompanied him on the voyage, were also listed on the *Silvain*'s roster as American citizens.[70]

During this trip to America, the enterprising but not always trustworthy Dumoussay, intent upon increasing his holdings in the Georgia sea islands, entered into the agreement with Richard Leake on February 15, 1791, to purchase Jekyll Island. However, Dumoussay, having purchased five islands in fewer than three years, had apparently overextended his economic resources and failed to pay the taxes levied against the property. As a consequence, the tax collector of Chatham County seized Jekyll and sold it at public auction on April 17, 1792. The buyer was another of the investors in the Sapelo Island deal—Nicholas François Magon de la Villehuchet. The émigrés were a close-knit community, and Villehuchet, by apparent prearrangement, conveyed portions of Jekyll Island to three other Sapelo investors, one-fourth to du Bignon, one-fourth to Chappedelaine, and one-fourth back to Dumoussay.

Well before the Jekyll sale, du Bignon, still planning to bring his little family to Sapelo and set up a new homestead, had acquired a seagoing vessel which he had christened *Le Sappello,* and set sail for France. He returned to Georgia in 1792 with his wife Marguerite and their children, Joseph, now seven, and Henri, who was four. A third child, an infant boy, apparently died during the voyage or shortly after their arrival in America. With them on the ship was Thomas Dechenaux, who would become one of Christophe's closest friends in America.[71] It was only after their arrival in Georgia that Christophe was greeted by the opportunity to buy the one-fourth interest in Jekyll Island, a proposition he accepted with alacrity on May 22.[72]

It would prove to be a fortuitous purchase, for, returning to Sapelo, du Bignon found the little colony in complete disarray. Not only had conflicts developed between the older and younger members of the group, but Dumoussay had also played fast and loose with the Sapelo Company's finances. As a consequence, du Bignon decided to settle his family on his newly acquired Jekyll property instead.

Unfortunately the Jekyll deeds had been lost at sea when Villehuchet sent them back to France "for the purpose of obtaining a renunciation of dower" from his wife. En route the vessel was "chased by an enemy," and the deeds and other papers were "thrown overboard and entirely lost."[73] The lost deeds did not seem a problem when on June 14, 1794, du Bignon signed an agreement to exchange his portion of Sapelo for the two-fourths of Jekyll belonging to Dumoussay and Chappedelaine.[74] However, three of the investors in the Sapelo Company died in 1794. Dumoussay succumbed to fever in September, and five days later, on September 15, Chappedelaine was killed by his uncle, Picot de Boisfeuillet, in a duel over a property dispute.[75] Villehuchet, on the other hand, had returned to France where he was guillotined that same year.[76]

In 1796 the heirs of the deceased Dumoussay and Chappedelaine began to demand that the issue of ownership be clarified, and du Bignon undertook efforts to have legal restoration of the lost deeds in order to gain a clear title to his three-quarters of Jekyll. In seeking to clear up the matter, he was able to wrangle a legislative enactment on February 19 to enable the Glynn County Superior Court to hear testimony and take depositions attesting to the sale of the island property and the transfer of the lost deeds. Thanks to du Bignon's friend Dechenaux and Charles Harris, both of whom had witnessed the 1794 exchange of the Sapelo lands for Jekyll property and who gave depositions and testified to that effect, the conveyance was finally legally recorded with the Glynn County Court.[77] On October 14, 1800, du Bignon purchased for $2,142.85 the other fourth of Jekyll from Grand Clos Meslé, who had shared it with Villehuchet and one Lewis Harrington, a planter acting also as attorney for his partner.[78] Thus by the end of 1800, Christophe Poulain du Bignon claimed sole ownership of the entire island.

In the meantime, du Bignon had made the long-neglected Horton House livable once again and had begun cultivating his land. He ran a substantial plantation with fifty-nine slaves, owned a house and lot in Savannah as well as a house in Frederica, and had additional land in Brunswick.[79] He also continued his seafaring ways by operating the sloop *Annubis,* which engaged in coastal trade between Savannah and Brunswick. In 1798 he wrote to a friend in France, "I am alone on an island of 5–6000 acres. I quarrel with no man. Here is truly the land of liberty."[80] He seemed for the most part satisfied with his lot. Only once did he try to sell Jekyll Island. On November 16, 1819, and for several weeks thereafter he ran an ad in the *Daily Georgian* offering the island "indisputably the finest property on the sea coast of the Carolinas or Georgia," the ad boasted, "for the cultivation of cotton or the enjoyment and preservation of health." It extolled as well the abundance of game and timber.[81] Apparently he had no takers.

The du Bignons were hospitable and charming and soon had a wide circle of prominent friends. They played host to the Coupers and Spaldings from nearby Saint Simons as well as their Savannah and Brunswick friends. However, life did not go as smoothly as they had supposed. The son of Marguerite du Bignon's previous marriage, who had become, like his father, a naval officer, had by 1815 fallen on hard times and sent his three daughters and a son to live with their grandmother. The boy did not long survive after arriving in Georgia, but Christophe came to despise the girls, whom he thought to be after his wealth. To make matters worse, the second daughter, Clémence, caught the fancy of her half-uncle Joseph who, despite his father's objections, married her on October 27, 1819.[82]

Christophe never forgave his son. The family were staunch Catholics, and even had Christophe not disliked the girl so intensely, he would no doubt have objected on the grounds of the Church's interdiction against consanguineous marriage. As a consequence of the marriage, Joseph du Bignon was virtually disinherited by his father. In his will, Christophe left Jekyll Island and his other properties to his younger son, Henri, while Joseph was left only eighty dollars a year and was pointedly mentioned in the will only after "my mulatto woman named Maria Theresa and her daughter Margueretta." To them he also left eighty dollars a year, their freedom, insofar "as the Laws of the Country will allow," and a slave of their own, "my Negro woman Nelly," under the care and protection of his executors, "who should allow them to leave the State if necessary for their comfort."[83] To his wife, he left six hundred dollars in annual income and "my Mansion House," along with its buildings, furniture, and house servants.

Christophe, although a slave owner, no doubt viewed himself as a benevolent one, declaring in his will "that my old Negroes be treated with all the humanly kindness accessory to their comfort." His relative kindness did not prevent his slaves, thirsty for liberty, from trying to escape. On September 5, 1810, Thomas Dechenaux, acting as du Bignon's agent, posted a wry ad in the *Savannah Evening Ledger* offering a ten-dollar reward for a runaway slave named Tom:

> Ran away about three weeks ago, from Jekyl Island, a NEGRO MAN, named Tom; about 36 years old; five feet, four or five inches high; has large whiskers, and is very artful. He took with him a small fishing canoe boat. The fellow is well known, and particularly remarkable from his being lame and disabled of the right arm, on account of a shot in the shoulder, which he received (being on the same errand) some time after his legal death and burial, about the year 1804; but notwithstanding, was found again, whereby the coroner was disappointed, having to return the fees. He was afterwards drowned; appeared again, and is again vanished. In the hope that he may once more re-appear, the above reward is offered and will be paid for him, on his being apprehended, dug or fished up, and delivered on the above island. . . .

Such desperation for freedom as that expressed by Tom's actions explains why, when the opportunity came during the War of 1812 for du Bignon's slaves to escape with the help of the British, they did not hesitate. Twenty men (one Tom among them), six women, and two children made up the twenty-eight slaves who boarded the British frigate *Lacedomonian* during its raid on Jekyll Island on December 1, 1814. The British plundered the du

Bignon home as well, taking away money, plate, jewelry, and clothing and destroying crops and livestock. A later claim filed against the British government attested to $69,418.50 in damages and loss of revenue. The claim was not settled until 1828, three years after Christophe's death, and even then for only $10,690, or about 15 percent of its declared value. John Couper from Saint Simons Island pursued the ship that had taken away both his and du Bignon's slaves as far as Bermuda, where he saw one of du Bignon's escaped slaves aboard the frigate *Brune,* to which he had been transferred. Others, he learned, had been sent to Melville Island and still others to Halifax, Nova Scotia.[84] Although one might hope that the freedom-hungry slave Tom was finally set at liberty by the British, it must be noted that one Tom, valued at $450, was listed among the slave inventory at du Bignon's death in 1825.[85]

Christophe's son Henri (now called Henry by the Americans)[86] had grown up on the island with only his brother and the slave children as playmates. Most of the settlers along the Georgia coast from Darien south were of English or Scottish descent, and marriageable young women of the Catholic faith and of French descent were rare indeed outside Savannah. Therefore, when a young Frenchwoman named Ann Amelia Nicolau, just his age, appeared as the house guest of John Couper on Saint Simons, it seemed a match sent from heaven.

Ann Amelia, originally from Bordeaux, France, had come to Saint Simons, separated from Jekyll by only a short boat ride across Saint Simons Sound, at the behest of her brothers Joseph and Bernard, the latter of whom was her guardian. The former had been shipwrecked off the Georgia coast and, once rescued, had liked it so much that he sent for his brothers, Bernard and Paschal, and eventually for their sister, Ann Amelia. Just prior to her arrival, however, her brother Joseph was drowned, and another brother, Bernard, had fallen sick with the malarial fevers that struck the coastal lands in the summer. When Ann Amelia arrived a short time later, she was given the hospitality of the Couper

Ann Amelia Nicolau (Mrs. Henri du Bignon). The miniature portrait was found on the body of her brother who drowned just before her arrival in Georgia. The miniature was partially defaced by the salt water. (Southern Historical Collection, Library of the University of North Carolina, Chapel Hill)

plantation. But according to a letter of Aaron Burr, who had taken refuge on the Georgia coast after fatally shooting Alexander Hamilton in a duel and who, as it happened, visited the Couper plantation during her stay there, the tragic news about the two brothers was kept from her until Bernard was out of danger from his illness.[87]

It was doubtless John Couper, a jovial and florid Scotsman, who introduced Ann Amelia to the du Bignon family. According to one source, they met when Christophe Poulain du Bignon called at the Couper plantation to express his condolences to a fellow countryman on her brother's death. He was, as the story goes, "so struck by her beauty and charm that he promptly offered her either of his two sons in marriage."[88] One may question whether

such a proposal would have been made on so inappropriate an occasion, though a young woman whose prospects looked a bit gloomy might well have found it welcome even then. Not only had she lost her brother, but she had also recently lost her parents, who were killed during a slave uprising in Santo Domingo, and most of her inheritance was either gone or in jeopardy. Still, even though Christophe may have been captivated by her fairness and grace, he must have waited until a later occasion to propose the match, for the marriage did not take place for three years.

When the prenuptial agreement was drawn up on April 30, 1807, between Henri Charles du Bignon, who was not quite twenty at the time, and Ann Amelia Nicolau, John Couper and her brother Bernard were among the witnesses, along with Christophe and his son Joseph. The agreement gave the couple ten slaves and forty acres of cotton land on Jekyll for their use. They were officially married on Monday, January 18, 1808, by the rector of the Catholic church of Savannah.[89]

During the next eighteen years Ann Amelia bore Henri du Bignon nine children, five daughters and four sons, one of whom she named for her benefactor John Couper. Their first daughter, Maria Louisa, born on March 31, 1808, said to be Christophe's favorite grandchild, would die in 1824.[90] By his own testimony he never ceased weeping for her until his own death in 1825. His death was followed by that of his wife in December of the same year, leaving his son Henri in full possession of the island and the "Mansion House."

The following year, 1826, Ann Amelia gave birth to her last child, named Henry Charles for his father, with the spelling thoroughly anglicized. Though his wife's beauty had no doubt faded from the incessant strain of bearing nine children, Henri du Bignon's star was at its peak. He had come into his full inheritance, and he would in the coming years rise to the rank of colonel in the local militia, which was part of the Seventh Battalion of Georgia's Third Regiment. In about 1814 he was chosen as a commissioner of Glynn Academy, the public school system of Glynn County. Clearly, duties on his plantation, which still included fifty-seven slaves, did not prevent him from taking an active part in community activities. In the mid-1830s, as Brunswick enjoyed a short-lived "boom," du Bignon was engrossed in efforts to promote the economic strength of the city. When the bank of Brunswick was established in 1838, he was elected to serve as its first president. As one article in the *Brunswick Advocate* stated, "Colonel du Bignon is extremely well-known and highly esteemed, and is in every way qualified to discharge the duties of the office." Although neither the bank nor the city of Brunswick thrived from his effort, Henri continued to be well respected, serving at one point as tax collector and being appointed Justice of the Inferior Court.[91]

As a sportsman as well, Henri du Bignon was in his prime. Like his father, he was drawn to the sea and cut a dashing figure in regattas and boat races along the Georgia coast with his racing vessels, the *Goddess of Liberty* and the *Sarah and Catherine,* named for two of his younger daughters.

What could have caused such a civic-minded man to flaunt community values and conventions in the following decade one can only speculate. In any case, in the 1840s, ten years before his wife's death, Henri took as his mistress an English widow, Sarah Aust, who had come with her young daughter, Mary, to Jekyll Island as a tutor to his children. She bore him three children between 1840 and 1848. Even prior to his liaison with Sarah Aust, he fathered by a slave mistress at least one child, Charlotte, who was acknowledged at her baptism as "a free colored person and illegitimate child of Henry Du Bignon," as the records of the Cathedral of Saint John the Baptist in Savannah describe her.[92]

Despite his infidelities, at Ann Amelia's death from pneumonia on May 4, 1850, Henri paid her all the honor that a grieving (or perhaps guilt-ridden) husband may have felt he owed his wife. Her death occurred in Brunswick, and her funeral cortege

back to the island was heart-rending. As one person has described it, "The funeral possession, the coffin in the first boat, the crew dressed in mourning garments, followed by a long line of boats filled with relatives and friends, the rowers chanting 'Spirituals' in low tones was an impressive sight, as it came down the river from Brunswick, crossed the sound, and slowly wound its way through the tortuous channel of the little creek to the old landing [named Margeret's Landing, presumably for Marguerite du Bignon]. . . . From there the cortege followed the coffin, walked to the little burying ground and . . . Amelie Nicholai [sic] was laid by the side of the old chevalier and of her brother, who had met so tragic a death years before."[93]

After his wife's death Henri du Bignon did not marry his mistress, Sarah Aust. Instead, in 1852 he wed her daughter, Mary. Mary Aust would bear him five more children before his death on December 7, 1866, at the age of seventy-nine.[94] When he married Mary Aust, they set up their home at Ellis Point just north of Brunswick on Yellow Bluff Creek, where he lived out the rest of his life with his young wife, their children, and some of the children born to him by his wife's mother. From the early 1850s, the island plantation was left under the management of his two unmarried sons, John Couper and Henry Charles.

Three years before Henri's death, his children by Ann Amelia Nicolau, two of whom were already caring for the Jekyll property and possibly invoking their mother's prenuptial agreement with their father, demanded that he deed Jekyll Island to them. Alarmed no doubt by his growing second family, they insisted that the division of the land be made during his lifetime rather than trust him to treat them fairly in his will. Therefore, in 1863, in the midst of the Civil War, Henri deeded over to his three surviving sons, Charles, John Couper, and Henry (his second son, Joseph, having died, like his mother, in 1850), and to Eliza, his eldest and only unmarried daughter, the various parcels of land on

Painting of the *Wanderer*, the ship that brought the last major shipload of slaves to the United States in 1858, an incident in which members of the du Bignon family were involved. (Courtesy of Jekyll Island Museum)

Jekyll, many thousands of acres to each of the sons, and thirty acres to his daughter.[95]

On November 23, 1858, John and Henry du Bignon posted a notice in the *Savannah Daily Morning News,* warning "All Persons. . . against landing on the Island of Jekyl . . . or in any way trespassing on said island" and discharged their white overseer.[96] One week later just before dawn on the morning of November 29, the *Wanderer,* a vessel belonging to well-known Savannah businessman Charles Lamar, landed at Jekyll Island with a cargo of 409 slaves. Because the United States government had outlawed the importation of slaves in 1808, the vessel had been surreptitiously outfitted and all arrangements for the slaving expedition kept secret. As soon as the African prisoners were unloaded at Jekyll, the ship was taken to the Little Satilla River and anchored out of sight of passing ships.

The du Bignons' brother-in-law, Robert Hazelhurst, husband of their sister Catherine, was the physician called in to attend the slaves, suffering from the ill effects of their voyage under excruciating and unsanitary conditions.[97] Only the healthy had survived, and almost eighty had died during the trip. From Jekyll Island the unfortunate captives were quietly sold to planters throughout the coastal area. In spite of their efforts at secrecy, news of the landing spread quickly, and a deputy was sent to Jekyll Island to serve a subpoena on John Couper du Bignon for complicity in the affair. Although no firm evidence exists, newspapers reported that the du Bignon brothers received up to $15,000 for their involvement in the *Wanderer* episode, which seemed to amount primarily to allowing Lamar to use the island as a way station for his illegal cargo.[98] Although both John and Henry du Bignon were indicted in the incident, John was found not guilty, and the case against his brother Henry, who had apparently not been living on Jekyll Island at the time the *Wanderer* landed, was not prosecuted.[99]

When the Civil War broke out in 1861, John du Bignon, like most other coastal planters, moved inland with his slaves. All of Brunswick was deserted as well. The Confederate army strongly fortified Jekyll Island against enemy attack, but by

February 10, 1862, Robert E. Lee had decided to order a withdrawal of the batteries at Jekyll and Saint Simons in order to concentrate his strength at Savannah.

On March 10, exactly one month after Lee's decision to evacuate Jekyll, Union leader H. W. Miller reported to his commanding officer that "I landed with the rifle company and marines of this vessel and hoisted the flag over the rebel batteries on Jekyl Island, guarding Saint Simon's entrance." [100] On Tuesday, April 29, Dr. Jacob Solis Cohen, acting assistant surgeon on the Union ship the *S. S. Florida*, went ashore at Jekyll and reported in his diary the condition of the du Bignon house, the former Horton tabby house. "Taking a short cut [from the beach where the party landed] through the brush & underwood we emerged into a military road leading inland from behind the fort. . . . Our road was strewed with a variety of beautiful wild flowers, among which were the blue bell & several beautiful flowers of scarlet & carnation tint. . . . We rested awhile, and then followed a road which within a few hundred yards brought us to an old ruin, formerly the family mansion of the DuBignons the owners of the island." [101] In all probability no member of the du Bignon family had occupied the tabby house after the departure of Henri du Bignon and his young bride about 1852 or possibly not since the death of Ann Amelia. It is known that members of the family constructed other dwellings on the island, though all have disappeared without a trace. In all probability John Couper du Bignon lived in one of these until the Civil War. After the war, he returned to the island and remained there, even after it was sold by his nephew John Eugene du Bignon to the Jekyll Island Club. Because of John Couper's attachment to Jekyll, where he had spent his entire life, the club permitted him to live out the rest of his life in what one club member described as a "tiny and ill-kept shack," which was located in the fields north of the west end of Wylly Road. [102]

The coming of the Civil War marked the end of the absolute control of Jekyll Island by the du Bignon family, but thanks to John Eugene du Bignon, the great-grandson of the island's patriarch, the family influence would briefly reassert itself in the 1880s, only to be relinquished once more in 1886 to the famous Jekyll Island Club. The "old tabby," as club members would call the house constructed so many years earlier by William Horton, continued to stand unoccupied, slowly deteriorating even beyond the "ruin" Cohen reported in his Civil War diary.

In 1898, members of the Jekyll Island Club undertook to restore and preserve the shell of the Horton House. The restoration work was finished in early May 1898, when Ernest Grob wrote to Stewart Maurice to report on the progress: "Tomorrow will finish up the 'tabby house.'. . . all the walls are up, and around the entire top has been put a layer of concrete, filling up the spaces which were broken out above the windows, the middle wall has been brought up one and a half story[,] the chimney put in, iron rods run through to brace it, and lastly a coat of cement over the entire outside. To my mind the picturesqueness has now been taken from the ruin, and it looks like a modern house. However it will last many years now." [103] Thanks to these primitive preservation efforts by club members, the Horton House is still standing, but it is only as a shell of its former splendor when it was the home of one of Georgia's earliest colonial settlers and a family of French aristocrats who made it their refuge from the violence and the economic privations of the French Revolution.

DU BIGNON COTTAGE

Owners: John Eugene du Bignon, 1884–86; Jekyll Island Club, 1886–1947

Constructed: 1884

Architecture: Stick style with some Queen Anne elements

Architect: Unknown

The du Bignon family continued to operate its sea island cotton plantation until the Civil War, when fears of invasion by Union troops drove most coastal planters to the mainland. In the midst of the Civil War, on August 3, 1863, Henry du Bignon deeded Jekyll Island to his three surviving sons and eldest daughter. To his son John Couper, he gave that portion of the island located north of the beach road and known as Rock Bois. To his son Henry Jr. he gave some three thousand acres north of Rock Bois to the extremity of the island. His son Charles received the southern portion of the island, about fifteen hundred acres. To his daughter Eliza went a thirty-acre plot known as Bryan's Old Field.

By 1884 only Eliza still owned her portion. John Couper had returned to Jekyll after the war and

The du Bignon House in its original location. (Courtesy of Georgia Department of Archives and History, original in Jekyll Island Museum)

lived on the land in one of the houses that had been constructed during his family's ownership of Jekyll.[1] Even though he apparently loved the island and never wanted to live anywhere else, the plantation after the war became a losing proposition. He and his brothers hung on as long as they could, but one by one the parcels were sold. John Couper kept his land the longest, but apparently needing the money, he deeded his Jekyll property on December 1, 1883, to Gustav Friedlander, a German immigrant and Brunswick dry goods merchant, and William A. O. Anderson, a local attorney. Henry du Bignon Jr. had conveyed his land to one Martin E. Tufts in 1876. And in 1879 the portion belonging to Charles du Bignon was sold at public auction by his widow, Ann.[2]

The highest bidder on the latter parcel of land, however, was John Eugene du Bignon, the son of Charles's brother Joseph who had died of fever in 1850 and had not, therefore, participated in the division of the Jekyll land. Although John du Bignon had his finger in many Brunswick pies, he saw a great potential for Jekyll and decided to construct "an elegant home" there.[3] By this time the Horton House which his great-grandfather had occupied, had fallen into disrepair from neglect.

Selecting a site three miles south of the Horton House and located on what the press called "steamboat channel," or Jekyll Creek (now Jekyll River), he constructed in 1884 a splendid stick-style house with the gabled roof, overhanging eaves, wooden wall cladding, and diagonal porch support braces (stickwork) typical of the style. The house also suggests shifting tastes and shares some characteristics of the slightly later Queen Anne style, with its bay windows and dominant front-facing gable. Using for the most part the local pine and oak, du Bignon's "elegant" new home was, in reality, a fine farmhouse, suitable for his small family and capable of absorbing a few guests when need be.

Du Bignon had in 1876 married Frances (Fannie) Schlatter Westmorland, a comely widow and the daughter of Col. Charles Lyon Schlatter. Her father, a civil engineer who had been chief engineer for the state of Pennsylvania, had come to Brunswick because of his health and in quest of a milder climate and, once there, had organized the Brunswick & Albany Railroad.[4] Du Bignon's bride, Fannie Westmorland, had been widowed, according to most accounts, on her wedding day, July 5, 1867. Courted by several young men in the area, she finally had made young Eardley G. Westmorland her choice.[5] Rejection so enraged another of her suitors that he shot and killed the young bridegroom just after the ceremony. Nine years later, John Eugene du Bignon became her second husband.

The couple had only one daughter, Josephine, named for John Eugene's favorite sister and born in 1878. She would prove to be as attractive as her mother and, on the occasion of her marriage to Williams Jennings Butts in 1902, was referred to as a young woman "noted for her beauty and charm." It was claimed at the time of her death in 1965 that she had once been voted "the most beautiful woman in Georgia."[6]

Du Bignon was, above all, an entrepreneur. Known as "a dominant personality in financial circles of Brunswick,"[7] he was involved in almost every major undertaking the city knew from the 1870s until his retirement from active affairs some forty years later. Already recognized as a leading citizen at the time of his wedding, he was elected a city alderman that same year and would during his lifetime serve in many civic capacities, among them as a member of the city's Harbor and Railroads Committee and Board of Education and as president of the Brunswick Club. His business activities were equally varied: He was president or director at various times of the South Atlantic Towing Company, the Southern Cement Stone Company, the Brunswick Savings & Trust Company, the *Times Advertiser* Publishing Company, the Brunswick & Florida Inland Steamboat Company, the Cumberland Route of the Brunswick & South Atlantic

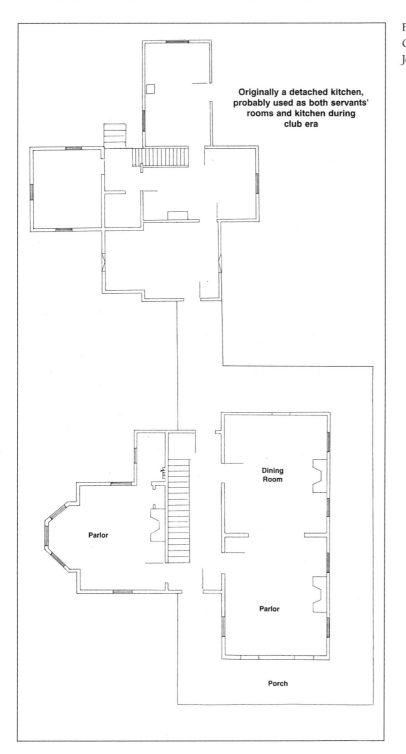

Originally a detached kitchen, probably used as both servants' rooms and kitchen during club era

Dining Room

Parlor

Parlor

Porch

First-floor plan of the du Bignon Cottage. (Based on plans in the Jekyll Island Museum)

John Eugene du Bignon was instrumental in the founding of the Jekyll Island Club. (Everett Collection, Coastal Georgia Historical Society)

Frances Schlatter Westmorland was the wife of John Eugene du Bignon. (Courtesy of Jekyll Island Museum)

Josephine Marie du Bignon, the daughter of John Eugene and Frances du Bignon, was renowned for her beauty. (Courtesy of Jekyll Island Museum)

Company, the Brunswick Foundry & Manufacturing Company, and the Saint Simons Transit Company. In addition, he also owned a principal interest in the Brunswick and Altamaha Canal property and a one-fifth interest in the Brunswick Street Railroad.[8] In 1884, at age thirty-five, he was nearing the peak of his entrepreneurial effectiveness. And certainly the deal he was able to work with the recovery of the Jekyll Island land was an excellent example of his skill.

His brother-in-law, Newton Finney, who had married John Eugene's older sister, Josephine, on April 17, 1860, just prior to the Civil War, was a kindred spirit. An equally enterprising northerner who had been dismissed from West Point in 1855 for insufficient academic prowess, Finney had joined the U.S. Coast Survey and had come south to chart the topography of the Georgia and Florida coasts. While in the Brunswick area he had been introduced to the du Bignon family, probably by John Eugene's future father-in-law, Charles L. Schlatter, now chief engineer of the Brunswick and Florida Railroad, who showed him "courtesies" and "assistance" during the time he was charting Saint Simons Sound. When war broke out, Finney clung to his government job as long as possible, and when he was finally forced at gunpoint by an armed committee from Bayport, Florida, to give it up, he returned to Brunswick and his bride. Writing to Confederate congressman Francis Bartow of Savannah on March 15, 1861, he requested a commission in the Confederate army. "Though by birth a native of New York, my . . . ties of Home and marriage are with the South," he contended. He wrote as well to Jefferson Davis and was successful in receiving an appointment, rising in time to the rank of captain in the Confederate army.[9]

After the war Finney, like du Bignon, had begun to cast about for new ways of making money. In December of 1871 he was appointed by the Brunswick City Council to go to New York to negotiate with steamship owners to establish direct communications between New York City and Brunswick.[10] By 1872 he had moved his family to New York and within two years had become a partner with Oliver Kane King in King, Finney and Company, railway bankers and merchants.

Du Bignon, in the meantime, had begun to consider the possibility of trying to acquire the rest of Jekyll Island and sell it for a tidy profit to some northern investor. Working through his brother-in-law in New York, he invited several groups of potential investers down for a hunt on Jekyll. Finally, in April 1885 dry goods merchant John Claflin with his cousin E. E. Eames came to Jekyll at the invitation of du Bignon. Not only could he take them on a hunt on the island, he could show them the warmth and hospitality of his new home there as well. Aware all his life of the value of publicity, du Bignon had touted Jekyll Island as a huntsman's paradise, and the *Brunswick Advertiser and Appeal,* in reporting the Claflin-Eames visit, reinforced these views: "Jekyl Island is probably the finest hunting ground in Georgia, the proprietors of the island having taken special pains to protect their game from the blunderbusses of the average gunmen, they are now able to entertain their friends with a hunt either for deer or turkeys, for the island abounds with both."[11]

Du Bignon's salesmanship was effective, and it did not take him long to persuade John Claflin to invest in Jekyll and to lend him the money to acquire the entire island. On June 16, 1885, du Bignon signed three promissory notes to Claflin, who loaned him in all $10,700, using as collateral "all of that certain tract of land known as Jekyl Island." On May 26 du Bignon had drawn up an agreement between himself and Martin Tufts to buy back the northern end of the island "together with all and singular, the houses, out-house, edifices, buildings, stables, yards, gardens, liberties, privileges, easements" for $3,500. A similar agreement for $4,000 was signed

Josephine du Bignon Finney, sister of John Eugene du Bignon, was the wife of Newton S. Finney. (Courtesy of Mrs. L. C. Liebrecht)

Newton S. Finney, with the help of his brother-in-law, John Eugene du Bignon, played a vital role as the founder of the Jekyll Island Club. (Courtesy of Mrs. L. C. Liebrecht)

on June 16 with William A. O. Anderson acting for himself and Gustav Friedlander for their middle section of the island, and finally on June 18 he agreed to pay his Aunt Eliza $100 for her thirty acres. Thus, for a total of $7,600 he purchased the rest of the island, which in turn he planned to sell, along with his southern portion, to Claflin.[12]

When du Bignon's brother-in-law, Newton Finney, learned of this scheme, he conceived an even better idea. Perhaps instead of selling it to one investor, they could sell it to a corporation of investors, organize a club for huntsmen, and thereby make a greater profit than one person would be willing to pay. He and his partner King, through their Union Club memberships, were well acquainted with many prosperous New Yorkers. He felt sure he could put together a corporate group who would be willing to purchase the island.

At the same time John Eugene set about from his vantage point in the community to "sell" the Brunswick area as a healthy and exceedingly pleasant location for a resort to offset northerners' fears of a miasmic climate and the malarial fevers that had struck the Georgia low country often in the past.[13] In addition, he set about to stock the island with the best possible game supply. Now "the happy owner of the entire island," as the *Advertiser and Appeal* congratulated him, he was "determined to keep up the supply of game on his island. He now has the finest hunting in Georgia, probably, but is not content to have the supply diminished." As a consequence, he was bringing in abundant quantities of quail, deer, and pheasants.[14]

Within a matter of months, Newton Finney had begun to organize what would become the Jekyll Island Club. It was incorporated in December 1885, and on February 17, 1886, Finney signed an agreement with his brother-in-law to purchase the island in the name of the Jekyll Island Club for $125,000, which would represent a remarkable profit for du Bignon.

The agreement gave Finney until April 1 to find fifty prospective members who would agree to take two shares of stock at $600 each, or the contract would be "of no effect." In fact, working with his partner King, he must have succeeded beyond his wildest imagining. The people who agreed to become members of the club included the cream of New York society, among them William K. Vanderbilt, J. P. Morgan, Pierre Lorillard, Henry B. Hyde, and Joseph Pulitzer. In Chicago as well they had heard about the club, and from there Marshall Field led a small but impressive list of new members. Members were also accepted from Philadelphia, Albany, Boston, Buffalo, San Francisco, and Athens, Pennsylvania. There was only one Southerner among them, and his name stood out prominently on the list—John Eugene du Bignon.

Before the first of April Finney had signed up fifty-three members, and the Jekyll Island Club became a reality. Du Bignon with his extraordinary profits from the sale of the island was able to pay back Claflin, who had himself become a member of the new club, and have a virtual fortune for the times, more than $100,000, left over.

He had, in the process, given up his new home to the fledgling club and moved once more into Brunswick, where for many years he lived in a dwelling at 901 Union Street. In 1887, prior to the completion of the new $45,000 club house, which had been designed by Chicago architect Charles A. Alexander, Finney had invited club members to visit the island and stay in "the small Club House," which was "open for the convenience of such members and their guests, as may desire to visit the Island before the opening of the New house."[15] He could only have been referring to the former du Bignon house, as it was the only suitable place on the island. Visiting committees and members who came down to inspect the progress on the club house no doubt stayed there. Once the new club house was completed, the club began to utilize the du Bignon house as the superintendent's cottage, and Richard Livingston Ogden, the newly appointed superintendent, who would oversee the club's development and first season, no doubt made it his residence, as did Ernest Gilbert Grob, who would serve forty-two years as club superintendent.

For many years du Bignon maintained an active interest in the club, making certain it got off to a good start with the press by personally escorting a Brunswick reporter to the island for a tour as soon as the new club house was complete. The journalist was duly impressed: "The elegant steam yacht Howland was put at our disposal and we were comfortably transported to the island, where we began the inspection of the Club House. . . . it is an elegant structure and unlike anything else in this section. From a distance it looks like some English castle with its square shaped windows and its lofty tower."[16]

As the only local club member, du Bignon played a major role in readying the island for its first season. For example, working in conjunction with Superintendent Ogden, he was authorized "to contract for the construction . . . of an artesian well." He and William B. D'Wolf served as a committee to outfit the stables that were to be constructed. With

Lewis Edwards he was appointed to build or purchase "boats, skiffs, sailboats and floats as may be deemed necessary."

Appointed along with Finney at the first meeting of the executive committee to take "general charge of the Island, its police protection, increase of the game and care and sale of the live stock," du Bignon finally carried out the task with Ogden, who was appointed at the second executive committee meeting to replace Finney, who had been elected permanent secretary at a handsome monthly salary of $300 instead. In short, du Bignon and Ogden were to act as "a local Board of administration on all matters pertaining to the general management and government and police of the island."[17]

In addition to his interest in the Jekyll Island Club, du Bignon was also a principal owner of the Oglethorpe Hotel in Brunswick, having put up the money to remodel the old Oglethorpe House. The new hotel was going to open in the same season as the Jekyll Island Club, and du Bignon had assured club leaders that the hotel could provide staff support as well for Jekyll's opening season. But when it became apparent that the Oglethorpe would do well to staff its own premises, Ogden was put to no little inconvenience trying to scare up kitchen help, waiters, and chambermaids and was forced to begin the season with an inexperienced staff.

Nevertheless, in the opening years of the club, du Bignon wielded significant influence simply because he was on the scene to take care of the many details that were necessary locally. He had even influenced the club to utilize the services of his brother-in-law, A. J. Crovatt, as club attorney, which they did for many years. But his influence quickly waned as the club gained momentum and increasing numbers of other members moved into official roles. After the club's formal opening in 1888, du Bignon served briefly as a member of the game committee but quickly fell into oblivion as far as club leadership was concerned. He used Jekyll facilties often during its first five years of operation,

but after 1892 he rarely came to the island, and in 1896 he gave up his membership altogether.

Some of his disillusionment with the club may have resulted from the fact that in 1895 his brother-in-law, Finney, had been forced by club officials out of his so-called sinecure office as permanent secretary.[18] Finney, who had made and lost several fortunes in his lifetime and had been forced to declare bankruptcy on at least one occasion, was severely affected by the loss of the club income, on which he had come to depend more than ever following his serious financial losses in the panic of 1893.[19] With the death of his wife in 1892, he simply lacked the heart to start again, and he never fully recovered from this series of financial disasters.

Du Bignon had suffered his own financial setback in the wake of the 1893 depression. As a daring entrepreneur, he made a great deal of money, but he also took great risks, and as a consequnce his fortune suffered occasional vicissitudes. At about this time he gave up his Union Street house and moved with his family into the Oglethorpe Hotel for a period of at least seven years.

Hoping to turn a quick profit, he had become involved in a rather daring, and illegal, gun-running trade to Cuba. As the "managing owner" of a vessel known as the *Dauntless*, he captured the interest of coastal residents during many months as his ship played hide-and-seek with government officials. Accused of defying the United States government's policy of neutrality in the Cuban uprising against a repressive Spanish government by smuggling "a number of men and a large quantity of arms and ammunition" to the Cuban insurgents, owners of the *Dauntless* were brought into court on September 29, 1896, at the very moment a furious storm struck the Brunswick area, killing at least seven people and doing an estimated $350,000 worth of damage. It interruped the controversial hearing by threatening literally to blow down the courthouse. Spectators and court officers fled the building and reconvened in the police courtroom, only to be driven out once more by the persistent leaking of the roof as the wind and rain continued to pound the city. But neither storm nor legal action could daunt the *Dauntless,* and, after paying a fine, its owners allegedly continued their smuggling activities until the vessel was finally fired on and captured on October 23, 1896, by the *USS Raleigh.* Far from damaging du Bignon's reputation in the area, it may well have enhanced it by providing an exciting summer and fall for the citizens of Brunswick, most of whom, like Americans in general, were sympathetic to the Cuban rebel cause. They had vicariously followed and cheered on the movements of the defiant vessel, which the local press depicted as a heroic and cunning "Artful Dodger."[20]

With these activities and their concomitant financial risks occupying the attention of John Eugene du Bignon, he allowed his membership in the Jekyll Island Club to lapse. In December 1896, two months after the capture of the vessel, his lucrative

smuggling trade at an end, his share of club stock was sold for debt.

That same year his former house on Jekyll was to be moved to make way for the construction of an apartment building, the Sans Souci, which was to include six apartments owned by various club members, among them Henry Hyde, William Rockefeller, and J. P. Morgan. The *Brunswick Times-Advertiser* announced on June 25, 1896, "the old duBignon residence, now used as the superintendent's headquarters is to be removed, and a large casino, costing well up in the thousands, is to be built on the site." The fact that du Bignon's newspaper reported that a casino rather than an apartment building was to be built suggests how far out of touch he was with club affairs at the time. On August 10, the paper reported, once again erroneously, on the intended use of the land, "The old duBignon cottage on Jekyl Island is being removed to-day in order to allow work to commence on a new

One of the earliest photographs of the Jekyll Island Club House, *left,* with the du Bignon House still in its original location, *right.* (Everett Collection, Coastal Georgia Historical Society)

Ernest Gilbert Grob, club superintendent for forty-two years, resided during the club's early seasons in the Superintendent's Cottage, as the du Bignon House was sometimes called. (Courtesy of Jekyll Island Museum)

intendent, was now, at least for the January to April club season, called Club Cottage and offered for rental to members and guests at a cost of $15 per day for two months or less and $300 per month for longer periods of time. Superintendent Grob described the cottage when he wrote to club member and prospective renter John G. Moore on February 9, 1898: "Club cottage contains five sleeping rooms, bath, parlor and three servants rooms, rents fifteen dollars per day linen, fire, light and service included." [23] Before Moore could reply, member J. Herbert Ballantine had already snapped it up.[24] By the time Grob described the property the following year, however, the use of the rooms had changed somewhat. Writing to A. E. Claflin, he listed the rooms as: "1st floor: -Parlor -Back-Parlor (which can be made into a bed-room should you require it) and Den. 2nd floor: -3 bed-rooms and a bath-room. Attic: -3 servants rooms. In the extension, there is a kitchen, laundry and a room for the colored woman (who takes care of the house) to sleep in. The house rents for $300. per month, the club furnishes woman care-taker, bedding complete, towels, light and fire. Rooms are heated by fire-places, halls by furnace. Hot and Cold water." [25]

One of Club Cottage's most famous guests was Theodore Vail, president of AT&T. Vail, recuperating there from a leg injury in 1915, celebrated on January 25 the opening of the first transcontinental telephone line with a hookup that included Vail at Jekyll Island, Pres. Woodrow Wilson in Washington, Alexander Graham Bell in New York, and Bell's assistant, Thomas Watson, in San Francisco. Throughout the years the cottage would serve as the residence of some of the nation's wealthiest men and their families.

Du Bignon's loss of membership in the Jekyll Island Club by no means severed entirely his association with its members or ended his attempts to use these contacts to feather his nest. In an effort to promote the club and ingratiate himself with Henry Hyde, president of the Equitable Life Assurance As-

cottage to be built on the ground on which it is at present situated." [21] The move of less than a hundred yards, accomplished by mules and wagons, cost $550 and changed the look of the house considerably.[22] The old foundation and basement were demolished, and the structure was lowered onto brick piers. The lattice work was taken off the porch, the house was repainted using drastically different colors, and ornamental brackets were added to the porch columns to reduce its old-fashioned stick-style appearance and enhance its Queen Anne features, in greater harmony with the club house.

With its refurbishment, the cottage, which had served primarily as the residence of the club super-

sociation in New York and Jekyll's so-called "czar" at the time, du Bignon conceived the idea of a special article about the club, to be published by his Brunswick newspaper, and first approached Hyde about it in December 1896. Hyde embraced the idea with enthusiasm. Never one to put off until tomorrow what can be done today, he wrote to du Bignon on Christmas Eve, asking how soon he could get the article ready. "I would like to get it as soon after the first of January as possible. The fact that Jekyl Island will be well advertised will be good for Brunswick also." [26] On January 15 du Bignon informed Hyde that the article would have to be delayed because of the absence of the staff member he wanted to work on it. By late spring it still had not been done, but the concept had been expanded considerably. On May 22, Superintendent Grob wrote to Hyde that du Bignon had informed him the day before that the *Brunswick Times* was going "to publish a 5000 copy paper and send it all over the country, writing up Brunswick, Saint Simons, Cumberland and Jekyl." [27] Du Bignon wanted to

The first official transcontinental telephone call was made from Jekyll Island in 1915 during Theodore Vail's stay in the Club Cottage. Vail is on the telephone, while William Rockefeller listens in. J. P. Morgan Jr., *third from left*, is standing behind Rockefeller. (AT&T Archives)

Du Bignon Cottage, also known as Club Cottage, is shown here after its move to its present location in 1896. (Everett Collection, Coastal Georgia Historical Society)

know whether the Jekyll Island Club would be willing to make a contribution toward its publication. Whether the special paper appeared at this time is not known, but a similar edition was published in 1909.

Du Bignon also worked on behalf of the club to arrange better railroad connections so that members might avoid the "uncomfortable change of cars at Everett." He reported to Hyde on January 15, 1897, that the Southern Railroad was willing to cooperate with cars coming from Atlanta.[28] New Yorkers, however, who took another route, would not benefit from the arrangement and would, throughout the club's history, have to change trains at Thalmann, a junction north of Brunswick.

In 1898 du Bignon contacted Hyde once more, seeking to borrow $25,000 and offering the Oglethorpe Hotel as security. Hyde declined, stating that his company had a rule against "loaning money on hotel property." Du Bignon wrote again, this time offering his dock property with a 540-foot waterfrontage as security. But this time Hyde's secretary responded with a sense of finality that did not invite further negotiation: "this Society has established a rule not to loan money on property outside of the City of New York."[29]

That same year du Bignon's wife, Frances, requested permission from club president Charles Lanier and treasurer Frederic Baker to "hold moonlight excursions" on or around Jekyll that the Brunswick Humane Society would sponsor. Permission was granted, as it was routinely for such requests.[30]

Overall, however, by 1896 du Bignon's real influence at the Jekyll Island Club had ended, and although he still continued to contact members for one thing or another, there are no indications that he ever visited the island again. He lived out his long and fruitful life in Brunswick, involved in its many activities. In 1919 he was struck by a policeman's motorcycle and seriously though not fatally

Interior of the du Bignon Cottage. (Courtesy of Jekyll Island Museum)

injured. Still viewed in the press as a "popular Brunswickian," he had most recently worked as head of the employment service for the U.S. government in the area. "Col. duBignon has always been in the foremost for the uplifting of the city and community and his hundreds of friends hope his injuries will not be found to be as serious as they appeared last night," the *Brunswick News* reported on January 30, 1919.

In fact, du Bignon, after a long recovery period at Clifton Springs, New York, lived on another eleven years and continued to lead an active life. Finally in the fall of 1929 he suffered a stroke from which he never fully recovered. At his death on February 1,

1930, he was recognized as a member of "one of south Georgia's most distinguished families," and his obituary alleged with good reason that "he was connected with every civic movement and a majority of large enterprises of the city."[31]

With the closing of the Jekyll Island Club in 1942 and the takeover of the island by the State of Georgia in 1947, the du Bignon cottage was rented for almost forty years to various employees of the Jekyll Island Authority. Restored in 1989 to its former "elegance" as it looked following the move in 1896, it was opened to the public and is now available for all to see as part of Jekyll Island's Historic District.

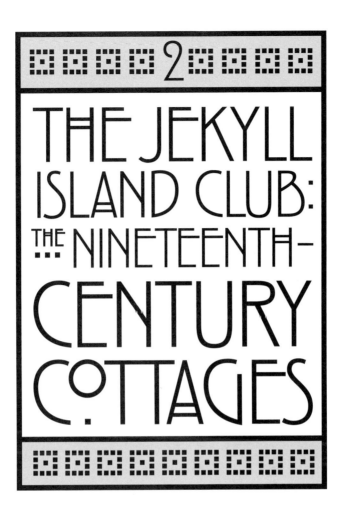

2

THE JEKYLL ISLAND CLUB: THE NINETEENTH-CENTURY COTTAGES

Owners: McEvers Bayard Brown, 1888–1926; Jekyll Island Club, 1926–ca. 1947

Constructed: 1888

Demolished: After 1944

Architecture: Queen Anne

Architect: William Burnet Tuthill

Of all the cottages built by Jekyll Island Club members, that of McEvers Bayard Brown, the first ever constructed, certainly has the most bizarre history, for it is the only one among them that was never occupied by its owner. Thirty-five-year-old Brown hired an architect and approved plans for its construction, then sailed away from the United States before it was completed, never to return again. Spending the rest of his life on his yacht anchored in the Colne River near the little town of Brightlingsea, England, he would become known as "the millionaire hermit of the Essex Coast."[1] Brown was from a prominent family of New York bankers who had as early as 1801 owned the commercial house and shipping concern of LeRoy, Bayard, and McEvers. The only child of Alexander Speers Brown and

The cottage built by eccentric millionaire McEvers Bayard Brown, who never occupied the house. (Courtesy of Georgia Department of Archives and History, original in Everett Collection, Coastal Georgia Historical Society)

Ruth Hunter Bayard, he was born July 5, 1852. His closest playmates as a child were his two first cousins Robert Fulton Cutting, who was born the same year as Brown and who would become a well-respected New York banker and economist, and William Bayard Cutting, two years older, who would be an equally distinguished New York lawyer as well as a financier and something of a reformer. Their closeness continued as adults. Both were, like Brown, members of the Jekyll Island Club. And until his death Brown gave as his legal address 32 Nassau Street in New York, which was the office address of his two cousins as well.

Little is known about Bayard Brown's early life. He was alternately listed in the New York City Directory as a lawyer or a banker, and he clearly had an active business career during his young adult years. By the time he was thirty, for example, he was serving as a board member for the Terminal and Danville railroad lines.[2] Conflicts within the Terminal board, however, prompted a split and a spate of resignations. When Bayard Brown refused to resign, William Clyde, who spearheaded the opposition, pushed through a resolution to oust him along with another newcomer, John A. Rutherford.[3]

Six years after the Terminal conflict Bayard Brown joined the Jekyll Island Club. Although not a charter member, he was elected within the club's first year, on September 15, 1886, having been proposed by Oliver Kane King, business partner to the club's founder Newton Finney, and one who assisted many ways in getting the new club off the ground. King must have thought Brown a desirable club member, for not only was he from a distinguished family but also, from all accounts, seems to have had a reputation for cutting quite a figure in society. According to a *New York Times* article about Brown in 1911, "Before he left New York in the late eighties he was a leader in the most fashionable set," belonging to the elite Union, Riding, and Knickerbocker Clubs. "He was then less than 40 years old and a very handsome man."[4]

A visitor to his yacht in the late 1890s described Brown as a man of about average height, "elegantly dressed," with a rounded figure, perfectly fitting clothes, and soft, white hands. His "iron-gray hair" was "brushed straight up from his broad handsome forehead," and his beard, also iron gray, "came to a round point beneath a chin well formed and determined." He had, the visitor proclaimed, "the alert gray eyes of an up-to-date New York business man," and "his voice was unusually pleasant, his accent that of a cultivated and polished New Yorker." That is, in fact, what he was.[5] What he became, however, would never be fully explained or understood by either his friends or his family.

Brown's father had died in 1886, and at the time he joined the Jekyll Island Club he had just inherited the family fortune. Wealth gave him the freedom to choose his own life style, and a peculiar one it would be. It seems likely that he was attracted to the Jekyll Island Club because of the relative seclusion from New York it provided. He purchased two shares of stock, one from George E. Gray and one from Newton Finney, the latter of which brought with it lot 71, located in a rather remote area, half a mile north of the club house. Had he chosen to do so, it would have been a relatively simple matter in the early days of the club to negotiate a more desirable building site closer to the club house and its conveniences. Brown, however, seems to have preferred the lonely site he purchased from Finney. He had come early in life to prefer solitude to the vicissitudes of human interaction, and the isolated plot of land, unlike any other ever selected by a member as a building site, suited him just fine and served to reflect his curious personality.

Here overlooking the incomparable Marshes of Glynn, which had been immortalized by Sidney Lanier in 1878, Brown would build the first cottage to be erected by any club member on the island. Its construction was under way by February 22, 1888, when Thomas C. Clarke visited during the club's opening season and wrote to Charles Stewart Mau-

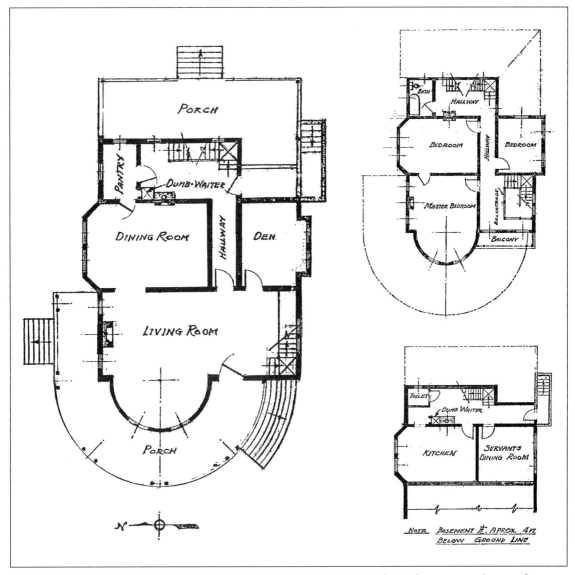

The first-floor, second-floor, and basement plans of the Brown Cottage were drawn from memory by one of its residents, E. P. Courier, in 1975. (Courtesy of Jekyll Island Museum)

rice that "One man has begun to build a cottage. What for I dont know. The club house is good enough for me."[6] But not for Brown, for whom the constant contacts at the club house would have been anathema. Mentioned for the first time in the club's executive minutes on March 14, 1889, the cottage must have been completed before the end of 1888, for it was carried for the first time in 1889 on the tax rolls, where houses were customarily included only after they had been completed for a full year. It was initially valued for taxes at $10,000, an amount that would decline over the years, no doubt reflecting a degree of neglect, until it stabilized in 1892 at $4,000.[7] The architect of the Brown house was, from all indications, the New York architect who also designed Carnegie Hall, the Princeton Inn, and the Columbia Yacht Club—William Burnet Tuthill. Tuthill, who had trained in the office of Richard Morris Hunt and was a founder of the Architectural League, was one of Brown's few guests on the island. It was he who oversaw the house from the time of its construction until the end of 1897, during which time he made at least three visits to the island, always as the guest but never in the company of Brown. A further piece of evidence is an erroneous entry in the *Dictionary of American Biography* which lists him as the architect of the Jekyll Island Club in 1888.[8] The architect of the clubhouse is well documented to have been Charles A. Alexander, and the clubhouse was constructed in 1887, not 1888. However, the entry is valuable in associating Tuthill with the Jekyll Island Club in 1888, exactly the date of the Brown house, the only cottage built on club property in that year.

In 1885 Tuthill had authored a book called *The Suburban Cottage: Its Design and Construction,* and the Brown house seemed to follow his recommendations in that work as precisely as possible. It conformed in practice to Tuthill's theoretical advice that a cottage "should be characterized by unity and directness, with truth and breadth of expression." As the book advised, the house faced northwest.[9] To take advantage of the spectacular view of the marshes, its northern and western facades were wrapped with a large rounded porch, which gave the impression of a great wing, like that of a seabird perched for flight. The cottage also followed Tuthill's more pragmatic ideas, such as his admonition to "place the bath-room over those parts of the story below which will be the least affected in event of leakage."[10]

Like the model house Tuthill sketched for his book, the Brown cottage made abundant use of verandahs and had both a dining room and bedroom with large bay windows and a single second-floor bathroom at the back of the house, with one additional toilet only for the servants. Such stylistic similarities and Tuthill's known oversight of the house from 1889 to 1897, at which time it was taken over by a New Yorker named Lyman Rhoades, make it virtually certain that he was its architect, a fact that the erroneous entry in the *Dictionary of American Biography* seems indirectly to confirm.

By the time the house was completed, Bayard Brown had sailed away on his yacht never to return. Brown's departure from the United States had ostensibly been intended to be only a two-year sea voyage. What prompted him never to return to his country has been the source of much speculation. According to the story most frequently told, Brown had built his Jekyll cottage for his bride-to-be, perhaps envisaging himself and his beloved like the mysterious lovers of Sidney Lanier's poem who

pace timidly down through the green colonnades
Of the dim sweet woods, of the dear dark woods
Of the heavenly woods and glades,
That run to the radiant marginal sand-beach within
The wide sea-marshes of Glynn.

Perhaps he, like the poet, saw the spot with its "Beautiful glooms" and "soft dusks in the noon-day fire" as one suited for "wildwood privacies" and "closets of lone desire."

If so, his bride-to-be, if she ever existed at all, was apparently less enthusiastic. Nothing is known about the young woman in question, and her identity remains a mystery. Some accounts claim she jilted him at the altar; others contend they were actually married when she ran away; still others question the story altogether. The legend was doubtless derived from a report that appeared at the time of his death of "the charred remains of a photograph of a woman" found in his cabin.[11] Although the story was repeated many times, the *Essex County Telegraph* called it "sensational" and reported that James Munson, who was Brown's steward, said the story was "all bunkum" and that no such charred remains were ever found. Whatever the truth, Bayard Brown's secret is lost among the legends that grew up around him. The *New York Times,* which dutifully reported the story, agreed: "There is the inevitable gossip about a love affair that drove Mr. Brown into exile, but somehow he did not act like a man thus disappointed."[12] All that is known for certain is that he fled the United States in the

summer of 1888,[13] ostensibly for a two-year cruise aboard his yacht, the *Lady Torfrida.* Eventually he found his way to the Essex coast of England, where he dropped anchor near the little town of Brightlingsea. There he would remain, a shadowy man living in lonely isolation from the world aboard his yacht until his death on April 8, 1926.

Brown had taken up yachting in the 1880s when he had bought the *Lady Torfrida* for $200,000 from Sir William Pearce, director of the Fairfield SB & Engineering Company, who had constructed the vessel for his own private use.[14] In 1889, he sold the yacht to a brother of the Russian czar[15] in order to purchase in 1890 a larger yacht, this one also from Pearce and also originally christened the *Lady Torfrida.*[16] The new yacht, whose name Brown would change to the *Valfreyia,* had allegedly been built for King Edward VII when he was prince of Wales. The prince refused the vessel, however, and negotiations

The west view of the Brown Cottage in 1915. (Courtesy of Jekyll Island Museum)

The Brown Cottage from the rear. (Everett Collection, Coastal Georgia Historical Society)

were under way to sell it to the czar of Russia, when Brown stepped in with an offer of £30,000, which was quickly snapped up.[17]

As early as 1894 stories about Brown's eccentric behavior began to appear in the press. The *New York Daily Tribune* suggested in August of that year that his antics had already "passed the border which separates eccentricity from insanity."[18] Still only forty-two years old and in possession of a sizable fortune since the death of his father in 1886, Brown seemed to waver between generosity toward the townspeople of Brightlingsea and what the *Tribune* interpreted as madness toward the crew aboard his yacht. Accounts of his generosity in Brightlingsea vary in magnitude, with at least one contending that his benefactions were up to a million dollars during his thirty-six years there.[19] In fact, his donations, doled out over a long period, were probably considerably more modest, consisting of annual contributions to Sunday school funds, thirty pounds here or there to repair the spire or purchase a peal of bells for the parish church,[20] and quiet contributions of wood or coal to keep poorer citizens warm during

the winter. His largest single contribution seems to have been £600 for the Bayard Recreation Grounds at Brightlingsea, which still bear his name. Nevertheless, townspeople viewed Bayard Brown as an important benefactor to the community, and his generosity reached even beyond Brightlingsea. The rector of Saint Mary's, in Southern Norfolk, for example, contended that Brown was "a most generous and kind man," adding that he had "a special regard for young people."[21]

There was another side to Bayard Brown, however, erratic and cruel, seen occasionally by would-be visitors to his yacht but best known to his crew. Whenever one of them had offended him in any way, he "waited until the victim was nicely in bed, and then suddenly dashed upon him with a stick, belaboring him until weary of the work, when he would bolt out of the cabin without saying a word." Second engineers were his special targets, and he delighted in "arming himself with the cook's poker and hunting the 'second' round the vessel." Wise men, it was said, "locked and barricaded themselves in their cabins." Some of his antics seemed more mischievous than cruel. A sport he seemed to enjoy particularly was dousing his men unexpectedly with water from a giant syringe used in England for washing windows. "Sometimes he would surprise an officer at dinner and give him the contents of the syringe full in the face." [22] The device was an unfailing source of merriment to the master of the *Valfreyia*. On occasion he would even dismiss the entire crew in a rage and sit for days, alone on his yacht, "without so much as a boy to clean his boots or cook his breakfast." [23]

Brown was also secretive about his mail, filing some of it behind locked doors but burning most of it himself as soon as it was read. Even the New York newspapers, which arrived at his yacht on a regular basis, were prohibited to the crew. Brown read them quickly and burned them in the galley stove, standing beside it until they were reduced to ashes, to make certain the crew did not get so much as a glance. None of his men was permitted to mention America in his presence, it was said, nor, they claimed, did he ever speak to them of his homeland. [24]

An element of paranoia also marked Brown's behavior. Suspicious that dynamite might be hidden among the coal in the ship's bunkers, he would, on occasion, have his crew throw all the coal overboard, thereby enriching the delighted coal dealers in the town. He also kept about him "a bodyguard of watchmen on duty day and night" to guard him against an unknown danger. And would-be visitors to the *Valfreyia* were sometimes questioned in a cryptic and puzzling fashion about warnings and signals, claims and penalties. [25]

Members of Brown's family, in spite of his odd behavior, considered him quite capable of looking after his own affairs. His cousin, Jekyll Islander William Bayard Cutting, when asked if the family had ever considered committing Brown to an asylum, replied: "Nothing of the kind has been thought of. Mr. Brown has been supposed to be able to look after his own affairs. He has managed his own estate,

and has written many letters to his agents in this city which have indicated that he was well posted in the affairs of his business." He hesitated, he said, to believe any reports of Brown's insanity. [26]

Cutting was right. Brown *did* seem able to manage his own affairs. His club dues and taxes were almost always paid on time by his New York agent, and he remained a member in good standing of the Jekyll Island Club until his death in 1926. In 1893, when the Jekyll Island Club, in an effort to fill its dwindling coffers, sold debenture bonds, most members purchased only $1,000 worth of the bonds. Brown's contribution to the effort, however, was $5,000, second only to that of Gordon McKay. [27] Only once did club superintendent Ernest G. Grob have to write to Brown's agent to inform him "I today paid the taxes ($54) on Mr. M. Bayard Brown's house to prevent it from being advertised 'for sale' as the taxes were due the 26th of December." [28] But on this occasion, notices had been sent to the architect Tuthill, who had evidently grown tired of handling the property of a man who showed so little interest in it himself and had turned the house over to a new agent, Lyman Rhoades of the Safe Deposit Company of New York. The delinquent taxes were apparently the result of some confusion as to who was responsible rather than indifference or neglect on the part of Bayard Brown.

Tax problems loomed ominously in England as well. After twenty-two years of Brown's yacht being anchored in the Colne River, the British government suddenly decided "that a habitation 200 yards from Brightlingsea is in England" and promptly served Mr. Brown notice that he was expected to pay income tax on the sizable revenues he received from his business interests each year. If Brown did suffer from insanity, he was not so insane as to fail to protest what he considered to be unjust taxation. Represented by one W. O. A. J. Danckwerts, he appealed to the courts, contending that "the income tax was for landlubbers and that a sea-going yacht, even though it did not go to sea, was not a residence."[29] The courts ruled against Brown, which brought Brightlingsea residents up in arms, for their greatest fear was that Brown would simply lift anchor and sail away, as he was threatening to do.

Bayard Brown had become to the town, suffering from a depressed shipping trade, the American goose who laid the community's golden egg. The tax decision, widely reported in the press, would, it was feared, "add to the unpopularity with which the income tax is already regarded at Brightlingsea." Over the years, the mysterious vessel and its eccentric millionaire anchored offshore had become something of a tourist attraction in the area and were, as such, regarded as one of the community's most valuable assets. "People come from afar out to look at the mysterious yacht," the *Times* contended, "and boatmen have made a profitable business of rowing visitors out into midstream for a closer view of the floating fixture."[30] According to an account published at the time of his death, Brown simply ignored, apparently without consequence, the ruling that he must pay taxes on his annual income.[31]

Although he was not fond of giving money to the government, he appeared to have little compunction about giving or even throwing it away, sometimes lavishly and in what appears to be foolish ways. Stories were told of his tossing handfuls of gold and silver overboard into the restless sea, sometimes in the middle of the night, sometimes in the direction of people desiring to come aboard his yacht. No doubt these stories contributed greatly to the popularity of tourist boating excursions to the vessel. At other times, however, visitors might expect, instead of coins, hot coals being tossed upon them. Everything depended upon the mood Brown happened to be in at any given time, and one approached the yacht at one's own peril. For a very fortunate few who found him in a particularly good humor, a ladder was lowered over the side of the ship, and the visitors were allowed aboard where Brown would "show them over the yacht from stem to stern."[32]

With Brown remaining in England, his Jekyll cottage sat for a time forlorn and empty. Finally it was decided that the house required a live-in caretaker, and for a time the job was turned over to the Jekyll Island launch captain, James Agnew Clark, who lived there with his mother and sister. However, in 1899, Brown decided to have the house refurbished, and the Clarks were compelled to vacate. The timing was propitious for Clark, for the following year he announced his intention to marry Minnie Schuppan, the club's head housekeeper, and expressed a desire to have a house of his own. When a later need arose for another caretaker, Clark was not interested. Not only was the location of the Brown house unsuitable for his new wife, who needed to be on call as housekeeper, but Captain Clark had also been burned by having made and paid for repairs authorized by Tuthill, for which the architect, already growing weary of looking after a house whose owner ignored it utterly, never got around to reimbursing him although a residence was part of his contract. More than a year later, when Lyman Rhoades took over the care of the cottage, Superintendent Grob was forced to remind him that the captain was still owed $165 for the work. In 1900 club officials agreed to build a house for the Clarks next door to the club cottage and conveniently located just behind the club house.

With the Clarks' departure, the redecorating and refurbishing of the Brown cottage began. The outside of the house was repainted a bottle green, with cream-colored trim and a red-brown roof. Brown was apparently making an effort to decide whether to sell or to rent. If it crossed his mind at this point to return for a stay in the cottage himself, the thought was short-lived. He decided to rent. The interior of the house was redone using both wallpaper and paint, with "light shades" in the bedrooms, a "chocolate color" in the main hall, and "maroon" for the den.[33]

Although there were a number of inquiries from various club members and guests, among them

The Brown Cottage was occupied by the island's boat captain, James Clark, and his family prior to his marriage to Minnie Schuppan, the club housekeeper. Captain Clark sits on the steps. (Courtesy of Georgia Department of Archives and History, original in Jekyll Island Museum)

former club president Henry Elias Howland, Julia Anderson, Walton Ferguson, Hugo Richards Johnstone, and Jesse Spalding, there were no takers. Grob set out at the beginning of 1900 trying to rent the house for $450 a month,[34] certainly a fair price by club standards. But, even though it was, according to Grob, "the only vacant house on the island," it was unacceptable and too remote for club members. In trying to rent the cottage to Johnstone, Grob wrote to describe it:

> This house has just been entirely done over inside and outside, it having been built several years ago, but never occupied, except by caretaker. If Mr. Brown should rent, the house is fully furnished, with exception of silver and cutlery, table linen, bed-linen and towels. There is also a stable attached to the house. It contains on lower floor a Main-hall or sitting room, dining room, butlers panty, and a Den or library. On the second floor are three sleeping rooms and a bathroom, the "attic" has a good floor, also good light, and can be used as a room for servants, also store room for trunks. The kitchen, also a servants bed-room[,] is in the basement. The house is lighted by "gasolene."[35]

This letter is the most complete description we have of the interior of the Brown house.

At the same time Grob was overseeing the redecoration, he had also taken care of minor storm damage caused by a recent "northeaster." He had the plumbing repaired, had an artesian well drilled so that there would be water for the house, and purchased needed additional furniture. In short, he put the cottage in tip-top shape. But no one was interested. By the beginning of the next season, he had reduced the rental price from the original $450 to $200, still without success.

In fact, in the entire history of the Jekyll Island Club, not one member or guest ever rented the Brown house. The only guest who may have occupied the cottage at all was its architect. The club register does not indicate where he stayed during his first visit, but during his second visit, which began March 5, 1889, the club register indicates cryptically that he stayed in a "cottage." Unfortunately, it does not specify the Brown cottage, and we will never know for certain. But during his next visit in 1890 he registered for a room in the club house. If he did use the Brown cottage during his 1889 visit, he, too, may have found the location inconvenient and a bit gloomy.

The house did not, however, sit empty and forgotten during the remainder of the club's history. At various times, other club workers, both black and white, occupied the cottage. When no renter could be found, Grob wrote to Lyman Rhoades that he would seek a caretaker for the house for not more than twenty-five dollars per month.[36] Whether at this time or some later date, John Francis Courier, licensed steam engineer for the club launch, and his family moved into the house and lived there until about 1920.[37] It was, in fact, his son, E. P. Courier, educated as an engineer at Georgia Tech, who drew up the only existing floor plan of the Brown house, which he did from memory, long after its demolition.

Bayard Brown continued to live peacefully on his yacht at Brightlingsea until World War I, when the British government, desperate by 1917 for seaworthy craft to use in the war effort, made an inspection of the *Valfreyia*. They found the yacht badly in need of maintenance and rejected it for military purposes. At the same time they ordered Brown to move it from his accustomed location to Wivenhoe, where the vessel was put in drydock for repairs. There she remained for nine years, with Bayard Brown and his crew still living aboard. According to one source, even when she lay in drydock with her plating removed, Brown lived aboard the ship sometimes with "nothing but a tarpaulin between his stateroom and the elements."[38]

Such neglect of his own physical comfort manifested itself in other ways as well. Described as a "social butterfly" in his youth, "noted for his good looks and fastidious mode of living," Brown had become an aging man who passed his days "smoking cheap sailor's shag . . . , eating treacle and jam out of a pot," and consuming a bottle of gin daily.[39] If that were the case, it was clearly by choice or indifference, for Bayard Brown died a wealthy man.

Thus he remained until his death from a heart attack suffered at 3:00 A.M. on April 8, 1926, at the age of seventy-three. Only his steward James Munson and his cook Edward Fieldgate, son of his captain of thirty-three years, were at his side. His body lay in state for nearly a week in its mahogany coffin in the *Valfreyia*'s elegant oak-paneled state saloon. On April 16 it was taken to the parish church in Wivenhoe for a memorial service to be conducted by the vicar of Brightlingsea. Even in death, however, the crew had difficulty in getting Bayard Brown off his beloved *Valfreyia*. The coffin, draped in the American flag, proved too wide for the gangway, and it was only with "some difficulty" and with the coffin's fittings removed that they were able to get Brown's body ashore.[40]

It was taken in a gusty rain to the little parish church, where the townspeople had packed the church to pay their final respects. Turning out in large numbers were officials of both Brightlingsea and Wivenhoe, among them a deputy mayor, aldermen, town clerks, assemblymen, the stationmaster, the postmaster, Essex County hospital officials, churchwardens, members of the *Valfreyia* crew, and myriad onlookers, some of whom stood outside the overflowing church in the rain to catch a glimpse of Brown's coffin.

After the services the body was taken to London to await shipment from Southampton to the United States. Back in New York, funeral services were held on May 4 at Grace Church at Broadway and Eleventh, with burial at Greenwood Cemetery in Brooklyn. Unlike those at the crowded church in Brightlingsea, only eighteen people attended the services in New York, and three cars followed the funeral cortege to the burial site.[41] New York had forgotten Bayard Brown, as he had tried to forget New York.

Despite Brown's peculiarities and tendencies toward both paranoia and manic depression, his crew remained, for the most part, intensely loyal. Captain Fieldgate had stayed with him from the time he left New York until his own death thirty-three years later. By that time, his son had also gone into Brown's service. His secretary, Maj. Percy Sturdee, was on Brown's staff for twenty-four years, and, though some had apparently deserted, many others among his eighteen-man crew had grown old in his service. Some had even died waiting for the orders to sail which, according to one source, came only once but were rescinded before the vessel had moved more than a few yards.[42] As the *New York Times* interpreted it, "To have kept the crew of his strange craft so well content with a job which most sailors would have found insufferably dull indicates uncommon talent for handling men."[43] It may also reflect the fact that the crew was uncommonly well paid. And some of them hoped for more. All of Brightlingsea and Wivenhoe waited with the crew members in anticipation of the reading of Brown's will. Rumor had it that he had made a new will only a month before his death, and they had high hopes that loyal service would be rewarded or that worthy charities would be remembered.[44]

The only will found, however, proved to be almost fifty years old. Dated February 15, 1878, it left half his worldly goods, which were considerable, to his surviving millionaire cousin, Robert Fulton Cutting, and the other half, since William Bayard Cutting, the other heir, had died in 1912, to be divided among his three surviving children, Justine Bayard Cutting Ward, Bronson Murray Cutting, and Olivia Cutting James, and one Iris M. Origo, who was living in the Tuscany region of Italy.[45] Brown's English holdings were valued at £13,559, and his estate in America was said to be possibly in excess of $20 million.[46] Following Brown's death, the *Valfreyia* was purchased at "a bargain price" by the Maharajah of Nawanagar, well known as a cricket player under the name of "Ranji." He had the vessel modernized and changed her name to *Star of India,* the name by which she would be known by various owners until she was taken into the service of the British Navy in World War II.[47]

The Queen Anne cottage that Bayard Brown had built on Jekyll Island continued to stand throughout the club era, but for members and guests it was little more than a landmark. Efforts to rent it finally ceased, and it was maintained as only a sometime residence for island workers. The house stood until the end of the club era, and in that final season of 1942, Marian Maurice reported in her diary on March 1 that she had "walked to Brown house after tea."[48] If it was still standing in 1947 when the state of Georgia took over the island for use as a state park, its dilapidated condition made demolition by the Jekyll Island Authority almost inevitable. All that remains now at the site on the edge of the Jekyll airport are the remnants of a chimney and a historic marker, reminding sightseers of the strange story of the millionaire hermit of the Essex coast.

SOLTERRA

Owners: Frederic Baker, 1890–1913; Frances Baker, 1913–14

Constructed: 1890

Burned: March 9, 1914

Architecture: Queen Anne

Architect: Unknown

Frederic Baker, who constructed the now-vanished cottage known as Solterra, was born about 1831, the son of Josiah and Abigail Bates Baker. He graduated in 1852 from New York University. About 1869 he entered into partnership in a warehouse company with James B. Williams, who had previously been a junior partner in a New York dry goods firm and then studied and practiced law before joining Baker. What Baker himself did between his graduation from college and the founding of Baker & Williams, for which he served as president, is not known, but one can only presume that

Solterra, the cottage of Frederic Baker. (Lanier Book, 1911)

he was gaining experience in some manner in the business world, for he was to head a very successful company.[1]

Baker and Williams began with a limited number of warehouses on Water Street in New York but gradually expanded to include a large group of storehouses on Washington, Greenwich, Vestry, West, Laight, South, and Front Streets. Baker had also, by the mid-1870s, obtained an interest in a tannery business in Watertown, New York, and was judged by financial analysts at the time as "respectable and reliable."[2] For much of his adult life Baker devoted himself exclusively to the development of his business, gradually expanding his interests to include a substantial amount of stock in the Northern Pacific Railroad, a firm in which his partner had been elected a director in 1879.

Sometime after 1884, when he was in his mid-fifties, Baker wooed and wed Frances Emma Steers Lake, the daughter of James R. Steers and widow of dry goods merchant George Graham Lake. She was in her forties and the mother of two nearly grown children by her previous marriage. Despite their late marriage, the Bakers had one daughter of their own, named Abigail for Baker's mother. Unfortunately, the little girl died in early childhood, and the couple never had another child. Baker, however, treated his wife's children as his own, and when his stepson, Henry Steers Lake, had sons of his own, he called one of them Frederic for his stepfather.

The Bakers had been married fewer than five years when he was elected to the Jekyll Island Club on May 22, 1888. They arrived the following January 1 to spend their first season on Jekyll, taking four rooms in the club house. It did not take them long to determine that they would like to spend their winters there on a regular basis and that they would enjoy their island vacations more in the spaciousness and homey atmosphere that could be provided only by a private cottage. Thus they made a decision by early March to construct a cottage at Jekyll, which they would use as a winter retreat from their Fifth Avenue home in New York City.

Baker had purchased one club share without a lot from club president Henry Howland, who had nominated him for membership. On March 3, 1889, he petitioned the executive committee for a plot of ground near the club house on which to build his cottage.[3] The executive committee, with the club still in its early stages, seemed exceedingly eager to have members construct houses, but all the lots closest to the club house had already been assigned. Therefore, one of the members of the committee, L. M. Lawson, offered to relinquish his lot 28, just north of the club house, in exchange for another (lot 58) of equal area but in a considerably less desirable location north of the club compound at an intolerable distance from the club house itself.

Baker wasted little time in getting started. On March 14, he brought down a New York friend, D. G. L. Robinson, presumably to look over the site. The house he planned was to be a splendid Queen Anne shingled design, complete with turrets and a gazebo. A contractor named M. A. Fuller was brought in from Jacksonville to undertake the construction, which was begun in 1890. According to Baker he did "good work at a reasonable price," always an important factor to most Jekyll Islanders.[4]

By the beginning of the following season, the house was ready, and the family occupied it for the first time on January 14, 1891. The largest house yet built at Jekyll, it was "a handsome two-story structure of 12 rooms, elegantly furnished," according to the *Brunswick Times*.[5] For the next twenty-three years, it would be much used, by both the Bakers and their guests. There is little question that, because of its location and graciousness, it was considered one of the most desirable houses on the island, and it quickly became an island social center, with Frances Baker as a willing hostess. In 1893, for example, it was the site of a tea held on February 16 to inaugurate the Jekyll season. "The house was handsomely decorated with azeleas [sic], hyacinths, ferns and palms," and virtually everyone who was on the island was in attendance.[6]

Frederic Baker and Elizabeth Claflin riding donkeys at Jekyll Island. (Southern Historical Collection, Library of the University of North Carolina, Chapel Hill)

Frederic Baker's original Jekyll Island Club share. (Courtesy of Jekyll Island Museum)

Frederic Baker quickly made himself indispensable to the club. Within a year of becoming a member, he was elected club treasurer to replace Lloyd Aspinwall, the ne'er-do-well son of the club's first president. Under Baker's tenure in office, the treasurer would in fact take on the executive responsibilities normally expected of the president. He held the job of treasurer until 1908, when he relinquished the post to George H. Macy to accept the less-demanding position of third vice president. He continued to hold the honorary post of third vice president for several years, though by 1912 he had stepped down from all offices in the club. During his almost twenty-year stint as treasurer, however, Frederic Baker made vitally important contributions to the Jekyll Island Club. By 1895 he seems to have been virtually running the organization. In April of that year he responded to a letter from

Henry Hyde, president of the Equitable Life Assurance Company in New York, the largest of its kind in the world: "Your letter did me a great deal of good; to see a waking up of members as to this island, its excellencies and its wants, is most encouraging." The primary responsibility, which "has been onerous," he contended," seems to have fallen to me. To see help coming gives me a great let up."[7]

Working closely together for the next several years, Baker and Hyde would bring about the greatest spurt of building and modification in the club since the 1890 spate of cottage construction of which Solterra had been a part. The two of them, along with another club member, New York contractor David H. King Jr. (see Chichota chapter), would oversee the remodeling of the club house, the construction of the Sans Souci, a large dwelling with six apartments, the building of a private

Solterra, *left,* the name of which means "Sunland," as seen from the Jekyll Island water tower. The cottage in the background is Chichota. The photograph was taken between 1900 and 1914. (Courtesy of Jekyll Island Museum)

Baker-Hyde stable, and the erection of a larger private stable to house the horses of various members. They would also lay the groundwork for an eight-apartment wing on the club house called the annex, which would be constructed in 1901, and for Faith Chapel, to be built in 1904. These last two projects, because of various disputes, were put on hold until after the death of Henry Hyde in 1899.

The construction of Faith Chapel in particular was a project dear to the heart of Frederic Baker, a staunch Presbyterian. A simple chapel, known as Union Chapel, had been constructed in the early 1890s and still stood on lot 38, once owned by Walter Rogers Furness and the site of the present Gould tennis court.[8] By 1897, however, it had been deemed inadequate by Baker and others who longed for a more worthy place of worship on the island.

By February 1897, a subscription list had been begun to guarantee construction costs, and pledges of a thousand dollars "and more if necessary" had already been accepted.[9] By March, Baker had contacted a New York architect, Howard Constable of Constable Brothers, to draw up the plans, which would be completed by March 15.[10] By June bids had been taken for the execution of Constable's plans, with the low bid of $4,452 coming from W. H. Mann, who over the years would do much construction work at Jekyll. The Bakers wanted it done right, with proper wooden pews instead of chairs, with cypress shingles instead of cedar. In a burst of enthusiasm, Baker had momentarily championed the idea of scrapping the simple plans for Constable's shingled church for a somewhat more elaborate and expensive Spanish-style structure with a red-tile roof. But, considering the difficulties he was having raising the money even for the more modest church, that idea was quickly dropped.

When insufficient funds had been pledged by August, Baker wrote to Hyde that the church with all its furnishings was expected to cost under $7,000. "I am willing to stand under one-half of this debt. Do you feel like taking the other half? It can be repaid out of collections and gifts." But Hyde was growing a bit crochety and had begun, albeit momentarily, to view the Jekyll Island Club as an endless drain on resources. He responded to Baker on August 24 that "I do not feel that I should assume any responsibility in the matter of finances in connection with the erection of the new Church," reminding him that he was still owed $14,500 for alterations to the club house. Baker, stung by Hyde's unexpected reply, wrote to Hyde and James Scrymser on September 1, "After a full survey of the matter of a new chapel at Jekyl, I feel that the project better be delayed for this year." They could, he asserted, probably raise $3,500, but a church like the one he wanted, "an edifice . . . worthy of the island and . . . durable" would, all told, cost a good deal more. "If we are to put up a cheap affair for utility only," he concluded, "the present one covers the ground."[11] Union Chapel was repaired in 1900,[12] and it continued to serve as the island's only place of worship until the construction in 1904 of Faith Chapel, presumably following the shingled design of Howard Constable. The old chapel at this time was moved north to the black workers' compound and served as their church for many years.

As a rule, Baker tried to get along with his fellow club members. While Hyde tended to be imperious and uncompromising, Baker made efforts to take others' views into consideration. Although he was outspoken and critical on occasion in private letters to Hyde, he was usually viewed as genial and flexible in public. It was typical of Baker that he would prefer to postpone the building of the chapel, which he and his wife badly wanted and in which they were willing to invest substantial sums, rather than risk any further controversy and unpleasantness. Club member Robert Weeks de Forest, himself an amiable and philanthropic man, viewed the club leadership during this period as "rather negative than positive," pointedly excepting only Frederic Baker from this judgment.[13]

Although Hyde's and Baker's efforts to improve the Jekyll Island Club continued into the 1898 season as though nothing had happened, the burdens

Faith Chapel, built in 1904, was a project long championed by Frederic Baker. (Lanier Book, 1911)

of office and the continued pressure exerted by Hyde continued unabated. Escaping for a time the burdens of Jekyll Island affairs, the Bakers took an extended trip to Europe and North Africa in 1898. Leaving for Europe in May, they were in Cairo in December, and evidently continued the trip into the following winter, for, uncharacteristically, they did not come to Jekyll for the 1899 season.[14]

While the Bakers were away, they offered their home to the president of the United States, William McKinley, who at the invitation of Cornelius Bliss was making plans to spend a vacation at Jekyll Island. He had been invited to come in 1898, but the attack on the *Maine* in Havana Harbor and the ensuing Spanish-American War had put an end to any vacation plans for the president. Now, however, with the brief war at an end and the Treaty of Paris signed on December 10, 1898, Bliss tried once again to get the president to come during the 1899 season, and this time he was successful. He eagerly accepted the Bakers' offer of their home for the president and his party.

In a letter to her aunt, Marian Maurice captured the reaction on the island to the president's impending visit: "Our great excitement here at present is over the arrival of the President & his party tomorrow." She announced to her that the party would include the president, the vice president, and their wives, who were to stay at the Baker cottage. They "will probably be [here] only for a day or two . . . as guests of Mr Cornelius Bliss one of our members who is here now, we also have Mr Reed the Speaker of the House & feel quite overwhelmed with all our celebrities."[15] McKinley and his vice president, Garret Hobart, did indeed arrive on March 20 with their wives in the company of Sen. Mark Hanna, whom they were later to visit at Thomasville, Georgia. They remained on the island until March 22, during which time the local newspapers overflowed with exuberance at their visit. "Jekyl Island has had the greatest crow in its history for the past few days," enthused the *Brunswick Call* on March 22.

"Every room in the clubhouse and every cottage has been occupied by millionaire guests. The president and vice-president of the United States, and the speaker of the house, have been guests of the club. The eyes of the world have been upon Jekyl."

Solterra, as the president's residence during his brief visit, was also the site of his reception on March 21 to meet club members, among them homeowners C. S. Maurice, H. K. Porter, and N. K. Fairbank with their wives, who came to pay their respects. Enjoying long rides around the island, a cakewalk performed by black club employees, and the hospitality afforded by club members at their best, President McKinley proclaimed the atmosphere at Jekyll "simply delightful."[16] It was Solterra's finest hour, though unfortunately its owner was not present to enjoy it.

The visit also had a political motive, as the presence of McKinley's adversary, Speaker of the House Thomas Reed, suggested and as the press was quick to note. During the visit, however, the president and Speaker Reed were reputed to have settled their differences concerning the future of the Republican Party and the 1900 election.

Jekyll Islanders were shocked two years later to hear of McKinley's assassination. Mary C. Hoffman, the wife of club member Dean Eugene Hoffman, wrote to Charlotte Maurice: "This terrible news about the President has almost paralyzed us here, and we are so stunned that we almost hold our breaths when we talk. Frightful. The poor man who committed the deed is only the tool of others. Could law and justice only get hold of the instigators, what a blessing it would be to see them all hanging by their necks."[17] Strong words for the wife of the dean of a theological seminary.

The Baker family spent many happy winters in Solterra, bringing with them not only numerous guests but also a sizable household staff, as they did in 1901. Almost a week before their own arrival, the Bakers sent down six women and two men servants by Mallory steamer from New York.[18]

They arrived on January 11 to open the house and prepare for the arrival on January 16 of Mr. and Mrs. Baker, Mrs. Baker's daughter Frances Lake, and her niece, a Miss Steers who evidently spent a great deal of time with them. In May after the club season had closed, Charles F. Maurice in New York commented in a letter to his mother that the Bakers had him and his sisters to dinner on a Friday night "and took us to the theatre afterwards and I wish I could have been less of a bore. . . . Miss Lake's and Miss Steers's 'vibration' does not act in harmony with mine, and . . . in their company I am always more than usually stupid."[19] A week later he called on them again and this time "had an unusually pleasant time for those circumstances and managed to make my 'vibration' get more in harmony with Miss Steers's."[20] By 1905 both Mrs. Baker's son and daughter had married, and the cottage began to overflow each winter with their spouses, children, and nurses, as well as with other guests.

In 1908, Frederic Baker, by now nearly seventy-eight years old, fell ill and was forced to remain in New York throughout the club season. However, Mrs. Baker came down without him, accompanied by only three servants "& the grandchild." They took "the Cottage" (presumably Club Cottage) as Charlotte Maurice noted and "are to live there & not open their own house. I think it bids fair to be an off year here."[21] But she was wrong about that. By mid-February guests were pouring in to Jekyll, and as the *Brunswick Journal* reported, "Authors, financiers, and leading lawyers are already enjoying the balmy climate and the crack of their guns in the game preserve can be heard every day." One of the authors in question was Winston Churchill, an American novelist who bore the same name as the British statesman.[22]

Frances Baker, who loved the island as much as her husband did, had become a club member in her own right in 1897 and continued to come to Jekyll each season, bringing with her most often her daughter, Frances, now Mrs. John Seymour Thacher, her grandson, Master Jack Thacher, and her recently hired companion, Miss M. W. Beatty, who would accompany her to Jekyll from 1907 until 1916.

Over the years Mrs. Baker developed a very special interest in the development of an island school for the club employees' children. In 1901 the Glynn County Board of Education authorized for the first time a teacher for the Jekyll Island school for white children, appointing to the post a thirty-year-old woman named Bertha Baker, who had taught for more than ten years in Brunswick elementary schools. Originally from Darien, just a few miles north of Brunswick, she was a well-respected young woman in the community and a talented musician who served for many years as organist for St. Mark's Episcopal Church in Brunswick.

The Jekyll school was a small yellow frame building trimmed in brown built on a tiny patch of unassigned land just north and behind the lot that would contain Faith Chapel. Although its teacher, Bertha Baker, was of no relation to Frances Baker, the latter became a "patron saint" to the little school, matching the $17.50 salary paid to Miss Baker by the county with an equal amount from her own purse. She furnished supplies and even firewood for the school and when the need arose paid for repairs to the schoolhouse. She was remembered by the children as a generous woman, not only to the school, but also to the families of Jekyll workers during the club's annual Christmas celebration. The daughter of one of the island fishermen recalled that on that occasion each year Mrs. Baker gave to each child a gold coin worth $2.50, but to their parents she gave a gold piece worth twice that amount, both substantial gifts in the early part of the century, when a number of island workers earned a dollar a day and when John D. Rockefeller was reputed to have handed out only dimes to the children.[23]

On the morning of March 9, 1914, Solterra caught fire from a faulty flue. Although firefighters struggled to extinguish the flames, the frame cottage burned quickly until nothing was left but the chimneys. (*Top,* courtesy of Georgia Department of Archives and History, original in Jekyll Island Museum; *left,* courtesy of Jekyll Island Museum; *right,* courtesy of John J. Albright)

The death of Frederic Baker on June 15, 1913, at his Fifth Avenue home in New York was said to be "unexpected" even though he had become a semi-invalid.[24] The news saddened members of the Jeykll Island Club, who knew that he had continued to come down and participate vigorously in club activities for as long as he was able. Even when he was physically incapable of making the voyage, he never forgot Jekyll, leaving in his will $3,000 to the club, which during his years as treasurer had always been in need of extra money to make up for its annual deficits. He also remembered the club superintendent, Ernest Grob, leaving him fifty shares of stock in Baker and Williams the exact legacy left to four members of his family.

The death of her husband did not put an end to Mrs. Baker's visits to the island. Indeed, she was entertaining a large number of guests in her cottage the following season when, on the morning of March 9, a fire broke out in the attic, caused, according to the newspaper, by a defective flue. Ironically, Frances Baker had contacted a local builder, George Cowman, not long before to get an estimate to repair the faulty flue, but the needed work had not yet been done.[25] Flames quickly consumed the frame house. Island employees rushed to remove all the furnishings they could, "but with the inadequate fire fighting apparatus at hand were unable to save the residence."[26] The island teacher, Bertha Baker, as one child recalled, "let us out of school when it burned."[27] But there was little anyone could do, and despite all efforts to save the house, it was too late. Frances Baker could only watch as her beloved Solterra was reduced to ashes.

On the day after the fire the Brunswick newspaper declared that "Mrs. Baker immediately announced her intention of rebuilding." But her resolve was short-lived. She was seventy-three years old and lacked the heart to begin again. Although the house had been insured for $30,000, Mrs. Baker evidently had some difficulty in collecting the insurance money, and a Brunswick contractor, W. H. Bowen, was brought in to mediate.[28] In the end, when the opportunity presented itself to sell her property to Richard Teller Crane Jr., she took it. Crane would build on the site in 1917 Jekyll Island's most splended "cottage."

With the loss of her cottage, Jekyll seemed to lose its appeal for Frances Baker, and she came only once more, staying in the club house with her companion, Miss Beatty, in February 1916. She occupied herself instead with building a new home in Southampton, Long Island, where she and her husband had for many years spent the summers. It was there that she died three years later on February 9, 1919.

FAIRBANK COTTAGE

Owners: Nathaniel Kellogg Fairbank, 1890–1903; Fairbank Estate, 1903–4; Walton Ferguson, 1904–19; Ralph Beaver Strassburger, 1919–23; Marjorie Bourne Thayer, 1923–42

Constructed: 1890

Demolished: by 1944

Architecture: Shingle style

Architect: Unknown

The Fairbank Years

While the name of Nathaniel Kellogg Fairbank, who constructed a cottage on Jekyll Island in 1890, may not be a household word to most Americans, it was one that "blaze[d] like a planet" among important Chicago businessmen and philanthropists of the late nineteenth century. He was described by his contemporaries as the man "who perhaps accomplished more than any other Chicagoan of his generation for the cultural and spiritual life of the city."[1]

He had come into the world with neither fame nor fortune. Descended from several generations of farmers, he was born on October 20, 1829, to

The Fairbank Cottage, west side facing Jekyll River. (Courtesy of Jekyll Island Museum)

Nathaniel K. Fairbank was one of the most prominent men in Chicago when he joined the Jekyll Island Club in 1886 as one of its original members. (Chicago Historical Society)

Stephen T. Fairbank and his wife, Mehitable Kellogg, who had recently come to Sodus, New York, a town barely emerged from the wilderness. His mother died when he was eight years old, and he attended school only until he was fifteen. He was then sent to Lyons, New York, to work as an apprentice bricklayer with his brother-in-law, who had the misfortune to be killed in a hunting accident only a few years later. Young Fairbank, known to his friends as Kell, moved on to Rochester, New York, where he took a job as a bookkeeper in a flour mill.

Despite his humble beginnings, Fairbank was ambitious. In a diary kept during his years in Lyons, he recorded his determination to succeed. "When I look around and see the many boys who have such good opportunities for improvement, splendid education, all the advantages of best soci-

ety, . . . it seems almost a pointless attempt to try and reach what I aspire to. *But try I will.*"[2]

In 1855 Fairbank obtained a position as western representative of the New York Grain Commission for David Dows and Company, a job that sent him to Chicago. It was his big chance. Chicago was a young, bustling community, with many opportunities the young man was quick to seize. Within a few years he was elected first vice president of the Chicago Board of Trade and had begun to make his fortune, amassing sufficient funds to provide the capital for the purchase of a lard and oil refinery known as Smedley, Peck & Co., eventually to become N. K. Fairbank & Co., which would at some future date include the manufacture of soap among its primary enterprises.

A dashing young man with "blue-black hair and side whiskers,"[3] Fairbank was quite popular with the ladies but resisted marriage until 1866, when he was thirty-six years old and sufficiently wealthy to support a family in style. During a vacation trip east to Rhode Island three years earlier, he had met a woman, younger than he by ten years, named Helen Livingston Graham, "a small shy person of great piety but with an engaging sparkle of humor."[4] She would become his wife and the mother of his eight children: Graham, who was born in 1867 but died before he was seven months old; Helen Graham, 1868; Kellogg, 1869; Wallace, 1872; Dexter, 1876; Margaret, 1878; Livingston, 1880; and Nathalie, 1883. Prior to his marriage, Fairbank bought a house on Michigan Avenue where he and his wife would live for the rest of their lives. Fairbank was considered an excellent family man and a "wonderful play-fellow" with his children.[5]

When the great Chicago fire of 1871 spread through the city, it fortunately spared the Fairbank house, but Kell, who was moving rapidly into a position of prominence, was appointed to the General Relief Committee to assist victims of the fire. Given his rising eminence in the business and social world, coupled with the fact that he was one of the founding members of the prestigious Chicago Club, an organization of which he would serve as president from 1875 to 1889, it is not surprising that he was among the small contingent of Chicagoans invited to join the Jekyll Island Club when it was established in 1886.

The Fairbanks registered for their first visit to the island on February 11, 1888, during the club's maiden season. By the following year their cottage was under construction on what would later be called "the most convenient and desirable site on the island,"[6] next door to the club house on lot 15, which he had purchased from his New York stockbroker and friend E. K. Willard, who had resigned from the club in 1888.

By comparison to the Fairbanks' more elaborate houses in Chicago and Wisconsin, the Jekyll house, which was demolished late in the club era, was a modest frame two-story structure, completely surrounded by porches. Whether its architect was Fritz Folz, the same architect who had fifteen years earlier designed The Butternuts, their vacation home in Lake Geneva, Wisconsin, is unknown, though certainly there is nothing in the styles of the two houses to suggest that this was the case. The new Jekyll cottage consisted of six bedrooms, all with fireplaces, two baths, a living room, a library, a kitchen, and two servants' rooms with a bath in common.[7] The cottage has many characteristics of the shingle style so popular in the 1890s, with wood shingles used for both wall cladding and roofing, an irregular, steeply pitched roofline, intersecting cross gables, and a half tower blended into the house. Its asymmetrical form and abundant use of porches are typical of this style.

While Fairbank enjoyed Jekyll Island immensely, his wife, Helen, never seemed to care for it as he did. One of her major problems was what she considered the lack of a suitable place of worship. She found Sundays there "a considerable chore . . . as she had to leave Jekyll at eight o'clock to go all the way to the mainland for morning service."[8] Throughout their years at Jekyll she made her weekly treks into Brunswick for church. Even though in the 1890s

there was a rudimentary church known as Union Chapel on the island, it clearly failed to meet her standards of what a church should be. Despite efforts on the part of some members to build a new church in 1897, disputes among the members put the project on hold, and Faith Chapel, which stands today on Jekyll, would not be constructed until 1904, after the deaths of both Helen and Kell Fairbank.[9] The need for an appropriate church was not a new preoccupation for her. In 1874 and 1875 when the Fairbanks had built their Wisconsin vacation home, one of Helen Fairbank's first activities in the area was to spearhead a drive to get a new Episcopal church built nearby.[10]

Kell Fairbank had no such reservations about Jekyll when he elected to become one of the club's original members. He loved the quiet pleasures of the island and joined heartily into the spirit of simplicity for which the club was known. One of his daughter Helen's recollections of Jekyll includes that of her father "standing in an old flatboat eating freshly fished-up oysters, still dripping with sea water." According to his granddaughter, he "thrived on the sociability of the place"[11] and was well liked by Jekyll members. For fifteen years, from 1888 until 1903, club members elected him as club vice president or as first vice president during the years when there were two vice presidents. During those same years he was also elected to the board of directors. Since the presidents with whom he served, Henry Howland and Charles Lanier, were frequently absent from the island, Fairbank assumed many of the presidential duties, such as greeting newly arrived members and guests at the dock. Knowing of his wife's reaction to Jekyll but trying to put the best face on the matter, he wrote to one of his daughters, "I think she likes the place though she may not like to admit it."[12]

In spite of Mrs. Fairbank's lack of enthusiasm for Jekyll, she dutifully came down every season with her husband and one or more of their children, until a yellow fever epidemic in nearby Brunswick in the summer and fall of 1893 effectively closed the club for the 1894 season, with only a very few members braving the dangers of the fever to spend their winter vacations on Jekyll. The Fairbanks were not among them. In fact, the only recorded use of the cottage even in the following year was that by a party of gentlemen hosted by Fairbank, including Chicago friends Marshall Field, Charles Fargo, and Marvin Hughitt. The Brunswick newspaper commented on the arrival by private railroad car of this "array of Chicago brains and millions bound for Jekyl. . . . It would be hard to get together a quartette representing more interests financial, mercantile, and social, than this one."[13]

In February of that same year, Henry B. Hyde of New York, who had taken over many operational aspects of the island, conceived the idea of constructing a splendid annex to the club house. Because of so many other building projects, however, the idea was shelved until 1897, when it was raised again. Hyde's idea was that Fairbank should give up thirty-five feet of his land so that the annex could extend at right angles from the club house. Fairbank objected strenuously that such a construction

would block his view of Jekyll Creek. He suggested instead that the annex be constructed obliquely across a small northeast corner of his lot. Hyde, who was viewed by his son and no doubt others as the "czar of Jekyll Island," was furious to be thus thwarted, writing to Frederic Baker that he thought Fairbank had "acted rather selfishly . . . and unbusiness-like" in not allowing the construction of the annex "which will be of benefit to the Club even if it is somewhat injurious to his cottage."[14] But Fairbank stood his ground, and, despite Hyde's fulminating, the matter was dropped for the moment. It was the only recorded dispute that Fairbank ever had with other club members. Only after Hyde's death was the issue raised again. This time, without Hyde's temperamental insistence on his own way, Fairbank's plan was adopted. He deeded the necessary land over to the club, and the annex was built in 1902, making a very attractive addition to the club house.[15]

In the spring of 1895, not long after her husband's return from Jekyll, Helen Fairbank had a sudden attack of appendicitis and, six painful weeks later,

The construction of the new annex, a matter of controversy between Henry Hyde and Nathaniel K. Fairbank in 1895, was finally built in 1902 after Hyde's death according to the plan proposed by Fairbank. (Courtesy of Georgia Department of Archives and History, original in Jekyll Island Museum)

in June 1895, she was dead of peritonitis. It was a difficult time for Kellogg Fairbank.

At the time he had constructed his Jekyll house, Fairbank had been a still dapper man of sixty-one. He smoked small black cigars and continued to sport his distinguished side whiskers. He had shown himself to be a man who could weather the financial storms that often beset men with a bent for speculation. He had, for example, invested $75,000 in a project for a Nicaraguan canal, before the Panama Canal project was begun. He had tried to take advantage of a projected wheat shortage in 1872 and lost heavily when the wheat crop proved abundant.[16] But most serious of all was an effort in 1893 to try to corner the market in lard. On August 2, the *Chicago Herald* carried the headline, "The Great Lard Deal Goes to Smash. The Collapse of the Corner Wrecks Commission Houses and Creates Liabilities of $4,000,000." The financial panic of 1893, which caused many failures, brought about the most serious financial setback of Fairbank's career. Following the incident Josephine Dexter, the wife of his good friend, Wirt Dexter, called upon him, knowing that he was alone, to provide sympathy at his losses. Upon her arrival, the door to the house was standing open. A letter from his daughter Helen described the scene: "She found him in his library, sitting alone by the window with a paper on his knee, but he was not reading, just looking out at the trees. . . . He told her he would probably lose everything that day—but he had failures before and had retrieved himself and made up his fortunes. But this time he knew it would be harder because of his age." And it *was* harder, as Helen noted, "but he gathered all his assets together and before he died had paid every cent he owed." The affair was, she surmised, "a great blow to his pride in his ability as a speculator."[17]

Unfortunately, that was not the only worry he had at the time. Fairbank was a man known for his philanthropic bent. He had been instrumental in cultural activities such as the construction of Chicago's Central Music Hall, but he had a particularly soft heart for the downtrodden and had made many generous contributions to such causes as St. Luke's Hospital and the Newsboys' Home. Sometimes his concern for the underdog had involved him in controversial causes. For example, he, along with his friend Wirt Dexter, had provided financial support for and staunchly defended the rights of the Reverend David Swing, a free-thinking minister who had been forced to resign from the pulpit of the fashionable Fourth Presbyterian Church in November 1875, when his views on such issues as evolution had obtained notoriety.[18]

To his later regret, Fairbank had become involved in another such unpopular cause during the period just before he began his Jekyll Island house. A recent divorce scandal, called by the *New York Times* "the most indecent and revolting divorce trial ever heard in the Chicago courts,"[19] had exonerated the husband but found a once-popular matron, Mrs. Leslie Carter, guilty of adultery, depriving her of her nine-year-old son and all support by her husband. Having no means of livelihood and having been raised only to be the wife of a wealthy man, she decided to become an actress and appealed to Kell Fairbank for help in providing temporary support and theatrical training. He agreed to help her until she could get back on her feet. However, wanting in no way to become publicly associated with the woman, he dealt with her only through bankers and lawyers, providing more than $50,000 between July 1889 and March 1891 in payments and "loans" to theatrical producer David Belasco, known as "the bishop of Broadway," who had agreed to undertake her training.

There had been no written contract, and as the months wore on, Belasco and Mrs. Carter requested more and more money from Fairbank, threatening him with unsavory publicity and legal action if he did not oblige. Finally, Fairbank refused categorically to provide any further support to Carter, whose career was apparently already well launched, albeit not to the greatest of reviews. Nevertheless, Belasco was unwilling to drop the matter. Finally, on June 3, 1896, the Supreme Court of New York began a twenty-one day trial of *Belasco v. Fairbank,* in which the producer sued the lard refiner for an additional $65,000 for his services. Fairbank seemed fairly confident of the outcome and wrote to his daughter Helen, "All my friends here are very kind, and at the clubs they take pains to come and say they admire my courage in making the fight. . . . The universal sentiment is that it is a blackmail suit and it will be strange if that sentiment and feeling does not permeate the jury, which is a very fair one. I am sure the Judge has made up his mind to that effect."[20] The jury, however, did not believe that an adequate case for blackmail had been made and brought in what the *New York Times* described as a "remarkable verdict."[21] They found in favor of Belasco and awarded him $16,000 on the grounds that to do otherwise would have branded him unfairly "as a perjurer and blackmailer."[22] The decision was, many thought, unfair to Fairbank, whom the *Times* described as "not only a very rich man, but a generous and public-spirited man"[23] who had apparently gotten himself involved in the affair only through a genuine desire to help "the underdog in the fight," as he himself had testified on the witness stand.[24] Almost twenty years later, in 1915, David Belasco wrote, "I never regretted anything more than being forced to bring suit against Fairbank. He was courteous, kind-hearted, mellow, and human."[25]

Those three years—1893, when Fairbank suffered his greatest financial loss; 1895, when he lost his wife and had his only contretemps at Jekyll; and 1896, when he lost the much-publicized court case against David Belasco—had been the most trying years of his life. But somehow he found the strength to go on. To help cope with the situation, he hired an Alsatian woman, Elisabeth Schmitt, as a companion-governess for his youngest daughter, Nathalie. And for a time his oldest daughter, Helen, and her hus-

band, Ben Carpenter, moved with their children into the Fairbank house, but by 1900 they had once again established their own household.

Fairbank and Nathalie, along with various other children on different occasions, continued to spend their winters at Jekyll. In 1900, he passed the winter season with his two youngest daughters and their governess touring Egypt, where Fairbank observed, as he explored the wonders of Egyptian ruins, "Hm! they'd much better have spent their money on irrigation."[26]

Back at Jekyll for the 1901 season, Fairbank spent the rest of the year divesting himself of his business activities and going into complete retirement. In April 1902, shortly after returning from his last season on Jekyll, where he enjoyed the company of his three youngest children, Nathalie, Margaret, and Livingston, Nathaniel Kellogg Fairbank suffered a paralytic stroke. He lived on for nearly a year, but finally on March 27, 1903, he died at the age of seventy-three.[27] His cottage was sold by his heirs to Walton Ferguson on March 20, 1904.[28]

The Ferguson Years

When Kellogg Fairbank and his daughters were in Egypt for the winter of 1900, Walton Ferguson of Stamford, Connecticut, was delighted to take the opportunity to rent their Jekyll Island cottage. The previous January Ferguson had been ill and hoped to convalesce on the island and even to bring his doctor with him. However, when his son, Walton Ferguson Jr., wrote to the club superintendent to inquire about accommodations, he had little luck. At first Superintendent Grob thought that the J. P. Morgan apartment in the Sans Souci, which rented for twenty-five dollars a day, might be available, but upon looking further into the matter he discovered that it was to be in use when the Fergusons wished to come.[29]

Evidently some satisfactory accommodations were found for the Walton Fergusons, for they checked in on February 25. That same day, however, Grob wrote to Walton Jr., who wished to join his father, that "Fourth floor best can do now, Better hold off until something better may come up."[30] He held off until March 8, when he finally arrived on Jekyll with his wife. After the difficulties of finding accommodations in 1899, Ferguson was delighted in late January of the following year to receive a letter from Superintendent Grob indicating that the Fairbank cottage would be available to rent for the season. Grob described it as having "6 bed-rooms, main hall and library, also a room for maid. It is fully furnished, rents for $15.00 per day, which includes the services of a colored woman who acts as chambermaid."[31] Ferguson snapped it up. It certainly appeared to be a bargain compared to the Morgan apartment, which contained only three bedrooms, a drawing room, and a bath, with two servants' rooms provided in the attic. Within four days Grob had written again to confirm his reservation: "Have put you down for the Fairbank cottage from Feb'y 15th. You need not bring anything, it is fully furnished. There are two (2) bath-rooms, one on each floor."[32]

In 1901, however, Fairbank and his daughter Nathalie returned to their usual routine of wintering at Jekyll, and their house was not available for rental. That year the Fergusons did not come to the island at all, but in 1902 Ferguson nominated his son, Walton Jr., for membership in the Jekyll Island Club. He was elected on December 2. With the Ferguson family attachment to Jekyll even more clearly affirmed, when Kellogg Fairbank died in March 1903, Walton Ferguson made an offer the following season to purchase the cottage from his estate. The inconvenience and difficulty of getting the accommodations he wanted when he wanted them had been a troublesome matter indeed. With Ferguson's son, now a club member, also determined to come to the island each season, reliable quarters became an even greater necessity. Evidently, the family had enjoyed the Fairbank house with its excellent loca-

Walton Ferguson purchased the Fairbank cottage in 1903. (Courtesy of Mrs. Alfred W. Dater Jr.)

tion adjacent to the club house. All of these factors no doubt influenced his decision to purchase the cottage, which he did on March 20, 1904.[33]

Ferguson was born July 6, 1842, in Stamford, Connecticut, the son of John W. Ferguson and Helen Grace Morewood, who had moved from New York only a few months earlier. He attended private schools and completed his education at Trinity College in Hartford. After his graduation, he went into business with his father in the firm of J. & S. Ferguson, a New York banking concern. On September 8, 1869, at the age of twenty-seven, he married Julia Lee White, the daughter of John Trumbull White of New York. She was three years his junior. Ten months later, in 1870, the first of their six children, Walton Jr., was born, followed in succession

Julia Lee White Ferguson, the wife of Walton Ferguson, wrote letters to her grandchildren about the creatures of Jekyll Island. (Courtesy of Mrs. Alfred W. Dater Jr.)

by Helen, 1872; Grace Carroll, 1874; Edward, 1876; Alfred Ludlow, 1879; and Henry Lee, 1881.[34]

Some ten years after his marriage to Julia White, Ferguson expanded his business interests to Pittsburgh where he became, with his brother, Edmund Morewood Ferguson, and Henry Clay Frick, one of the three partners who constituted the original firm of H. C. Frick Coke Company. This firm was later incorporated into the H. C. Frick Company, of which a one-half interest was later acquired by Carnegie Steel Company. In February 1901, the business was merged with the United States Steel Corporation. As years went on, Ferguson was involved in a multiplicity of business concerns, including railroads, gas companies, and electric light companies. He was one of the organizers of the Brooklyn Edison Company and the founder of the Kings County Electric Light Company, which was later absorbed into the former concern. He was a director of the People's Gas Company of Chicago; the Virginia Iron, Coal, and Coke Company; the Virginia and Southwestern Railway; and the Detroit and Mackinaw Railway. He was active in the establishment of the Union Carbide Company for which he served as a director, and he was president and one of the organizers of the Stamford Trust Company, a director of the First National Bank of Stamford from 1878 until 1921, and chairman of the Board of the Stamford Gas and Electric Company. In addition to his business activities, he was president of the Ferguson Library, established by his older brother, John Day Ferguson, who had died in 1877.[35]

Walton Ferguson divided his leisure time between his home on Strawberry Hill in Stamford, his summer home on Fisher's Island, New York, and his new winter home at Jekyll Island. He also enjoyed many pleasant hours on his steam yacht, *Christabel,* which he had first chartered about 1901 for a cruise on the Mediterranean, setting out from Villefranche, France, passing through the Aegean Sea, pausing for stops at various Greek islands, and continuing to the mouth of the Nile River, where the party temporarily left the yacht to take a *dahabiah* up the Nile.

During the cruise Ferguson "fell in love with the yacht," which had been twice chartered to the Kaiser of Germany. He struck up a friendship with the captain and discovered that the owner was an old gentleman who was not expected to live much longer because of an injury he had sustained in doing a back dive from the bridge deck. On a whim, Ferguson wrote to Lloyd's of London, asking that they notify him should the yacht ever come up for sale. Some time later the executor of the *Christabel* owner's estate wired him offering to sell the yacht but without fixing a price. Ferguson sent a trial offer of $50,000, which, to his surprise, was immediately accepted, and Ferguson found himself in 1903, the same year he acquired his Jekyll Island cottage, the proud owner of the vessel.[36]

By 1916, when he was seventy-four years old, he had begun to tire of the yacht, which he found too expensive to maintain for the limited use he was making of it. "It was all very well when I bought the ship to pay a foremast hand $9 to $11 a month with keep," he commented, "but now to have to pay $15 to $17; I simply cannot warrant such an expense!"[37]

That same year, in March 1916, a heater evidently caused a small fire in the Ferguson cottage at Jekyll, and Walton Ferguson took the opportunity, when he was going to have to repair the damage anyway, to do some additional remodeling, adding three bathrooms and two closets and reroofing the entire cottage—all done for what today sounds like a remarkably low cost of $1,151.70.[38] He came down in 1917 to view the results, but that season marked his last recorded visit to Jekyll Island. His son, Walton Ferguson Jr., vacationed with his wife on the island for the 1918 season, but he had begun to lose interest in the club and had long since sold his Jekyll share (in 1906) to his uncle, the Reverend Henry Ferguson, rector of Saint Paul's School in Concord, New Hampshire, who had been elected to membership that same year.

Walton Ferguson and his wife, Julia, had enjoyed the island for many years. Julia had written many letters home to her grandchildren telling them of Jekyll's pleasures, of "the mockingbirds [that] sing all day long," the "many cardinal red birds & bright blue birds, all chattering away," and of the squirrels that were always scolding the birds who invaded their territory, and above all, of her special character Bill Lizard who had been created for her grandson, Philip Dater, during a period when he was confined to his bed.[39] But the days of mockingbird song and Bill Lizard were over. Ferguson's health had begun to fail, and in 1919 he made the decision to sell his cottage to Ralph Beaver Strassburger. Walton Ferguson lived on until April 7, 1922, when he died, just three months shy of his eightieth birthday, at his Strawberry Hill home, where he had been "an invalid for many months."[40]

Walton Ferguson's yacht *Christabel*. (Courtesy of Mrs. Alfred W. Dater Jr.)

The Strassburger Years

On January 10, 1919, naval Lt. and Mrs. Ralph Beaver Strassburger with their three-year-old son, Peter, his governess, and a maid, checked into the Ferguson house as the guests of Mrs. Strassburger's father, Frederick Gilbert Bourne, who had served as president of the Singer Sewing Machine Company and who was currently president of the Jekyll Island Club.[41] The armistice that ended World War I had been signed on November 11, 1918, and the Jekyll Island Club was enjoying its first postwar season. The Strassburgers had visited the club three times before, in 1910, 1914, and 1918. Having made up their minds, apparently, that they enjoyed wintering at Jekyll, they decided to purchase the Ferguson house, which had recently come up for sale. Ralph Strassburger was elected to club membership on April 8, 1919, and purchased the Ferguson cottage on December 10 of that same year.[42]

Born May 25, 1883, the eldest son of Jacob Andrew Strassburger and Mary Jane Beaver, Strassburger had graduated from the naval academy in 1905, was commissioned as an ensign in February 1907, and served briefly on the navy's presidential yacht *Mayflower* during the administration of Theodore Roosevelt. In 1909 Strassburger left the navy to take a position in the marine department of the Babcock & Wilcox Company, which manufactured steam boilers for naval vessels around the world. One incident of his personal courage is recorded during this period in his life. On a trial run of the newly built U.S. battleship *North Dakota,* "a header blew out causing the death of two men and scalding several others." Strassburger, ignoring the risk, went into the chamber and isolated the boiler, "thereby saving many lives and, in all probability, the ship itself."[43]

In West Wickham, County Kent, England, on May 11, 1911, Strassburger married Mae Miller Bourne, known as "Mike" to her family. Two years later he entered the diplomatic corps, serving first as consul general and secretary of legation to Ro-mania, Bulgaria, and Serbia, but soon promoted to the post of second secretary of the embassy in Tokyo, Japan. His diplomatic career was cut short by the election of a Democrat, Woodrow Wilson, as president in 1912 and the subsequent appointment of William Jennings Bryan as secretary of state. Strassburger, an ardent Republican, resigned from his embassy post. Other disappointments followed close on the heels of his dashed diplomatic career. On October 16, 1913, the Strassburgers lost their first son at birth. Then the following year, when he ran for Congress, he was narrowly defeated by Henry W. Watson.

The world soon turned around for the Strassburgers, however, when a second son, Johann Andreas Peter, the only surviving child of their marriage, was born on January 13, 1916. The couple was understandably protective of the boy, as Mae Strassburger reveals poignantly in a letter to her sister Marion, written just after their arrival at Jekyll on January 31, 1920: "The trip down was very comfortable although I kept my weather eye on Peter all night for fear that he was uncovered or too warm. Consequently I feel dead tired tonight—having had next to no sleep." They had been met at Thalmann junction by a special train. "'Twas luxurious [sic]," she noted, "as we were the only ones there." But most of her thoughts were of Peter. "The trip over in the boat was pretty rough. Poor little lamb was sick and I think that concerns about him kept me up." They were met on the dock by various friends, "but I had no time to be with them as I rushed Peter right up to the house (first Strass and then I would carry him) & to bed."[44]

The Strassburgers made their permanent home on a large estate called Normandy Farms in Gwynedd Valley, Pennsylvania, where they raised thoroughbred horses as a hobby. Strassburger's postwar vocation was that of a newspaper owner and publisher of one of Pennsylvania's oldest daily papers, the *Norristown Herald,* founded in 1799.

After the outbreak of war in Europe, Strassburger, fearing that America would be forced into

Ralph Beaver Strassburger was the third owner of the Fairbank Cottage.
(Courtesy of Library of Congress)

Mae Bourne Stassburger, wife of
Ralph Beaver Strassburger, was one
of the daughters of Frederick
Gilbert Bourne, president of the
Singer Sewing Machine Company as
well as of the Jekyll Island Club.
(Courtesy of Strassburger Family)

Peter Strassburger was the only son
of Mae Bourne and Ralph Beaver
Strassburger. (Courtesy of Florence
H. Hughes)

the conflict, felt strongly that "the best defensive method . . . would be the building up and the strengthening of the Navy rather than the forming of a large Army." To support that idea, he became active in the Navy League.[45] With war raging in Europe and the United States having broken off diplomatic relations with Germany, Strassburger offered his services once again to the navy and was assigned to U.S. naval intelligence. He also served on the overseas transport *Louisville* and was assigned to special duty with the Fourth Naval District. For his wartime efforts he received a letter of commendation from the secretary of the navy. Following the war he stood in staunch opposition to United States participation in the League of Nations.

That postwar season of 1919, with Ralph Strassburger still bearing his wartime rank of lieutenant, would prove to be Frederick Gilbert Bourne's final season as the much-beloved president of the club, over which he had presided since 1914. Unfortunately, he never made it to the club for his final season, for he lay suffering from an unnamed "stomach ailment" in New York during most of the club season. It is clear that his family did not at first realize the seriousness of his illness. Mae Strassburger wrote to her sister Marion on January 28, "I am so sorry Father has had such a siege and feel that if he can only stand the trip down the change will do wonders for him. It is not wildly gay here but probably as winter finally sets in people will rush to get south." Even as late as February 18, she was still hoping for her father to come to Jekyll: "Everybody asks after Father and hopes that he will be able to get down later."[46] But that was not to be. Bourne took a turn for the worse and on March 9 died of uremic poisoning. The executive committee voted to halt a golf tournament then in progress on the day of his funeral, and the club would later dedicate to his memory a magnificent stained-glass window designed by Lewis Comfort Tiffany and installed in Faith Chapel, which had been built on the island in 1904, the final fulfillment of Helen Fairbank's dream.[47]

Despite their father's death, Bourne's children continued to cling to the Jekyll winters that they had enjoyed since 1901. Shortly thereafter, two of his daughters became members of the club. Marion C. Bourne was elected April 23, 1919, and her sister, Marjorie Bourne, was elected the following year on March 6, 1920. Although Mae Strassburger never joined the Jekyll Island Club in her own name, she nonetheless enjoyed its benefits through the membership of her husband.

While the three sisters shared in Jekyll's pleasures, apparently all was not always harmonious among them, a lapse that caused Almira Rockefeller, wife of William Rockefeller, to comment in a letter written from Jekyll Island to her daughter Emma on January 14, 1920: "I do hope when father and I are gone our children will not quarrel among themselves. . . . There are three or four members of the Bourne family coming to the Club and all are at loggerheads."[48]

Such disputes, if Mrs. Rockefeller had correctly perceived the situation, seem to have been brief. Although there does appear to have been a property dispute following the death of their father in 1919, it did not take on the proportions of those that occurred in the family of Jay Gould (see Chichota chapter), nor did it tear the family apart. Nevertheless, Frederick Bourne had left seven surviving children, three sons and four daughters, and a massive estate valued at over $40 million, a situation that tended to create friction. The *Herald Tribune* reported on November 28, 1926, for example, that the Long Island estate, Indian Neck Hall, "was sold to a syndicate because of disagreement among Commodore Bourne's children as to its disposition." They engaged in litigation that seems to have gone on for a number of years, "apparently preferring to divide the estate with a score or more of lawyers than with each other," as the April 10, 1942, *News of Sayville*, New York, suggested.

At the time the Strassburgers bought their cottage, whatever disagreements may have occurred among the Bourne children were no doubt just be-

Frederick Gilbert Bourne, father of cottage owner Majorie Bourne and the Jekyll Island Club president from 1914 to 1919, rides at Jekyll. (Courtesy of Florence H. Hughes)

ginning, but they were evident enough to be noticed by their Jekyll neighbors. Perhaps it was the burgeoning family dispute that prompted Strassburger to decide he had had enough. When he and his wife and son arrived on the island on January 31, 1920, Marjorie Bourne accompanied them, as she frequently did on their voyages. Marion Bourne, who had taken over the Sans Souci apartment her father had purchased from Julia Anderson in 1903 (apartment two, first floor, north) arrived on February 27 with her maid and menservants. The presence of yet another of the Bourne offspring on the island may have served to increase the tension and strain on household nerves.

Whatever the reason, one season of cottage ownership proved quite sufficient for Ralph Strassburger. Although he remained a club member until 1924, he put his Jekyll house up for sale in the summer of 1920—only a year or so after he had purchased it. Eager to unload the property as quickly as possible, he printed announcements describing the house and its desirability and sent them to all club members. In view of the fact that, in later years, the cottage would be demolished, the description of the house's interior is particularly valuable.

This cottage is of frame construction with large porches front, sides and rear. The ground floor contains a commodious living room with large open fireplace, small library, two bedrooms and bath, and kitchen. On the upper floor are four bedrooms and four connecting baths. In the rear are two servants' rooms with stationary washstands and servants' bath.

The bedrooms have been entirely refurnished this year; all rooms have been repainted or retinted and are in first-class condition. The house is entirely screened.

He reminded members of "the proximity of the cottage to the Club House" and of the grounds "well stocked with shrubbery" containing "an area of about twenty-five thousand (25,000) square feet." He concluded that "Undoubtedly this is the most convenient and desirable site on the Island," being "of easy access in rainy weather."[49] The house and its contents, the announcement stated, would be sold as a whole.

Cyrus Hall McCormick was one of those who responded with an inquiry about the cottage's location, which he could not remember. Strassburger sent him a surveyor's sketch, noting that he had "modernized the bathrooms," three of which had been installed only three years earlier. "There is no question," he wrote, "but what this cottage is the most desirable one on Jeykl [sic] Island. Mr. Richard Crane, of Chicago, had it for several years and always told us that they would have bought it and not built their house had it been available for purchase at the time they had it under lease."[50] McCormick took almost a year to respond, at which time he returned the surveyor's sketch and had his secretary indicate that he "does not now care to consider he purchase of a home at the club."[51]

Times were changing, and so were architectural tastes. The modest shingled cottages of the early 1890s had given way to more modern Italian, Spanish, or Mediterranean style houses like the Shrady,

Gould, and Goodyear cottages. And certainly anything looked modest and simple by comparison to the recently constructed Crane villa. In short, Strassburger had the house on the market for three years with no buyer. They continued to use the cottage themselves, coming down, again with Marjorie Bourne in their party, in March 1922, and then without her in March 1923. Despite her absence from Jekyll in 1923, it was she who purchased the Strassburger cottage that same year.

The Bourne-Thayer Years

Marjorie Bourne, born in 1888 and nicknamed "Hooley" by her family,[52] was the youngest child of Commodore Frederick Gilbert Bourne and his wife, the former Emma Keeler and, of course, one of the coheirs to his wealthy estate. Despite the family's legal disputes in sorting out their inheritance, she seems to have maintained a close relationship with her sisters, particularly Mae and Florence, and her brother George, known to family members as "Ginty." Not only did she join the Strassburgers at Jekyll and take the cottage off their hands when they were unable to find a buyer, but she also traveled with them on occasion to Europe. Two years after purchasing the cottage, for example, in July 1925, while she was in France with her sister Mae and her brother-in-law Ralph Strassburger, she was involved in a railroad accident at the Gare de l'Est in Paris, in which two persons were killed and twenty injured. Majorie Bourne, however, escaped unharmed.[53]

As for Marjorie's relationship with her sister Florence (Mrs. Anson Hard), she was asked to be godmother of Florence's daughter and namesake, who was born in 1925 and who described days with her Aunt Hooley as "never a dull moment."[54] Recognized in West Sayville, Long Island, for her generosity, she, along with her brother Howard, handed out hundreds of Christmas gifts each year to the village's children.[55]

At the time she bought the Strassburger cottage, Marjorie Bourne was thirty-four years old and still unmarried. Her single status gave her a singular freedom of movement, and she divided her time between Deauville, France, her home in Gwynedd Valley in Pennsylvania near that of the Strassburgers, and Dark Island Castle, the magnificent estate that her father had built for her mother in the Chippewa Bay of the Saint Lawrence River between 1901 and 1905. She had joined the Jekyll Island Club just a few years earlier, and her purchase of the cottage gave her still another option for vacations.

By October 1926 rumors were abroad that she was engaged to marry Alexander (Alec) Dallas Thayer, the son of Brig. Gen. Russell Thayer and Mary Homer Dixon of Chestnut Hill, Philadelphia. Marjorie Bourne staunchly denied it: "There is no truth to the report. I can't imagine who started the rumor. I have known Mr. Thayer a long time and we are friends."[56] Photographs of Marjorie Bourne taken at the time show a stylish flapper with little evidence of spinsterhood about her. She clearly enjoyed the freedom of movement and action to which she was accustomed.

Indeed, she had been known as something of a daredevil in previous years, having the family's penchant for enthusiastic and daring motoring, and the *New York Times* of June 4, 1908, reported in a front-page story a five-mile race that pitted her speeding chauffeur-driven automobile against the South Shore express on Long Island. At one point the automobile pulled ahead of the speeding train and dashed across the tracks just a few feet in front of the racing engine. However, despite all efforts and risks, the train pulled into the station its full length ahead of her vehicle. Apparently, racing the trains was common practice for members of the Bourne family, and thus far, they had beaten every locomotive on the line except this one. But whether she won the race or not, the incident had clearly caught the imagination of the country, and it was front-page news in every major New York newspaper,

The Bourne family departing from the island aboard the Jekyll yacht. *Left to right,* Marjorie Bourne (fourth owner of the Fairbank cottage), club president Frederick Gilbert Bourne, his wife, Emma Keeler Bourne, Ralph Strassburger, and Mae Bourne Strassburger. (Courtesy of Florence H. Hughes)

among them the *New York World*, which reported the "sight of a pretty girl standing up in a speeding auto urging the chauffeur to put daylight between his car and the fastest train on the Long Island Railroad." [57] Marjorie Bourne was also reputed to be a crack shot, and the same *Times* report suggested that she had "recently won a villa from her father in a rifle match."

Evidently, however, Marjorie Bourne had decided that it was time to settle down, and despite her October denials, her engagement to Alec Thayer was indeed formally announced at the Strassburgers' Normandy Farms on November 28, 1926. No date was set for the wedding. Nonetheless, on the following Friday, December 3, the couple quietly

slipped away to be married in the Episcopal Church of the Messiah in Gwynedd Valley, accompanied only by Miss Bourne's young nephew, Peter Strassburger; Countess Stephanie Beniezky, wife of a former Austrian prime minister; and Henry D. Bradley of New York. The marriage, according to one reporter "marked the culmination of a romance of long standing." [58]

Marjorie Bourne's new husband, Alec Thayer, was born January 29, 1888, and was a dashing and attractive man of thirty-eight, less than a year older than his bride. His primary recognition had come from his athletic prowess, and he gained particular notoriety as the quarterback on the football team at the University of Pennsylvania, where he was lauded especially for the excellence of his punting and drop kicking. He also played center field on the baseball team. He left the university in 1910 to take up an active sporting life, especially on the tennis court. With his sister Molly, he earned mixed-doubles championships in Delaware, Pennsylvania, and Eastern States tournaments, though he was a championship singles player as well.[59] According to the *Philadelphia Record* of December 4, 1926, he was also "known in lawn tennis and cricket circles."

During World War I, like his new brother-in-law, Ralph Strassburger, he had served in the military, enlisting in 1917 as a pilot; training at Ellington Field, Texas; and serving afterwards as an instructor at Fort Sill, Oklahoma, and Selfridge Field in Detroit, Michigan. From September 1918 to February 1919, he was overseas, serving in France as an aviation instructor and, after the armistice, in Strasbourg. At the time of his wedding, Thayer was identified as being in the insurance business, though he also worked for a time as a stockbroker.[60] Marjorie and Alec Thayer made their primary home at Marjorie's five-hundred-acre Gwynllan Farm, where she raised prize German shepherds at their forty-seven-acre Gwynllan Kennels and he focused on Guernsey cows for their dairy farm.

The Thayers did not visit their Jekyll Island cottage together until 1930, when they arrived on January 15 for their first stay. The season was characterized by a flood of guests, beginning with Alec's mother, accompanied by his brother F. Eugene D. Thayer. On January 26 still more family members and guests poured into the cottage, among them Marjorie's brother, George, and his wife, the former Nancy Potter, along with other members of the Potter family. Then on February 12 arrived Alec's sister-in-law, Mrs. Edmund Thayer, and her two children.

Following that first active season, the Thayers used the cottage only on rare occasions, and in fact, it was the Strassburgers who occupied it the following season. Instead of Jekyll, their new yacht, the *Queen Anne*, purchased in 1931 and reputed to be one of the largest in the country, captured their interest, and they took up yachting in earnest. No visits to Jekyll Island by any member of the Bourne or Thayer family are recorded again until 1936 when Alec's brothers Russell Jr. and Joseph came with their respective families to stay in the cottage. Marjorie and Alec Thayer did not arrive until March 4. They sailed in on the *Queen Anne* with a large party of people that included young Peter Strassburger, now seventeen years old, George Bourne, and several friends. Then on March 22 Alec's brother Edmund arrived with his family, and the cottage overflowed with life for one brief, final moment. No other visit by Alec and Marjorie Thayer is recorded in the Jekyll Island guest register. Although the cottage was used in 1937 once more by Alec's mother, it seems to have stood empty thereafter until it was finally demolished at some point near the end of the club era. A 1944 survey shows only what is referred to as the "old Thayer plot."[61] Its last owner, Marjorie Bourne Thayer, lived until 1962, and two years after her death, her widower, Alexander Dallas Thayer, married her sister Florence.[62]

Owners: Walter Rogers Furness, 1890–97; Joseph Pulitzer, 1897–1911; John J. Albright, 1912–30; Jekyll Island Club, 1930–47

Constructed: 1890

Architecture: Shingle style

Architect: Furness, Evans, & Co. (probable)

The Furness Years

Walter Rogers Furness, born in 1861, was at age twenty-five the youngest original member of the Jekyll Island Club. He hailed from a distinguished Philadelphia family, whose members had attained prominence in a variety of fields. His grandfather

William Henry Furness was well known as the first regular minister of the Unitarian Church in the city and as an abolitionist of some eminence. Two of the Reverend Furness's sons attained equal distinction in their own fields. Horace Howard Furness, the father of Walter, editor of the *New Variorum Shakespeare,* was said to be "the world's greatest Shake-

The Furness Cottage at its original location. The cottage was moved three times, once by each of its last three owners. It was moved to its present location to serve as a club infirmary. (Courtesy of Georgia Department of Archives and History, original in the Jekyll Island Museum)

Walter Rogers Furness, from a prominent Philadelphia family, was the youngest of the Jekyll Island Club's original fifty-three members in 1886. (Courtesy of Wirt Thompson Jr.)

speare scholar," a proclamation made by writer Owen Wister, grandson of actress Fanny Kemble and her Georgia plantation-owner husband Pierce Butler, at the time of Furness's death.[1] Helen Kate Rogers Furness, Walter's mother, was also involved in the work, compiling a concordance to Shakespeare's poetry. Furness's brother Frank was a famous Philadelphia architect, who had worked in the atelier of William Morris Hunt and whose work influenced a number of younger noteworthy architects, among them Louis Sullivan, the mentor of Frank Lloyd Wright.

Walter Rogers Furness unfortunately was not a chip off the old block. As the oldest child of Horace Howard Furness and Helen Kate Rogers, he seems to have been a fun-loving, devil-may-care young man to whom life had given every advantage. Considered handsome and charming, he came from a family that was not only prominent socially but also provided a rich cultural environment. Sunday afternoons at Lindenshade, the family's country home, overflowed with stimulating activity and visitors with the best minds in the land.[2] But such intellectual têtes-à-têtes were of less interest to the young man than a pleasant afternoon on the racquets court or in a hunting party with his chums. Often those afternoons would end with a pleasant drink among friends, an activity frequently prolonged into the night. He once made the assumption that a comrade, and apparently a rival for his future wife's affections, "looked on me very coldly" because he "refused to take a parting drink with me."[3] Such attitudes were a harbinger of things to come.

In 1879 Furness began his college years at his father and grandfather's alma mater, Harvard University. When his mother died during his senior year 1883, he inherited considerable property from the estate of her father, Evans Rogers. Now financially independent of his father, he was free to make his own way and follow his interests. He did not return to Harvard and never finished his degree. Nor did he immediately enter the working world.

For a few years he pursued an avid interest in photography, writing and privately publishing in 1885 a book entitled *Composite Photography Applied to the Portraits of Shakespeare*. The subject of the book, with its focus on the Elizabethan bard, may have been an effort to regain his father's favor after his failure to graduate from Harvard. For a brief time it may have worked, but not entirely to his satisfaction. He wrote to his bride-to-be on February 12 of the following year: "Tonight I have spent my first evening at home for many months and I find it intolerably dull, this prodigal son business is not what it's cracked up to be I can assure you. The governor [his father] has not put a purple robe on my shoulders neither has he given me a ring. What is the use in being good if you don't get rewarded for it." [4]

Such would be his philosophy in the years to come, and one that provided him with little character for dealing with life's adversities. Nor, evidently, was his reconciliation with his father permanent. One of the things he had inherited from his grandfather's estate was the family house at 222 Washington Square. His parents had lived there before Helen Furness's death, and Horace Howard Furness had a niche made on one wall to contain a mask of Shakespeare. When the house came into the possession of young Walter Furness, however, the new owner replaced the mask of Shakespeare with a plaster cast of an orangutan, "for fun," according to a reminiscence of his son, but one cannot miss the deliberate mockery of his act.

A man of weak resolve could hardly fare well in the Furness family, where expectations of achievement were high and the competition was great. Walter's brother Howard would carry on the scholarly work of their father, while his other brother, William Henry, would become a physician. Walter himself seemed to have no vocation and to lack the will to develop his talents in any area. Family albums, for example, reveal his effort to carry on a family tradition of caricatures. Whereas his uncle Frank and his father had inserted extraordinary caricatures into their correspondence, his own remained crude and amateurish. He had no propensity toward scholarship and but limited interest, so it seems, in architecture.

For a time, however, things went well in Furness's life. On June 2, 1886, he married Helen Key Bullitt, the attractive daughter of John Christian Bullitt, a prominent and wealthy Philadelphia lawyer who could trace his ancestry back to the nation's founders.[5] Walter had sought to ingratiate himself with Helen's father in order to win her hand and wrote to her of one encounter with him: "I saw your respected Pa in the street the other day & he looked

Helen Key Bullitt, wife of Walter Rogers Furness, exemplified the hourglass-figure ideal of the late nineteenth century. (Courtesy of Wirt Thompson Jr.)

pretty chipper notwithstanding your absence. [She was visiting in Washington, D. C. at the time.] I fairly sweep [sic] up the street with my hat when I bowed to him for fear he [would] put me on his black list." [6]

In the same year he married Helen Bullitt he joined the newly founded Jekyll Island Club. His mother's brother, Fairman Rogers, had heard about the club and determined to join as one of its charter members. Learning from his uncle Fairman of the Georgia island with its bounties of game and the "fairy-tale" promises of its founders, as one new member described them, Furness, always ready for a good adventure, decided to join as well and

Helen Bullitt Furness playing croquet. (Courtesy of Wirt Thompson Jr.)

Walter Rogers Furness, *left,* and J. W. Fassitt, a member of the Furness, Evans, and Company architectural firm, pose for a photograph in Savannah with their hunting dogs, *left to right,* Dan, Pat, Isaac, and Zulu. (Courtesy of Wirt Thompson Jr.)

became the youngest of the club's original fifty-three members.

Despite his Jekyll membership, he did not visit the island for several years. He and his wife, Helen, did much traveling, and he hunted in Thomasville, Georgia, and fished for tarpon in the Gulf of Mexico. These were good years for the young family. As his son would write later about the period surrounding his birth in January 1889, "The family was good, about at its peak, with enough money to live nicely and a wide circle of relations."[7] Within three years of the marriage the couple would have two children, Helen Kate Furness, named for Walter's mother and Helen herself, and Fairman Rogers Furness, named for Helen's brother.

A little over a month after his son's birth, Walter Rogers Furness visited Jekyll Island apparently for the first time, accompanied by a friend named J. W. Fassitt. Fassitt was employed by Frank Furness's architectural firm, Furness, Evans and Company. Undoubtedly the trip to Jekyll was connected with the construction on the island of the new Furness cottage, which would be completed in 1890. Whether Fassitt himself was the architect or was merely there to oversee construction of a house designed by Walter's uncle Frank cannot be said with certainty since the plans have apparently not survived; however, there can be little doubt that the house was designed by someone connected with the well-known architectural firm of Furness, Evans and Company. Frank Furness seems to have done all the Philadelphia architectural work for the family, including work for Walter's father, Horace Howard, his uncle Fairman Rogers, and Walter himself. It is very likely, therefore, that it was he who drew the plans for Furness's charming Jekyll cottage as well, although it cannot be determined for certain.[8] Its shingle-style design is typical of an architecture that has been said to be that "most wholly wedded to the landscape."[9] Its wall cladding of wood shingles, its extensive use of porches, including the rounded tower-like structure with the

Furness children at Jekyll Island, 1890, with the tower of the Jekyll Island Club in the background. (Courtesy of Wirt Thompson Jr.)

upstairs porch, and its asymmetrical facade and roofline make it the purest example in the cottage colony of this architectural style that was popular between 1880 and 1900.

The cottage seems to have been virtually completed by the end of 1890 or early 1891. Evidently, however, a few finishing touches were still needed on the house when the family arrived on December 10, 1890, for they moved into the club house upon arrival. The architectural firm's representative, J. W. Fassitt, stayed only briefly but returned twelve days later, presumably to look over the finished house and take care of any minor additional details. The following year the family arrived once again on December 11, in advance of the club's official opening, and checked into the club house with their two children and their nurse Maggie O'Brien.[10] Two days before Christmas, Helen's brother John arrived. In the ensuing weeks, various other guests joined them on the island, and the cottage was well used for the season. Once the

Helen Bullitt Furness with her
children, Fairman and Kate.
(Courtesy of Wirt Thompson Jr.)

following year, Walter was able to persuade even his father to come for a visit.

Thus their pattern was established. Each season the Furness family would arrive shortly before or after Christmas and would spend all or most of the club season hunting on Jekyll. Helen Furness hunted alongside her husband and sometimes independently, on at least one occasion, March 3, 1893, bringing down one of the island's elusive and wily boar.[11] The family came every year from 1889 until the 1894–95 season. Walter Furness was also active in club activities, serving on the game committee from 1891 to 1897, clearly reflecting his primary interest in the hunting at Jekyll. He was chosen to serve on the board of directors for 1894–95 and as secretary pro tem in 1897.

Their pattern of annual seasonal participation in the club's activities was disrupted, however, in 1896. For the first time since building their cottage, they did not spend the winter on Jekyll. The endless leisure that they had enjoyed had come to an abrupt end, and for the first time in his life, Walter Rogers Furness had become gainfully employed. He had been taken in as an active partner with the architectural firm of his uncle, Frank Furness. Although he was not a trained architect, a position had been created for him to which he could devote his attention. Recognizing that with his new job he would have little time to spend at Jekyll, Furness sold one of his club shares to A. S. Van Wickle in July 1895.

In 1896 he sold his cottage as well to newspaper magnate Joseph Pulitzer, who would occupy it until he completed a larger brick house the following year. As part of the transaction Furness acquired Jekyll lots 33 and 34, which he subsequently sold to Henry B. Hyde, president of the Equitable Life Assurance Corporation and which would eventually be the site of Edwin Gould's Chichota. Once Pulitzer had completed his new house in 1897, he would use the Furness cottage for his family's servants, as

Kate Furness with her mother, Helen, in 1902. (Courtesy of Wirt Thompson Jr.)

would John J. Albright, who acquired the Pulitzer property after Joseph Pulitzer's death in 1911.

Walter Rogers Furness came for only brief visits to Jekyll Island after selling his property there, returning twice, both times with his wife, on January 13, 1897, and on March 6, 1898. They stayed in the club house during both vacations. Not long after his visit of March 1898, however, a turning point came in the life of Walter Furness. During a game of racquets he was struck in the eye by a speeding ball and permanently blinded in that eye. He seemed unable to accept and overcome the disability. The year 1898 is the last in which he is listed in the Philadelphia City Directory as a partner in the firm

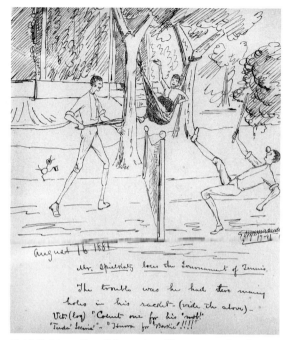

August 16 1881

Mr. Spielkatz loses the Tournament of Tennis.

"The trouble was he had too many holes in his racket (vide the above)—Veto (log) "Count one for his 'nut'!" "Tuda' tennis" – "Hurra for 'Barkis'!!!!"

C. N. B. Macaulley did a series of humorous sketches depicting Walter Furness as Mr. Spielkatz. One of these, dated August 16, 1881, curiously foreshadows the eye injury that would cost Furness dearly. (Courtesy of Wirt Thompson Jr.)

of Furness, Evans and Company, and it was the beginning of the end of his happy life with his family.[12]

It marked the end as well of his association with the Jekyll Island Club. On January 21, 1899, the club superintendent, Ernest Gilbert Grob, wrote to Furness: "I am extremely sorry to hear about the injury to your eye, and that you do not think of coming down. Am also sorry that you want to dispose of your share, but will be pleased to put it forward, should I hear of a buyer. I am of the opinion that there will be several shares sold this winter."[13] By January 1901, however, the share, valued by Grob at between $1,500 and $2,000, had still not been sold, and Furness was growing increasingly impatient. He had informed Grob that, because of his in-

jury, he would never be able to hunt again, and once again Grob assured him that he would make every effort to sell the share.[14] By this time Furness, weary of paying the expensive club dues and assessments for a club he never again intended to use, simply stopped paying them. He had been lax for some time about keeping up his dues and assessments, and in 1899 E. C. Purdy, the club's assistant treasurer, wrote to Henry B. Hyde, the executive committee member who had taken control of club affairs, sending him a list of club members who were in arrears for dues for 1897 and 1898, as well as for recent assessments. Furness's was the only name that appeared on all three lists. He was carried on the club roster until 1901, when at a joint meeting on April 8, the board of directors and the executive committee adopted a resolution that because of Furness's failure "to pay dues, assessments, or other indebtedness to the Jekyll Island Club," and after "repeated written notification thereof from the treasurer," Furness's shares were to be "forfeited" and sold at public auction and that his membership in the club should "cease."[15] The share, sold at auction that same year, was bought in by the club, which later sold it to a syndicate headed by Frederic Baker of New York.[16]

Things went from bad to worse in Furness's life from this point on. Repeated bouts with alcoholism brought about strained relations with his family. When his son, Fairman, entered the diplomatic corps as third secretary to the Russian embassy in 1912, he wrote his letters home only to his mother. Helen Key Bullitt Furness died on January 2, 1914, of "a complication of diseases," no doubt exacerbated by her worries over her husband. She was only forty-seven years old. After her death, with young Fairman still at the embassy in Saint Petersburg, only Furness's daughter, Kate, was left to cope with her father's rampant alcoholism.

The death of his wife, which must have brought him a painful dose of both grief and guilt, only in-

Walter Rogers Furness and Helen Bullitt Furness. (Courtesy of Wirt Thompson Jr.)

tensified Walter Furness's despair at the turn his life had taken. He outlived Helen by little more than a month, dying on February 17, 1914, at age fifty-three. Although his obituary gives Bright's disease as the reason for his death, the real story was told in a sad letter from Kate Furness to her brother in Russia, telling of their father's last days: "As you may know we have had an awful time with him. Twice he was brought out from the Racquet Club in a dreadful condition or all bruised up and I don't think he had one sober day [until he was brought to the hospital]. . . . he never stopped talking & never slept & never ate[.] Then he started on Delirium Tremors and he yelled & talked for 36 hours without stopping until he exhausted himself and his heart just gave out and of course you can not help thinking that it is a good thing."[17] It was a painful and tragic end for one who seemed in his youth to have much to live for.

The Pulitzer/Albright/Goodyear Years

After the Furness cottage passed into the hands of Joseph Pulitzer, it would be subsequently owned by John J. Albright and briefly by Frank Goodyear, the latter of whom donated it in 1930 to the Jekyll Island Club for use as an infirmary in memory of his mother, Josephine Looney Goodyear. Each of its new owners would have the cottage moved to a new location. Thus in its history it was displaced three times from its original site. Pulitzer, who purchased the cottage in 1896, used it only a short time for his personal habitation. When he constructed his brick house in 1897, he had the Furness Cottage moved approximately 125 feet "in a South-westerly direction" to make room for the new structure.[18] Under the ownership of both Pulitzer and John J. Albright, who purchased it in 1914 from Ralph Pulitzer, the cottage was relegated to use as servants' quarters from 1898 to 1930. After Albright purchased the Pulitzer property in February 1914, and as he made the necessary alterations to prepare it for his own

purposes, he had the cottage moved once more in April 1915 "about 50 ft. to the south & then 50 ft. to east."[19] There would reside the Albright servants, among them the coachman, Keyes, and in later years the chauffeur, Dumbleton.

When Frank Goodyear purchased the cottage to be dedicated as an infirmary in memory of his mother, Josephine Looney Goodyear (see Goodyear Cottage chapter), the Jekyll Island Club provided him a lease on December 20, 1929, to the new plot of land at the eastern end of Shell Road. The cottage was moved to its current location on January 21, 1930. It was then deeded from Frank Goodyear to the newly incorporated Josephine Goodyear Memorial Infirmary.[20] The February 1930 Report of the Executive Committee to the annual stockholders' meeting announced the "splendid gift" that was "dedicated to the relief of the ill on the Island and cares for both black and white, in separate wards, of course."

The State Era

When the state of Georgia acquired the island in 1947, the cottage was still fully outfitted and supplied for use as an infirmary. However, the Jekyll Island Authority dismantled the infirmary and in the mid-1950s leased the cottage for $70 a month to William McMath of Dawson, Georgia, who served briefly as construction superintendent for the Jekyll Island Authority and was one of only three stockholders in the Jekyll Hotel Corporation, which ran the club house as a hotel from 1956 until 1971.[21] With his partner, state senator Jimmy Dykes (see Mistletoe chapter), McMath was involved in a number of financial undertakings during the early years of state ownership of the island. After McMath's departure, the Jekyll Island Authority leased the cottage to various island employees, the most recent being Etienne (Al) Elfer Jr., who lived there from 1979 until 1996. At present, the cottage is leased to Jekyll Books and Antiques, Inc.

HOLLYBOURNE

Owners: Charles Stewart Maurice, 1890–1924; Margaret Stewart Maurice,[1] 1924–47

Constructed: 1890

Architecture: Jacobethan (Tudor subtype)

Architect: William H. Day

The Maurice family, who built the cottage Hollybourne, was the only family associated with the Jekyll Island Club from its founding in 1886 until its final legal dissolution in 1948. Charles Stewart Maurice was born on June 29, 1840, at Perth Amboy, New Jersey, the son of Charles Frazier Maurice and his wife, Cornelia Joline. Maurice had Georgia connections through his grandfather Benjamin Maurice, who had been a Savannah merchant for a number of years before moving to New York and finally Perth Amboy. Financially ruined during the Napoleonic Wars when England imposed restrictions on American trade and the U.S. retaliated with its own trade restrictions, Benjamin Maurice was further hurt in business when his partner John Patrick allegedly cheated him. In his son's words, "skinflint Patrick did him out."[2]

His son, Charles Frazier Maurice, entered business as well, but in 1842 "at the earnest solicitation of a number of friends," he opened a private school

Hollybourne Cottage. (Courtesy of Thomas Maurice)

Charles Stewart Maurice, who would become one of the nation's foremost bridge-builders, shown here in his Civil War uniform in the 1860s. (Southern Historical Collection, Library of the University of North Carolina, Chapel Hill)

fall of 1861 to study marine engineering, covering both sophomore and junior curricula in a single academic year, and on November 17, 1862, he was commissioned third assistant engineer (midshipman) in the U.S. Navy and reported for duty aboard the *Ossipee,* then stationed in the Washington Navy Yard. Throughout his life Maurice was dyspeptic, and repeated attacks of indigestion in the summer of 1863 sent him home on sick leave. However, he rejoined the navy in the fall and, this time, was assigned to the gunboat *Agawam.* Thus Maurice spent the spring and summer of 1864 on the James River, where "a small fleet of ironclads and gunboats was keeping open a line of communication with General Grant, and was under frequent fire from enemy batteries and sharpshooters along the banks." [3] Before he ended his service in the navy on December 21, 1865, he would serve as well on the steam frigate *Colorado* and the *Malvern,* the flagship of the North Atlantic Squadron.

Maurice turned down an appointment as assistant professor of mathematics at the U.S. Naval Academy in Annapolis, Maryland, to turn his attention to the business world. He was first employed as an engineer by the Lower Hudson Steamboat Company, designing engines for the company's vessels. In the fall of 1866, however, he opened a tannery with a boyhood friend, Eugene Underhill, in Athens, Pennsylvania, though in 1869 he sold his interest in the business to his partner and returned to his father's home at Briarcliff, New York. In that same year on April 28, he married Charlotte Marshall Holbrooke, daughter of John G. Holbrooke and his wife, Marian Marshall, both from families of great distinction. Charlotte Holbrooke claimed no fewer than eleven ancestors who had crossed the Atlantic on the *Mayflower* to found Plymouth Colony.[4]

Stewart Maurice, who now had a wife to support, was still casting about for what was to be his life's work. He began to supply timber to the Oswego Midland Railroad for the construction of bridges, a pursuit that led to a lifelong interest in bridge-

at Napanock, New York, which he later moved to Sing Sing (now Ossining), New York, to merge it with Mount Pleasant Military Academy, which became one of the best-known private schools of its time. Stewart Maurice received his early education there, before entering Williams College in Williamstown, Massachusetts, as a sophomore in 1858. He graduated as class salutatorian and Phi Beta Kappa in 1861, just in time to take part in the Civil War.

In order to prepare himself to enlist in the navy, he entered Rensselaer Polytechnic Institute in the

building. With Charles Kellogg, who had patented a combination of wooden and iron bridges and was seeking to expand his application of the process, he formed a partnership on July 1, 1871, for "manufacturing and building Road and Railway Bridges."[5] The firm of Kellogg and Maurice would be one of the pioneer companies in the building of iron bridges and the second company to build them of steel. Their first major accomplishment was the construction of a bridge over the Tombigbee River in southern Alabama. They also built a section of the Third Avenue Elevated Railroad in New York, as well as bridges in Nova Scotia and Brazil, a Platte River Bridge at Plattsmouth, Nebraska, and the Thames River Bridge at New London, Connecticut.

The partnership was dissolved in 1884 in order to merge on March 1 of that year with other bridge-building firms to form the Union Bridge Company. Among Maurice's new partners were George S. Field and Edmund Hayes from Buffalo, New York, Charles MacDonald from New York City, and Thomas C. Clarke of Seabright, New Jersey.[6] The new firm would construct some of the best-known bridges of the time, among them the Poughkeepsie Bridge over the Hudson River, the Cantilever Bridge over the Niagara, the Cairo Bridge over the Ohio, and the Memphis Bridge over the Mississippi.

As Maurice's fortune grew, so did his family, and during the course of their marriage Charlotte and Stewart Maurice would have nine children: Archibald Stewart (born in 1870), George Holbrooke (1871), Marian Bridge (Mamie, 1872), Charles Frazier (1873), Cornelia (Nina, 1876), Charlotte Marshall (1880), Margaret Stewart (Peg, 1883), Albert Touzalin (1885), and Emily Marshall (1887). All of them grew to adulthood except Charlotte's namesake, who died in infancy on October 10, 1881.[7]

The following year, to accommodate their growing family and perhaps take their minds off the loss of their baby daughter, the Maurices did extensive remodeling on their home in Athens, Pennsylvania. They engaged the New York architectural firm of William H. Day, De Baud and Company who made

Charlotte Marshall Holbrooke, the wife of Charles Stewart Maurice (in the 1860s). (Southern Historical Collection, Library of the University of North Carolina, Chapel Hill)

every effort to meet their requirements, as De Baud made clear to Maurice: "It has been our aim to reconstruct the house in as quiet a manner as possible, avoiding all pretense and newness. In color and detail it will be our endeavor to still add to its simplicity—giving it character and dignity that it may grow more and more to your liking day by day; thus being in every sense of the word—a 'home.'"[8] Such efforts no doubt reflected the Maurices' desires.

When Maurice joined the Jekyll Island Club as a founding member in 1886, he originally purchased two club shares but sold one of them to his friend Albert E. Touzalin, president of the Chicago, Burlington, and Northern Railroad, before the club was chartered. He brought with him into the club not only Touzalin, for whom he had just named his youngest son, but also two of his partners in the Union Bridge Company, Thomas Curtis Clarke and Edmund Hayes. Eventually another partner, George Spencer Field, would join the club in 1891.[9]

Clarke was the first of the group to go to the island, which he did during the club's maiden season, 1888. He wrote to Maurice on February 22, glowing with enthusiasm after three days on the island, "The [club] house is a very handsome one, beautifully furnished and appointed, and in such a manner as to give it a very home-like effect, rather than that of a hotel. The cooking also is like that of a private home. We have delicious oysters and plenty of fresh fish." The weather he found "perfectly delightful," the rides and drives "very beautiful" and the hunting, with the exception of ducks which were scarce, excellent. "I think if you come here next December with a dog you will have all the pheasant and quail shooting you could wish."[10]

Touzalin, who had not yet visited the island, seemed less enthusiastic and suggested to Maurice on July 25, 1888: "About our Jeckyl [sic] shares . . . , I think this is a good time to sell if we are so disposed." He had heard reports from two friends who had been there, and had reached "the belief that it will be a good Club for rich and young New Yorkers, but hardly for staid old fellows like you & I."[11] But Touzalin died suddenly in September 1889 without having sold his share.

He could not have been more wrong, however, as far as Maurice was concerned, for the latter's enthusiasm for Jekyll was unbounded. His philosophy of simplicity, reflected in the remodeling of his Athens home, coincided beautifully with that espoused by the Jekyll Island Club, and he became profoundly interested in the flora and fauna of Jekyll, as well as in the island's history. In fact, for the rest of their lives, both Stewart and Charlotte Maurice were among the island's staunchest boosters, and together they collected its history and legends, which Stewart Maurice would eventually have published.[12]

Maurice made his first two trips to the island alone in January 1889 and evidently liked what he saw. It was obvious from the outset that rooms in the club house would never suffice for his large family, with two of his eight children, Al and Emmy, still barely past the toddler stage. By early May he was already making plans for the construction of a cottage. Charlotte Maurice wrote to her son Arch on May 15, "I was to have gone with Papa to New York a week ago yesterday for a couple of days as he wanted me to look over the Jekyl plans a little more closely."[13] Her trip had been unfortunately delayed by little Al's falling ill with scarlet fever. They had turned once again to the New York architectural firm that had redone their Athens home, with architect William H. Day designing the house that would prove to be the most interesting, architecturally speaking, of any ever built in the island's cottage colony.

On January 19, 1890, Maurice took his wife to look over the island and the site of their new cottage, which they would call Hollybourne and which would serve as the family's winter home for more than fifty years.[14] Day's design is a very early example of an eclectic Tudor style built from about 1890 until 1940 in the United States. Influenced by late medieval and renaissance buildings popular during the reigns of Elizabeth I and James I of England, the style has been variously labeled by architectural historians as Jacobethan or pseudo-Jacobean. Typical of the style were the shaped Flemish gables, paired chimney flues, and patterned stonework that characterize the cottage.

In many respects, however, Hollybourne is unique. The cottage is the only one in the club era to have been constructed using the island's native "tabby," the same mixture of lime, sand, and shell of which the Horton House was built in colonial

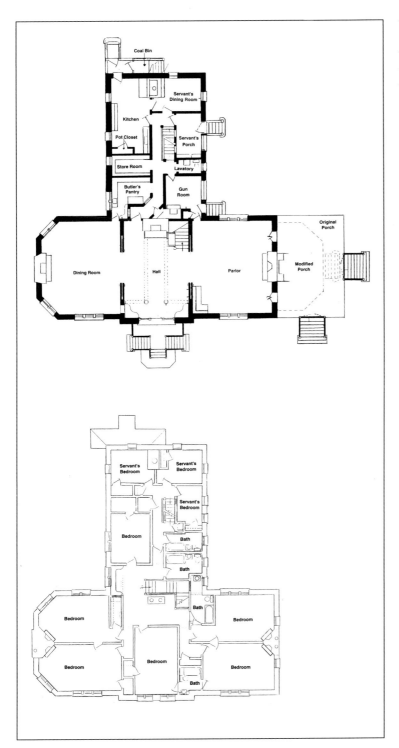

Hollybourne, first-floor and second-floor plans. (Based on original plans by William Day in Southern Historical Collection, Library of the University of North Carolina, Chapel Hill)

The truss in the attic of the Maurice cottage reflects the bridge-building techniques that Maurice required from his architect. (Photo by Jack Ross)

days. One island worker referred to it as "compromise cottage," for the compromises in architectural principles that the bridge builder, Maurice, worked out with the architect, Day. The use of steel in the house's support system, the solid base of nineteen brick piers in the basement, and the system of trusses that help to distribute the weight and support the twenty-eight-by-twenty-five-foot living and dining room ceilings without the use of beams or pillars are all typical of bridge construction techniques and reflect Maurice's knowledge of and confidence in the building principles of his own profession. The architect had the good sense to engage a local contractor, Burr Winston, who was no doubt familiar with the use of tabby in the area. For $18,000 he was able to build a cottage, the first floor of which contained a hall, a dining room, parlor, butler's pantry, gun room, servants' dining room, kitchen, a storeroom, large porch with a fireplace, and a servants' porch. The second floor consisted of nine bedrooms, five of them large and four small, with two baths.[15]

By December 1890 the house was complete, and the Maurices set out with their entire family for their first stay in their new Jekyll cottage, leaving Pennsylvania on December 16. Charlotte's father de-scribed the scene with apparent merriment: "They went off in good spirits. 5 horses, 4 dogs a cow and two men went a week ago and 16 humans followed yesterday."[16] By the time they arrived eighteen people were in their party, including the Maurices, all their children except Charles, who rarely came to Jekyll, Mr. Maurice's parents, a Miss Taylor, two nurses, and two unidentified men, probably servants. The Misses Chandler and Touzalin, from New York and Boston, respectively, had evidently joined their party en route and registered with them for a stay at the club house. Even their nine-bedroom house could not accommodate such a group, and Mr. Maurice's parents and his two oldest sons, Arch and George, were also obliged to stay in the club house.

Every single year between 1890 and 1942, with the sole exceptions of the 1894 and 1895 seasons, some members of the Maurice family arrived to spend all or part of the winter at Jekyll Island. An epidemic of yellow fever ravaged Brunswick in the summer of 1893, preventing the club's opening for the 1894 season. People left town by the droves, stores closed, and trains and steamers stopped running. The only contact between the people of Brunswick and the outer world was by wagon to Waynesville, where they were quarantined for fifteen days before being allowed to continue. Club superintendent Ernest Grob wrote to Maurice about the situation on August 25, indicating that "there is likely to be a famine here" and that he had taken "the liberty to have a deer killed today, as we have been a week without any substantial food."[17] Charlotte Maurice was dismayed, writing on November 17 to her son Arch, "It is uncertain as yet whether the Club will be opened this Winter or not on account of the yellow fever this summer at Brunswick and some people seem to fear going South. This is nonsense after they have had frost, as it kills all germs at once."[18] Nevertheless, the club did not officially open, and the Maurices did not go down.

Hollybourne, February 1905, still showing the original front steps and side porch. The individual chimney pots, patterned brickwork, and parapeted gables are typical of the substyle of Tudor architecture called Jacobethan. (Southern Historical Collection, Library of the University of North Carolina, Chapel Hill)

The dining room of Hollybourne, where the Maurices entertained frequently during the club season. (Southern Historical Collection, Library of the University of North Carolina, Chapel Hill)

During the 1895 season, for the first of only two occasions, the Maurices permitted their cottage to be rented—by Joseph Pulitzer. On December 12, 1894, before the Pulitzer retinue arrived on December 29, Mrs. Maurice came down and checked into the club house, accompanied only by her son George. Apparently uneasy about renting out Hollybourne, she did a detailed inventory of everything in the cottage during the two-week interval, down to the smallest kitchen utensil.[19]

Usually, however, the Maurices arrived in December to celebrate Christmas on the island and stayed for the entire club season, which ordinarily ended in early April. The trip from Athens, Pennsylvania, to Jekyll Island was not always ideal. There were frequently long delays and occasional mishaps en route, as Marian reported in December 1901. They had arrived "five hours late," not reaching Brunswick until 8:00 P.M., and in the meantime "we had to change at a miserable junction called Thalman where Papa had a bad fall owing to the fact that in one place the platform was six feet from the ground, no railing & not a sign of even a hand lantern on this pitch dark night. It was a wonder he was not seriously hurt but . . . escaped with only a badly bruised back from which he has now recovered."[20]

Nevertheless, the trip was worth the effort. Their Jekyll Christmases, in particular, soon drove away all thoughts of hardship the trip might have caused. Cornelia described their family traditions in a delightful letter to her Grandmother Holbrooke after the Christmas of 1898: "The children have a little tree every year which is put in my room beside the fireplace & all the stockings suspended from the mantel. . . . I think the older children enjoy it nearly as much as the smaller ones. . . . I lighted a fire in the fireplace & the candles on the tree which together give plenty of light to open the stockings, for it was still dark outside. Then everyone assembled in dressing gowns & slippers & George wrapped in a blanket caused a great deal of fun."

After the opening of the stockings, the family dressed and took the boat to Brunswick for church. Then came their usual Christmas dinner, for which they always included the club superintendent, Ernest Grob, and, until their marriage, the club's head housekeeper, Minnie Schuppan, and the boat captain, James Clark. This particular year they had prepared a special surprise: "We arranged a small tree in the centre of the table & around it a present for each one with a ribbon attached to it & the pile in the centre about the tree covered with holly. When dinner was over each one pulled the ribbon nearest them & out came the presents from their hiding places. It caused a good deal of surprise & fun." Such memories had left an indelible impression on all the children. Emily, the youngest of the Maurice children, also wrote to her grandmother that year, dutifully recounting her Christmas treasures: "a little train with a lot of track and a freight station, a dear little toy spinning wheel, a silver comb, three books, a little candle-stick and a very pretty doll."[21] The train was clearly intended for both Emily and Al, who received among his bountiful gifts that year "a little bridge a switch house a lamp a lantern and and [sic] an extra car for a little railroad Emily and I have."[22]

The family expanded its generosity to others on the island as well. In 1901, for example, they "had a Christmas tree for all the Island employee's children, 17 of them, of all ages . . . from six months to 11 years & they gave us a very lively two hours. . . . The only interval of quite [sic] was the period during which they were consuming large quantities of ice cream & cake & how they did enjoy it! It was great fun to watch them."[23]

For many on the island the Maurice cottage was the very center of Jekyll life during the club season for the next two decades. They entertained almost daily with simple teas and sumptuous dinners in their cottage, and Mrs. Maurice kept a menu diary for every single dinner served on the island. On one of these occasions on February 26, 1893, her

The servants of the Maurice family, among them Elizabeth, *middle,* who was the wife of Ernest Grob's assistant Otto Lederer, and Mary, *right,* the cook. (Courtesy of Jekyll Island Museum)

mother-in-law complained peevishly to her grandson that they had "sat one and three quarters of an hour at the table—[I] sat in the parlor and look thru' at them and wonder what can possibly keep them so long eating."[24]

Only rarely was their entertaining disrupted. In the fall before the 1898 club season, for example, they had the interior of the house painted. To everyone's dismay, "they managed to change the color of the dining room from the soft pretty greyish green it used to be, to such an unpleasant combination of purplish blue & sickly yellow" that Charlotte Maurice "decided she could not stand it & the only way to get back anything like the old color was to have

it done while we were here." While the painting was being done, the family had to take its meals in the hallway. "The children regarded the[se] four days . . . as a delightfully prolonged picnic but I am afraid the elder members of the family were not quite so appreciative & were much relieve[d] when we were finally able to return to the dining room for dinner on Friday night."[25]

The Maurices spent many hours as well enjoying the natural pleasures of the Georgia coast, walking beneath the live oaks and pines, hunting seashells on the beaches, riding bicycles and horses, enjoying carriage rides after tea, or even taking a rare dip in the ocean when the weather was warm enough.[26]

Archibald Maurice, *right,* after a hunting trip at Jekyll. (Courtesy of Georgia Department of Archives and History, original in Jekyll Island Museum)

Evening activities included games of whist, playing and singing in the parlor, and, of course, reading and letter writing. Marian Maurice in letters to her grandmother recorded many delightful occasions, like the oyster roast on the south end beach in 1898: "After lunch we danced a Virginia Reel in which all, old & young, took part, one of the gentlemen being 89 years old, others of them children only 8. It was very jolly." Black employees, she indicated, provided "fiddle" music for the dancing. "After the Virginia Reel we had a cake walk in which the oldest & most dignified took part & made themselves as ridiculous as possible."[27]

They also enjoyed excursions to the neighboring islands. Marian wrote to her grandmother of a trip to Cumberland Island the following season to visit the Carnegie estate Dungeness. Her letter, describing their outing of fourteen people, captures a glimpse of Dungeness when it was more than the ruin it is today: "The house is gray stone very large & handsome & comfortable & luxurious in every way & the grounds beautifully kept. The house

looks almost as large as our club house & they say Mrs Carnegie often has thirty guests with her at one time." She found Cumberland Island to be "very much the same as Jekyl only much more beautiful . . . as there are many more pine trees & the painful evidences of the dreadful storms which have so disfigured our poor Island are not so apparent there."[28]

Charlotte Maurice seemed to be an untiring hostess, who thought little about entertaining large numbers of people in her home and at one time invited the entire Brunswick chapter of the Daughters of the American Revolution to the island as her guests. Among the Maurices' many friends were several families from the local area, none who grew closer to the Maurices over the years than the Dents from Hofwyl Plantation. Marian Maurice recorded visits to the Dents' plantation in 1898: "Nina & I went up to the Dents [sic] plantation & spent three days with them. They are such very pleasant people to stay with & we enjoyed our little visit very much." The weather had been cold and windy during their stay, but that had not prevented their drives, during which they visited "the old plantations of Hopeton & Altama" where they found some "very picturesque ruins of the old plantation house & a sugar mill which were built out of tabby," although they found the "house at Altama . . . still in fairly good repair & they have put it in order & are living there."[29]

On occasion they also visited the Dents in Savannah, as Nina indicated to her Grandmother Holbrooke: "They have a rice plantation a little way from Brunswick and a house in Savannah which is old fashioned and had a good many interesting old things in it." In Savannah they had met many people, among them "one of Grandpa Maurice's old scholars who had been also a great friend of Papa." She went on to tell of another adventure: "Yesterday we all went over to St. Simons Island in the club's naptha launch. The sail over the water was very pleasant and while on the island we went up to the top of a big lighthouse from which we had a very fine view. . . . I was quite surprised to find they used kerosene lamps. We saw the old foundations of a smaller light tower built in 1811 out of tabby."[30]

The Dents, to whom Marian referred as "our rice plantation friends,"[31] were regular visitors at Hollybourne, as the Maurices were at Hofwyl, and over the years the two families formed an intricate friendship, with Emily Maurice rooming with Ophelia Dent at school. On at least one occasion (February 15, 1909) Ophelia's brother Gratz escorted Emily to a dance in Brunswick. In 1910, however, the Dents encountered a serious financial crisis, to the extent that they were contemplating selling their plantation.[32] When Stewart Maurice discovered their situation, despite the fact that he himself was only beginning to recover from losses he had incurred in the panic of 1907, he wrote to his daughter Marian, who had informed him of the matter, that he would be "very glad to extend financial aid," though he could not do much until he had paid off "the balance of my own indebtedness." Even so, he offered to send "$1000 this month and, unless something unforeseen occurs, I could spare $2000 or $3000 without much inconvenience between Jan. 1st & Feb. 1st."[33] The friendship between the two families continued until the end of the club era.

The Maurices were a close-knit family, and when Al was sent off to school after the 1898 Christmas holidays, Emily, who had been his playmate and constant companion, was like a lost soul. "Emily didn't know what to do with herself the first few days," her sister Nina reported, "but I think she will be all right after a little when some of the small girls she knows come to the Island."[34]

The Maurices' visits to the island were not, however, merely months of uninterrupted idleness and pleasure seeking. For example, Stewart and Charlotte Maurice, who were more than any other single club members interested in the island's history, had taken the lead, along with fellow club member John Mason Loomis, in the restoration of Captain Horton's house, which club members called "old tabby," and the du Bignon cemetery in 1898. (See Horton House chapter.) At least some of the work was done by Brunswickian W. H. Bowen and was completed on May 3, 1898.[35]

Like other members of the club, the Maurices regretted the lack of a suitable church on the island.

Albert Maurice after the hunt, on the front porch of Hollybourne. (Courtesy of Thomas Maurice)

During the 1893 season Mrs. Maurice's father, John George Holbrooke, complained of having to go into Brunswick with Dean Hoffman for church, because there was no regular service at Jekyll. "It was a tiresome trip and I content myself at home." [36] His sentiment no doubt expressed the feelings of many, and sometime between 1893 and 1898, though the date is uncertain, a simple church known as Union Chapel was constructed on the island. Charlotte Maurice took as her special project the duty of making certain that ministers were there to preach each Sunday's sermon. [37] She contacted Bishop Nelson of Georgia who helped her to arrange for a supply priest to come to the Island each Sunday, even obtaining a commitment from the bishop himself to try to come once a year the third Sunday in March whenever he could work it out. [38] He was true to his word and by March 1899 had begun to make the necessary arrangements for priests to come to Jekyll for Sunday service, even going so far as to recommend the "customary honorarium" of $25. [39] Mrs. Maurice had known Bishop Nelson when he was rector of a church in Bethlehem, Pennsylvania, when her sons were in school there. "[W]e . . . like him very much," wrote Marian Maurice, "& when he makes his yearly visit to Jekyl he always stays with us." [40] But Charlotte Maurice did not limit the clergy solely to Episcopal priests. Her ecumenical attitudes brought in ministers of many faiths. On one occasion in 1899 she invited a Mr. Perry, the minister of the black church in Brunswick, to the island. "Our service was very pleasant indeed and with a good number of colored men we had quite a congregation, though there are hardly a dozen people in the Club House, and only two cottages occupied." [41] That same month she invited to the island a Catholic priest named P. J. Luckie, whom she had befriended during his mission work in Brunswick. [42] He would later speak of her as "the truest, best and noblest of the friends that I a Catholic priest ever had." [43] Certainly she was much beloved on the island and seemed to be a friend to all, regardless of religion and race. As one of her con-

temporaries described her, "No one was too poor or too humble to be noticed [by her]; she was just as gracious to the meanest mendicant as to the highest celebrity." [44] No doubt the building of Faith Chapel in 1904 was welcomed by Charlotte Maurice as well as other members of the club, and she continued to see to the bringing in of clergymen, as she had done in former years, to keep her guests and other club members from having to make the long trek into Brunswick for Sunday services.

Despite their commitment to the island, it was not always the perfect place to the Maurices. At one point in 1903, they even considered selling Hollybourne and giving up their winters at Jekyll because of a controversy that stemmed apparently from Maurice's desire to build a private stable on the island. In 1900, both he and Frederic Baker had appealed to the executive committee for leases "granting to them the use of land outside the enclosure for the erection of private stables." Their request, seeming to meet with little opposition, was approved on April 12, and by April 26 the lots were being surveyed. [45]

Initially, the club seems to have granted Maurice the right to build a stable on club land without payment for a lot lease. Some members obviously felt that such a practice could only undermine the financial stability of the club, which already had its own stables where members' horses could be boarded. Maurice was clearly disheartened by the controversy, which he wanted to avoid at all costs, even if it meant giving up his beloved Hollybourne, but Frederic Baker urged him to "stay, and we'll fight it out. . . ." He recommended that Maurice apply to the board of managers for a deed to the stable lot. "You as well as myself will be obliged to pay a small sum . . . say $150 to $200." Baker expressed dismay that the situation might mean "the abandonment of Jekyl so far as your family is concerned," arguing that "The associations are too pleasant to relinquish. Too many heart to heart talks in that sofa near the fire in the south east room, too many good dinners, too many good chats after dinner—

I do not forget the cherry cordial—to be relinquished." Even he, however, felt nostalgic about more harmonious times, musing wistfully, "I wish Jekyl was the old Jekyl." [46]

In the end, Maurice decided not to sell, to the delight of Baker, who wrote again on April 20, 1904, to express his satisfaction as well as that of his wife and many friends at the decision "not to sell your house at Jekyl, but to remain one of the cottage colony. Albeit said colony, as some of its backbiters assert, does not pay into the club its share of expenses, and wants to conduct matters quite in its own interest. But I'll tell you all about this when we meet." [47] There is no question that the stables were built at some point, because there are records of the builder George Cowman working on them at various times. [48]

The contretemps at an end, life continued for the Maurices on the island as it had in the past until April 1909, when Mrs. Maurice came down unexpectedly with typhoid fever, contracted at Jekyll Island. By mid-May she seemed to be recovering and by July appeared almost well, but a relapse in August would prove to be fatal. John Claflin wrote to Stewart Maurice in 1909: "Dr. Brown has just told me of his visit to Athens. I had thought Mrs. Mau-rice entirely out of danger and I am deeply grieved to learn of the serious illness following the typhoid fever." [49] Letters of concern came daily from Jekyll Islanders and friends in Brunswick. Gratz Dent wrote to Mrs. Maurice from Hofwyl Plantation on September 2: "You have had a dreadful siege of it all, and it seems a cruel turn of fate that you should be selected for a case of typhoid fever, because don't you remember the last precious day I was at Jekyl, a Sunday evening before you left for the North? Mr. Grob was dining with you, and the discussion of typhoid came up, with you a champion for the island? I often think of that. And two weeks later you were ill with the disease." [50] Two days after he posted his letter, she was dead. Condolences poured in from all sides and especially from members of the Jekyll Island Club. Ernest Grob, the club superintendent, who had become an old family friend, was stunned by her death and wrote in disbelief: "I do hope it is not so. The last I heard of her was that she was on the road to complete recovery. . . . I too feel as though I have lost a mother, as she was all that to me." [51]

Although Charlotte Maurice's was not the first case of typhoid among club members and staff, it was her illness that spurred club officials to begin

Charlie Hill, driver and caretaker for the Maurice family, holds the horse for Stewart Maurice. Marian Maurice sits behind. (Courtesy of Thomas Maurice)

to investigate the source of typhoid on the island. On April 28, 1909, club physician William H. Merrill suggested that the problem might have resulted from their method of disposing of sewage and garbage. He also recommended screening the club house but did not rule out the possibility of a chronic typhoid carrier on the island.[52] However, it was not until 1912 when six members of the club came down with typhoid that the club finally took action. Once again the problem was diagnosed, this time by Dr. William W. Ford, as sewage disposal too near the oyster beds. When the club finally installed a modern new sewage system, the problem ceased.[53]

After Charlotte Maurice's death her family made every effort to carry on as before with their old Jekyll traditions, though it was sometimes difficult. The first Christmas after her death, they "had the little tree up in Nina's room & hung up our stockings as we always do. But we all missed Mother greatly & even poor little Em's brave spirits rather gave out toward the end of the day & she longed for Mother quite pitifully."[54] Nevertheless, Emily was among those who clung most tenaciously to the old traditions, writing to Marian on December 31, 1912, "Your Christmas night letter came Sat. and had been eagerly watched for, for I did want awfully to hear how you survived. . . . I'm glad Mr. Grob was pleased. The tree must have been rather nice this year too. . . . Oh Mamie dear, isn't it the devil to care so really *terribly* about family customs—it makes me feel more than ever that we *cannot* and *must not* give up Jekyl ever."[55]

Their mother's death marked the first of many changes for the Maurice family. Two of the older sons, George and Charles, as well as their sister Cornelia, had married before their mother's death, and not long thereafter even the youngest children began to choose their life mates. Emily, who had come to Jekyll since she was three years old, was now twenty-four. When she agreed to marry twenty-six-year-old Charles Whitney Dall in 1911, she planned for the ceremony to take place in Faith Chapel, which her mother had cared for so diligently during her lifetime. They were married at noon on December 19 by the Reverend R. E. Boykin, with Ophelia Dent as one of her bridesmaids. A wedding breakfast in Hollybourne followed the ceremony.[56] She spent her first Christmas thereafter with the Dalls but wrote joyfully to her father on October 15, 1913: "Mrs. Dall vows it's *my duty* to go to Jekyl this year for Christmas. Hurrah!"[57]

Albert, who had graduated from Princeton in 1906, continued his education at Columbia Law School, and taken a position in the firm of Joline Larkin & Rathbone, had begun to court a charming young woman named Eleanor Fowler in 1910.[58] They too were married in 1911, spending their honeymoon on Jekyll before returning on December 27 to their home in New York.[59] In mid-February 1913 they had their first child, Albert Touzalin Maurice Jr. Al's childhood playmate, Emily, gave birth to her first child the following month, on March 21, 1913.[60]

On Sunday night, January 20, 1918, a fire broke out in Hollybourne. No doubt fearing the kind of conflagration that destroyed the Bakers' cottage in 1914, staff came almost instantly from the club house. The chef and his assistant rushed to the scene and were the first into the cellar, where the fire had evidently begun, and were later joined by two bellboys. Members of the Maurice family pitched in as well, with Mr. Maurice putting out the fire that was starting in the woodwork. Thanks to their quick action, the fire was contained and the damage minimal, estimated by George Cowman to be well under $300.[61]

Stewart Maurice, who had always been something of a naturalist, indulged this hobby even more fervently after his wife's death. He was often consulted by club members about various facets of the flora and fauna on Jekyll. Club member Howard Elliott, president of the Northern Pacific Railroad, captured this unique role Maurice played in the club: "to me he was always an integral part of Jekyl. He loved it

Charles Stewart Maurice, *center,* with the two brides, his daughter Emily, *left,* and his daughter-in-law Eleanor, *right.* (Courtesy of Thomas Maurice)

The two sets of newlyweds on their honeymoons at Jekyll, December 1911. *Left,* Whitney and Emily Dall, who had their wedding in Faith Chapel, and, *right,* Eleanor and Albert Maurice. (Courtesy of Thomas Maurice)

Members of the Maurice family and friends enjoy a picnic at Jekyll. Among those present are Albert, *standing, left,* Emily, *seated, right,* Whitney Dall, Emily's husband, *standing, second from right.* (Courtesy of Thomas Maurice)

so—he knew it so well—its birds—its flowers, its trees—its shrubs—its paths and all its history and development. He was really Jekyl Island in many ways—and his kindness and hospitality to me I shall never forget."[62] He was a man "to whom conversation was an art" and whose "gift of incisive speech, kindly yet caustic wit, and terse expression of opinion upon men and things" caused him to be much admired among club members."[63]

Maurice's final year was saddened by a rupture in his relationship with his son Albert, apparently caused by the young man's brief involvement with a "Mrs. Lewis."[64] Stewart Maurice was furious with his son. At first, the children banded together to assist Al financially, and Cornelia's husband, Rob, had evidently given him much pro bono legal

time.[65] Al was aware of his father's wrath and wrote to Marian from Jekyll Island on February 17, 1924, where he had been with his wife, Eleanor, for more than a month and where he had evidently gone for recovery. "I wish that you could see me now so that you would realize the changes that this stay had done to me. Ernest [Grob] says that he hasn't seen me look so well in twenty years." In that same letter he wrote: "Of course I want to come up to Athens and see Papa, but from my telephone conversation with you weeks ago, I got the impression strongly that he didn't care to see me. Let me know about this at my office. I expect to leave here tomorrow."[66] Three days later his father was dead.

Unfortunately, the matter did not end there, for Stewart Maurice, in a codicil added to his will on

December 26, 1923, had disinherited Albert, leaving part of his one-eighth share of the estate in trust for Al's sons, Albert Jr. and Thomas, to pay for their support and education until they reached the age of twenty-one. At that age they would receive the income from the trust annually until the age of thirty-five, at which point the whole of the income and principal would be paid to them. The balance of Albert's portion would go to his wife, Eleanor, for "as long as she remains his wife." [67] It was an unpleasant situation with which Archibald and Marian, eldest son and eldest daughter, named as executors of the will, would have to deal.

Otherwise, the will had provided for all real estate to be held in common by the heirs. It allowed for the winter home and stables at Jekyll to be sold if the executors so desired, but clearly no one wanted to sell Hollybourne. The Jekyll share, which had to be held in a single name, went to Margaret, though Arch, Emily, Marian, and Cornelia all agreed to share equally in the "dues and assessments on Margaret's membership and share." [68] One might suppose that those heirs interested in the Jekyll Island Club drew lots to see who was made the official member but that all who wished were to partake of the club's pleasures. The estate executors sold the Maurice lot and cottage to these same five children of C. S. Maurice on October 29, 1924, for $5,245. [69]

Al's situation continued to plague the family. Arch, as one of the executors of his father's estate, showed a certain ill will toward Al, who apparently persisted in the situation that had so enraged his father. When Arch arrived on the island on March 13 and heard that Al planned to return to Jekyll later that month for a stay in the club house, Arch's immediate reaction was to refuse him a guest ticket. "Mr. Grob doesn't advise this," Emily wrote to her sister Marian. "Says Al would just get it from someone else. Arch feels we will have to make a break with Al sooner or later (I suppose he means over the trust question) & it might as well be now. . . . Mr. Grob advised Al to bring Ellie [Eleanor his

Albert Maurice, *right,* on a red bug, with his two sons, Thomas, *left,* and Albert Jr., *center.* (Courtesy of Thomas Maurice)

wife] with him—whether because there has been slight gossip about them already, I don't know." [70] Archibald's viewpoint may well have prevailed, for Albert's name does not appear in the guest register at any time for the rest of the club season.

Rancor apparently continued for a time, and Albert brought suit against the executors of his father's estate, who agreed, undoubtedly with the acquiescence of all heirs, to give him $2,500 "for professional services rendered." In acknowledging receipt of the check, Albert's lawyer, John S. Sheppard, wrote to Archibald, "I have arranged for the entry of an order discontinuing Albert's suit without costs." He went on to give a little paternal advice: "From my conversation with Albert this morning, I got the distinct impression that he is anxious to eliminate some of the conditions which have troubled you all, but that he finds some difficulty in the process. I believe it would be helpful if you and the other brothers and sisters could let Albert feel your fraternal feeling for him and your desire to assist him in any way you can." [71]

The story was not long in coming to a happy conclusion. Albert evidently put an end to the situation and moved with his family to Aiken, South Carolina, where he became president of the Southeastern Clay Company. He was welcomed back into the family fold with open arms, for Al and Eleanor, along with their two young sons, spent Christmas at Jekyll with the rest of the family in 1927, and the following year various members of the family visited him in Aiken on December 29, 1928.[72]

It may have been the losses that continued to plague the family that made them realize how much they meant to one another. Two years after his father's death Charles Maurice died of pneumonia in 1926. Charles had seldom come to Jekyll, and several Jekyll Islanders commented in their letters of condolence that he was the only member of the Maurice family whom they had never met.[73] Then two years later, in July 1928, Archibald died as the result of an auto accident. In February 1931, only

four years after moving to Aiken, Albert, the youngest of the sons, died suddenly at age forty-six of a heart attack.

Of all the children's deaths, his was the one that touched Jekyll Islanders most, perhaps because they had known him since he was a very young child. Ernest Grob, who had only recently resigned his position as club superintendent, wrote: "he was always 'my boy' to me. I never knew that he had been cautioned as to his heart—he was always so gay and put his soul in anything he undertook. . . . you have been unfortunate in the loss of brothers— three in four years is a great many, and I consider that they all died young."[74]

Al's last visit to Hollybourne had been the year before his death. In late January 1930 Marian and Margaret had visited Al and Eleanor in Aiken. They all returned together to Jekyll Island on February 1

Marian Maurice, *second from left,* and friends picnic at the beach. (Southern Historical Collection, Library of the University of North Carolina, Chapel Hill)

and celebrated Al's birthday at the cottage with Mr. Grob and Dr. Firor in attendance. During that last season, Marian and Al took long walks together, and everyone seemed happy. Al and Eleanor stayed with Marian and Margaret until April 5.[75] In a final gesture of family harmony, Marian and Margaret left the island the day of his death to return home to Pennsylvania to make arrangements for him to be buried in the family plot at Tioga Point. Marian Maurice described it in her diary as "a beautiful inspiring service . . . Al's last wish to me fulfilled."[76]

Marian and Margaret Maurice were the only two children who remained unmarried. They still came faithfully to Jekyll every season, arriving in early January to remain until April, opening Hollybourne to all who cared to visit. But even there they found things changing, their familiar world collapsing. Ernest Grob had continued to visit them and dine with them regularly. But the 1930 season had been his last as well. And when Marian and her sister arrived on January 2 the following year, she commented in her diary "Melancholy arrival with Mr. G[rob] gone. Many changes. Captain C[lark] not running boats."

Nevertheless, the Maurice sisters faithfully continued their annual trips to Jekyll. Only their aging caretaker, Charlie Hill, who in his youth had been their father's carriage driver, remained to remind them of the old days. When they arrived on January 3, 1936, they found Charlie Hill ill with pneumonia, which he could not seem to shake off for many months. They saw that he was well cared for in the island infirmary, where they visited him daily. Marian Maurice gave constant reports on his condition in her diary. By the following season, she reported happily that he "appears to have made complete recovery."[77]

To visit many of their old friends, they had to go into Brunswick, which they did from time to time to pay a call. On March 30, 1940, they visited both Captain Clark and Ernest Grob, the latter of whom

The family of Charlie Hill. *Left to right,* his daughter Anna, Charlie, and his wife Angie. (Courtesy of Jekyll Island Museum)

they found "very weak [and] broken." But it was Captain Clark's death of which they received news the following morning. He too had been "very low. So very sad." The news came as a shock, but the two aging sisters, by this time accustomed to such sorrows in their lives, attended his "beautiful simple service," and the club launch *Jekyll Island* flew its flag at half mast.[78]

When the United States declared war on Japan in December 1941, the announcement seemed at first to have little effect on the club, which opened as usual for the season. The Maurice sisters were on

The Maurice sisters at their beach house on Jekyll. (Southern Historical Collection, Library of the University of North Carolina, Chapel Hill)

the island receiving visitors with their customary grace. Al's son Thomas F. Maurice and his wife arrived from Aiken on February 27, and Emily joined her sisters at Jekyll on March 1 from her home in Cedarhurst, Long Island. Visitors continued to come throughout the season. On March 6, 1942, however, Marian announced in her diary that she had been informed of the "early closing of [the] club." Although the Maurice sisters continued their walks to the beach and their drives after tea, they nevertheless soon began to pack their things for an early departure. The care and extensiveness of their preparations and the fact that they had hired a moving van to send many of their household possessions home to Athens suggest that they knew they would not be coming back the following year. The movers came for their things on March 15, but still the sisters stayed, as though they could not bear to leave their island home.

They finally departed from Jekyll on March 26 aboard the club launch *Sydney,* pausing in Brunswick for a brief visit with Captain Clark's widow before going on to Hofwyl Plantation where they planned to spend several days with the Dent sisters. March 29 was Palm Sunday, and Ophelia Dent drove them into Brunswick for services at Saint Mark's Episcopal Church and then on to the Cloister on Sea Island for lunch. Marian Maurice's reaction was, "Beautiful planting. Good lunch, but oh! the contrast to Jekyll." [79]

The Jekyll Island Club did not reopen for the duration of the war, and although the two sisters expressed a desire to return in 1945, they were denied access. Clearly they were unhappy about the situation, and a friend consoled them: "It is a shame that the privilege of going there has been denied to you and I do hope this will straighten itself out before long." [80] But the sisters were never again to be allowed to return to their Jekyll cottage for their annual vacations. The only access they were finally permitted was for the purpose of sorting through and packing up the rest of their belongings.

By the end of the war many of Jekyll's structures had fallen into disrepair, and the club, which had almost always operated with annual deficits even in its best years, simply did not have the financial resources to reopen. Its president, Bernon Prentice, along with several other club members, explored the idea of reopening as a more commercial resort, but none of the plans seemed feasible, particularly after the death on January 13, 1945, of Frank Miller Gould, whose wealth had been a key factor in the plans.

In August 1946 the state of Georgia began to explore the possibility of condemning the island for use as a public park, and after a great deal of posturing and protest, club officials agreed to cooperate, with the price of $675,000 as compensation for the entire island and all improvements being decided upon by the court.

The club's lawyer John Gilbert indicated that "two of the stockholders of the Club have expressed considerable dissatisfaction over the proposed condemnation by the State and over the Club's position, especially its offer to cooperate."[81] One of these was Margaret Maurice, speaking for herself and her sisters. Not only were they disconsolate about the prospect of losing Hollybourne, where they had wintered for more than fifty years, but they were also evidently unhappy about the compensation they were being offered for the cottage.

Assessors selected by the state of Georgia and the various defendants in the case originally estimated the value of the Maurice property at $12,000. Bernon Prentice, eager to mollify the Maurice sisters, who were in opposition to the entire proceeding, proposed that the Maurice properties be increased in value to $15,000, with the club properties being decreased in value by an equal amount to compensate.[82] Evidently, even this increase was not sufficient to make them happy, nor, for that matter, could any amount have compensated them for the loss of their beloved cottage. In the end the Maurice sisters were awarded $20,000 as their share of the total compensation paid by the state, which took physical possession of Hollybourne along with the rest of the island on October 7, 1947.

J. D. Compton, president of the Sea Island Company, wrote to Margaret Maurice on October 13 that the state was moving quickly and was expected to "have between 100 and 200 convicts on the island within the next couple of weeks" to begin work on the island's roads and structures. He suggested that she "come down here at an early date, to make arrangements for the removal of the furniture and furnishings from your Jekyll Island house."[83] Margaret Maurice wrote back that they expected to arrive on October 23, "the first day we could get Pullman spaces from New York." They anticipated that sorting through their belongings that would need to be sent to several different places would be "a complicated matter," and they requested help for Charlie Hill in moving his possessions as well. "Charlie is sick, not able to work, and is trying to get men to help us when we come down."[84]

The sisters spent the nights at Sea Island, coming to Jekyll only during the day, bringing a box lunch with them, for there was no water or electricity in their cottage. The task of "dismantling our dearly loved house" was a painful one, though Compton did all he could to make things easier for them. After it was all over, Marian Maurice wrote to thank him for his efforts "to ease for us the arduous, heartrending task" and especially for seeing to the careful packing of the seashells that had been collected for more than fifty winters. "They will be a lovely memory of Jekyll and I know that I will never look at them without a grateful thought for their respite of peace and comfort afforded us . . . in the old cottage of which we have many memories of past days of happiness on Jekyll." They had felt their trip south, "formerly so familiar" to have been this time "a leap in the dark" but expressed their gratitude for his "efficient thoughtfulness." They declared that "many times we have asserted that when Jekyll was lost to us we wanted never to see the coast of Georgia again."[85]

In fact, after that trip they never did return to Georgia, and, according to their nephew Thomas Maurice, they would go through Alabama en route to Florida rather than pass through the state. Their bitterness was easy to understand. Margaret Stewart Maurice had been only seven years old when her family constructed Hollybourne. Her sister had been eighteen. Now they were sixty-four and seventy-five, respectively, and had lost the cottage that had been so much a part of their lives. Since their final departure in 1945, no one has occupied Hollybourne and, despite occasional partial restoration efforts, it has fallen into a state of sad disrepair, a consequence of persistent problems from moisture and termites. In 1996, the Jekyll Island Museum stabilized the cottage and opened it in October of that year for special architectural tours. Though the efforts are only a beginning for the cottage that had been closed to public view for more than fifty years, perhaps they will help to hasten the day when Hollybourne will once more be fully restored to reveal the warmth and hospitality it once held as the much-loved winter home for the Maurice family.

INDIAN MOUND

Owners: Gordon McKay, 1892–1903; McKay estate, 1903–5; William Rockefeller, 1905–22; Rockefeller estate, 1922–24; Helen Hartley Jenkins, 1924–34; Jenkins estate, 1934–37; Jekyll Island Club, 1937–47

Constructed: 1891

Architecture: Anonymous (Historic American Building Survey designation)

Architect: Unknown

The McKay Years

Gordon McKay was already over seventy years old when he joined the Jekyll Island Club on March 24, 1891, and began preparations to build his new winter home in the style that the Historic American Buildings Survey sponsored by the National Park Service calls "anonymous" architecture, designed "primarily for convenience, comfort, and economy."[1] At the time McKay was rebounding from his second unsuccessful marriage, which had ended just the year before.

He was a man who had made his own fortune by dint of hard work and an enterprising nature. Although he had little formal education, he came from a distinguished family. His maternal grandfather, Samuel Dexter, a Boston lawyer of great eminence, had served as both secretary of war and secretary of the treasury in the cabinet of Pres. John Adams. McKay's paternal grandfather had been a

The McKay cottage as it looked originally. (Courtesy of Georgia Department of Archives and History, original in Jekyll Island Museum)

captain in the British army and later, briefly, a professor of French at Williams College, which would award Gordon an honorary degree in 1851 in gratitude for his generosity toward the college.[2]

Gordon himself, however, had been forced at an early age to give up his formal schooling and earn his own livelihood. His father, Samuel M. McKay, a cotton manufacturer from Pittsfield, Massachusetts, his mother, Catherine Gordon Dexter, and his two brothers had all fallen victim to tuberculosis, which, in spite of his delicate constitution, somehow Gordon managed to avoid. When his father died, Gordon, who was only twelve, took his first job with the Lowell Machine Company. His cleverness and inventive nature drew him toward a career in engineering, and at age sixteen he went to work with the engineering corps of the Boston and Albany Railroad and of the Erie Canal.

When he was twenty-four years old he returned to his home town of Pittsfield, Massachusetts, to open his own machine shop for the repair of paper and cotton mill machinery. After seven profitable years in a business that had grown to include about a hundred employees, McKay accepted a position as treasurer and general manager for the Lawrence Machine Shop in Lawrence, Massachusetts, a post that he held for only four years before once again striking out on his own. Although sources list Gordon McKay as an inventor, his primary talents were an uncanny knack for perceiving the potential of and improving upon the inventions of others as well as for quickly understanding and capitalizing on new manufacturing methods.

Just a few years before the Civil War, McKay encountered the major invention that was to change his life. It was a device concocted by a Boston cobbler named Lyman Blake for sewing together the outer soles of shoes, the upper, and the insoles. By the time McKay saw the machine and had a chance to evaluate its significance, other manufacturers from Lynn, Massachusetts, a town noted for its excellent shoe productions, had already made the

cobbler an offer of $50,000. Although McKay was willing to pay $70,000, Blake felt honor bound to accept the Lynn offer if they came up with the money by the option deadline. When the rival bidders failed to arrive at the appointed time, Blake sold the patent to McKay, who was waiting in the shop with $8,000 cash and an agreement to pay the additional $62,000 from his profits. The Lynn men arrived shortly thereafter, money in hand, to find their prize had slipped away. Determined to get it back, they brought suit against McKay. After a seven-year legal battle, during which time McKay had already begun to capitalize on the patent, he was finally given clear rights to the Blake patent.[3]

His timing could not have been better in acquiring the invention, for with the coming of the Civil War, McKay took advantage of the opportunity to press for a government contract for army shoes and boots. With the help of Blake and Blake's brother-in-law, Robert H. Mathies, McKay adapted the machine to army requirements and found himself with an order for 25,000 pairs of "bootees," as the government brogans were called. When President Lincoln heard that a pair of shoes could be sewn in thirty seconds on McKay's machine, he remarked to Peter Neal, mayor of Lynn, Massachusetts: "Friend Neal, go home and buy real estate. The day of little country shops is coming to an end. Shoes will be made in big factories in cities."[4]

He could not have been more right. McKay and his associates continued to improve the machine until each one could turn out six hundred pairs of shoes a day. By the end of the war, McKay was operating two factories, at Rayham and Farmington, New Hampshire, and was already a wealthy man. Even before the Civil War ended McKay had begun to make additional profits renting his machinery to other companies in exchange for royalties. By 1876 he was making $500,000 a year in royalties, a figure that ultimately increased to $750,000.[5] In the meantime, in 1872 he applied for an extension on his patent, estimating that his machines had produced

Gordon McKay made his fortune during the Civil War after patenting a shoemaking machine that supplied boots for soldiers. (Harvard University Archives)

200 million pairs of shoes at a savings of eighteen cents a pair over the cobbled variety. Despite a howl of protest and threats of violence from other shoe manufacturers, the patent was extended.

But the McKay Association, as it was known, did not have the only shoe manufacturing machinery in the country. A welt-shoe sewing machine was controlled by Charles Goodyear, and by the mid-1870s the two companies were in fierce competition and frequent litigation. Finally in 1880 they decided to join forces, with McKay handing over his turned-shoe machinery patents to Goodyear and the latter assigning McKay the rights to his machines.

In 1895, however, four years after joining the Jekyll Island Club, Gordon McKay sold out his interests to Goodyear and retired. He had in the process of his career acquired patents on more than forty inventions, which had brought him a fortune estimated at up to $40 million.

Unfortunately McKay's fortune did not bring him happiness. In 1845 he had married a young woman from Pittsfield, Massachusetts, named Agnes Jenkins, but the couple divorced some years later without having had children. In about 1868 McKay hired a housekeeper named Ann Eliza Tyler Treat, a thirty-five-year-old widow with two daughters aged twelve and ten. Despite her position as McKay's housekeeper, Ann Treat was a woman of old New England stock, solidly middle class, and a descendant of a revolutionary war colonel, Andrew Tyler, of Frankfort, Massachusetts. She was the widow of a sea captain and shipbuilder from Frankfort, Maine, by the name of Robert Crosby Treat. Captain Treat had died at sea on October 4, 1867. Rather than accept the charity of others for her support, Mrs. Treat took the position of McKay's housekeeper, the highest female rung of the Victorian domestic staff and one that required a great understanding of the gracious life.

As the Treat children grew up in Gordon McKay's household, the younger of the two, Marion Hubbard, known as "Minnie," caught the wealthy man's fancy. According to one newspaper source, "He educated her in private schools and showered gifts upon her."[6] When she was twenty-one, he asked her to be his wife. At fifty-seven Gordon McKay was still vigorous and relatively attractive. The *New York Times* described him as "light complexioned, square shouldered, and affable of manner. . . . He travelled all over the world, was an admirer of art, a clever violinist, and liked company in a quiet way."[7] To the young woman, he and the life style his wealth provided must have seemed glamorous and appealing. She accepted his proposal, and they were wed in 1878.

Many might have thought the match doomed from the start. Even Gordon apparently realized the May-December marriage to the daughter of a member of his domestic staff would create quite a stir in society. On September 27, 1878, anticipating family reaction, he wrote to "ma cousine," most likely Josephine Dexter, the wife of his cousin Wirt Dexter: "You see I Persist in the relationship and claim the consequences. . . . I shall be married next Tuesday to the prettiest and sweetest young lady the world has produced of the marriageable persuasion since Wirt Dexter . . . persuaded his wife." Anticipating her response, he urged, "Suspend judgement until you are a man the other side of fifty and see the brightest eyes and loveliest face in the world smiling on you. . . ."[8]

Once again, no children were born for a number of years into the marriage. Then, on May 10, 1886, in Florence, Italy, Minnie gave birth to a little boy, whom she named for herself, Marion Victor McKay. The following year on May 3, 1887, a second child, Robert Gordon McKay, this time named for her husband, was born in Paris, France. The birth of the two children, however, did not strengthen the marriage, for Gordon McKay apparently did not believe the children were his.[9] Nevertheless, the four of them seemed to be living harmoniously as a family as late as 1889, when they received a visit at their Newport home from John MacKay, an author who wrote under the pen name of Ben Reay. Gordon McKay was, he concluded, "a most interesting man" and his wife was "charming." "They have two children," he noted.[10] There was no hint of the rupture that would come the following year. However, other indications suggest that McKay was already distressed about the situation.

In November 1887, the same year that Robert was born, Gordon, who was worth more than $40 million, made out his will, leaving Minnie only an annual annuity of $9,000 and annuities of $2,000 each to his mother-in-law and his sister-in-law. For the two little boys, however, whom the will refers to pointedly as "*her* son[s]" (emphasis mine), he left only $500 per year with payments ending when they reached age twenty-one. It was hardly the bequest of a doting father.[11] The will made modest annuity provisions for eleven other people as well, all women, but left the bulk of his estate to Harvard University.

Marion Treat McKay, the second wife of Gordon McKay, was known to her family as "Minnie." (Courtesy of Amy McKay Kahler)

Victor McKay, son of Marion Treat McKay. (Courtesy of Amy McKay Kahler)

Robert McKay, son of Marion Treat McKay. (Courtesy of Amy McKay Kahler)

As Gordon seemed to be preparing for death, Minnie, on the other hand, was stretching toward life and becoming increasingly aware of her beauty. Gordon's will made the tensions between them obvious and may even have been a factor in their impending separation. It must have come as no surprise to those who knew them well when they announced their intention to divorce in 1890. Gordon was almost seventy at the time, and his wife was only thirty-three.

After the divorce McKay drew up a codicil to his will canceling all previous provisions for Minnie, her mother, and her sister, and reducing the annuity for the children to $100 a year. He also insisted that Minnie assume all expenses of education, maintenance, and care for "her two children," as he always referred to them in his will and subsequent codicils. The frequent revisions from 1890 to 1892 reflect the agitation and indecision that Gordon McKay must have felt during this period. In the end he relented and provided for Minnie a house in Washington, D. C., valued at not less than $35,000 in addition to the annuity of $9,000, which "shall continue during the whole of her natural life, notwithstanding her remarriage." [12] He also left annuities of $1,200 each to her mother and sister and made provisions that permitted her to provide annuities of $2,500 for each of her sons.

After the divorce and his subsequent retirement, McKay continued to occupy his home in Cambridge, Massachusetts, where he enjoyed the college community, with summers spent at Newport and winters at Jekyll Island. Despite his marital trials, he remained an affable and generous man with a wide circle of friends, and his divorce from Minnie Treat, however much it may have wounded him, did not put an end to his social life.

In the year following his divorce McKay joined the Jekyll Island Club. His cousin Wirt Dexter, who had been a club member since its founding in 1886, had died suddenly on May 17, 1890, and N. K. Fair-

bank of Chicago, who had been a close friend of Dexter, nominated McKay. Upon election in 1891, he purchased the required share, from W. B. D'Wolfe, along with the lease for lot 14 that came with it. [13]

The cottage he built upon the lot seems to have been constructed between April 1891 and January 1892, when McKay registered for his first stay there with his good friend Harvard geology professor Nathaniel B. Shaler, who had been instrumental in persuading McKay to leave the bulk of his fortune to Harvard. [14] The house's architect is unknown, and plans for such "anonymous" residences were "adapted from plan books that circulated throughout the nation." [15] The shingled structure was plain and clearly designed for comfort rather than charm, for one can see in the design a primary concern for utility that well suited a man like Gordon McKay. It was box-like, with wide eaves, abundant porches, and little in the way of ornamentation; in short, it was an expression of the man himself, who enjoyed a quiet elegance but was not given to "ostentatious display." [16] The design of the McKay cottage was also in clear harmony with the club's philosophy of simplicity. [17]

Although Gordon's ex-wife never saw the cottage, she must have been much on his mind when it was being built, as she would be for the rest of his life. There is no question that she had a haunting loveliness, for she was, according to the *Newport Herald*, "thought to be one of the most beautiful women of the times." [18] In the years to come, she flitted annually with her eighteen trunks between her splendid new home in Washington and the continent of Europe. [19] In 1899 she married Baron Adolph von Brüning, secretary to the German Embassy in Washington. Although her reasons for marrying Gordon McKay in 1878 can only be guessed at, she left her own testimonial as to why she wed the baron. A letter to her mother during one of her excursions to Aix-les-Bains in France explains:

"Mr. Von Brüning has asked me to be his wife. He will have to get the Emperor's consent & if he does not gain it he says he will leave the [diplomatic] service[.] Now comes the question of what is best and most expedient. He is very rich of good family & noble and good position. He could give me all I wish . . . from a worldly point of view. I want position a social position more that anything in the world [.] Shall I let such a chance slip by? I may never have another."[20] In fact, Kaiser Wilhelm II did not give his consent, and the baron, separated from his embassy post, "was in deep disgrace for several years" before being forgiven and returned to diplomatic service.[21] According to the *Newport Herald*, an extraordinary gift of $100,000 bestowed upon the couple by the bride's former husband, Gordon McKay, was a factor in angering the Kaiser, although a later account contradicts this version, claiming rather that the gift helped return the baron to the Kaiser's good graces.[22]

Minnie's training to be a baroness had also been in large measure a consequence of Gordon McKay's generosity. Her excellent education at his expense had prepared her well, and the Treat sisters had learned to move with ease in the most elegant society. Even during her years as a divorcée, Minnie entertained the "best people" at her frequent teas and luncheons in Washington.[23] Florence and her mother felt comfortable calling upon Mrs. William McKinley in the White House, as they did on May 7, 1896, to find her "sitting in a high old fashioned chair looking like death and knitting red socks." She confided to them that she had knit about 3,500 pairs in all. "No wonder the poor woman has fits," Florence remarked wryly in her diary.

Although Gordon and Minnie, who was calling herself Marion by the time of her marriage to Baron von Brüning, carefully avoided crossing each other's paths any more than was absolutely essential, he remained on friendly and hospitable terms with her mother, Ann Treat, and her sister, Florence, inviting them frequently to dine when they were at Newport. Florence Treat recorded in her diary a number of such instances, noting on May 23, 1896, when they all dined at McKay's Marine Avenue house, "It seemed so strange for us all to be there . . . without Minnie." Gordon McKay, who was an accomplished violinist, still enjoyed an occasional afternoon of music with Florence at the piano, as he did on June 12 that same year. Somehow they had all come to terms with a situation that, for most people, would have been extremely awkward, but McKay seemed to harbor no bitterness toward Minnie or her family.

Thus it was no surprise to Ann Treat and her daughter when, on March 21, 1895, during a visit to Saint Augustine, they received a letter from him inviting them to be his guests at the Jekyll Island Club. The bitter winter had turned back upon itself, and they had just had word that it was "too cold to go North." They accepted gratefully, leaving for Jekyll on March 28.

It turned out to be a miserable trip. Victor, who often traveled with his grandmother and aunt and was frequently in their care, was motion sick throughout the trip. They missed their connections in Waycross and, arriving too late to get a boat to Jekyll, were compelled to spend the night at the Oglethorpe Hotel in Brunswick. The following morning went little better. They arose early for the scheduled 8:00 A.M. departure of the club launch, but it failed to arrive on time. Finally at noon the porter "sent us off in a carriage to catch the boat." But their ordeal was not yet over. "We sat on the wharf on the sun until two o'clock furious then," Florence noted in her diary, "but our sail of an hour to Jekyl was so lovely that we forgot our long wait."

Because McKay's house was closed since he had not come down that season, they were given rooms in the club house. "The view from my window is the finest of all with views along the west side and beyond the river and marshes," Florence wrote. It was late in the season, and few people were still on the island—among them the Porters, N. K. Fairbank, and Mrs. [Annie Lee] Wister, "who was celebrated as the translator of Marlitt's delightful romances." They whiled away the time playing games of whist, taking long drives through the woods and along the "wonderful beach . . . hard as concrete," or merely "enjoying "the perfect stillness and . . . loveliness."

One day in particular, Friday, April 5, proved unforgettable. It was Ann Treat's birthday, "and Victor presented her with a bunch a azalias [sic] and made her a wreath of wild pear blossoms." They took an afternoon drive along the riverside and then down the beach. The driver, wanting to show them something really special, turned the carriage to Oglethorpe Road "to see the resurrection ferns." However, they began to encounter small brush fires burning along the drive. Suddenly there loomed just ahead a larger blaze, with "smoke and flame across our road." It was Florence who made the decision that there was little else to do but drive through it "as fast as possible. . . . We bowed our heads to escape the heat," she wrote, "and rode through although I was quite sure I felt the heat on my back and after I got back I found a spot burned in the lining of my woolen sleeve which must have been burnt by a spark." "I was never so frightened," she confessed. "But in spite of the fright it all appeared that it is the most beautiful spot on earth."

Mrs. Treat, Florence, and Victor left the club, which was by then nearly deserted, on April 8 to return to Washington. Although they had not stayed in Gordon McKay's house, they did make a point of going over and peeking in the windows. They made no comment about what they saw, though after having visited so often in McKay's home in Newport, they may have found his Jekyll house to be unassuming and a bit disappointing. Whatever their reaction, they professed to find the club house "most attractive" and the spot as a whole "as beautiful as a dream." [24]

Florence Treat's diary account is the only known surviving "family" record of a visit to the Jekyll Island Club. They never came again, though they continued to see McKay throughout the remaining seven years of his life. McKay himself came to Jekyll Island almost every year from the beginning of his membership in 1891 until his death in 1903, failing to appear only in 1893, when the club was officially closed because of a yellow fever epidemic; 1895, when his former in-laws visited; and 1897. McKay's last recorded visit to the Jekyll Island Club began on January 29, 1902. After he returned north, he fell ill at his Newport home and lay bedridden throughout the remainder of the year and most of the following year until his death.

McKay's generosity was legendary at Jekyll Island, where his contributions and support almost always exceeded those of better-known wealthy members. For example, on July 1, 1893, when debenture bonds were issued to raise money for the Jekyll Island Club, five members took $1,000 in bonds; one member (Bayard Brown) took $5,000, and Gordon McKay, the only other subscribing member, took $30,500. When efforts were being made to construct a chapel in 1897, most members gave pledges for $100. Henry Hyde, president of the Equitable Life Assurance Company, who was pushing hard for many improvements at Jekyll, suggested to club treasurer Frederic Baker, "I believe that if Mr. McKay were approached and you were to tell him exactly what you have raised and what you still want he might contribute $500 or $1,000 if the thing struck him right." [25] Again when Hyde was seeking to raise funds for the first Jekyll Island golf course, he informed Baker: "I have talked the matter over with Mr. Pulitzer and Mr. McKay. My idea was to raise $10,000. I think Pulitzer would have given two or three thousand and Mr. McKay would have acted very liberal." [26] McKay paid for the construction of a bicycle path, which he himself very likely never used, and participated in an 1899 stable association, in which he owned four stalls.

He brought horses and carriages down by Mallory steamer on a regular basis, perhaps mainly for his guests, for by this time he was almost eighty.

McKay was, by all accounts, a generous man, establishing among his benefactions the McKay Institute in Kingston, Rhode Island, for the education of Negro boys. His most generous gift, however, was his million-dollar bequest to Harvard in his will, plus an annual 80 percent of the balance of the net income from the remainder of the estate. The McKay endowment was designated to promote applied sciences and mechanical engineering and to provide scholarships and construct buildings for this purpose.[27] To the great disappointment of N. S. Shaler, then dean of Harvard's Lawrence Scientific School and the man who had single-handedly turned McKay's "serious dislike" of Harvard into benevolence toward the college, Harvard elected in 1904 to initiate negotiations with the Massachusetts Institute of Technology to divert a large portion of the income from the McKay endowment from the Lawrence Scientific School, which, according to Shaler, McKay had called "his School," to M.I.T. Shaler felt betrayed, and his efforts to see that McKay's bequest was honored "brought him into collision with the authorities of both institutions."[28]

The controversy would continue long after Shaler's death in 1906 and result ultimately in a lawsuit brought against Harvard by Harvard alumni and members of the bar who felt that "the sanctity of trusts and wills had been attacked in a most insidious and dangerous way" (*President and Fellows of Harvard College v. Attorney-General et al.*).[29] In 1917 the Massachusetts Supreme Court ruled that Harvard indeed had not acted in accord with Mr. McKay's bequest and "cannot lawfully carry out this agreement" with M.I.T.[30] The fund was subsequently used in the founding of the Harvard Engineering School in 1919, which became the Graduate School of Engineering in 1935 and in 1951 a part of the Division of Engineering and Applied Science, now known as the Division of Applied Sciences. Harvard also used the endowment for the construction of the Gordon McKay Laboratory of Applied Science and a series of professorships, with as many as thirty-five professors being supported simultaneously by the endowment, one of the largest in Harvard's history.[31]

The McKay-Shaler friendship had begun in 1865, and Professor Shaler and his wife were frequent visitors at McKay's Jekyll home as well as in Newport and Cambridge. Shaler was described by a contemporary as a great teacher and a "humanist, philosopher, naturalist, and engineer," who "glowed with poetic imagination and kindly humor."[32] During the early years of their friendship, Shaler professed to find McKay a man of "great dignity and kindliness" who "could imaginatively project himself into any large enterprise."[33] In his final years, however, McKay came increasingly to rely on Shaler, who painted a sad picture of the invalid who "summoned him by telegraph" at inconvenient times, compelling him to make "hurried visits to Newport" where McKay lay bedridden from 1902 until his death. During these taxing visits, according to Shaler, McKay's "mind groped eagerly at business details" that "freed him for the moment from the gloomy consideration of his decrepit state."[34] His death came as a final liberation on October 19, 1903. He was eighty-two.

On March 20, 1905, the Gordon McKay estate sold McKay's cottage to William Rockefeller, one of the club's original members.[35]

The Rockefeller Years

William Rockefeller was born in Richford, New York, on May 31, 1841, the child of William Avery Rockefeller and his wife, Eliza Davison. He was the younger brother of John D. Rockefeller and the third of six children. Named for his father, whom he resembled in appearance and personality, William had a "robust physique and expansive good nature."[36] A business partner who later became a severe critic described him as a "solid, substantial, sturdy gentleman with the broad shoulders and strong frame of an Englishman."[37] Like his father, he loved horses and "good living," was a jovial and sociable man who excelled at the art of salesmanship, and was aggressive in business.[38] Unlike his father, around whom floated rumors of philandering, there was never a breath of scandal about William's domestic life. He was a devoted family man, said to be "a lover of nature and little children especially."[39] Even one of the most savage critics of his financial tactics considered him to be "a good, wholesome man made in the image of his God,"[40]

Although brought up in the Baptist church and an active member during his early adult life, he attended the Episcopal church in later years.[41] H. L. Mencken once wrote that "Most Americans when they accumulate money climb the golden ramparts of the nearest Episcopal Church. But the Rockefellers cling to the primeval rain-God of the American hinterland and show no sign of being ashamed of him."[42] William, however, obviously decided to "climb the golden ramparts" even though his brother John held fast to the old-time religion.[43]

His upbringing was such that he adhered from first to last to the popular Horatio Alger maxim of his day that hard work, frugality, and clean living were the prime ingredients of success. Born into a solidly middle-class rural New York family that moved to Oswego in 1850, William attended Oswego Academy with his elder brother, John. In 1853, the family moved to Cleveland, Ohio, where William attended high school. Upon graduation, he went to work as a bookkeeper and by 1859 was employed by the firm of Hughes and Lester, commission merchants. When the Civil War broke out in 1861, both William and John considered enlisting but ultimately allowed their younger brother Frank to uphold the family military honor. During the war John entered the oil refining business, while William did so well in his commission house that he became a partner in Hughes, Lester, and Rocke-

feller, subsequently Hughes, Davis, and Rockefeller.[44]

On May 25, 1864, twenty-three-year-old William Rockefeller, already an up-and-coming young man about Cleveland, married twenty-year-old Almira Geraldine Goodsell, called Mira, whose occupation was listed as "housekeeper" on her marriage license. The following year their first child, a son, was born, though he tragically died in 1866 before he was two years old. They would lose a second son at age five in 1877. Four of the children born to the Rockefellers between 1868 and 1882 survived to adulthood: two boys, William Goodsell (born 1870) and Percy Avery (1878), and two girls, Emma (1868) and Ethel Geraldine (1882).

The period from 1865 to 1882 was important to the Rockefellers not only because of family growth but also for William's business career. In 1865 he decided to enter his brother's oil business, then known as Rockefeller and Andres, already one of the largest refineries in Cleveland. In 1866 William was sent to New York in a daring move to broaden operations into the world market. He succeeded brilliantly in his mission, proving himself to be "one of the ablest export managers in America."[45] Simultaneously, the Rockefellers expanded in other directions, absorbing rival refining companies in Cleveland, New York, Pittsburgh, and Philadelphia into their corporation, which in 1871 became known as the Standard Oil Company of Ohio. John D. was the president and William the vice president of the firm.

Ten years later in 1882, in conjunction with their partners, they created the Standard Oil Trust and shortly thereafter moved the company headquarters to 26 Broadway in New York City. When in 1892 the trust was ordered by the Ohio Supreme Court to dissolve for violation of an antitrust law, the Standard Oil combination simply reorganized into separate entities with interlocking directorates. William thus became president of Standard Oil of New York, a position he held until 1911, while his brother John headed Standard Oil of Ohio and Henry M. Flagler directed the fortunes of Standard Oil of New Jersey.[46]

In all these complicated organizational activities, which made Standard Oil the most powerful oil producing, refining, and distributing industry in the world, William Rockefeller played a vital part. His natural charm and geniality as well as his business acumen attracted capital and new partners for the firm. In the process, he amassed an enormous per-sonal fortune in excess of $150 million and much valuable real estate, including a Fifth Avenue town-house and a country estate called Rockwood Hall overlooking the Hudson River and adjoining his brother's country place near North Tarrytown, New York. Here he raised prize Jersey cattle, roses, and carnations.[47]

He also bought a 50,000-acre forest preserve in the Adirondacks, where he developed a summer lodge and camp at Bay Pond and maintained a small

William and Almira Rockefeller during their later years at Jekyll Island. William, the brother of John D. Rockefeller, was president of the Standard Oil Company of New York. Almira shunned the ostentatious display that characterized some members of her social class, preferring the simpler joys of family life. (Courtesy of Rockefeller Archive Center)

army of men to keep poachers away from the fish and game that abounded in the area.[48] His efforts to prevent trespassing on his preserve aroused the ire of the local citizens and led to prolonged lawsuits and even, it was reported, to bloodshed. In the end, the law upheld Rockefeller, though the ruling, as the appellate court noted with some regret, "deprives the public . . . of the pleasure and profit of fishing and hunting in a very large portion of the Adirondack forest, and gives to men of great wealth, who can buy vast tracts of land, great protection in the enjoyment of their private privileges."[49]

Both in the Adirondacks and at Rockwood Hall, Rockefeller indulged his love of nature, taking long walks and often stopping to chat with one of his employees' children. A friend of the family, writing to his daughter, recalled: "Your father was the first one who ever made me see the birds and trees with real interest. I used to take long walks with him around 'Rockwood' and no one ever saw so much on a walk as he did."[50] Unlike many of his wealthy contemporaries, Rockefeller was not prone to support the great philanthropic institutions of his day, though his presence on the board of trustees of the Museum of Natural History attests to his love of the natural world.

Another valuable piece of land acquired by Rockefeller was located in Greenwich, Connecticut, where his son, William Goodsell, would subsequently make his home. Here the elder Rockefeller developed a sixty-acre park adjoining his farm and stocked it with imported deer. Some of these were shipped to the Adirondacks while others were donated to the Bronx Zoological Garden and to the Jekyll Island Club.[51]

The Rockefellers were a close-knit family who shunned the gaudy display and social pretension characteristic of some member of their class. Mira Rockefeller was in large measure responsible for this relatively unassuming stance. Despite a personal fortune of over $3 million including strands of pearls valued at $157,000, diamonds, and furs, she apparently never forgot her middle-class origin and

upbringing. She insisted that she was just an "ordinary mother" who used "common sense" rather than faddish "theories as to child culture" to raise her offspring. In her opinion, they were "just four ordinary boys and girls." To be sure, she sent them to private schools rather than to public institutions, but not, she explained, because of snobbery. New York schools were crowded, hence, "It is only the fair thing that parents who can afford to should send their children to private schools, and thus keep their places in the public schools for those children who must depend upon the public school system for their entire education."[52]

Women's clubs held no interest for Mira, and she had little patience with giving fashionable parties even for relatives. "Now do not wear yourself out over entertaining," she admonished her daughter Emma. "It is not worth while. All this rush of entertaining is nonsense."[53] Though basically down-to-earth and "kind and thoughtful" toward others, she still was a woman of stature, seen as "charming" and "queenly" in her bearing.[54]

If Mira was something of a homebody, at least while her children were young, her husband by contrast and by virtue of his business affairs mixed in the club world of men, joining the Union League, Metropolitan, and Riding Clubs and in 1886 becoming an original member of the Jekyll Island Club. His brother John evidently also considered becoming a member, and his name was actually written on the original subscription list but subsequently crossed out and replaced by the name of E. W. McClave.[55] Of course, by this time in his career, William Rockefeller was already a wealthy, prominent, and respectable corporate head, just the sort of man the club organizers sought to attract.

The Rockefellers came to Jekyll for the club's opening season on March 12, 1888, and took rooms in the club house.[56] A month later William sold one of his two club shares to James J. Hill for $3,500, for a profit of $2,900, and did not return to the island again until March 1896.[57] But from that date on he took more than casual interest in the club. To begin

The Rockefeller children in a carriage on Jekyll beach in March 1905. Taken from the Geraldine Rockefeller McAlpin baby book. (Courtesy of Rockefeller Archive Center)

with, in 1896 he invested in the private apartment building called the Sans Souci, located next to the club house and ready for occupancy in 1897.[58] In 1897 he purchased four stalls in a newly constructed private stable on the island owned in conjunction with J. P. Morgan, Joseph Pulitzer, James J. Hill, and seven other members.[59] Although he neither held club office nor served on any committee prior to 1914, he did agree in 1896 to become a director, serving in this role until his death in 1922.

A regular visitor to the island, Rockefeller demonstrated his commitment to the club in various other ways. He invested in club bonds (1896), made donations to the chapel and the Horton house restoration funds (1897–98), built a bicycle path at his own expense for the enjoyment of the members (1901), contributed generously to the construction of an electric power plant (1903), and, though not a golfer, did not hesitate to subscribe to the club's first course in 1898 and to the upkeep of another one laid out in 1909.[60]

The event that signaled his decision to make Jekyll Island his permanent winter vacation home came in March 1905 when he bought Gordon McKay's cottage and share of club stock.[61] The house was seldom used during the next eight years, but following his retirement from the presidency of the Standard Oil Company in 1911 and especially after the trying Pujo investigation of 1912 and 1913, he began to use the residence more regularly and intensified considerably his active involvement in Jekyll affairs. Indeed, in his twilight years, Jekyll became a virtual haven for an often besieged and ailing Rockefeller.

From 1899 on, the operations of the Standard Oil Company, which were controlled by a gigantic holding company created in that year, had been the target of muckraking magazines and newspapers. Furthermore, William Rockefeller's financial machinations outside the oil industry had come under public and legal scrutiny. In branching out into other enterprises, notably copper, gas, and railroads, he had allied himself with Henry H. Rogers and with James Stillman of the National City Bank in New York, whose daughters married Rockefeller's sons and who was himself a member of the Jekyll Island Club. Stillman and Rockefeller made strange bedfellows. The latter was warm, affable, and happily married. The former was cold, reserved, and separated from his wife. Yet the two men got along famously and cooperated in a number of speculative ventures, one of which, involving the Amalgamated Copper Company, was so unethical as to cause Thomas Lawson, an associate in the scheme, to attack it in a series of lurid newspaper articles in 1904 and in a book entitled *Frenzied Finance* published in 1905, in which he accused the corporation of having destroyed the lives and fortunes of no fewer than fifty "previously reputable citizens."[62]

Inevitably the financial shenanigans of the "Standard Oil Gang," a label tacked on the Rockefeller-Rogers-Stillman trio by the press, and the monopolistic practices of the Standard Oil holding company soon came under governmental investigation and were subjected to antitrust proceedings. William's son, William Goodsell, assistant treasurer of the company, was forced to testify in 1906, and the following year William himself and his brother John were hauled into federal court in Chicago in a case presided over by Judge Kenesaw Mountain Landis. Finally in 1911 the Standard Oil holding company was dissolved by court order, and William withdrew from further activity in the organization.[63] In fact, he began to curtail all his business activities except for an interest in the Chicago, Milwaukee and St. Paul Railroad and a few other railroad investments.

The decision to reduce his role in the business and financial world resulted in part from his declining health, which the strain of unfavorable publicity and legal action only exacerbated. He was confined to bed with an attack of lumbago in February 1911, took a trip on his Milwaukee line in August during which he was ill for several days, and in October decided to go abroad in hopes of recovering his former vigor.[64] Rockefeller had suffered from chronic throat problems since 1895. In spite of having undergone surgery for the condition six times, his health seemed no better when he departed for Liverpool with his wife and physician, Dr. Walter F. Chappell, under whose care he had been for the past decade.[65]

The trip to Europe did little or nothing to improve Rockefeller's throat ailment, and he was still weak in 1912 when confronted with news of a subpoena from the U.S. House of Representatives Committee on Banking and Currency (popularly known as the Pujo Committee), which was investigating the possible existence of a money trust in the United States. The committee was interested not only in J. P. Morgan's banking practices but also in the financial affairs of the Rockefeller-Stillman alliance.[66]

Despite the fact that House Sergeant at Arms Riddell, backed by droves of process servers and detectives, staked out Rockefeller's home at Rockwood Hall and his townhouse in New York, the oil magnate somehow managed to slip away undetected to Jekyll Island.[67] Rumors of Rockefeller's whereabouts drifted to the ears of the sergeant at arms. Emily Maurice records the event in a letter to her sisters on January 6, 1913, noting that she was amused "to read one day in the Times last week that Mr. Sergeant-at-Arms Riddell announced he had sent members of his staff to . . . Jekyl Island & had found the rumors of Mr. Rockefeller's presence there absolutely unfounded (it was the first I knew he was supposed to be there), then to open Mamie's letter & hear that Dad had had the gentleman in question out driving all a.m."[68]

Later in January Rockefeller left the island for a cruise to Nassau but upon returning to the mainland submitted to an examination by Dr. Charles W. Richardson, an independent physician representing the Pujo Committee. Richardson reported that Rockefeller's throat condition was serious indeed—just as Dr. Chappell had been claiming all along—and that any testimony should be restricted in length. As a consequence, the committee and Rockefeller's lawyers worked out an arrangement for testimony to be taken privately on Jekyll Island by Chairman Arsène Pujo and Committee Counsel Samuel Untermyer.[69]

The date set for Rockefeller's hearing was February 7, 1913. The place was a parlor in his Sans Souci apartment. Dr. Chappell stood in readiness, his instruments and a box of pills set out on a table in case of a throat seizure. Representing the committee were Pujo and Untermyer; Rockefeller had two lawyers present, John A. Garver of New York and A. J. Crovatt of Brunswick, the club attorney. Frank R. Hanna, the Pujo Committee stenographer, was also there assisted by Edith Ferguson of Brunswick, who was "under instructions to record Mr. Rockefeller's testimony."[70]

Rockefeller, who had been waiting in an adjoining room with his daughter Emma (Mrs. David H. McAlpin), entered the parlor wearing a gray suit, wine-colored bow tie, and slippers and looking very pale. He took a seat in a large rocker near the stenographer, and the proceedings began. Rockefeller answered four rudimentary questions (where he lived, what sort of exercise he took, and two queries about when the Amalgamated Copper Company was organized) before being seized by a violent coughing fit that brought the hearing to an end. Dr. Chappell administered a pill, and though Rockefeller's spasm ceased, his physician insisted "that the ordeal should go no further." Pujo agreed.

Rockefeller shook hands all around and retired to his bedroom to rest while Pujo went to the club house to issue a statement to awaiting newsmen. Returning to Brunswick aboard the club yacht, he was hounded by reporters who wanted to know whether Rockefeller was feigning illness and had pulled "a job" on the committee. Pujo responded with indignation that he wanted it "distinctly understood that I don't think there was the slightest taint of malingering in what occurred to-day."

Rockefeller remained on Jekyll Island until mid-March recovering from his ordeal. He briefly considered the possibility of moving from the Sans Souci apartment to his cottage next door, but since the season was so far advanced, he decided against it and continued to recuperate in the Sans Souci attended by his wife and his second daughter, Ethel Geraldine (Mrs. Marcellus Hartley Dodge), who joined him on February 20.[71] It was clear, however,

William Rockefeller was briefly examined by the Pujo Committee in his Sans Souci apartment on the second floor, north end, of the Sans Souci. (Courtesy of Edwin J. Gould family)

Indian Mound with trellises during Rockefeller era. (Courtesy of Jekyll Island Museum)

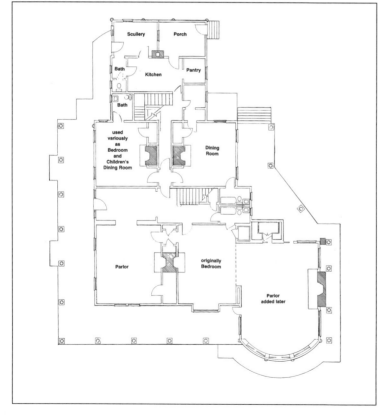

The first-floor plan of Indian Mound after it was remodeled by the Rockefellers. (Based on plans in Jekyll Island Museum)

that Rockefeller intended in the future to make his cottage the center of his activity on Jekyll Island. The year before he had obtained plans, specifications, and estimates for a major renovation of his house, including rewiring and installing an electrical bell system at a cost of $8,169.[72] Implementation of the project was apparently delayed, but by the summer of 1913 the remodeling work was well underway. The "William Rockefeller residence on Jekyll Island," reported the *Brunswick News*, "has been practically rebuilt and will be refurbished throughout for the coming winter, new plumbing now being installed."[73] In fact, between 1913 and the fall of 1917, not a year went by without some new construction on the Rockefeller cottage, including a porte cochere, upstairs porch, and dormer windows on the north side; a new rounded addition on the southwest side facing Jekyll Creek; an east wing extension with an upstairs sewing room; and a totally remodeled verandah with new columns and pipe trellis.[74]

In 1915 the cottage was reshingled from top to bottom, each shingle being dipped in barrels of stain but certainly not in the mixture of buttermilk and creosote that one legend alleges.[75] Nor were the grounds around the house ignored. Flower beds adorned the south and west flanks of the cottage, and Cherokee roses and Carolina jasmine clung to the porch trellises.[76] In 1916 Rockefeller put in a seawall along his property line on Jekyll Creek. Noting this development, the *Brunswick News* reported: "During the summer Mr. Rockefeller had many improvements made to his already beautiful place. Among these was the building of a bulkhead on Jekyll Creek just in front of his home. It is said this alone cost something over $35,000, while many other parts of the estate received very costly attention."[77]

The cottage, virtually transformed since the days of Gordon McKay, even received a new name, Indian Mound, recorded in the club register for the first time on February 7, 1914. According to the recollections of Charlie Hill, a long-term employee

The towel warmer in the master bedroom bath at Indian Mound. (Courtesy of Jekyll Island Museum)

of the Maurice family, a mound ten feet high containing what was once thought to be Indian bones but which proved to be only oyster shells once stood in front of the cottage. Although it was lowered to improve the view of Jekyll Creek, from this mound the name allegedly derived.[78]

From the time of the Pujo investigation until the end of his life, Rockefeller never missed a season on Jekyll, and his health seemed to improve with every passing year. "Mr. Rockefeller never feels so well," the *Brunswick News* was informed, "as when he is enjoying the secluded and exclusive life which only this paradise on earth affords."[79] Indeed, even though he could still hardly speak above a whisper, his condition was so much better that in 1914 he came to Jekyll without a physician in tow and, what is more, agreed for the first time to serve on the club's executive committee, a position he held until his death in 1922. He was also appointed chairman of the committee on roads and forestry, an appropriate appointment in light of his interest in nature and his love of motoring.

William Rockefeller with his daughter Emma Rockefeller McAlpin on the porch of Indian Mound in 1921. (Courtesy of Rockefeller Archive Center)

Other than daily walks, Rockefeller's only outdoor sport was automobile riding. He had taken an auto tour of Europe in 1909, commuted regularly by car between Tarrytown and his office in New York City, and, even when surrounded by the Pujo Committee's process servers in 1912, had managed to slip out for motor rides.[80] To Jekyll he brought an electric car (three of them in 1916) and could be seen on any given day driving with his wife or daughter.[81] A typical entry in Emma McAlpin's diary in 1921 read: "Walked around long block with Father after breakfast. Clear & crisp. Took a ride with him in the electric on the beach. All went to the movies in P.M. Father's first movie."[82] On another such occasion, she recorded: "Took electric ride with Father & car was stuck in the sand."[83] For all his love of motoring, Rockefeller was not insensitive to the noisy nature of cars on an island whose chief attraction was its naturalness and whose former modes of transportation had been horses, carriages, and bicycles. Therefore, as a member of the executive committee, he had been willing to vote to restrict automobiles to the beach and the Shell, Wylly, Plantation, and Howland Roads.[84]

Rockefeller's commitment to the club was by no means confined to committee work. He pledged $5,000 to help fund a series of club house improvements and paid particular attention to the island's dairy operation. In 1920 he brought B. M. Hawk, his Rockwood estate manager, to the island to deal with an outbreak of fever, caused, it was thought, by improperly sterilized mechanical milkers. "Mr. Hawk is spending a good deal of his time at the dairy at father's wish," noted Mira Rockefeller. "Father is busy all the time and it is a good thing for himself and the club."[85]

The Rockefellers never came to Jekyll alone. During the heyday of their membership in the club, they were always surrounded by children and grandchildren and a host of other relatives, friends, and employees. Dr. Walter B. James, club president from 1919 to 1927 and one of a team of physicians who had removed William Rockefeller's appendix in 1900, was married to Helen Goodsell Jennings, Mira's niece.[86] As noted earlier, Rockefeller's two sons had married club member and business associate James Stillman's daughters, and his daughter Geraldine was married to Marcellus Hartley Dodge, nephew of club member Helen Hartley Jenkins, who would subsequently purchase Indian Mound. In addition, Robert and George Brewster and Edward S. Harkness were club members and sons of Rockefeller's Standard Oil business partners. These were by no means all the extended Rockefeller clan.

Clearly a season on Jekyll with the Rockefellers was a family reunion.

The 1920 season, however, would be the last for Mira Rockefeller. She and her husband registered on January 5 and promptly threw themselves into the island routine. Mira, who had not been well for several years, suffered from angina pectoris and neuritis. While on Jekyll her neuritis had practically disappeared, and though she had "a few twinges at night," she felt no discomfort during the day. On January 17, however, she awoke early and was so ill that she was forced to return to her bed. Shortly thereafter she died of heart failure. Her body was transported from Brunswick to New York for burial, with the train being met during a snowstorm by her daughter and son-in-law, Emma and Hunter McAlpin.[87]

In the wake of the death of Mira Rockefeller, the family descended on Jekyll Island in force the fol-

lowing season in a show of support for William. The weeks went by in the usual manner. Emma took long walks and rides in the electric with her father, spent quiet evenings with him at the cottage, participated in hymn singing at the club house, and attended church services at Faith Chapel. They saw movies at the tea house and were entertained by employees' children at the island school house. To these tranquil forms of entertainment were added endless rounds of auction bridge, dinner with the Jameses, tea with the Cranes and Maurices, and pleasant chats on the club house porch with Dorothea Harding and Marjorie Bourne. The younger set, including Rockefeller's granddaughter, Geraldine McAlpin, and her friend Routh Ogden, rode bikes and little motorized vehicles known as red bugs, played tennis, and frolicked on the beach. On February 18, 1921, Geraldine fell from a bicycle and injured her foot. An X ray in Brunswick the next

Like his predecessor in Indian Mound, Rockefeller was generous toward the club and funded the Rockefeller Bicycle Path at Jekyll Island. (Courtesy of Jekyll Island Museum)

day disclosed that she had a broken fibula. She spent the rest of her vacation on crutches, though she managed to hobble to the club house for lunch and dinner and to the beach for a picnic. Routh Ogden also was injured during her stay and for a time had her arm in a sling, but her mishap was minor, for she partnered with Dr. Dandy, the club physician, in a tennis tournament on March 4, two days before leaving the island.[88]

Rockefeller spent one last season on Jekyll in 1922, a season that in most respects was a repeat of the previous year, except that fewer young people from the family were present and Rockefeller's health was failing. On June 24, 1922, not long after returning to Rockwood Hall, he died. Funeral services were held in the music room of his residence on Fifth Avenue in New York City, and his body was escorted by motorcade to Tarrytown for final burial beside his wife in Sleepy Hollow Cemetery. As the procession was pushing its way out of Manhattan, a car carrying officials of the Standard Oil Company was struck by a reckless driver. Fortunately, no one was injured, and the occupants went on to the graveside ceremonies riding in another automobile.[89] From club members and others, letters of condolence poured in, including one from Elizabeth Claflin who wrote to Emma McAlpin: "Your father's genial, kindly nature endeared him, I am sure, to all who knew him. It is to me one of the pleasantest memories of Jekyll."[90]

The Rockefeller House on Jekyll Island remained empty during the 1923 and 1924 seasons. In March 1924 it was sold to Helen Hartley Jenkins of Morristown, New Jersey.[91]

The Jenkins Years

When Helen Hartley Jenkins purchased Indian Mound, she was sixty-four years old and the wealthy widow of George Walker Jenkins, former president of the American Deposit and Loan Company. She

had inherited much of her fortune upon the death in 1902 of her father, Marcellus Hartley, founder of the Union Metallic Cartridge Company, which later merged with the Remington Arms Company.[92] Helen Jenkins, nicknamed Nellie, and her sister Grace were twins, born to Hartley and his wife, Frances Chester White, on August 16, 1860. The couple also had an older daughter, Emma. Helen Jenkins outlived both her sisters. Her twin, Grace (Mrs. James Charles Stokes), died in her mid-thirties, only four months after the death of her twelve-year-old daughter of appendicitis. And Emma, who became the second wife of Norman Dodge, died giving birth to her son, named Marcellus Hartley Dodge for his grandfather. Her older sister's death was a particularly important event in the life of Helen Jenkins, for she became, in effect, the boy's surrogate mother. Because the child's father traveled extensively in his work, Marcy, as he was called, came to live with his grandparents and his Aunt Nellie. Helen Jenkins, who did not marry until Marcy was over twenty, virtually reared the boy in her sister's stead.[93]

When Helen Hartley finally did marry George Walker Jenkins in 1894, she gave birth subsequently to two daughters of her own, naming them Helen and Grace for herself and her twin. Her older daughter, who bore her mother's full name, Helen Hartley Jenkins (though she was called Babs by family members), was born about 1895. She graduated from Barnard College in 1915, married Francis Hunt Geer the following October, and died in 1920, still in her twenties.[94] Mrs. Jenkins's second daughter, Grace, was born in 1896 and would outlive her mother.[95]

At the time of her election to the Jekyll Island Club in 1909, Helen Jenkins, forty-nine years old, had already been a widow for more than a decade. Robert Weeks de Forest of New York nominated her for membership at a board of directors' meeting on October 27. That it was de Forest who proposed

Helen Hartley Jenkins with her nephew, Marcellus Hartley Dodge, son of Norman Dodge and Emma Hartley. (Courtesy of Helen Mead Platt)

her for membership is not surprising, for the two of them knew each other well and shared mutual interests. De Forest was widely recognized as New York's leading philanthropist, and Jenkins, likewise, was known to be one of the nation's major female philanthropists, having founded, among her many benefactions, the School of Nursing at Teachers College of Columbia University. No doubt through their charitable efforts and especially through a common interest in the penal system, Helen Jenkins had come to know de Forest and had won his respect, most specifically for her support of New York's Association for Improving the Condition of the Poor, which had been founded by Helen Jenkins's grandfather, Robert Milham Hartley, and was one of de Forest's special charities.

In 1907, her nephew, Marcellus Hartley Dodge, married the youngest daughter of William Rockefeller, Ethel Geraldine, and Helen Jenkins became the closest thing to a mother-in-law that Geraldine ever had. Thus Mrs. Jenkins had other connections on the island as well. In her early years as a club member she visited Jekyll only irregularly and had no fixed residence. Although she stayed sometimes in the club house, whenever possible she rented an apartment, for she was frequently accompanied by friends and by her daughter Grace, who in 1922 married Winter Mead. During the 1922 season, for example, Helen Jenkins rented an apartment in the Sans Souci, and in 1923 she stayed in the annex apartment of her friend de Forest. However, for 1924, since no apartments were available, she was compelled to take rooms in the club house for herself and her guests.

When the opportunity arose that year to purchase the Rockefeller cottage, Indian Mound, she no doubt considered both the increased space it would provide for her family and friends and the certainty of always having suitable lodgings. With little hesitation, she decided to take it, buying the cottage fully furnished, including silver, china, and bedding.[96] Her first stay in Indian Mound, now designated in the club register as "Jenkins cottage," began on January 25, 1925, and her visits to the island thereafter became more regular. It was her habit to arrive in mid to late February, bringing with her not only her daughter Grace and her family, but friends as well, often including various members of the faculty at Columbia University, the frequent beneficiary of her generosity. Among them was Adelaide Nutting, a leader in the field of nursing, who had been lured away from the Johns Hopkins Hospital to serve as the first chair of Columbia University's new School of Nursing, founded, along with two professorships in nursing, through the initiative and generosity of Helen Hartley Jenkins.[97]

Another frequent visitor to Indian Mound was Professor Edward Lee Thorndike, famous for his many books on psychology and language but perhaps best known for his popular Thorndike's dictionaries.[98] It may have been he (though Helen Jenkins also counted Columbia's president, Nicholas Murray Butler, among her friends) who convinced her to donate $350,000 to build Philosophy Hall and to make a joint donation with her nephew, Marcy Dodge, upon his graduation from Columbia University in 1903, of a new dormitory, Hartley Hall.

One of her particular favorites among the Columbia faculty and her frequent guest at Jekyll was Michael Idvorsky Pupin, a Serbian immigrant who had become a well-known professor of physics at Columbia and who had designed the device known as a "loading coil" that permitted the famous 1915 transcontinental call that AT&T president Theodore Vail made from Jekyll Island.[99] It was certainly at his instigation that she "endowed and equipped the Marcellus Hartley Physics Laboratory, where Professor Pupin conducted many of his major experiments." Pupin, who was two years her senior, built what was called a "Serbian house" in the Berkshire country of New York. The "colorful architectural design" of this house so delighted Mrs. Jen-

"Walking up from the Ferry," *left to right,* Helen Mead (age four), Grace Jenkins Mead, Helen Hartley Jenkins, the resident Jekyll doctors, Dr. George Berry, and Dr. Warfield M. Firor. Dr. Berry would become famous later for having survived Parrott sickness. (Courtesy of Helen Mead Platt)

kins that she constructed a similar cottage "on a wooded hillside not far away." [100] When Austria invaded Serbia in 1914 at the outset of World War I, Mrs. Jenkin's sympathies went out to her friend's native land. Her aid to the Serbian cause was such that she was awarded the Order of St. Sava, the Serbian Red Cross, and a medal from the National Slavonic Society.

The list of Helen Jenkins's philanthropies by no means ended here. She gave generously to many medical facilities, including Grace Hospital in Banner Elk, North Carolina, in memory of her twin sister, and to Polyclinic Hospital on West Fiftieth Street in New York. She was active in prison welfare work, serving as a member of the executive committee of the New York State Prison Council and of the National Prison Association and counting

among her friends the warden of Sing Sing prison, Lewis E. Lawes. Because the welfare of children was equally important to Helen Jenkins, she established Hartley Farms in Towaco, New Jersey, as a summer playground for underprivileged children and adults and served as a director of both the New York Nursery and Child's Hospital, a branch of Morristown Memorial, where the school of nursing was also named for her as a principal benefactor. To address many of these concerns she served as president of the Hartley Corporation of Hartford, Connecticut, which she had established for "philanthropic purposes."

Through one of her many benefactions, she made the acquaintance of Virginia C. Gildersleeve, the first female dean of Barnard College. When Helen's eldest daughter, Babs, died in 1920, Helen and her

The chauffeur watches over the Mead children, grandchildren of Helen Jenkins, as they look for shells on Jekyll beach. (Courtesy of Helen Mead Platt)

second daughter, Grace Mead, gave an "entrance gateway" bearing Babs's name to Barnard, her alma mater. Soon Virginia Gildersleeve and Helen Jenkins became fast friends and, joined by Professor Pupin, frequently lunched together on weekends.

Dean Gildersleeve, who described Jenkins as "an enthusiastic, somewhat crusty and faintly alarming old lady with a multitude of irons in the fire and a keen, ironic brain,"[101] was one of the guests who joined Helen Jenkins during the first season in her newly acquired cottage. Grace Mead, Adelaide Nutting, Mrs. John Purroy Mitchell, wife of a former New York mayor whose election as a reform candidate Jenkins had supported strongly in earlier days, and Marcellus Hartley Dodge were among the many others who came to visit that year. Dean Gildersleeve visited Jekyll frequently in the years to come and remembered it fondly in her memoirs. Here she would come to rest "after the strenuous work of 'putting the budget through,'" and would be greeted at the club dock by Helen Jenkins and the rest of the household, including her two West Highland terriers, Wolvey and Sandy. "My throat would tighten, " related Dean Gildersleeve, "for since my parents' death no household had ever displayed such a universal welcome." She remembered Jekyll in her autobiography in rather poetic terms as being like "a setting for Shakespeare's *The Tempest*," with the tall "long-leaved pines [that] formed forest aisles inland, . . . the dull shimmer of oaks, the radiance of huge magnolias, the sun glow of wild oranges, the Cherokee roses and wisteria."

The cottage into which Dean Gildersleeve was welcomed was always filled with people: servants, friends, and relatives. Helen Jenkins's granddaughter remembers the "public rooms" (parlor, main living room, entrance hall) as being carpeted in red "with extremely heavy lined red velvet curtains in the doorways."[102] Four of the six bedrooms were also carpeted in red, but the other two were graced

Helen Jenkins with Dr. D. McEachern on a Jekyll Island red bug. (Courtesy of Jekyll Island Museum)

Dean of Barnard College, Virginia Gildersleeve, with Helen Jenkins's terriers at Indian Mound in 1925. (Courtesy of Mrs. Winter Mead)

with oriental runners and Spanish hand-tufted rugs. Mahogany furniture predominated throughout the house. The servants' quarters were modestly furnished with single beds, dressers, table desks, and scatter rugs. Although the cottage contained a kitchen, dining facilities, and a breakfast room used to serve meals to the children, and though a cook was part of her staff, Mrs. Jenkins and her guests took many, if not most, of their meals at the club house.[103]

Besides acting as hostess for her houseguests, Helen Jenkins socialized broadly, embracing newcomers to the club as well as the older members. On one occasion she invited Dessie Randall, daughter of Blanchard Randall, who had recently joined the club, to make a fourth at bridge. "I played bridge with Mrs. Jenkins," she informed her mother, and "another lady Miss [Lillian] Hudson (Miss Nutting's understudy at Columbia) and Dr. Pupine [sic] and beat them all to pieces it was all luck of course but Dr. P. who is really a shark was very complimentary. He is a most delightful person."[104] On another occasion the Blanchard Randalls were invited to Indian Mound where they were served "delectable Chinese tea" and were shown a beautifully carved solid ivory Mah Jong set that was much to be envied. However, the afternoon ended on a somewhat sour note when some remarks made by Mrs. Jenkins were interpreted by the Randalls as mean-spirited. Despite the fact that she had shown them every hospitality in her Jekyll home, the Randalls persisted in viewing Helen Jenkins as a "character," or as Virginia Gildersleeve put it, "something of an enfant terrible."[105]

There is no question that Helen Jenkins had a strong personality, though an addiction to jewelry was perhaps her greatest eccentricity. Emily Randall described her rather unkindly as "wild as ever smothered in diamonds & sapphires & crazy as a loon."[106] On the contrary, Mrs. Jenkins had a keen mind, as her friendships with college professors, deans, and presidents attest, but even her friends

and family found her adornments excessive at times. "With huge cabochon rubies on her breast, her fingers glittering with heavy rings, her tongue afire with the energy of her thoughts," wrote Dean Gildersleeve, "she could frighten some people witless," and clearly the Randalls were awed by her formidable presence. "But," she continued, "her daughters and I loved her and no one ever found her dull."[107]

Two accidents forced Helen Jenkins to miss the 1928 season on Jekyll. She was badly scalded when a tea urn overturned, spilling its contents on her, and while recovering from this mishap she had a fall and broke a rib. As a consequence, she was bedridden at her Park Avenue home in New York City for five weeks, attended by her physician and friend, Dr. Samuel A. Brown, who with his wife had been her guest at Jekyll in 1922.[108] Although she returned to the island in 1929, it would be her last season at Indian Mound, for her health was not good. In 1930 she suffered a series of psychological shocks which did nothing to improve her condition. In late August 1930 she learned that Marcellus Hartley Dodge Jr., the twenty-two-year-old son of her beloved nephew, had been killed when the automobile in which he was riding struck a tree near Bordeaux, France.[109] This blow was followed on October 20 by a fire that partially destroyed her mansion in Morristown, New Jersey, and caused her "to be carried to safety."[110] Then, a year after the death of her grandnephew, her chauffeur struck and seriously injured a pedestrian on Park Avenue in New York. Fortunately, the car was in good mechanical order and the driver was not held criminally liable. The accident was particularly ironic since her Hartley Corporation made "a special study of the causes and prevention of motor vehicle accidents."[111] Her health failing progressively over the next several years, Helen Hartley Jenkins died at age seventy-three at her Morristown home on April 24, 1934. Her daughter, Grace Mead, and her nephew, Marcy Dodge, were with her at the end.

Her cottage was closed temporarily after her last stay at Jekyll in 1929, but during the 1930s it was used by a variety of visitors to the island. The Jenkins estate resigned her club membership in 1935. Although her will had left Indian Mound to her nephew, Marcy, he had never had enough personal interest in Jekyll Island to become a member of the club. As a consequence, on November 7, 1934, he "forever renounced and refused title to said property," a renunciation reiterated in Brunswick on June 29, 1937, shortly after the executors had conveyed the cottage to the Jekyll Island Club on April 26, 1937, in exchange for all debts and taxes currently owed.[112] Club officials rented the cottage every year from 1937 until 1940 to various club members during the peak of the season, among them the David Ingolls and the George Whitneys. During the war years Indian Mound remained closed as did all property on the island, undoubtedly deteriorating as a consequence, so that in 1946, after the war ended, it was estimated that an expenditure of $8,950 would be necessary to make the cottage once again habitable for guests. At that time some thought was still being given to the idea of a postwar reopening of the club as a sort of "public Inn and resort, catering to a selected and restricted clientele, rather than on a club. . . . basis."[113] Under the "public inn" scheme, Indian Mound would have accommodated eleven persons in the main bedrooms and additional guests in the servants' quarters.[114] However, the plan never took effect. Instead, the island was condemned by the state of Georgia in 1947 and converted into a public park under the management of the Jekyll Island State Park Authority.

The State Era

In 1951, during a period when the island was "in a closed-down status," the authority debated the possibility of opening Indian Mound to sightseers but decided against it.[115] Three years later in 1954,

Tallu Fish, first curator of the Jekyll Island Museum, on a red bug that was part of the early museum collection, on the porch of Indian Mound. (Courtesy of Tallu Fish Scott)

Tallu Fish, a recent widow who had grown up in Waycross, Georgia, and was then serving as editor of the *Democratic Woman's Journal* of Kentucky, was given a lease and permission to operate Indian Mound as a museum, with herself as curator. The authority agreed to clean, rewire, and heat two rooms in the house for her use and to install a kitchen in her living quarters with the understanding that she would open the cottage as a museum by December 11 of that year, the date scheduled for the official opening of the causeway that would connect Jekyll Island with the mainland. She would also be allowed to charge admission (twenty-five cents for adults and fifteen cents for children), retaining 75 percent of the profits over $100 for herself and the rest going to the authority. In exchange, Mrs. Fish promised to add "all other mementos and records of the Jekyll Island Club, to the collection now in the Rockefeller House."[116] Many "items of historical interest, including books and china from the old Jekyll Club" had been placed earlier in the vault of Indian Mound for safekeeping, the very vault in which Helen Jenkins had undoubtedly kept her splendid jewels while vacationing on the island.[117] Tallu Fish thus became the first curator of the Jekyll Island Museum, which was, in essence, limited at the time to what she called the "Rockefeller Museum," and she was vigorous in her effort to create an interest in the historical importance of the club. The new museum was opened as scheduled on the same day of the official opening of the causeway. Tallu Fish lived in Indian Mound for more than eight years, until the 1960s when she finally moved into her own house on Bliss Lane, where she resided until her death in 1971.

Repairs and maintenance on the cottage in the early years of state ownership were done, for the most part, with unskilled convict labor. The first major renovation of the house since the days of William Rockefeller began in 1968 under the direction of Roger K. Beedle.[118] At the time of this restoration, water, termites, and dry rot had done considerable damage to the structure. A new roof was added "using a specially constructed asbestos-perlite-cement shingle" which had the appearance of "weathered wood shingles." The interior walls were covered with gypsum board over which was applied "a factory finished cotton fabric very similar to the original canvas." The interior trim was refinished and replaced "as originally installed," and most of the original light fixtures were retained, although fixtures in the living room and library were pirated from nearby Mistletoe cottage.[119]

Landscaping had been generally neglected during the early state era. Indeed, a report by landscape architect Clermont Lee, hired in 1970 to make a landscaping plan for the club compound, indicated that "Village trees have received very little care during the last 25 years." Lee's landscape design, however, was never fully implemented, a failure due in part "to changed uses of the area," in part to a lack of accurate historical information, and finally because the Jekyll Island Authority felt at the time that maintenance of the grounds would be too costly.[120]

Nevertheless, the restored cottage was opened once again in February 1971 and has remained one of the few cottages consistently on view to the public. In recent years, Indian Mound has undergone, under the direction of Warren Murphey, a complete historic restoration to its post-1917 appearance and has been refurbished once again with original paint colors and porch trellises. Thus the cottage looks today much as it did when William Rockefeller and his family made it their winter home.

MOSS COTTAGE

Owners: William Struthers Jr., 1896–1911; William Struthers estate, 1911–12; George Henry Macy, 1912; Kate Carter Macy, 1912–21; William Kingsland Macy, 1921–47

Constructed: 1896

Architecture: Shingle style

Architect: Unknown

::

The Struthers Years

William Struthers Jr., who built Moss Cottage at Jekyll Island, was the owner, with his brother John, of one of the nation's most important marble firms. Located in Philadelphia, the firm had been founded by their grandfather John Struthers, who had emigrated with his young family from Scotland about 1816 and taken a post in the architectural firm of William Strickland. Struthers, who had served as superintendent of construction for the well-known United States Bank in Philadelphia,[1] was very suc-

Moss Cottage was built in 1896 by William Struthers Jr. In 1899 Struthers made several modifications to his cottage, adding a bay window at the north end and a conservatory at the south end. (Everett Collection, Coastal Georgia Historical Society)

cessful and eventually established his own firm, J. Struthers & Son, located at 1022 Market Street, which specialized in marble, sandstone, and imported Scotch granite. When George Washington's body was moved to its final resting place at Mount Vernon, it was John Struthers who designed and erected at his own expense the new vault.[2]

Known as "an architect's office and a marble yard"[3] and reputed to be the oldest and largest of the kind in Philadelphia, and a "first class business," it passed at John Struthers's death into the hands of his son William, "a careful prudent man & a popular bus[iness] man"[4] who took his own sons into partnership and operated the firm under the name of William Struthers & Sons. After his death in 1876, the firm continued to function as William Struthers' Sons, under the supervision of William Jr. and his brother John.[5]

William, who dropped the Junior after his father's death in 1876, was the younger of the two brothers. Born in 1848, he joined the family firm about 1870, when he was twenty-two years old, though he was erroneously included as a member in the 1866 R. G. Dun financial report, where he was described as "a young married man."[6] In fact, he did not wed his childhood sweetheart until January 18, 1870. She was a heartbreakingly beautiful young woman who bore the romantic name of Savannah Durborrow and was said to always wear a blue ribbon in her hair.[7] "Vannie," as she was known to her family, was born in Griffin, Georgia, about 1849 but had moved at a young age with her parents to Philadelphia. She and William Struthers were said to be inseparable from their school days. Even as adults, they were rarely apart, and when his beloved Vannie died on November 23, 1911, the inconsolable William would survive her by less than a month, succumbing to his grief on December 12.[8] As a young man Struthers had taken a great interest in the Pennsylvania National Guard and had risen to the rank of major. He was also a man of many clubs—among them the Philadelphia Club and the Radnor Hunt Club.[9] It is not surprising, therefore, to find his name on the Jekyll Island Club roster.

Struthers was nominated for membership in the club by his brother-in-law Rudolph Ellis on April 4, 1887, the year after the club was founded. He was seconded by Oliver Kane King, a business partner of the club's founder, Newton S. Finney, and one who was helping Finney with the organizational aspects and membership drive. Struthers was elected on May 20 but seemed to take little interest in the club. When, by November of 1890, he had still not come down, he resigned his membership. There seemed little reason to continue to pay the high dues and assessments when he never used the facilities. Ellis, who was married to Struthers's sister Helen, did not give up, however. In February 1893, he persuaded the Strutherses, with their twenty-two-year-old daughter Jean, to be his guests at Jekyll Island for the first time. Again in February 1895, they came down as his guests. Ellis's repeated attempts to lure Struthers into the club were successful, largely because Struthers liked and admired his brother-in-law. By the mid 1890s, club facilities had expanded and were about to expand again under the leadership of Henry B. Hyde. Jekyll had become a splendid and well-known resort, with excellent hunting grounds and several fine houses that had been constructed by various club members.

Only seven months after the 1895 visit, Ellis was able to persuade Struthers to allow him once more to nominate him for membership, which he did on October 23. Seconded by the club's founder Newton Finney, he was reelected on November 13, 1895. This time Struthers decided to make a real commitment to the club and wasted little time in preparing plans to build a cottage on his Jekyll lot 1.[10] The architect of the house, which he named Moss Cottage, is unknown, but there is a possibility that Struthers himself or someone from his firm may have designed the house. He was, as noted above, in the building trade and had an "architect's office." Although his firm specialized in marble-facaded pub-

William Struthers Jr. was the owner
of an important marble works in
Philadelphia and one of the few
Jekyll Island Club members who
joined the club not once, but twice.
(Courtesy of Struthers family)

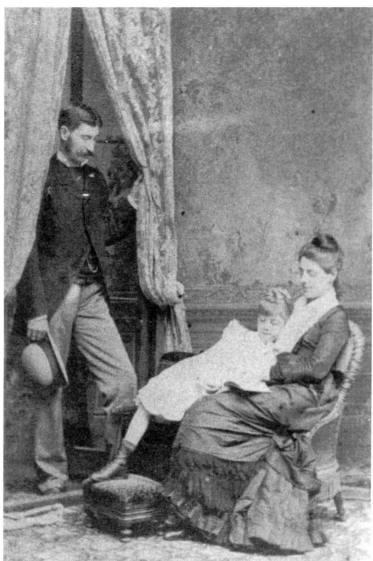

Struthers with his wife, Savannah, and their daughter, Jean, about 1880.
(Courtesy of Struthers family)

Struthers's wife, Savannah
Durborrow, was born in Griffin,
Georgia, but moved with her family
at a young age to Philadelphia
where she met William Struthers
Jr., who became her husband.
(Courtesy of Struthers family)

Jean Irvine Struthers in her pony cart on Jekyll Island. (Courtesy Struthers Family)

lic buildings such as those it had built for the city of Philadelphia, some domestic architecture is listed among the company's designs and constructions.

The cottage, with its nineteen rooms and five baths (including the third floor servants' rooms), was an excellent example of the shingle-style architecture popular in New England resorts from about 1880 until 1900. With its generous porch and wood shingles used for both wall cladding and its steeply pitched roof, it is a classic example of the style. The cottage clearly reflects its owner's interest in the innovations and technology that were about to reshape America. Moss Cottage was, from all appearances, the first to be wired for electricity at Jekyll and may well have been served by a private generator, since electricity was not generally available on the island until 1903. In fact, no evidence indicates that the house was ever equipped with gas fixtures. Struthers's interest in modern technology was also suggested by the fact that on the day after Christmas in 1900, he was the first club member to bring an automobile to Jekyll Island. The noisy vehicle created a furor among members, and the executive committee, which had previously passed a regulation against motorized vehicles, compelled him to have it sent back to Philadelphia by Mallory

steamer. Only two weeks later, however, the committee reconsidered the issue and voted to allow automobiles on the island, though limiting their speed to six miles an hour and only permitting them to be driven on roads relatively far from the club house between 10:00 A.M. and noon and from 2:00 to 7:00 P.M.

Moss Cottage is first mentioned on December 15, 1896, when William and Savannah Struthers arrived with their daughter Jean, her maid, and two members of the Gerhard family. Still more guests arrived on Christmas Eve, and the Struthers family apparently remained not only through Christmas, but also, as would be their custom, through most of the club season.

The house suffered only slightly from the hurricane of 1898 with nothing more than a little soiling of the wallpaper from the "rain beating through some of the windows."[11] Nevertheless, some redecorating was necessary. The following season, Struthers had the house re-wallpapered and the electric bell system repaired. In the fall of 1899 he decided to make several modifications to the structure, adding a bay window in the den at the north end of the house and a conservatory at the south end. In later years, however, the conservatory was removed, and the cottage today looks very much as it did when Struthers built it.[12]

William Struthers had been only forty-eight years old at the time he constructed his house. Nevertheless, he had already been retired for at least twelve years. In about 1883 he had moved his family from their Philadelphia home on South Twenty-first Street to Woodlea, the wisteria-covered country house they had built near Bryn Mawr, Pennsylvania, not far from Philadelphia, and had left his brother, John, to run the family business. In spite of his young age, Struthers had already made a tidy fortune. During his working years he and his brother were awarded a contract in excess of $5 million, said to be the largest in Philadelphia history at the time, to construct new public buildings in the city.

This was only one of the many substantial public and commercial contracts they won over the years. The firm had at various times constructed the Merchants' Exchange, the Philadelphia Exchange, the Pennsylvania and Reading Railroad buildings, the Newkirk building, the Farmers and Mechanics' Bank, the Continental Hotel, and numerous other buildings in Philadelphia, Boston, Mobile, and Natchez.[13]

Thus Struthers, well off and retired from an active business career, was free to enjoy the quiet outdoor life with the wife and daughter he adored. He loved to hunt, with duck hunting being his favorite pastime, and he indulged the activity with enthusiasm within the context of the Jekyll Island Club. The Strutherses were usually among the first to arrive

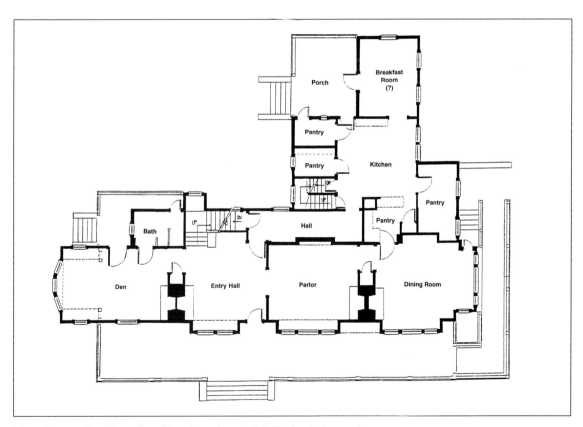

Moss Cottage, first-floor plan. (Based on plans in Jekyll Island Museum)

Drawing of Jean Struthers said to be by the impressionist painter Mary Cassatt and still in the possession of the family. (Courtesy of Struthers family)

on the island, sometimes as early as mid-December to take advantage of the hunting.[14] In 1898 he was named to the club's game committee and by 1904 had risen to chairman of the committee and assumed a place on the club's board of directors.

The Strutherses' daughter, Jean Irvine, born in August 22, 1871, was a popular and active outdoorswoman in her own right. Relatively athletic for that Victorian era, she participated in various club competitions and frequently came away the winner. In March 1897, for example, she proved victorious in both the hundred-yard bicycle spoon and egg race for ladies and the clay pigeon match in which she had to compete against both men and women.[15]

Her attractiveness and independent spirit captured the eye of several Jekyll Island Club members, and rumors circulated among club officers in 1897 that she was engaged to marry David H. King Jr., who had been widowed two years earlier. That same year King constructed his own house on the island, and Jean's father ordered a number of citrus trees on behalf of King for his landscaping. The two were on the island from early December until April, arriving and departing within days of each other. While King may have courted the comely Jean Struthers during the club season, the romance was apparently short-lived, for he did not return to the island the following year, and there was no further talk of an impending marriage.

That Jean enjoyed male companionship and that men enjoyed her company and conversation is certain. In 1904, the Strutherses' next-door neighbor on the island, Joseph Pulitzer, in the absence of his wife, invited her to join him for early morning horseback rides, during which he poured out his complaints about the constant barrage of telegrams he received on the island and his overwork, most of which was clearly of his own creation. But Jean listened sympathetically and sent him occasional little notes expressing her concern and, on one occasion, thanking him for a little bouquet of violets.[16]

Though she encouraged such harmless friendships, she seemed skittish about marriage. Henry Francis Sears pursued her for years, according to family lore, always keeping an engagement ring in his pocket in the hope that one day she would accept his proposal.[17] Finally, in 1904 she agreed. The couple was married on Lake Geneva, Switzerland, at the Château d'Hauteville, on September 14, 1904. One of those who attended the wedding was Mary Cassatt, the well-known impressionist painter who hailed from Philadelphia but was now living in Europe and who some years earlier had done a

Jean Struthers with her husband, Dr. Francis Sears, and daughters, Jean Struthers Sears, *left*, and Emily Esther Sears, *right*. Emily, who would later become Mrs. Henry Cabot Lodge, was christened at Jekyll Island in Faith Chapel in 1905. (Courtesy of Struthers family)

charming sketch of Jean as a young woman playing a mandolin. Both the Strutherses and Cassatts were prominent Philadelphia families who socialized with one another, as is evident from the fact that Mary's brother Alexander and his wife, Lois, were guests of Struthers's sister Helen and her husband, Rudolph Ellis, at Jekyll Island in March 1895. Lois Cassatt returned again in February 1907 as a guest of the Ellises.

The marriage of Jean Irvine Struthers, who was thirty-three at the time, to forty-two-year-old Henry Francis Sears would result in the birth of two daughters and a son. Emily Esther, born July, 15, 1905, was christened at Jekyll Island on April 1 of the following year in the newly completed Faith Chapel by Rev. Endicott Peabody of Groton School.[18] She was one of only two members' children ever christened there. Emily Sears would later become Mrs. Henry Cabot Lodge. Her sister, Jean Struthers Sears, born on November 25, 1907, would marry Archibald Alexander. Their brother, Harry, was not born until 1913 and never saw his Struthers grandparents.

After their marriage, Jean and Henry Francis Sears visited her parents on the island every season with their little daughters and their nurses. Jean was devoted to her parents, and in 1908 when her mother was not well, their friend Charlotte Maurice noted in a letter to her son Arch that "Mrs. Sears is bringing all her servants and is to keep the house and Mr. & Mrs. Struthers are to be as it were her guests."[19] That pattern of family vacations continued until the year of the poignant deaths of Jean's mother and father within the span of a single month in 1911. Sears, who was a Boston physician, had himself become a member of the Jekyll Island Club the year after his marriage to Jean Struthers but had resigned in 1910. Jean Struthers Sears would return to the island only once after her parents' death, in 1927, as the guest of James Byrne of New York.

Thus ended more than fifteen years of quiet pleasures the Struthers family had enjoyed at Jekyll. Moss Cottage was sold on March 1, 1912, to

George Henry Macy, who transferred the deed to his wife, Kate, on March 6, and, under the care of the Macy family, the cottage would begin an entirely new era.[20]

The Macy Years

When George Henry Macy purchased the Struthers house in 1912, he was fifty-eight years old and just two years away from retirement from his position as president of Carter, Macy & Company of New York, Chicago, and San Francisco, as well as of its overseas subsidiary, George H. Macy & Company, which had worldwide operations in India, Ceylon, China, Japan, Formosa, and London. The parent company, Carter, Macy & Company, one of the country's largest and most important tea importers, had been founded by Macy's father-in-law, Oliver Stanley Carter. The tradition of marrying the boss's daughter continued into the next generation, when Helen, Macy's oldest daughter, married Irving Kent Hall, who would become a partner in Carter, Macy & Company. Like most Jekyll Islanders, Macy was a busy man, who in addition to his primary business concern served as a director or trustee of many other corporations, among them the Atlantic Mutual Insurance Company, the Commonwealth Insurance Company, the Saint Louis Southwestern Railway, the Seamen's Bank, and the Sterling Salt Company.[21]

He had been elected to the Jekyll Island Club ten years before on March 5, 1902, having been proposed for membership by John S. Kennedy and seconded by C. Ledyard Blair. Even though he had purchased apartment 6 in the annex from Morris K. Jesup in 1909, when the Struthers house became available in 1912, he decided to acquire it for his large family who were always crowded in the annex. No doubt he already knew the house, for he had been well acquainted with William Struthers from their joint service on the club's game committee. In fact, it was Macy who replaced Struthers

Kate Louise Carter married George Henry Macy in 1880. (Courtesy of Robert Macy Finn)

George Henry Macy, president of Carter, Macy and Company, was fifty-eight years old when he purchased Moss Cottage. (Courtesy of William Kingsland Macy Jr.)

when he stepped down as its chairman. Macy did not immediately give up his annex apartment, but, like Rockefeller, continued to own both his house and his apartment for several years, thus providing more space for entertaining guests. He finally sold the apartment in 1915 to James W. Ellsworth.

The George Macys had become by that time an important part of Jekyll's social life and were, according to one who knew them, "the most hospitable people I ever saw in my life."[22] They provided a welcoming atmosphere, not only to their family and friends but even to the companions, tutors, and nurses who sometimes accompanied the millionaire families to the island. One such was Kate Brown, who served both as tutor to the chil-

dren of Edith Carpenter Macy and Valentine Everit Macy, also a club member, and as social secretary to Mrs. Macy. Visiting Jekyll with her employer in 1917, Kate enjoyed frequent visits to the George Macys' home. She was invited often to dine, to play the piano, and to participate in whatever activities the family was enjoying. "[T]hey are absolutely kind in every way," she wrote, "always thinking of some new nice thing to do for people. They have a large house and have their meals there. Even the butler seemed unusually pleasant."[23]

George Macy's wife, whom he had married in January 1880, was Kate Louise Carter, described by Kate Brown as "the kindest soul that ever lived."[24] Of the Macys' five children, four of them, Helen,

Kate Brown visited Jekyll Island as tutor of the Valentine Everit Macy children in 1917 and left a valuable and articulate record of her impressions of the club and its members. (Courtesy of Katherine Owens)

Eight-year-old Kathleen Macy at Jekyll. Kathleen would become a talented artist and the wife of James Anthony Finn. (Courtesy of Robert Macy Finn)

Thomas Ridgway, William Kingsland, and Oliver Carter, did not accompany their parents to Jekyll that season. Only their youngest, twenty-one-year-old Kathleen, was with them. She was, Kate Brown contended, "a very sweet girl" but was in "much discussion and high conflict" with her parents over her future. Kathleen wanted to be an artist, but her parents "are too conservative and old-fashioned to like the idea," Brown concluded. "There is also a love affair and various complications." [25] In the end, Kathleen Macy would prevail, and she became what

one member of her family has called a "talented artist and etcher." [26] She went on to marry a New York banker, James Anthony Finn, and give birth to their eight children. The Macys' eldest son, Oliver Carter Macy, was at the time recently divorced, "and most people's sympathy is with the wife," noted Kate Brown in one of her letters to her family. [27]

Macy's youngest son, Kingsland, was married to Julia Dick, the daughter of his friend John Henry Dick, who was nominated for membership in the club by its president, Frederick Gilbert Bourne, seconded by Macy himself, and elected on January 24, 1916. Thus the Macys frequently enjoyed not only the presence of their children on the island, but that of their in-laws and cousins as well, typifying the extended family connections among club members.

George Macy, who was especially interested in hunting and golf, found Jekyll to be quite suitable. He hunted virtually every day, according to his daughter Helen, who was often at his side. "We took our own hunting dogs down as well as my horse," she wrote. "I used to hunt every day with my father and was a pretty good shot, birds, pheasant, etc. also wild boars. I remember taking a baby white one back to the house and keeping it for some time."[28] In 1908 Macy was named chairman of the game committee, a post he held for a number of years. Reporting on Jekyll's hunting conditions for 1913,

he quoted from the report of the game keeper, Brett, "The Island was never in better shape, and the prospects are good for a good all around hunting season." He had, in March 1910, with the approval of the forestry committee, undertaken a policy of selected burning of underbrush and grass in the hunting areas in order to ensure the best conditions for the propagation of game and for shooting. In addition to the abundant pheasants and quail, Macy reported, still quoting from the Brett report, "There are more large ducks than I have seen for many years, and less coots and blue-bills. The Deer and Hogs have also done well and are in fine shape. I think this is due much to the burning," which had, of course, been his idea.[29]

Helen Macy, who did not visit Jekyll after 1910, did not remember a golf course on the island. Al-

George Henry Macy, *left,* on a hunting party at Jekyll Island. (Courtesy of William Kingsland Macy Jr.)

River Road and the live oak tree in front of Moss Cottage. (Courtesy of William Kingsland Macy Jr.)

though there had been since 1898 what Robert Todd Lincoln derisively referred to as "a place where one could make a pretence [sic] of knocking balls about,"[30] it was George Henry Macy who, in 1909, spurred the committee on golf and sports, to which he had been named in 1908, to plan for another, more modern course. He oversaw the construction of the course in every detail, from obtaining the original estimate of $8,500 to burning off the savannah where the course was to be constructed to choosing the type of grass to be planted there.[31] It was also Macy who took the lead in seeking a golf professional for the club. He had contacted a well-known golf expert, Walter Travis, for recommendations and obtained the name of a Canadian champion, Karl Keffer, who would be Jekyll's golf pro for the next thirty-two years.[32] Writing to Cyrus Hall McCormick on March 10, 1909, he indicated his desire to have the links ready for play by the beginning of the next season. "It is hardly necessary for me to repeat the advisability of getting the Golf Links ready by the first of January, 1910," he stated, "as we might be able to attract a good many people to Jekyl during that month, when there are few members there, and this would go a long way towards reducing the expenses of the Club."[33]

Macy's interest in promoting new memberships in the club sparked a membership drive that would be continued under the administration of Charles Lanier through at least 1911. On November 10, 1909, he wrote to McCormick that "We have been getting up some invitations to parties whom we think would be desirable members of the Club and would be acceptable to the Governors." In the letter he asked McCormick to "send in the names of a few of your Chicago friends."[34] In an effort to attract desirable members, the club waived dues for 1910 for newcomers. "It really makes the purchase of a share very attractive, and we want to select the people that we feel are going to be a benefit to the Club," contended Macy.[35] Among those he had just recruited were banker Eugene Delano of Brown Brothers & Company; Edwin Hawley; Hugh Grant, former mayor of New York City; and E. T. Stotesbury, head of the firm of Drexel and Company of Philadelphia.

Unfortunately, Macy's health began to falter, as he suffered increasingly from high blood pressure and heart disease. In November 1910, club president Charles Lanier informed the membership that "Mr. Macy's ill health has compelled him to resign as Treasurer."[36] By 1912, however, Macy's health had improved sufficiently for him to become once again vigorously involved in club activities. That year he assumed the dual roles of third vice president and chair of the executive committee. He would rise to second vice president in 1914 and first vice president the following year, a post he would hold for the rest of his life. He got along well with club president Frederick Gilbert Bourne and, on at least one occasion, in 1914, accompanied him to Jekyll on his steam yacht, the *Alberta*.

The Macys did not come to Jekyll Island in 1916. But in 1917 they arrived early in the season on January 9 to stay for several months in Moss Cottage, bringing with them their daughter, Kathleen, and

friends Dr. Charles B. Slade and a Miss Mellin. On Valentine's Day, Macy's nephew, Noel, arrived and moved into the cottage as well. His parents, Valentine Everit and Edith Macy, with their daughter Edytha, her new tutor Kate Brown, and a friend, Mrs. F. Louis Slade, whom Kate judged to be "attractive [and] clever," had come down from New York with Edwin Gould in his private car, the "Dixie." Arriving on January 19, they took an apartment in the Sans Souci. With the Great War raging in Europe, Jekyll Island was enjoying an unusually busy time, with many families vying for the limited accommodations.

In spite of the war and the burning issue over whether or not America should get involved, it was a delicious season. Picnics on the beach, games of golf, and leisurely drives filled every day. "After lunch Mr. Geo. Macy took Edytha and me in his car up the beach and back by a lovely road through the Island," wrote Kate Brown on February 20. He could not resist stopping "at a kind of farm to see the game birds (used as decoys) and animals that are kept there. . . . Then we went back to the Macys, had tea with the charming daughter aged twenty-one and a Miss Delafield, played the piano, and then continued the ride till driven home by rain." It was for them all a pleasant, leisurely winter, marred only by the unfortunate death of Edwin Gould's son, Edwin (see Chichota chapter), who, Kate Brown claimed, had been "quite mad about Kathleen Macy and . . . proposed to her every other day."[37]

On March 14 Kate Brown announced their impending early departure. "Mr. Geo. Macy is far from well," she wrote, "and worries a great deal. He is afraid of the railroad strike, among other things, and as he is not well enough to travel without a good deal of care, the Everit Macys think they must go with him."[38] They were going to White Sulphur Springs, West Virginia, where "In case the strike comes off we shall be within motoring distance of N.Y."

White Sulphur Springs would prove to be quite a contrast to Jekyll, for there, as at most other resorts for the elite, a greater formality prevailed. At Jekyll, however, as Helen Macy noted, "We dressed for dinner but the idea [at other times] was to be equipped for hunting or riding not dressed up." Even so, to Kate Brown, despite the de-emphasis on sartorial splendor, life at Jekyll seemed quite elegant. Edith Macy "wears a new evening gown every night and new costumes every day—always perfectly appropriate and kept in the perfect condition which only a maid's constant attendance can achieve," wrote Kate Brown. Her own idea of a vacation "would not mean a place where we had to spend several hours a day in dressing. But they are so used to it that I suppose they don't mind."[39]

Clearly it was all relative, and Kate Brown anticipated with some apprehension the greater elegance that she expected at White Sulphur Springs. Still writing from Jekyll, she exclaimed, "They all call it so simple here, as to clothes and all that, but heavens, what must it be at White Sulphur Springs then! Where they say people dress a good deal. It will be an awful strain on my one evening gown! I am darning it already."[40] Her worst fears were realized when they reached the West Virginia resort, which, although pleasant enough, Kate found excessively expensive and ostentatious. "Here we are and I begin to see that life at Jekyl Island was simple—positively *rural* compared to this! This is the sort of thing I don't care for, an enormous hotel, quantities of people, all trying to outdress and outshine the others, and money, money everywhere."[41]

On March 25 while the Macys were at the Greenbrier Hotel in White Sulphur Springs and not long after leaving Jekyll Island, George Macy enjoyed his fifty-ninth birthday. He was, according to Kate Brown, "a very successful business man, liked by everyone, jolly and generous by nature but of late years made to worry over every thing by some kind of a shock which makes him a half invalid."[42] That birthday would prove to be his last, for he died on January 18, 1918.

None of the Macy family came to Jekyll for the 1918 season. The war continued on, and Valentine Everit Macy was too deeply involved in wartime activities with such groups as the National Council for Defense to break away for long periods of time. His son, Valentine, joined an ambulance corps and sailed for France on May 26, 1917. "What anxious times these are for millions of families!" wrote Kate Brown of his imminent departure. And the women of the household set to work knitting sweaters for the boys in service.

The estate of George Henry Macy held his club share from his death in 1918 until September 7, 1921. Kate Carter Macy, came down only once after her husband's death, renting a room in the club house on January 27, 1920, since her cottage was being used at the time by the Edmund Hayes family. Perhaps it was a final trip down to determine whether or not she wanted to retain the property and assume her husband's membership in the club. But the decision was never made because of her death the following year (May 14, 1921). It was her son, Kingsland Macy, known to his friends as King, who in 1921 assumed the membership under article II, section V, of the club constitution, which permitted such inheritance. And it was Kingsland Macy to whom the Macy heirs deeded Moss Cottage on October 7, 1921.[43]

Born November 21, 1889, Kingsland Macy had graduated from Harvard in 1912 and begun his career with his father's Union Pacific Tea Company, as it had come to be known, serving from 1919 to 1922 as its president, a post he held at the time he joined the club.[44] Shortly thereafter he disposed of his grocery business to become a partner in the brokerage firm of Abbott, Hoppin & Company, from which he withdrew in 1928. He was the fourth generation of the Macy family to serve as a senior trustee of the Seamen's Bank.

Macy entered a colorful political career as a consequence of a battle with New York State, which was

William Kingsland Macy, president of Union Pacific Tea Company and a colorful figure in New York politics, became a member of the Jekyll Island Club and inherited Moss Cottage in 1921. (Courtesy of William Kingsland Macy Jr.)

seeking to take over his estate, along with neighboring properties, in Islip, New York, for use as a public recreation area, much as the state of Georgia would do with Jekyll Island in 1947. Macy and his brother-in-law, Horace Havemeyer, had other ideas, for they were intending to subdivide the property into smaller building lots. Although Macy lost the battle and his estate when the area became Hecksher State Park, he was sufficiently politicized by the event to take an active role thereafter in the Republican Party and become a reformer in state politics.

He was elected chairman of the Suffolk County Republican Committee in 1926, a post he held until 1951. From 1930 to 1934 he also served as chairman of the New York State Republican Committee. He used the post to set wheels in motion for a legislative investigation in 1932 that toppled the administration of the colorful mayor of New York City, James A. Walker, and in 1933 Macy supported the successful candidacy of Fiorello H. La Guardia for mayor. He was equally successful in his efforts to secure the dismissal of Republican Joseph McGinnies as speaker of the New York State Assembly, thereby making many enemies within his own party. Working from a power base in Suffolk County and owning eight weekly newspapers there, he wielded significant influence in the state. He sought the Republican nomination for the state senate in 1940, without success, but was appointed in 1944 to serve out an unexpired term there. His work in the New York State Senate brought him a successful election in 1946 to the U.S. Congress from the First New York District, which included Suffolk County. He would serve in Congress until 1951.

Recognized in academic as well as political circles, Macy was appointed in 1940 to a twelve-year term on the Board of Regents for the University of the State of New York. He had attended Groton School and graduated from Harvard in 1912. In 1944 he was awarded an honorary LL.D. degree by Alfred University in New York.

Known as "a vivid and vigorous conservative, with a tart tongue and pungent pen,"[45] Kingsland Macy is best remembered for his various political feuds. He picked worthy opponents, among them Thomas Dewey and Franklin D. Roosevelt. It was, however, his split with Thomas Dewey in 1950 that would eventually strip Macy of both his political offices and his appointment to the Board of Regents.[46]

Kingsland Macy had married Julia A. Dick on October 3, 1912. Both had visited Jekyll with their parents before their marriage, and they returned for the 1919 season. With their three young children—five-year-old Julia Kingsland, three-year-old William Kingsland Jr., and two-year-old John Henry Dick—and their nurses, they nearly filled Moss Cottage. Writing on January 29 to a friend, Chauncey Anderson, who was vacationing that season in Florida, Macy invited him to stop over on the way north for a visit. "If you come up alone I can easily put you in our cottage, as my large family occupies all but one single room in the house. Should Mrs. Anderson or anyone else come with you, if you will let me know sufficiently far in advance, I can almost surely make arrangements to put you up at the Club."[47] Anderson accepted readily, inform-

ing Macy that he would arrive with another friend, Bob Gillespie, for a visit from February 18 to 20.

The men evidently spent the few days hunting on the island during their visit, for Anderson left behind a shotgun, which Macy was obliged to ship home to New York.[48] The Macys registered again for a stay in Moss Cottage on February 24, 1924. Julia's brother, William K. Dick, and his family came down as well and were, in fact, regular visitors after the death of John Henry Dick, their father, in 1926, when William took over his father's membership. They did not, however, stay in Moss Cottage, which, even with its six bedrooms (plus servants' rooms) could not accommodate both families comfortably. Instead, they rented an apartment in the Sans Souci.

Macy continued his membership in the Jekyll Island Club until the early years of the Great Depression, when many members, in an effort to conserve their resources, resigned. Macy, who had not been to Jekyll since 1926, resigned his membership in 1930. In that year the executive committee reported that "The Club has had a full membership until the last fortnight, when Mr. Kingsland Macy's resignation was accepted as he had made plans to transfer his house to a member of his family, who is likewise a member of the Club, pending a sale. A candidate for membership has already taken an option on this share and it is probable that in a fortnight our list will again be complete." That optimistic prediction was short-lived. Macy's departure began a spate of resignations that continued throughout the 1930s.

In 1933, under the presidency of J. P. Morgan, the club established a class of Associate Members, with dues only $150 a year, as compared to $700 for the Founding Members. As a consequence, Macy rejoined the club in 1934 as an associate. After rejoining the club, Kingsland Macy never became as deeply involved in its operations as his father had been, and the Reginald Huidekoper family used the Macy cottage extensively during the late 1930s and early 1940s. Nonetheless, Kingsland Macy contin-

Julia Dick Macy, wife of W. Kingsland Macy, with her three children, *left to right,* Julia, Dick, and Bill, in 1923. (Courtesy of William Kingsland Macy Jr.)

ued to own his property through 1941 and the beginning of World War II. In the 1942 tax records, issued after the club had closed, only four homes were still listed as owned by individuals. Kingsland Macy's is not among them. Sometime between December 1941 and the end of 1942, it had been turned over to the Jekyll Island Club. He was therefore not compelled once again to sit by while the state condemned his property for public use, as Georgia would do in 1947. The Macys' connection with the Jekyll Island Club continued for forty years, from 1902 until its close in 1942. The last Macy club member, Kingsland, lived until July 15, 1961.

For a time after the state's takeover of the island in 1947, the cottage stood empty, until James L. Asher, appointed island manager in the late spring of 1956, began to use it as his residence. He lived there with his wife, Alice Leney, and their children, Peter, Alan, and Alice, for about a year, from June 1956 until June 1957. Roy W. Mann of Summerville, Georgia, leased the house on January 21, 1957. The lease was ratified by the Jekyll Island Authority on February 20, subject to his allowing Asher to remain in the house until December 31 (although the family moved out six months earlier).[49] Moss Cottage was used in the 1980s to house the Jekyll Island Museum. The historic preservation staff of the Jekyll Island Museum has restored it to its 1903 appearance. It was officially opened for public viewing on May 9, 1997.

CHICHOTA

Owners: David H. King Jr., 1897–1900; Edwin Gould, 1900–1933; Gould Estate, 1933–41

Constructed: 1897

Demolished: 1941

Architecture: Italian Renaissance

Architect: Clarence Sumner Luce (probable)

The King Years

Today only a ruined swimming pool, guarded by two stone lions, stands where a graceful 1890s revival of Italian Renaissance architecture in America once stood. The original owner of this fine architectural structure, the only one-story house built during the club era, was a well-known New York contractor named David H. King Jr., who was viewed by Jekyll Islanders as a man meticulous in his work and reliable in his dealings with others. Although King must have known many of the New

Chichota not long after construction, before the stone lions were added. (Courtesy of Georgia Department of Archives and History, original in Jekyll Island Museum)

David H. King Jr. was the well-known New York contractor who in 1897 built the cottage known today as "Chichota." (Courtesy of Carol Stevens)

ers, among them Cornelius Bliss, Charles Lanier, and James Stillman.

King had become intimately acquainted that same year with Henry Hyde, when Hyde engaged King to construct the New York office building to house his Equitable Life Assurance Company, then the largest of its kind in the world. However, it was neither Pulitzer nor Hyde who nominated King for membership in the Jekyll Island Club. He was proposed on March 25, 1889, by the club president, Judge Henry Elias Howland of New York, seconded by club founder Newton S. Finney, and elected by the membership on May 18. During his first visit to the club on February 2, 1892, King brought as his guest the well-known New York architect Stanford White, from the architectural firm of McKim, Mead and White. He and White had been working together during the three preceding years on the construction of Madison Square Garden and the Washington Memorial Arch in New York.

For several years as a new member, King enjoyed club benefits without assuming responsibility in its leadership. He was busy in New York with a developing career and an expanding contracting firm. Recognized by 1891, according to Dun and Bradstreet reports, as "one of the leading men in his line," he was entrusted with "large and profitable jobs."[3] In addition to his work on Madison Square Garden in 1891 and the Washington Arch in 1889, he had worked with several architects, among them McKim, Mead and White; Bruce Price; and Clarence Sumner Luce in constructing a group of model houses owned by King in the then-posh section of New York known as Harlem. He had also been the contractor who built the Mills Building on Wall Street (where King had his office), the Bank of America Building, the Manhattan Athletic Club, the Manhattan Opera House, the Manhattan Club, the New York Times building and the New York Herald building.[4] In January of 1894, King and his wife, Mary Lyon King, had reached the economic and social level that permitted them to purchase

York members before joining the club in 1891, he had had special dealings with two of them—Joseph Pulitzer and Henry B. Hyde.

In 1886, prior to joining the club, he had come into contact with Pulitzer in their mutual efforts to raise the Statue of Liberty, a gift from the people of France, in New York harbor. While Pulitzer was a vital factor in collecting funds with publicity campaigns through the *New York World,* King was the contractor designated by the American committee in charge of the project, not only to construct the masonry base designed by Richard Morris Hunt, but also to erect the statue itself, for which he had been awarded the contract on May 5, 1886.[1] In short, as one engineering journal stated it, King "had general charge from the laying of the first stone of the pedestal to the driving of the last rivet."[2] At the banquet held at Delmonico's on October 28, 1886, to celebrate the statue's completion, he would have encountered a number of other Jekyll Island-a house in Newport and move smoothly into that elite society. They spent their first season that year in the elegant surroundings of Whitehall, the newly acquired estate of Dexter Bradford on Catherine Street. King completely remodeled the house for his wife and children, three daughters, Ruth, Jeanne, and Dorothy, and one son, Van Rensselaer. The *Newport Daily News* speculated that the house, which in its earlier days had had "quite a reputation for sumptuous entertainment," would enjoy under the ownership of the Kings a revival "of some of the former splendor of the place."[5]

In the spring of the following year, just before a fateful trip to Europe, he was tapped by Jekyll "czar" Henry Hyde for a special role in the club. Hyde wrote to him on May 22, 1895, that he had gone to see Frederic Baker, club treasurer, the evening before for a long talk about Jekyll. "I put you on as one of the Directors for the ensuing year," he informed King. "We want to make that thing 'hum.'"[6] Although elections would not be held for several weeks, being personally chosen by Hyde was tantamount to election. He had won Hyde's respect during the construction of his Equitable Building and had been put in charge of modifications to Hyde's New York home since that time. Hyde was a man who was domineering and meticulous in overseeing every aspect of the work, and gaining his confidence was no mean accomplishment. In the next several years, King would serve on both the board of directors and the executive committee, as well as secretary to the Jekyll Island Club. Unfortunately, his favor with Hyde would prove to be short-lived.

The year 1895 represented both the height and the depth of David H. King's life. Not only was he firmly ensconced at both Newport and Jekyll, but his talent was also publicly acknowledged by a prestigious appointment in New York. In mid-February of that year a distinguished commission of four men was selected to oversee the continued welfare and development of New York City's parks, among them the splendid green expanse of the new Central Park

that had been elegantly laid out by Frederick Law Olmsted, the country's leading landscape architect. The mayor appointed one Republican, Augustus D. Julliard, and two Democrats, James A. Roosevelt and George Griswold Haven. These three would have the power to select the fourth man, who would be named president of the board at a salary of $3,000 a year and would be the only committee member who would receive pay for his work. The only stipulation imposed by New York's mayor was that "he must be capable and a Republican."[7]

The three distinguished New Yorkers wasted little time in making their choice—David H. King Jr.—and their own continued service was based on his acceptance of the post. King was vacationing at Jekyll Island when he received a telegram from Mayor Strong offering him the post. The press announced his acceptance on February 18. Although King was not a very active Republican, he had nonetheless "warmly supported" Mayor Strong and the reform ticket in New York's fall 1894 election, and the mayor seemed pleased with his acceptance.[8]

As luck would have it, the foursome would serve but briefly, with all four commissioners tendering their resignations the following September. A summer vacation trip the Kings made to Europe ended suddenly with the death of King's wife, Mary, on August 9, 1895. Her death was a "great blow" to King, and he pleaded the state of his health and his desire "to go to the Adirondacks to obtain a needed rest from business cares" as his reasons for resigning from the board.[9] The other three commissioners, who had agreed to serve only on the condition that King serve as president, turned in their resignations as well.

The death of his wife would radically alter King's life style. He moved from his 514 Fifth Avenue home into his Hotel Renaissance on West Forty-third Street, a hotel that he had had designed by Clarence Sumner Luce and built in 1891.[10] Shortly after his wife's death King also decided to sell the magnificent art collection that he and Mary had

David H. King Jr., *right,* and his son, Van Rensselaer King, *left,* by 1899 a student at Harvard, visited Jekyll in that year to arrange to prepare the cottage for sale. (Courtesy of Wirt Thompson Jr.)

been acquiring during their trips abroad from 1885 to 1895. Without his wife, King lost interest in preserving the collection, which included masterpieces by such well-known artists as Holbein, Corot, Rembrandt, Gainsborough, and Sir Joshua Reynolds. Its sale on February 17 and 18, 1896, at Chickering Hall created quite a stir in New York.[11]

With his withdrawal from other activities, however, King's interest in Jekyll Island seemed to increase. By December 1895 he was standing in on occasion for Henry Hyde and had been appointed to various important positions in the club structure. Hyde had been treating him as an intimate in club affairs since earlier in the year when he had written him on April 3, 1895, that "At the meeting in May I think you and I should make every endeavor to establish reforms in the management of the Club." He confided to him his intent to get rid of the "$5,000 sinecure office" held by Newton Finney, the club's founder who had seconded King's nomination as member. He talked over intended modifications to the club house including his desire to add an annex, which he labeled a "barracks," to give each owner member "the privilege of enjoying a house to himself."[12]

By the end of the year King was working closely with Hyde and club treasurer Frederic Baker and assuming more and more responsibility. He took on such tasks as sending telegrams notifying vendors of the need for cigars at the Jekyll Island Club, writing Hyde of insurance needs for club property, accepting responsibility with Baker for the sale of debenture bonds to fund the necessary improvements and repairs to club property, and working with Hyde to establish new room and board rates for club members and guests.[13]

On February 10, 1897, however, Hyde wrote King a letter that foreshadowed a change of tone in their relationship. It began jovially enough, "My dear David," whereas his other letters typically began "My dear Mr. King," but there was a biting undertone that reflected Hyde's lack of tolerance for anyone who failed to do his bidding. "Are you aware that I consider you a fraud of the very first water? You promised to come down with me on the 21st of January, and now in your letter you speak of getting here after the 20th of February. I have no use for such a man! We are thinking of leaving you off the Executive Committee, electing another man in your place as Secretary, and in many other ways reducing you to the ranks."[14] The letter went on to inform him about club activities and his own personal reaction to the many changes taking place, which clearly underscored the tongue-in-cheek tone of the earlier charges, but the words were nonetheless a harbinger of things to come.

Two projects had just been completed in which Hyde and King had been deeply involved: the remodeling and expansion of the club house and construction of the apartment building that would come to be known as the Sans Souci. King had decided not to become an associate in the apartment complex, however, and was instead in the process of planning a house to be built next door to Baker's Solterra. In addition, he and Hyde were working together on the plans for a new stable, to be built by a group of "associates." It was this latter project that would bring about the split between Hyde and King.

On May 4, 1897, Hyde wrote to King informing him that "I have been trying for twenty-four hours to get you on the telephone, which seems impossible to do." He was writing to ask King's immediate attention to the stable matter: "If we are going on with the matter of building the stable at Jekyl Island—you to attend to the building; I to attend to financial part—it is necessary that we should take some steps in the matter." He was eager for King to meet with the architect, Charles Alling Gifford, and get the plans drawn up. Hyde, never able to let well enough alone, took one last jab: "I have done a great deal of work on Jekyl Island matters and will now value your assistance very much, if I can get it."[15]

King apparently complied with the request and agreed to take charge of the stable construction, and on June 1, Hyde named him chairman of the building committee. King's first act as committee chairman was to designate a site for the stable and order the land to be cleared. Objections to the site King had selected, however, were promptly raised by another committee member, James Scrymser, and on June 2, King notified club superintendent Grob to "suspend clearing site for stable until further orders."[16] What should have been a minor dispute accelerated in the weeks to come into a major contretemps, resulting in King's threat to resign from the committee. Hyde was losing patience and wrote to King on June 16 that he had once again been unable to contact him. "I do not wish to displease you," he wrote, "but I assure you, my dear Mr. King, I would just as soon go on alone and build the stable as to try and find you at your hotel." Unable to locate King, he had discussed the conflict with Scrymser, who had agreed on the compromise of leaving the choice of stable sites to the club's superintendent, Ernest Grob. "I trust this will be satisfactory to everyone," Hyde stated.[17] His wife, Annie, confided to her son, James Hazen Hyde, known as Caleb, that "Pa . . . seemed angry about King [and] Jekyl Island."[18] The compromise was evidently not satisfactory to King who was still fuming in his New York hotel suite and refusing to take an active role in the stable construction. Hyde confided to the architect on July 2 that "Mr. King has practically resigned from the Stable Building Committee because he was not particularly pleased in regard to the location of the stable."[19] On July 14 King did resign.[20] And on July 24, he informed Hyde's secretary that he was sending him a check for his stalls in the stable but requested that they be offered for sale "as they will be of no use to me."[21] Hyde relieved King of his obligation and simply built the stable with fewer stalls.

In late May before the stable matter had come to a head, Hyde had sold King his rights to lots 33 and 34, which he had owned for several years, and King set out to construct his house.[22] Unfortunately, the identity of the architect of King's cottage is not known for certain. His close association over the years with Stanford White, as well as White's visit to the island in 1892, make it tempting to believe that he may have designed the splendid Italian Renaissance structure. Certainly White was known to have done other buildings in the style, and his name was associated with its revival in the 1880s. However, it was Clarence Sumner Luce to whom King had turned in New York when he needed an architect for his Hotel Renaissance, and that decision, in addition to the architectural similarity, in that both structures were built around a central open atrium, make him the more likely architect. King was evidently very pleased with Luce's design of his hotel, for he chose to repeat the atrium pattern in his Jekyll house, which in this case enclosed the only privately owned swimming pool in the cottage colony and perhaps the first one in the state of Georgia.

While plans were proceeding for King to build his house at Jekyll Island, Frederic Baker, who had the Queen Anne style house next door, raised an objection about the plans and complained to Hyde, who informed him that he had made no restrictions when he offered to transfer the lots to King. "I think the best way is to let him alone and permit him to build," he wrote.[23] In his response, Baker, apparently reconciled to the construction, nonetheless grumbled, "David King is a good enough fellow unless he gets on top of you."[24]

This new concern may have resulted in part from the fact that King was considering the possibility of building his own stables on a lot that he had acquired from Rudolph Ellis, located behind those he had purchased from Hyde and nearer to Baker's Solterra than he cared to have them. But Ernest Grob, ever the diplomat, wrote to Hyde on September 8 that "I am quite certain from what conversations I have had with Mr. King, that he will not put up a stable on the lot he purchased from Mr. Ellis if it be objectionable to the Club, in fact he said he would put it outside the fence line if they wanted him to." [25]

Evidently the matter was worked out, because within a matter of weeks, King had begun work on his house and had contracted for the drilling of an artesian well. The house was all but completed by the end of December 1897, and Grob wrote to Hyde on December 27 that "Mr. King's house is progressing favorably, [and] he will move into it on Friday next." [26] By early January King had begun to landscape his lot, and Hyde wrote to Frederic Baker that "Mr. King has leveled off his lot and no doubt the grass will be up in a short while. It is too bad he has cut down so many trees; there are only a few left, but after the grass is up and he has planted some

trees and the ground looks green it will be a decided improvement to your location." [27] In the months to come, King put in palms, orange and lemon trees, a fruit orchard, and flower beds, and the following year he ordered special California privet to use as hedges around his circular drive. [28]

The earlier dispute had apparently calmed, for as Hyde informed Baker, "Mr. King is here and evidently wishes to be agreeable." [29] Although he had resigned from the stable committee and association, King remained a member of the club's executive committee and continued to take an interest in club affairs. When the Maurice family and Col. John Mason Loomis headed up a subscription committee to preserve the Horton House in April 1898, King along with many other members pledged the prescribed twenty-seven dollars. He was also

The facade of Chichota. (Courtesy of Helen Mead Platt)

consulted when the United States government requested permission on April 9 to construct a temporary battery at the north end of Jekyll Island to protect the entrance to Brunswick harbor during the Spanish American War. It was he and Frederic Baker who responded to the request from Capt. Cassius E. Gillette, giving him permission to build the battery and prepare for the defense of Saint Simons Sound, should the need arise.[30]

While it may have been his preoccupation with his new house that had calmed King's anger and drawn him to Jekyll, he may also have had another reason for arriving earlier than the official 1898 season and remaining until its very end. In July 1897 Henry Hyde had reported to Frederic Baker a rumor he had heard from a gentleman in Savannah that King had become engaged to Jean Struthers, the only daughter of club member William Struthers of Philadelphia (see Moss Cottage chapter).[31] In fact, the Struthers family had arrived on the island on December 2, 1897, with King arriving the very next day. Both stayed until mid-April 1898, with King departing on April 15 and the Strutherses leaving only a few days later.[32]

There is no reason to believe that King would not have continued to come to Jekyll had disaster not struck the island and had the alleged "engagement" with Jean Struthers worked out favorably. Evidently, whatever romance may have existed between King and Struthers's daughter, if it was not a figment of Hyde's active imagination, burned itself out rather quickly, and Jean Struthers would several years later marry Henry Francis Sears.

To hasten his desire to leave the club and sell his property, in early October 1898 one of the worst hurricanes in Jekyll history slammed into the island, and King's property was particularly hard hit. Although the house was left standing, the splendid new fruit orchard was "all knocked down" and the palms "twisted" by the storm. Ceilings in two of the bedrooms collapsed, and the cellar was full of water, as it was in almost every rain.[33] The damage was not irreparable, but the hurricane, if not his failed romance, seems to have taken the heart out of King's interest in Jekyll Island. He did not come for the 1899 season and would, in fact, come to the island only once more.

When the storm damage had been repaired, King instructed Superintendent Grob to do nothing more to his house "except the necessary work to keep it from going to ruin."[34] Problems with the house had been there since its construction but had been intensified by the storm damage. Although neither the architect nor the contractor is known for certain, it is possible that King oversaw the construction himself, which would help to explain some of the problems. He was accustomed to building for northern winters, not Georgia summers, and the materials used in the house were incompatible with their environment, not taking into account the frequent shifts in the water table and the moist island air. The basement, already close to sea level, filled with water in every rain; the pool sprang a leak; casements expanded in the damp weather, causing doors to jam; and the roof leaked. King was eager to sell the house, and although he would remain a club member until 1903, he had clearly lost interest in Jekyll.

He briefly considered the possibility of putting in an appearance for the 1900 season but quickly changed his mind, deciding instead to come down before the season opened in November 1899, with his son Van, then a student at Harvard, for a ten-day stay to make arrangements to have the house renovated and "put in shape to be sold." He put it on the market furnished for $35,000, including in the price all three lots he had purchased from Hyde and Ellis. After going through the house with Grob, he decided to paint and paper and repair the increasing number of cracks that had appeared in the walls but basically to spend as little as possible on it.[35] Curiously, the first person to ask about the price of the King house was William Struthers, who indicated that he had a friend thinking of joining the club and buying a house.[36]

The Gould Years

Whether the friend of Struthers was Edwin Gould, who eventually purchased the house, is unknown, though the two men certainly knew one another and were good enough friends to go on hunting expeditions together at Hofwyl Plantation near Darien, Georgia,[37] If so, the sale of the house did not materialize immediately, and King was obliged to maintain the empty house for yet another year, with Grob tending to the seemingly endless stream of repairs and maintenance of the cottage and grounds. It was the following December that Edwin Gould finally purchased the cottage.

Gould had been nominated for membership by John C. Barron of Boston and seconded by William Rockefeller on November 21, 1899. He was elected to membership on December 13. He was the second son of the notorious financier Jay Gould. Of all Gould's sons, Edwin, born February 25, 1866, was said to be in temperament most like his father, with none of the flamboyance and indiscretion that characterized his older brother, George, whom his father saw, nonetheless, as his heir apparent. Edwin was, like his father, a family man with a quiet nature and a good head for business. He had attended Columbia University's School of Mines but had left in 1887, the year before his graduation, to enter the world of Wall Street, where he made his first million within a year. He went on to make a large fortune independent of his father's, among his many business interests serving as president of the Saint Louis Southwestern Railway, the Western Coal and Mining Company, the Diamond Match Company, and the Seventh National Bank of New York.[38]

He was the first club member to arrive on the island for the 1901 season, registering in advance of

the official opening on December 14, 1900. Within five days he had purchased the King house and lots and begun to modify and update the cottage and provide for the latest in modern conveniences, under the supervision of architect Charles Alling Gifford. New gas lines were run to the house, and Gould had it prepared for the electricity that the club expected to install in the near future. He also made plans to implement a new "hot water arrangement."[39] Even though King had recently refurbished the cottage, a crew of six painters was brought in to redecorate. In all, fourteen men were at work on the house.[40]

As Edwin Gould was overseeing the preparation of the cottage itself, his wife Sally was equally busy, making a trip to New Orleans to buy furnishings for the new house. "In one Royal Street antique shop, she spent $4,000 in a few minutes one day," according to one source, "buying furniture and bric-a-brac," including "a 200-year-old mahogany sideboard, a grandfather clock of the Revolutionary period, side chairs that predated Andrew Jackson and the War of 1812, a solid silver piece that once belonged to the unfortunate Joseph Bonaparte, a mahogany davenport, and a cordial set from one of the pre-war Louisiana plantation mansions."[41]

Whatever flaws the King house may once have held, they were quickly repaired, as Edwin Gould began to turn his new winter home into an island paradise for his young family. Although a recent member, Gould had already come to love the island and spared no expense to prepare the cottage.

Edwin's older brother, George, had been a member of the Jekyll Island Club since 1895, although he rarely came down. With his wife, Edith Kingdon, a former actress, he enjoyed the glittering social life of New York and Newport, the glamour of the theater and society parties, and festive dinners at Delmonico's. Jekyll, with its philosophy of studied simplicity, was not his cup of tea. It is surprising to find him among the Jekyll members at all, and the

Edwin and Sarah Gould on the steps of Chichota. (Courtesy of Edwin J. Gould family)

year after his son George was born to his mistress, Guinevere Sinclair, a fact well known in New York social circles since George Gould was never particularly discreet, his name quietly disappeared from the club rosters.

Jekyll was perfectly suited, however, to the quiet tastes of both Edwin Gould and his wife, Sarah Cantine Shrady, the daughter of Hester Cantine Shrady and the stepdaughter of a prominent physician, George Frederick Shrady. The couple had met in February 1892 at Helen Gould's coming-out reception, and after a relatively brief engagement they were wed on October 26, 1892, when Sally was only eighteen years old. It was a quiet ceremony, "a family affair" in the Shrady parlor, which had been gloriously decorated for the occasion by the Gould's gardener with boxwood, chrysanthemums, geraniums, and roses.[42] Their marriage would prove to be, in contrast to that of the George Goulds, a lifetime commitment of two people who were genuinely compatible. Like Edwin, Sally Gould preferred a quiet family-centered life rather than the social whirlwind that George and Edith enjoyed. For them Jekyll was paradise, and their passionate attachment to the island club would endure for nearly two decades.

Edwin was thirty-three years old when he joined the Jekyll Island Club, and his wife was twenty-five. They had two young sons, the elder, Edwin Jr., only six years old and the younger, Frank Miller, not yet a year old. Their first official stay in their newly redone cottage began at the height of the season on March 6, 1901. On that day Gould arrived with his wife and signed the guest register for the first time with the cottage's new name, Chichota, presumably in honor of a Creek Indian chief. Sally Gould's mother, Hester Shrady, had arrived three days earlier with her grandson Edwin Jr. and a female companion. It was the beginning of a large housewarming party to which the Goulds liberally invited friends and relatives alike. Throughout the

month of March guests continued to pour into their cottage—more than a dozen in all. Even though they preferred the quiet life, Edwin and Sally Gould enjoyed entertaining in the relaxed atmosphere of Jekyll, where the pretentions of such fashionable resorts as Newport were unwelcome.

It was hardly an ambiance to enthrall his brother-in-law, the foppish Marquis Marie Ernest Paul Boniface de Castellane, more popularly known as "Count Boni," who had wed Edwin's sister Anna in 1895. The couple visited once and only once, arriving with valet and maid in tow on February 19, 1903. Even in New York at its best, the marquis had curled his lip at what he considered to be the bad taste of American society, whose "ideas and customs . . . jarred on my sensibilities." To such a one who believed that "any outdoor existence . . . numbs the soul and destroys intelligence," the natural environment of Jekyll, the vision of the Goulds splashing with their children in their pool, and the constant diet of the island's bounties of game, oysters, and terrapin must, indeed, have been an ordeal. The Jekyll pastime of hunting, in particular, he found distasteful, for he contended that men given to hunting and sport were "in danger of developing into the most boring individuals imaginable." Although it is not surprising that Count Boni never returned to Jekyll, the Goulds continued for many years thereafter to entertain with their same unassuming grace a great variety of people, among them Italian marchesas, lords, and ladies.[43]

Even though Jekyll was the ideal family retreat for the Goulds and an especially wonderful environment for their young sons, they were acutely aware of the dangers the island afforded their children, who were never allowed to explore it unattended. More than fifty years after the fact, one of Frank Miller Gould's boyhood companions from Browning School in New York, Ernest Stires, remembered his visit to Jekyll and the protective restrictions placed upon him by his hosts during his

Frank Miller Gould in front of Chichota, about 1903. (Courtesy of Edwin J. Gould family)

Edwin Gould Jr. was killed in a tragic hunting accident during a visit to Jekyll Island in 1917 when he was in his twenties. (Courtesy of Edwin J. Gould family)

The Albright children learn to swim at the Chichota pool. (Courtesy of John J. Albright)

visit between Christmas and the New Year in 1911: "I had brought my bathing suit . . . but was told that the ocean was too cold in late December. I begged and wheedled a few governesses and my hosts and eventually was allowed to enter the Atlantic at the wonderful Jekyll beach, and found it not too cold at all. Nobody else swam with me. . . . There was a swimming pool at the Goulds' house, and this I was told was the proper place to swim. What I did not get away with was to escape from a very watchful governess. . . . Wherever we went in a sort of Irish jaunty cart . . . some sort of adult supervision was in attendance. Irksome."[44] What appeared to the boy to be excessive caution no doubt resulted from the Goulds' fierce love for their sons and a determination to protect them from harm, a desire that in the end would come to naught.

Edwin Gould with his sons, Frank Miller, *left,* and Edwin Jr., *right,* on Jekyll beach. (Courtesy of Edwin J. Gould family)

Their awareness of the ever-present dangers had been heightened during their first season at Jekyll when they crossed from Brunswick to the island on an evening in late March. The aging club launch, the *Howland,* which had been built in 1887, grounded on a jetty at the mouth of Jekyll Creek, and the Goulds were stranded some forty-five minutes on the darkening water. The club superintendent later commented that "had it been a rough night, it might have been a very serious affair."[45] Their second season as well brought about a somewhat more serious mishap. As the Goulds were returning north on their yacht *Nada* in late April 1901, the engineer of the vessel caught his hand in the engine's machinery, and the group had to put in at Savannah to have the man attended to and a finger amputated.[46] In all probability it was the Goulds, ever vigilant to protect their children, who installed protective railings around their cottage pool.

For the most part, the Goulds came to the island not on their yacht, but on their private train car, the Dixie, traveling to Brunswick and taking the club launch from the wharf. Ernest Stires recalled his own trip down on the Dixie. They traveled all night,

attended by "numerous and efficient stewards." The train arrived in Brunswick in late afternoon, and the Goulds, perhaps not wanting to risk being stranded once again on the jetties of Jekyll Creek, decided to spend an unscheduled night in the Oglethorpe Hotel and wait until the following morning to take the steamer to the island.

The Goulds, Stires recalled, were "wonderfully unassuming and quiet." As for the others he may have encountered, "I was dimly aware of odds and ends of famous names, but when I returned home my family were exasperated because I couldn't re-

Walkway to the Gould boat dock. (Courtesy of Jekyll Island Museum)

On the steps of Chichota, Frank Miller Gould, *seated, left,* and Edwin Jr., holding camera and dog. (Courtesy of Edwin J. Gould family)

member the names of anyone outside the Gould family, except a few first names of some boys and girls I played with." Nevertheless, for a northern boy, even given the constant adult presence, life must have seemed a winter dream, with daily tennis games, pony rides, swimming, and fishing. Only hunting was forbidden to the younger members of the family and their guest. Despite the protectiveness of their parents, Eddie Gould and his little brother would on occasion manage to give their tutor the slip and sneak away to play with the workers' children on the Jekyll Island school yard.[47]

Before the end of January 1901 Gould was making plans for the construction of a private wharf, longer even than the club dock, and a boathouse.[48] Anticipating still greater expansion of land and facilities, he began in March 1901 to acquire additional surrounding lots to add to the three he already owned. Intending to build the stable that King had never got around to constructing ("of course it is understood that it should be on the east side of the fence line," Grob informed club president, Charles Lanier), he had requested from the club another lot (38), which Baker and Stickney had agreed to sell him for $300, if it met the approval of the executive committee.[49] He also acquired lot 44 from John C. Barron, who had nominated him for club membership, and tried as well to purchase lot 32 of Walter Gurnee. But Gurnee refused to sell, and Gould had to wait until his death in 1904 to make the purchase.[50]

In 1902 Gould built a bowling alley, to which in 1913 he would add a covered tennis court, designed by Walter D. Blair of New York and built by local contractor George Cowman. It was said to be "one of the handsomest and costliest in the country"[51] It would be known as a "casino," like the similar though more elaborate facility his brother George had built at his Lakewood, New Jersey, estate, Georgian Court, in 1899. By the time of its completion it included, in addition to the bowling alley and tennis

Employee (possibly Charlie Hill) in front of the Gould cottage at Jekyll Island. (Courtesy of Jekyll Island Museum)

court, a rifle range, attendant's room, locker room, and restrooms. Later even a greenhouse would be attached to one side. As time went on, Gould added to his family's holdings a private stable, a beach house, and a two-bedroom cottage (April–June 1913) for his gardener and caretaker, Page Parland, and his wife, Aleathia, who oversaw the domestic aspects of the Gould cottage. Clearly, the Gould complex, eventually including real estate both on and off the island, was the most elaborate of any private property on Jekyll.

A rare shot of the interior of the Gould bowling alley inside the "playhouse" at Jekyll. (Courtesy of Jekyll Island Museum)

Gould's caretakers, Page, *right,* and Aleathia Parland, *left,* pose for the camera in front of Cherokee, the home of Edwin Gould's mother-in-law, Hester Shrady. (Courtesy of Jekyll Island Museum)

In 1904, as soon as he had acquired Gurnee's lot, Gould submitted plans to the club's executive committee for the construction of a cottage for his in-laws, the Shradys, to be built on the lot in question. (See Cherokee chapter.) It was abundantly clear by this time that Gould's intention was to make Jekyll Island a comfortable home for his entire family, for they spent most of the winter season there as a rule. The Brunswick press, reporting Gould's arrival at the extremely early date of October 12, 1906, "in his private car" and with "the usual retinue of servants," commented that "Mr. Gould is always an early visitor and generally is one of the last to leave Jekyl." [52] He often sent down his yacht, the *Nada*, to spend a portion of the time cruising in southern waters, and often times the Goulds came and went throughout the club season. [53] In 1914, having become interested in flying, Gould not only "offered the Aero Club of America the site for a landing field on one of his properties near Jekyl Island," but he also brought down his own plane, flying "with courageous members of the Jekyl Island colony as nervous passengers." [54]

Edwin Gould was a valued member of the club who was willing to expend his considerable resources for the general benefit of the members, funding among other things two new golf holes overlooking the sea and prefiguring the famous "dune" course built in 1926. [55] The city of Brunswick was also in his debt for such things as a "handsome ambulance," which he gave about 1910. [56] At the end of 1913, Gould expanded his holdings in the Brunswick area and the club's hunting options by purchasing a small island known as Latham Hammock, located across from the Jekyll wharf in the famous Marshes of Glynn. The three-thousand-acre island contained only about seventy acres of dry ground on which Gould and a group of men, who incorporated on January 6, 1913, as the Latham Hammock Club, intended to build a hunting lodge. [57] Rumors immediately began to circulate that a rift had developed among Jekyll Island Club

The Gould family arrives in Brunswick. *Left to right:* Eddie, Frank Miller, Sarah Gould, Cousin Ada, and Edwin Gould. (Courtesy of Edwin J. Gould family)

Edwin Gould toasts with lady tennis players. (Courtesy of Edwin J. Gould family)

Sarah Gould, *right,* with her dog and a friend on Jekyll beach. (Courtesy of Edwin J. Gould family)

members and that Gould planned to withdraw to form a rival organization. Nothing could have been further from the truth. Their real purpose, according to the Brunswick newspaper, was two-fold: First, by purchasing Latham Hammock, Gould would eliminate the possibility of having anyone else buy the property to "build a factory on it or erect some other buildings which would mar the outlook from the Jekyl Island Club"; and second, the lodge would "afford men of smaller means" than those associated with the Jekyll Club a place to hunt and fish.[58] Gould himself also viewed the hammock as an expansion of Jekyll's hunting grounds and made it available to club members. Certainly the Goulds themselves used it for hunting, and the Maurice family records describe outings and picnics there on more than one occasion.

The purchase of Latham Hammock was, in short, just one more manifestation of Gould's commitment to the Jekyll Island Club and its future.

Further evidence of the intended permanence of his association with the island was his promotion of his son Edwin Jr. for membership. It was highly unusual for a young man of his age—only twenty-one—to be accepted as a member of the organization while his parents were still alive, but the Jekyll Islanders were certainly not willing to deny the wishes of one so dedicated, influential, and generous as Edwin Gould. Edwin Jr., nominated by Edmund Hayes and seconded by W. D. Woodruff, was elected to the club on November 25, 1914. Edwin Jr., or Eddie, as he was known, had loved the island since his boyhood. Now that he was an adult, his freedom was no longer restricted as it had

Edwin Gould, *right,* with bicycle. His son Edwin Jr. is fifth from right, *standing.* (Courtesy of Edwin J. Gould family)

been when he was a child. Perhaps the overprotectiveness of his parents had made him rebellious, perhaps it was merely his nature to crave freedom, or perhaps he simply lacked academic aptitude. Whatever the reasons, he had not gone to college. He had always despised the structured academic life. Just as he had fled his tutor as a boy on Jekyll Island, so he had run away from his preparatory academy, Pomfret School in Connecticut, after only three weeks. And even when his younger brother went off to Yale, Eddie Gould refused to go to college.

By December 1916, however, his father had decided that it was time for his idle existence to come to an end, and he was making arrangements for him to learn about the business world at Guaranty Trust Company. Thus when Eddie Gould arrived with his father at Jekyll two days after Christmas, it was to be his last vacation for a long time. With them were Frank Miller, on Christmas vacation from his freshman year at Yale, and four young friends, Radcliffe Swinnerton, W. H. Brown, E. McCormick, and Phelps Phelps.[59]

Eddie Gould, prohibited from hunting as a child on the island, had as a young man developed a passion for the sport. During the days after Christmas he hunted ducks and doves with Swinnerton and McCormick, who were, to his regret, obliged to return to school with the end of the holidays.[60] He found few other distractions on the island, though he must have been delighted on January 9 by the arrival of the George Macys, not only because he was smitten by their daughter, Kathleen, but also because Mr. Macy provided him with a new hunting partner.[61]

With the arrival on January 17 of the Tracy Dows family, young Gould had struck up a friendship with the Dows children's tutor, Noyes Reynolds, and he, too, had soon become a hunting companion for young Gould. Edwin Gould Sr., who had left the island for a time, returned on February 19, bringing with him a relative who was frequently his guest on

Oglethorpe Road. (Courtesy of Edwin J. Gould family)

Jekyll—Nelson B. Burr. Also on the train coming down was another branch of the Macy family, Valentine Everit Macy with his family and their new tutor, Kate Brown. Sally Gould did not come with her husband, for her mother was ill in New York, recovering from a bout with pneumonia. She planned to join him in a few days when Mrs. Shrady's health improved. The two men remained briefly on the island and then left on a business trip to Saint Augustine, Florida, In the early evening of February 24, Eddie Gould and Noyes Reynolds went on another of their hunts. They had earlier set traps on Latham Hammock and set out about 1:00 P.M. to see what they had caught and to do a little early evening hunting.[62] Kate Brown, tutor to the Macy children, recorded what happened in a letter to her family written the following day:

> There was a dreadful accident here last evening which makes us feel sad today. Eddy Gould, the one young man in the twenties on the Island and son of the Mr. Gould who brought us down here, went out last night to visit his coon traps. He had set them on a lonely island separated from Jekyl by a mile or more of water and marsh, and the only person who went with him was a young man who is tutoring the Dows children. It was a very dark night and Eddy Gould bent over a trap which was sprung to see what it had caught. In bending he knocked against his gun which he had carelessly left cocked and it went off, shooting him through the stomach and killing him.[63]

Newspaper accounts differ somewhat, with the *Brunswick News* contending that he was "impulsively attempting to put a hurt coon out of misery with the butt of his gun," and the *New York Times* reporting that he was following "the custom of the natives, who kill trapped animals with a club in order not to injure the hide." The butt of his cocked gun was serving as his club. In any case, his gun, an "old Scott double-barrel hammer gun," which young Gould preferred to the "new automatic . . . pump repeating gun" and the "handsome double-barrel hammerless" that he also had with him on the

Two stone lions guard the ruins of the cottage called Chichota. (Photo by Jack Ross)

island, discharged into his groin, "tearing an ugly hole in the body." He moaned once, "O, my God," and dropped to the ground.

Noyes Reynolds was horrified. He frantically tried to carry Gould to the canoe in which they had arrived, but when he realized that Gould was already dead, he abandoned the body, and, struck with panic, set out alone in the boat. The Brunswick newspaper account is vivid: "In his excitement and haste to reach Jekyl for help, Reynolds fell from the canoe into the little creek, and for several minutes struggled in the water, finally succeeding in uprighting the boat. . . . finally people on Jekyl heard him screaming. At first those who heard the cries of the young man did not know who or what it was, but the cries continued . . . and a launch in charge of Captain J. A. Clark was quickly speeding toward the little canoe. . . . It was nearly midnight when the party finally returned to Jekyl with the remains." Edwin Gould, contacted in Saint Augustine, gave instructions for his son's body to be prepared for shipment back to New York. He did not return to Jekyll Island but went directly from Saint Augustine to Savannah, where he met the train carrying his son's coffin. His train car, Dixie, now became the funeral car that would carry Eddie's body home.

"It is an awful thing for him," Kate Brown had written, "for he was devoted to this boy." But the hardest part was still before him, trying to comfort Sally Gould for the death of one of her two beloved sons, on whom she had lavished such care and affection and who had been the very center of her life. According to the *New York Times,* she was "so prostrated by the news that she was placed under the care of a physician." The *Brunswick Times* had described young Gould in a headline as a "Popular Lad with Promising Career." Kate Brown, on the other hand, had spoken of him cryptically as "not quite like other people, mentally." Whatever the case, his parents were, as she attested, "devoted to him," and his death was a terrible blow.

After the accident, a legend grew up that the Goulds never again returned to Jekyll Island. Like most legends, this one has only a kernel of truth. Sally Gould, it is true, never returned to Jekyll. Even the memory of the many happy years they had all spent there together could not erase the terrible thought of the island as the place her son had died. Nor did she want others in her family to come down. Edwin Gould finally returned in 1921, but it would never be the same for him again. The man who had been accustomed to spending several months on the island every winter came back only four times in the sixteen years between his son's death and his own in 1933.[64]

The loss of Edwin Jr., one of the sons on whom he and his wife had doted, seemed only to intensify his love for children and his desire to see them protected. Encouraged by his warm friendship with his mother-in-law, who was herself a benefactor of the Messiah Home for Children in New York and who encouraged him in his outpouring of interest in children's welfare, Gould established the Edwin Gould Foundation for Children in 1923 and spent much of the last ten years of his life and a good portion of his fortune in seeing that disadvantaged children got a good start in life.

Chichota sat empty for many years. Members of the club were permitted to use the Gould tennis courts until 1920, when the family asked that they be closed.[65] Although Gould was beginning to cut his ties to Jekyll, he nonetheless gave a $1,000 donation for a new golf course in 1928, and he never sold his island property during his lifetime.[66] Only Frank Miller Gould, whose happy boyhood memories proved stronger than their tragic end, continued to come to the island on a regular basis. In 1928 he would build his own house on the island (see Villa Marianna chapter), leaving his father's cottage more forlorn than ever. On January 5, 1941, Marian Maurice, who had come to the island every year for more than forty years, recorded Chichota's final days in her diary: "Mr. Gould's house being demolished," she wrote, "a sad sight."[67] Only a leaf-filled pool remained with two stone lions, erect and ferocious, to keep their endless vigil.

PULITZER COTTAGE

Owners: Joseph Pulitzer, 1897–1911; Ralph Pulitzer, 1911–14; John Joseph Albright, 1914–31; Albright Estate, 1931–34; Jekyll Island Club, 1934–47

Constructed: 1897

Architecture: Eclectic

Architect: Charles Alling Gifford

Demolished: 1951

The Pulitzer Years

When Joseph Pulitzer became a charter member of the Jekyll Island Club in 1886, he was at the peak of his career, though his frenzied work pace was beginning to take its toll. Nervous exhaustion, lung trouble, and failing eyesight forced him into semi-retirement in 1887, and he gave up his personal management of the *New York World,* though he would never completely relinquish control.

Pulitzer's life to that point, had it not been for his health, was every immigrant boy's dream. His background was not unlike those of thousands of Europeans pouring into New York at the time. His father, Philip Pulitzer, was a merchant-class Hungarian Jew; his mother, Louise Berger, a Catholic. Born on

The final design of the Pulitzer Cottage as it looked after two additions, one in 1899 and the second in 1904. (Lanier Book, 1911)

Joseph Pulitzer, one of the nation's most prominent newspapermen, constructed his cottage on Jekyll Island in 1897. (*King's Notable New Yorkers*)

April 10, 1847, in Mako, Hungary, he had grown up in Budapest. In quest of a military adventure and having been refused by the Austrian and British armies and the French Foreign Legion because of his weak eyesight, he arrived in September 1864 in a United States in the midst of the Civil War and in need of soldiers no matter what their condition. On November 12, 1864, he was mustered into the Union Army into a predominantly German unit that had been organized by Gen. Carl Schurz. It was this same Carl Schurz who gave Pulitzer his start in the newspaper business when the war was over. With his partner, Emil Praetorius, Schurz owned a German-language newspaper, the *Westliche Post*, in Saint Louis, Missouri. He offered young Pulitzer

his first job as a reporter in 1868. The young man proved to be vigorous and relentless in his quest for the news and, like so many other young immigrants, eager to get ahead. Within three years he became a part owner of the newspaper. He moved rapidly in the world of journalism, buying for a song small newspapers in financial difficulty and turning them to a profit. One of these was the *Saint-Louis Dispatch,* which he acquired in 1878.[1]

Paralleling his journalistic career at this point was a political career. He was elected to the Missouri legislature in 1869, when he was still too young to serve. A disappointed supporter of Horace Greeley and the Liberal Republican movement in the late 1870s, he became an ardent Democrat, a political allegiance from which he never wavered. He was also elected to the United States Congress for a two-year term from 1885 to 1887, but he detested the job and served only a few months before resigning his congressional seat and returning at full tilt to the newspaper business. In 1883 he bought from financier Jay Gould the *New York World,* which would become his pulpit for many causes. There is no question that he reached many people, for he increased the circulation of the *World* tremendously by appealing to the masses through his "yellow journalism" techniques. It was the *World* that had made him a rich and famous man at the height of his career by the time he joined the Jekyll Island Club in 1886.

He was in many respects an unlikely Jekyll Islander. Whereas most club members were Republicans, he remained for the most part a loyal and outspoken Democrat. Most had been born to wealth and were of old colonial families, while he was a recent immigrant. Whereas most had ancestral origins in the British Isles, Pulitzer was an East European of Magyar descent. Most were Episcopalians and Presbyterians, considered the "elite" religions of nineteenth-century America, whereas Pulitzer was by background half Jew, half Catholic. (That he joined the Episcopal Church was never enough to make many forget his Jewish ancestry.) Finally, whereas most ascribed to the so-called "Gospel of Wealth," Pulitzer, despite his own lucrative income and spendthrift ways, was outspoken in his newspaper against the "aristocracy of money." He proclaimed the *World* to be, rather, the organ of the "aristocracy of labor." [2]

It was curious for Pulitzer, whose political and philosophical orientation was so antithetical to that of most members of the club, to be able to maintain his membership there despite occasional open attacks against other members. For example, the father of club member William Rockefeller and his brother John D. was an intriguing mystery to Pulitzer, and he promised special rewards to the reporter who could gain information about the father. Although it took several years, the tenacity of one of Pulitzer's reporters finally paid off, and the *World* published a story about Mr. Rockefeller, alleging that he had been a bigamist who had recently died out west. Neither John D. nor William Rockefeller deigned to respond to the story, either to confirm or deny it. Similarly, Pulitzer openly lampooned fellow club member J. P. Morgan for his 1894 gold deal with the government. Yet Pulitzer was able to become a member and maintain his membership, even though his newspaper was banned from many New York clubs and libraries.

There were many reasons why Pulitzer would have been considered an asset to the club and why Newton Finney, the club's founder, had been willing to give up his own shares to Joseph Pulitzer, while settling to split those of his brother-in-law, John E. du Bignon. First of all, Pulitzer was wealthy and well-known. He was clearly making efforts to move into more elite circles, joining such organizations as the Manhattan, Reform, Racquet, and American Yacht Clubs in New York, and taking time to attend elite social functions both in New York and in Bar Harbor, where he hobnobbed with the wealthy and would eventually purchase an estate called Chatwold. Certainly, neither of the

Pulitzers spurned elite society. And finally, Pulitzer espoused the philanthropic activities dear to the hearts of many of the nation's wealthier families.

Although he proclaimed himself to be a Democrat who championed the working class, he not infrequently sided with monied interests in economic issues. For example, he opposed the strikers during the Pullman Strike of 1894, and he joined his fellow Jekyll Islanders in supporting the gold standard and opposing free silver. As a consequence, William Jennings Bryan, who was a staunch supporter of free silver, attacked Pulitzer as one with too much money. "He used to be a socialist when he was poor," Bryan proclaimed in 1904, "but now that he has acquired wealth he is just like the rest of the capitalists." [3]

Not least among Pulitzer's assets among Jekyll Islanders, or at least in his initial acceptance in the club, was his wife. In his rise to fame and fortune, Joseph Pulitzer had the good sense to take time to woo and wed a Washington belle by the name of Kate Davis, a distant relation of Confederate president Jefferson Davis. Both the Pulitzers possessed a great personal charm. Kate was the daughter of a Georgetown judge, William Worthington Davis. Her astonishing beauty and intelligence not only had attracted Joseph Pulitzer, but also was a great value in New York society, which Kate enjoyed with unalloyed pleasure.

Unfortunately, Kate never enjoyed Jekyll Island, complaining constantly while there of the heat and sandflies. She never understood her husband's delight in the place. To Pulitzer it was a salubrious and tranquil refuge, where he felt better than he ever could in the northern winters that caused him such discomfort. On January 31, 1892, his son Joseph, not quite seven years old, wrote to his sister Lucille: "Papa has been ill with asthma but seems all right again now. He would go out if the weather were better but the wind is very cold and we have had snow and ice. Papa talks of going to Jackal [sic] Island and taking me with him but

Edith Pulitzer, on the day of her wedding to William S. Moore, seated beneath the portrait of her mother, Kate Davis Pulitzer. (Courtesy of Mrs. William C. Weir)

Three of Joseph Pulitzer's children. *Top to bottom,* Ralph, Herbert, and Constance. (Courtesy of Mrs. William C. Weir)

Mamma says she will not go. I don't quite know where it is, as it is not on the map but I believe it is in the Gulf of Mexico off Georgia U. S. America."[4]

Even though Joseph's geography was a little shaky, he had clearly perceived his father and mother's difference of opinion about Jekyll. Kate Pulitzer would never change her mind about the island. While her husband spent his winters there, sometimes in the company of one or more of his children, she preferred the comforts and amenities of Paris or voyages to more exotic places like Cairo. And although the Brunswick newspaper would announce on December 13, 1894, news of the impending arrival of Mr. and Mrs. Pulitzer and their daughters, the truth was that Pulitzer arrived accompanied by only his children, a friend, and a secretary, Alfred Butes. During this stay, when he rented the Maurice cottage on one of only two occasions it would be rented out, he would be joined by no fewer than nine other people but not by Kate.

One of those who came down that season was Col. Charles H. Jones, who arrived on February 4, 1895, to sign an agreement, witnessed by Butes and Harry D. Macdona and notarized by the club superintendent, Ernest Grob, that would give him management and control of the *Saint Louis Post-Dispatch* for five years at a salary of $10,000. According to the contract, Pulitzer also sold Jones one-sixth of the stock in the Pulitzer Publishing Company for $80,000 and agreed to elect him (Jones) director and president. Controversy would later surround this document, for the board of directors, apparently led by Pulitzer himself, refused to recognize it as valid, arguing that it was a personal agreement with Pulitzer, not legally binding to the Pulitzer Publishing Company. Jones felt he had been tricked by the newspaper magnate, and the two men began a name-calling contest in the press, with Pulitzer referring to Jones as a "wild ass colt" and Jones retorting that Pulitzer's editorial was "bumptious."[5] In the end, Jones petitioned the court to restrain the directors from interference with his management of the *Post-Dispatch* and their threats to dismiss him.

Despite the controversy Pulitzer apparently enjoyed his stay at Jekyll and determined that he needed his own cottage there where he could come and go as he liked. Thus he hired architect H. Edwards-Ficken to prepare a preliminary design for a new house. The architect made a trip to the island at Pulitzer's request to look over the site in March 1895 and subsequently produced a house plan for Pulitzer. Pulitzer, however, was not satisfied with the plans and decided not to engage Edwards-Ficken to do the job. Nevertheless, the architect sent him a bill for $792.05, including travel to Jekyll and time spent there, as well as $600.00 for the plans themselves. Pulitzer was outraged. He had earlier informed the architect that he "was uncertain whether he would build at all, that he wished you [the architect] to do nothing but think over the problem and make suggestions with a rough sketch." Pulitzer had originally agreed to pay only $100.00 for Edwards-Ficken's expenses. However, he ultimately did remit $192.05 to cover the architect's time and travel but refused adamantly to pay for the plans that, Pulitzer's secretary informed the hapless architect, "he never saw & never ordered, [and] which you had no right to make."[6]

Instead of building the house Edwards-Ficken had designed, Pulitzer decided in 1896 to purchase the home no longer used by Walter Rogers Furness. Two years later, however, Pulitzer had grown dissatisfied with the Furness cottage. Eyeing the fine new house next door recently completed by William Struthers, he decided that he, too, required a new residence. He did not, however, engage Edwards-Ficken to do the job. Instead, the contract went to the New York architect then involved in the extensive remodeling of the club house, Charles Alling Gifford. Gifford, who did fine work and whose fees were considerably more reasonable than those of Edwards-Ficken, designed for Pulitzer a stately brick house, unlike any of the other island resi-

Lucille Pulitzer, photographed here in June 1889, died in 1898, the year after Pulitzer constructed his house at Jekyll Island. (Courtesy of Joseph Pulitzer Jr.)

dences. It was, from the outset, eclectic in style, combining features from several types of architecture, including classical revival and Queen Anne.[7] In its final state, Pulitzer's house at Jekyll Island reflected his restless, never satisfied personality.

The contractor, W. H. Mann of the Stewart Contracting Company, came recommended by Henry Hyde, whose demanding personality lent additional weight to such a recommendation. "He is a very

thorough, conscientious man," Hyde wrote, "and I have had no occasion to find fault with him."[8] Coming from Hyde, who could find fault with almost anyone, including Pulitzer himself, this was high praise indeed. The house was built between October and December 1897 at a cost of approximately $15,000. One feature that was absolutely essential was soundproofing. Pulitzer suffered from a variety of ailments—rheumatism, failing eyesight, a nervous condition, and asthma—but none more so than hypersensitivity to sound. As a consequence specifications for the construction included various "deafening" techniques including a double thickness of "sheathing Quilt" between floors and walls, double layers of felt beneath floors, and double doors with a space between them for Pulitzer's bedroom.[9]

In 1898, not long after the completion of his cottage, Joseph Pulitzer suffered the loss of his daughter, Lucille, as Henry Hyde reported to his son from Jekyll Island on January 26: "I dined last night with Mr. Pulitzer. He is very much cut up on account of losing his daughter; she was the only one of the children who possessed his mind. Very confidentially, I think he feels his boy [Ralph] will never make a business man. I said all that I could to comfort him and came home early."[10]

In 1899 Pulitzer once again hired Gifford and the Stewart Contracting Company to add an addition to the house. Pulitzer was willing to spend only $5,000 for the addition and gave Gifford the go-ahead provided he could get it done for that amount. The estimate from the construction company came to $4,680, excluding gas, wiring, and heating.[11] Work on the new addition began in October 1899 and was to be completed for the 1900 season. Pulitzer was informed on November 21 that "Today the 'colored' carpenters went out on strike."[12] Nevertheless, despite the strike, the work, which included a six-room addition joined to the main house by a forty-two-foot glass corridor, was completed by December 27, with only finish work and decoration still required.[13] As it turned out, Pulitzer did not come to Jekyll for the 1900 season, and he did not see the new addition until 1901. When he arrived for the 1901 season, however, Rose McManus, Pulitzer's housekeeper, wrote to Kate Pulitzer that Mr. Pulitzer "was very much dissatisfied with [the] new addition to the house. The morning he arrived, he was so mad, that he danced a polka on the lawn but he is getting over it now."[14]

Still not satisfied, Pulitzer began planning for yet another addition to his house in 1903. The "principal object of the addition," as Pulitzer's secretary would later remind him, was "to enable the family to be with you."[15] In fact, he meant Kate, for only she refused to come down. She had come once in 1892, during Pulitzer's first visit to the island, but since that time she had adamantly refused. The children, on the other hand, came frequently. Pulitzer hoped that improvements in the cottage, including a special bedroom for Kate and a music room, at a cost of $11,500, would make it more attractive to her and lure her to spend the winters with them at Jekyll.

As it turned out, the plans alone apparently proved sufficient to bring her down. The editor himself debarked on the island, with a party of eight, including two of his children and Dr. Hosmer, on January 19, 1904. On March 1, Kate wired him of her impending arrival. Her message was rather flirtatious in tone: "Don't worry . . . have arranged to go and going with pleasure. I leave Thursday/ have

Joseph Pulitzer added a new wing to his house in 1899. (Courtesy of Jekyll Island Museum)

arranged everything/ expect you to welcome me with Joy or will leave on first raft." [16] She registered on Friday, March 4, and on the following Monday, Brunswick contractors Bowen and Thomas accepted a contract to build the addition, which would almost double the size of the original cottage. [17] The final specifications had apparently been delayed until Kate had an opportunity to look them over and give her approval. But her interest in Jekyll was short-lived, and she would not return again until 1906. Even then, she could not bear it for long. Back in New York after scarcely two weeks with her husband, she complained: "It is snowing, snowing, snowing, and looks as though it would never stop . . . My only consolation is that there are no sand flies." [18]

Pulitzer consoled himself in Kate's absence with his children's presence, his morning horseback rides, and carriage rides in the afternoon. Jean Struthers, the daughter of William Struthers, Pulitzer's next-door neighbor on Jekyll, joined him on occasion for early-morning rides along Jekyll's moss-hung bridle paths. In January 1904, she wrote him a note thanking him for the bouquet of "beautiful violets" he had sent her. Their morning rides continued throughout the season, and in February 1904 she wrote another note commiserating with him about the "work and telegrams that worry you." On a more positive note she added, "And with pleasure I will ride with you any day next week." [19] Perhaps it was, after all, news of these early-morning rides rather than the plans for the new addition that brought Kate hurrying to Jekyll "with pleasure." But Kate had little to fear from Jean Struthers, who was no doubt busily planning her wedding with Henry Francis Sears for September 14 of that same year. Nevertheless, Kate had little tolerance for any hint of flirtation between her husband and any other woman. Although she spent as much time away from him as possible, or so it seemed, she teased him nonetheless with her jealousy. After her return from Jekyll in 1906, she

Joseph Pulitzer, *third from left,* seated between Andrew Carnegie, *right,* and Frederick Gilbert Bourne, *second from left,* enjoys a dinner on Jekyll Island. (Courtesy of Jekyll Island Museum)

wrote him: "Do you miss us I wonder? Do you ever wish you could hear the rustle of a feminine skirt or feel the touch of a woman's hand on your head? If you do, be sure it is mine or beware!"[20] And she tantalized him with such statements as "I wonder if you will like to hear that I miss you & should like to make you a call at Jekyll if I had a wishing carpet & if I could be guaranteed against sand flies."[21]

The new addition, more than twice as expensive as the previous one, included in addition to Kate's new bedroom and the music room a porte cochere, two additional bedrooms, and a billiard room, to be attached to the main house. The original facade designed by Gifford would have to be elongated to accommodate the new rooms, thus throwing the dimensions of the house somewhat out of proportion, though they added to a more symmetrical effect. Efforts were made to have the material of the addition harmonize with those of the rest of the house in such a way that it would seem to be part of the original structure. The result, overall, was a large, meandering, albeit comfortable structure.

In general, Pulitzer seemed to get along well enough with other members of the Jekyll Island Club, participating in their meetings and joining them for dinner. However, on one occasion, at least, he raised the ire of other members by trying to hire away from the club Ernest Grob, its competent and reliable superintendent, for his own purposes—to take charge of his houses at Bar Harbor, in London, and at Jekyll. He had offered Grob an annual salary of $5,000, which was well in excess of what he was currently being paid by the club. At that point in time, Grob was also a bit disgruntled that the executive committee had taken from him the responsibility for hiring the chef and head waiter, a move that he thought undermined his authority. Frederic Baker wrote to Henry Hyde expressing his annoyance with Pulitzer, whom he uncharacteristically labeled "the dirty Jew," and proposing to raise Grob's salary to $300 a month and give him au-

thority over the hiring for the positions in question.[22] Evidently, whatever the club offered was acceptable, for Grob remained in his position for another thirty-two years.

On another occasion Pulitzer annoyed Henry Hyde by failing to pay promptly and in full for the ten stalls for which he had contracted in the new club stables, constructed in 1897. In March 1899, he had still not paid the balance of $617 he owed. Only through the intervention of Ernest Grob was the amount finally paid in April 1899.[23]

Pulitzer continued to come to Jekyll without his wife, Kate, for the most part, until 1909, when he spent his last three-month visit there, from January 10 until April 8. He was accompanied by his usual large retinue, including his youngest son, Herbert, and a governess, Elizabeth Keelan. Pulitzer had arrived that year for the first time in his new yacht, the *Liberty*, which he had purchased during the previous year. Upon hearing of the vessel, Kate had written to her husband, "I am more than glad to hear that the yacht is a success. I hope you will pass many days of comfort and happiness on her."[24] Her words were prophetic, for, except for the final visit to Jekyll, he spent most of his remaining days aboard the *Liberty*.

During these final years of his life, Pulitzer all but turned over the management of his newspapers to his sons Ralph and Joe. He replied to a woman seeking a job on the *World* that he no longer handled such matters, describing himself as "an invalid spending most of the time at sea in order to avoid the worries that would reach me if I were on shore."[25] Indeed, the vessel was for him a moving home where he could continually escape the bad weather to which he frequently attributed bad health. He was familiar with every nook and cranny of the yacht, and, therefore, in his blindness felt more comfortable at sea than on land. In March 1910, he hired a "literary companion," who would be a reader and conversationalist, but unfortunately

Joseph Pulitzer's yacht, *Liberty,* where he spent most of the last years of his life and where he died, en route to Jekyll Island, in October 1911. (Courtesy of the Mariners' Museum, Newport News, Virginia)

the poor man contracted smallpox, and the yacht had to dock in Gibraltar where Pulitzer had it fumigated and himself vaccinated.[26]

He planned one more visit to Jekyll. However, aboard the *Liberty,* en route to Jekyll Island, during a six-day stopover in Charleston harbor to wait out a hurricane warning, Joseph Pulitzer died from heart disease on October 29, 1911.[27] Kate, who had rushed from New York when she heard of his illness, and his son Herbert were at his side. His oldest son, Ralph, was the only one of Pulitzer's children to take any interest whatever in the club, and his interest was fleeting. In the same will that founded the Columbia University School of Journalism and the famed Pulitzer Prizes, Pulitzer had left one share of Jekyll stock to Ralph and one share to Joseph. The latter chose not to become a member of the club. Ralph, however, allowed his name to be put forward for membership, a mere formality as he virtually inherited his father's place on the club roster. He remained a member, however, for only a little over two years, resigning in 1914 and selling his father's house to Buffalo millionaire John J. Albright for $10,000.[28]

The Albright Years

John J. Albright, who purchased the Pulitzer house fully furnished on February 25, 1914,[29] was born into a well-to-do family at Buchanan, Virginia, near Natural Springs, on January 18, 1848. He was descended from Andrew Albright, a gunsmith who supplied arms to the troops of the Continental army, and a convert to the Moravian faith who had come to America from Germany in 1750.[30] John J. Albright's father, Joseph, was an iron manufacturer and eventually president of the First National Bank and coal agent for the Delaware and Hudson Canal Company and the Delaware, Lackawanna and Western Railroad. The younger Albright was educated at Williston Academy and Rensselaer Polytechnic Institute, from which he graduated with a degree in mining engineering in 1868.[31]

Three years later, following in his father's footsteps, he entered a business venture in wholesale coal with Andrew Langdon, first in Harrisburg, then in Lewiston, Pennsylvania. In 1873 Albright and Langdon became agents for the Philadelphia and Reading Coal and Iron Company and moved to Washington, D.C., where Albright also began dabbling in real estate.[32] There he wooed and won Langdon's sister Harriet, the daughter of J. LeDroit Langdon. She became his wife on December 4, 1873.

The children followed not long thereafter, with Raymond King's birth in 1875, Ruth's in 1879, and Langdon's in 1880. Albright's marriage to Harriet Langdon brought him into close contact with Amzi Barber, who had wed Harriet's sister, Julia Louise Langdon, as his second wife in 1871. Barber was a professor of natural philosophy at Howard University at the time but resigned his position to enter the real estate business with Albright. The two men were also briefly partners in the asphalt business at a time when paved streets were becoming essential in American cities, and they participated in the paving of Washington, Scranton, and Buffalo. Barber continued in the business even after Albright turned to other ventures, and by 1896 the Barber Asphalt Pavement Company had surfaced half of all the paved streets in the country, including Washington's Pennsylvania Avenue.[33]

Albright's coal interests, however, led him in other directions. When in 1883 the Philadelphia and Reading Coal and Iron Company established direct rail communication with Buffalo to ship their coal west, Albright moved his family to Buffalo to

At the insistence of his family, John J. Albright purchased the Pulitzer Cottage in February 1914. (Everett Collection, Coastal Georgia Historical Society)

oversee the operation, forming there a double partnership with T. Guilford Smith of Buffalo.[34] Albright devised a scheme of shipping anthracite to the western states and bringing the coal cars home filled with grain, a venture that netted him $100,000 in his first year alone. His father made the prophetic comment, "You will die poor, because this money came too easily."[35] Indeed, Albright did so well within the first five years of these ventures that he decided to retire and take his family on a fourteen-month tour of Europe and Egypt in 1888 when he was only forty years old.[36]

It did not take him long, however, to realize that retirement was not for him, not when there were so

Susan Gertrude Fuller, the second wife of John J. Albright, about 1891, when she was still a student at Smith College. (Smith College Archives)

many ways of making money in a rapidly expanding country. He turned his attention to another growing need in America—the providing of electricity. In 1896 Albright joined Jekyll Island Club member Edmund Hayes and others to construct a hydroelectric development on the Madison River in Montana. Two years later they carried out a similar plan on the Hudson River near Mechanicsville. These two projects were but preliminary experiments for their real goal—to harness the power of Niagara Falls. As one company prospectus had stated it: "Here is power, almost illimitable; constantly wasted, yet never diminished—constantly exerted, yet never exhausted; gazed upon, admired, wondered at, but never hitherto controlled."[37] It was irresistible to Albright and his partners. Work began on the powerhouse of Ontario Power Company of Niagara Falls, located just below Horseshoe Falls on the Canadian side, in 1902.[38] By 1906 the company was delivering electric power as far east as Syracuse. Although the passage of the Burton Bill in 1906 limited the diversion of water from the river and the importation of power, thus curtailing some of the company's activities, Albright never lost his strength of vision and merely encouraged the harnessing of other waterways to provide the needed power.

Vision and foresight were always Albright's greatest virtues as a businessman, failing him only once toward the end of his life. Anticipating the nation's growing need for steel at the turn of the century and acting as an agent for the Lackawanna Iron and Steel Company, he began quietly to purchase land around Buffalo for the purpose of constructing a new plant for what was to become the Lackawanna Steel Company, which later merged with Bethlehem Steel. Edmund Hayes, who had been at Jekyll when the project was conceived, joined in with relish when he returned home, and both he and Albright were named to the company's board of directors.[39]

Not long after returning from his extended tour of Europe, Albright had been invited to become a member of the Jekyll Island Club in 1890 by his partner Edmund Hayes, who had been a charter member. But John and Harriet Albright came down only once after he joined the club, in 1893. Amzi Barber and his wife, Julia, visited as well with a party of ten aboard the steam yacht *Sapphire* as the guests of Albright and Hayes. Barber would himself join the club in 1901.

Life seemed good for Albright, and his business ventures were thriving. However, with the premature death of his wife in 1895, he suddenly found his life at loose ends. Left with three minor children, though his oldest son, Raymond, was already twenty, he was especially concerned about his daughter Ruth, who was only sixteen and at an age when the companionship and mothering of an older woman is critical in a young girl's life. He therefore wrote to Smith College officials, asking them to suggest a young woman as a companion for Ruth. As luck would have it, they recommended a recent graduate, Susan Gertrude Fuller, of Lancaster, Massachusetts, who two years later would become his wife.[40] She is described by one of her classmates as "a quiet soft-voiced girl, who went through college doing what was expected of her." Her graduation photograph in 1891 reveals the pleasant face of a rather timid-looking young woman, who apparently would blossom with self-confidence in later years. Her friend remembered her as a woman of "wide and varied interests" with "sympathy, good taste, and . . . [a] keen sense of . . . responsibility." She was admired in later years for "her sincerity and friendliness and the same unaffected simplicity that characterized her in her younger days."[41]

Although she was younger than her employer by more than twenty years (he was forty-seven, and she was twenty-six), Susan Fuller and John Albright were married on March 23, 1897. The marriage would last more than thirty years, until her death in 1928. The couple spent their honeymoon at Jekyll Island, checking into room 37 of the club house on March 27. Remembering the pleasures of the island during that honeymoon stay, the Albrights began to think in 1900 of spending the entire winter at Jekyll with their rapidly growing family. On November 18, Susan Albright wrote to Charlotte Maurice asking her advice about accommodations. They wanted to come to the club about the end of February, she indicated, for a stay of about six weeks, "taking with us Ruth and the three babies. Do you think it would be possible for us to get an apartment and if so are the apartments suited to the needs of such a family? You realize what the demands of such a nurseryful are and that we would need rather commodious quarters and also would wish to feel assured that we were not encroaching upon the comfort of others by being in too close proximity."[42] At the time, however, few apartments were

Interior of the Albrights' apartment, # 3, in the club annex. (Courtesy of John J. Albright)

available, and the Albrights, apparently unable to arrange suitable accommodations, did not come to Jekyll that season.

With the construction of the club annex in 1902, their problems seemed to be solved. The couple purchased annex apartment 3 and began making annual visits to the island that were to last for the next thirty years. Their first recorded stay in their new apartment began on February 21, 1902. Even with the greater space an apartment could provide, the quarters in the club annex became increasingly crowded over the next several years, not only with Susan and John Albright and the children from his earlier marriage, but also with the offspring their own marriage had produced, including

The Albright children and their coachman, Keyes, arrive in Brunswick. *Left to right,* Nancy, Keyes, Susan, Elizabeth, and Fuller. (Courtesy of John J. Albright)

John Joseph Jr. (1898), Elizabeth (1899), Fuller (1900), Nancy (1905), and Susan (1907). When all their children came with them to Jekyll, a relatively rare occurrence, a second apartment or additional rooms were always necessary. Thus when the Pulitzer cottage, with its twenty-six rooms, became available in 1914, the children were ecstatic, and, at their pleading, Albright did not hesitate for long before purchasing it. He kept the annex apartment until 1917, however, when he sold it to Walter B. James, soon to become the club's president.

Life settled into a comfortable routine for the Albrights in their new cottage, and a family descendant described Albright's typical day at Jekyll: "After the family had gathered for a large, leisurely breakfast, Albright would sit for a while in the sun parlor, reading his newspapers and watching the birds. And then he might bicycle to the beach or get into a game of doubles on Frank Gould's indoor tennis court. In the afternoon, a drive along the shell trails or a game of golf was always followed by a lengthy tea, accompanied by good conversation. After dinner, to which they were conveyed by the Club carriage in bad weather, the men generally went to the smoking room for real talks, or Albright would organize a rubber of bridge."[43] For the most part, the Albrights enjoyed their family and the simple pleasures of Jekyll, and Albright did not, according to his grandson, mingle much with hard-driving businessmen like J. P. Morgan and George

Fisher Baker, whom he found generally uninteresting. In speaking of one Jekyll family he contended "that he felt they led dull lives, not necessarily because they had so much money, but because they did not use it wisely for the enrichment of life. Therefore, he felt somewhat apart from many of his fellow millionaires." [44] He spent much of his time relaxing and bird-watching in the "corridor" that Joseph Pulitzer had built to connect the two parts of his house.

His wife, Susan, was much interested in literature, and it may have been as a result of her tastes that the Albrights struck up a friendship with the poet laureate of England, Alfred Noyes, and his wife, who visited them at Jekyll in March 1914. During Noyes's stay, Albright "took him on a round of visits" to introduce him to William Rockefeller and other Jekyll Islanders who were at the club. As they made their way around the island, they came across a pond infested with alligators, where Albright is said to have pointed out "with some glee" their "striking resemblance" to some of the millionaires. [45] Susan, the youngest of the Albright children, remembered Noyes as a man who was not only "very British and read poetry in the evenings" but who also "was nice to children, which is the way I assessed guests." [46]

Albright's philosophy of wealth was that one must be its good steward, and he instilled into his children a sense that "money was a responsibility, never something to be used ostentatiously." [47] In fact, while many Jekyll Islanders may have lived extravagantly, at least away from the island, many shared his view that money brought with it responsibility, and their philanthropies had an enormous impact on the charities, museums, and educational institutions of the nation. One Buffalo reporter compared Albright to Lorenzo de' Medici, for he "gathered the beautiful things of the world about him," and his "aestheticism overflowed to give the city its noted temple of art." [48] He was referring specifically to the construction of the Albright Art

Gallery dedicated in 1905 in Buffalo's Delaware Park, for the construction of which Albright gave more than $1 million. Among his many notable benefactions were important contributions for the construction in 1897 of Welcome Hall, a community settlement house in Buffalo built in memory of the first Mrs. Albright, as well as liberal gifts to Rensselaer Polytechnic Institute and the University of Buffalo. As he had honored his first wife, so he honored his second, with generous gifts to her alma mater, Smith College, to which he gave $9,000 toward the construction of Seelye Hall and $60,000 toward the endowment of the L. Clark Seelye Chair of Classics during the academic year 1899–1900, $6,700 to endow a scholarship in 1913, and various other donations that resulted in enriching the scholarship fund. During fall term 1900, a residence hall, named Albright House in honor of the college's benefactor, was completed. [49] In 1929 the University of Buffalo awarded Albright the Chancellor's Medal for his contributions to culture and education in that city.

Albright's generosity extended as well to friends in distress, and he was not infrequently drawn into various business enterprises to assist them. One such effort to help would have a dire consequence in that it would ultimately result in the loss of his fortune in the late 1920s before the depression began. One of those he had sought to aid was his brother-in-law by his first marriage and fellow Jekyll Island Club member Amzi Barber, who had incorporated the Locomobile Company in 1899. According to Birge Albright, Barber was in debt by 1903 "to the extent of half a million dollars, and to keep the Locomobile Company afloat, he surrendered two real estate companies to Albright, who agreed to endorse $300,000 worth of Locomobile commercial paper and give Barber an annuity of $12,000. Albright made this agreement over the strenuous objections of several of his friends, who predicted that he would regret it." [50] He also paid the remaining $100,000 Barber still owed for his

The coachman, Keyes, *right,* with Susan Albright, mounted on the horse, and Nancy Albright on a bicycle.
(Courtesy of John J. Albright)

$300,000 yacht, the *Lorena,* and although Albright became the yacht's nominal owner as a consequence, he still allowed Barber its full use. Albright would later offer it for sale without success to the King of Portugal, the Russian navy, and the German Kaiser and would eventually sell it in 1906 to George J. Gould—a fellow Jekyll member.[51] When Barber died in 1909, Albright became the primary owner of the Locomobile Company as a consequence of the 1903 agreement. He allowed Barber's son-in-law to remain president of the company until his death in 1915, when he made his own son, Raymond Albright, president. Unfortunately, the young man would preside over the company's failing years as the expensive Locomobiles progressively lost ground to the cheaper vehicles being produced by Henry Ford.

A second person whom Albright helped was one of his young business associates, William H. Gratwick, to whom he allegedly lent more than a million dollars.[52] The young man invested the money in the Terminal Properties Company of Cleveland, an enterprise of O. P. and M. J. Van Sweringen. When the Locomobile Company began to fail, Albright, desperately in need of money, apparently called in the loan, but Gratwick was in no position to repay it in cash. Instead, he made payment in Terminal Properties Company stock, which Albright sold back to the Van Sweringens for $800,000. The amount would be paid in annual installments and would represent the bulk of Albright's income for the rest of his life.[53]

When Alfred Noyes visited Albright in Buffalo in 1927, the latter had already been forced to curtail his expenses, and Noyes found him "living, with the simplicity of a Thoreau, in a small frame house."[54] It was a real comedown for a family accustomed to a life eased by five maids, two cooks, a laundress, seven gardeners, and Keyes, their coachman, or in later years, Dumbleton, the chauffeur.[55] Susan Albright recalled her father's financial collapse: "Father put good money after bad, and with

his age it was VERY damaging to him. . . . Moving out of the house was so SAD, and that was before Mother died."[56]

In their days of plenty, the Albrights had not only their mansion in Buffalo and their cottage at Jekyll Island but also a chalet at Wilmurt Lake in the Adirondacks, where several other Jekyll Islanders, among them his partner Edmund Hayes, also had cottages and where Albright loved to fish for brook trout. Still feeling secure and comfortable in his wealth in 1912, Albright took his family on another grand tour of Europe where they "took over a whole floor of a pension in the Swiss Alps, and the two youngest children stayed there with 'Fräulein' [their German governess], while the others took trips into the Dolomites, Austria, and Germany in the Locomobile."[57]

But in the late 1920s John J. Albright's world came crashing down. Not only did he lose his fortune, he also lost his beloved wife Susan. He and Susan made their last trip to Jekyll together in March 1928 before her death in Baltimore on June 19, 1928, at only forty years of age. Ernest Grob, writing to Marian Maurice, characterized her death as "a great loss to Mr. Albright" and wondered "if it will keep them from Jekyl."[58]

There is no doubt that his wife's death and his financial setback forced him to rethink his use of the Jekyll Cottage. In 1930 Albright hired the Buffalo architectural firm of Edward B. Green & Sons to draw up plans to subdivide his cottage into six apartments. However, the scheme was never carried out, for Albright was not well. After undergoing an intestinal operation in July 1931, he grew progressively worse for the next six weeks and finally died in Buffalo on August 20, at the age of eighty-three.

After Albright's death, the taxes on the Jekyll Island property went unpaid for 1932 and 1933, and the state levied $1,297.71 against the property on February 8, 1934. On March 6, the Jekyll Island Club, the highest bidder in a sheriff's sale, purchased the property for $1,357.18.[59] There is no record of the Albrights' cottage being used after 1932.

During the war years, the Albright cottage, like most of the others, stood completely neglected. Susan Albright Reed, who had managed to visit the island with her husband during World War II, provides a rare glimpse of what it was like at the time. "I remember every detail of the house," she writes. "The last time I saw it was during the war when it and others had been abandoned,—windows broken, vines growing into the rooms, some furniture dilapidated, but the wisteria outside my room more beautiful than ever. The Navy had taken it over and gave my husband a car, complete with large gun, to go anywhere he wished except to the beach which was being closely guarded. . . . We went all through our house, and it was one of the saddest days of my life,—equal to the day that our house in Buffalo came under the auction gavel."[60] The family nevertheless recalled their Jekyll days with fondness. In fact, Susan's sister, Nancy Albright Hurd, returned for a brief time in the early 1980s to serve as part-time curator for the Jekyll Island Museum, though her family's cottage had by then disappeared.

When the state of Georgia acquired Jekyll Island in 1947, the cottage was still standing. However, a fire damaged the interior in 1951, and as funds for restoration and repair were unavailable, the Jekyll Island Authority decided on June 23 to demolish it.[61] Thus today one can only imagine the rambling house beneath the magnificent live oak trees before which one of America's most famous newsmen once "danced a polka" on the lawn.

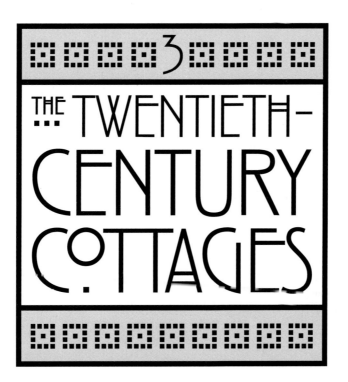

3

THE TWENTIETH-CENTURY COTTAGES

MISTLETOE

Owners: Henry Kirke Porter, 1900–1921; Porter Estate, 1921–24; John Claflin, 1924–38; Elizabeth Claflin, 1938–40; Jekyll Island Club, 1940–47

Constructed: 1900

Architecture: Shingle style (gambrel-roofed variant)

Architect: Charles Alling Gifford

The Porter Years

The first owner of Mistletoe Cottage was locomotive manufacturer Henry Kirke Porter. He was born in Concord, New Hampshire, on November 24, 1840, the son of George Porter and his wife, Phoebe Clarissa Ayer. The father was a hardware merchant in Concord and eventually a founder of Dilworth, Porter & Company, a Pittsburgh firm that made railroad spikes. Young Porter graduated from Brown University in 1860 and began to study for the ministry at Newton Theological Seminary in 1861. Unlike most Jekyll Islanders, who tended to be Episcopalians or Presbyterians, Porter was a Baptist.

Mistletoe Cottage is shown here closed for the winter season. (Everett Collection, Coastal Georgia Historical Society)

Henry Kirke Porter had studied to be a Baptist preacher but gave up the ministry in favor of business. (Archives of Industrial Society, University Library System, University of Pittsburgh)

Throughout his life he would remain extremely active in the Baptist Church, serving in such capacities as president of the American Baptist Home Mission Society (1895–97) and of the American Baptist Missionary Union (1901–4). But he would never be a minister.

He interrupted his theological studies to enlist as a private in the Forty-fifth Massachusetts volunteers during the Civil War, rising to the rank of corporal before he was mustered out in July 1863. Although at the close of the war he resumed his studies for the ministry at Rochester Theological Seminary, it took only a year for him to decide that he was better suited to the business world. Returning to Pittsburgh he formed an association with John Y. Smith, and the two men founded the firm of Smith & Porter, which would later become Porter, Bell & Company in 1871, H. K. Porter & Company in 1878, and finally the H. K. Porter Company in 1899. The firm specialized first in light locomotives, later adding heavy engines to its inventory. By the time of Porter's death in 1921 it was making some six hundred locomotives annually, sold not only in the United States but throughout the world.

Porter was especially known for his progressive views on the relationship between employer and employee. He pioneered such revolutionary ideas as a system of profit sharing with his workers, group insurance for his employees, and a workday in his plant reduced from ten to nine hours. Needless to say, he was popular with his workers.[1]

Porter's wife, Annie DeCamp Hegeman, was four years older than he and a thirty-nine-year-old widow with two children when she married him on November 23, 1875. She was born on May 27, 1836, a member of an old Huguenot family. Previously married to a widower, George Rutgers Hegeman, on October 9, 1856, she had two children by her first marriage—Annie May Hegeman, born May 9, 1859, and Joseph Perrot Hegeman, born July 17, 1862.[2] All accounts of Annie Porter suggest that she had an intelligence to match her husband's and that she was an attractive and highly cultivated woman. An artist herself, she was a founder in 1891 of the Shinnecock Hills Art Academy, one of the first art programs in the United States to encourage open-air painting and the impressionist movement. A contemporary account that described her as "brilliant" went on to elaborate: "She is an exceedingly intelligent woman with more brains than most people are endowed with; a sparkling conversationalist, a highly talented artist, and one of the most delightful of hostesses."[3] Certainly her social talents were important assets in the Jekyll Island cottage colony, and one of her lawn parties at Mistletoe has been caught by a photographer's camera. Unlike her Baptist husband, Annie Porter was a member of the Protestant Episcopal church.

When Henry Porter first visited Jekyll Island with his wife on March 27, 1890, as the guest of club president Henry Howland, he was fifty years old and at the very height of his career. Clearly club life pleased him, for the following year, 1891, he allowed his name to be put forward for membership. On that first visit they were joined two days after their arrival by Mrs. Porter's daughter, Annie May, who often vacationed with them on the island and who was adjudged by a contemporary to be one who was "fond of society and goes out a great deal."[4] The Porters had no children of their own, though Henry Porter welcomed his wife's son and daughter with apparent pleasure.

At first the Porters rented rooms in the club house, but as time went on they wanted more space for their lengthy stays on the island. First, they sought an apartment, as Ernest Grob makes clear in a letter in 1898 to Sans Souci apartment owner Julia Anderson: "Should you decide to rent, Mrs. H. K. Porter will be glad to take it; she has already spoken to me about an apartment, should one be vacant."[5] But by 1899 Porter was evidently already considering the possibility of constructing his own cottage, as the *Brunswick Call* reported on April 6, 1899: "By the opening of next season it is very probable that three elegant new cottages will be ready for their owners. It is stated that Cornelius N. Bliss . . . N. R. [sic] Fairbanks [sic] of Chicago, and H. K. Porter, of Pittsburgh, will have cottages erected on the island during the summer."[6] In fact, N. K Fairbank had long since constructed his own house on Jekyll in 1890, and Cornelius Bliss would settle for an apartment in the newly constructed club annex in 1902. Only the Porters were seriously considering building at the time. During the 1900 season, however, their cottage was still only a dream, and the Porters spent their winter vacation in the club cottage (see Du Bignon Cottage chapter).[7] By early April, however, Henry Porter had begun to look about for a suitable lot on which to build. Eventually he fixed upon lot 7, owned by George Bleistein

of New York, south of the club house, and next door to the McKay cottage. About April 19 or shortly thereafter, he acquired the lease from Bleistein for $2,500.[8]

Porter lost no time in engaging the New York architect Charles Alling Gifford, who had recently designed the Pulitzer Cottage, the new club stables, and the Sans Souci on Jekyll and who came highly recommended. By June of 1900 plans were evidently complete, for the architect and his contractor were making arrangements to come to the island in mid-July to begin construction.[9] By August work had begun, as was announced by the *Brunswick Evening Call* on August 7, 1900. Although the cottage is sometimes described as Dutch Colonial, its side-facing gambrel roof is not typical of the style at the turn of the century when front-facing gambrels were most common. It is far more typical of the gambrel-roofed variant of shingle-style architecture, although this type as well tended more often than not to have front-facing gambrels. Nevertheless, the dramatic use of windows, the wall-cladding of continuous wooden shingles, and the extensive use of porches relate it far more closely to shingle style. The gambrel-roofed design of the cottage was distinctive and different from that of any other house built on the island during the club era. Shingle-style houses were never very common in the South, and a contractor from New York, William J. McDermott, was brought in to supervise the job. By November builders were working on the interior trim and the primer coats of paint.[10] Although there was still much detail work to be done and some of the materials, among them balusters for the porch railing and doors, had not yet arrived, the three-story cottage with its fourteen rooms and five baths was nearing completion.

By the end of December the house, which had cost about $28,000 to build, seems to have been virtually finished, though the Porters still had before them the responsibility of decorating and furnishing it.[11] Crates of goods to outfit the cottage had

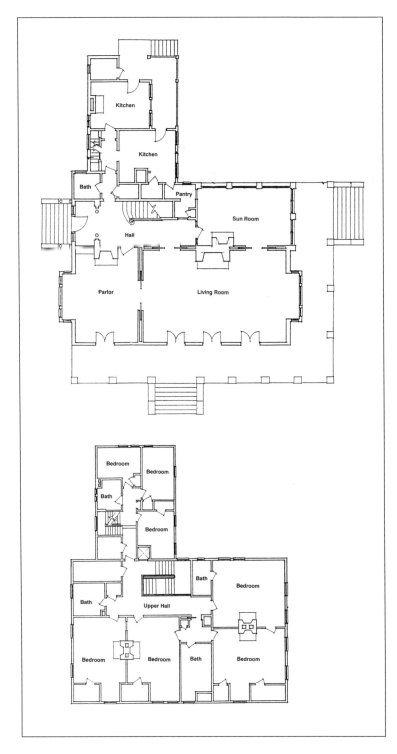

Charles Alling Gifford, architect who designed Mistletoe, Pulitzer Cottage, Sans Souci, and the club annex. Gifford also remodelled the club house.

Mistletoe, first-floor and second-floor plans. (Based on plans in the Jekyll Island Museum)

begun to arrive from England and France by January 20, 1901, but the Porters still had not put in an appearance.[12] When they did arrive, even though the structure was complete, they seem to have followed Ernest Grob's advice and used the club cottage for the 1901 season to "let the new house dry out thoroughly" and to take time to decide how to furnish it.[13] Thus the first time they formally registered for a stay in their new cottage, which they named Mistletoe, was on February 11, 1902.

In the fall of the year that Henry and Annie Porter settled into their new winter home on Jekyll Island, he was elected to the United States Congress from the thirty-first Pennsylvania district. He served only one term, however, 1903–5, and was not reelected thereafter. Even so, the Porters had evidently enjoyed their stay in Washington, for they maintained a home there from 1903 on, as well as a residence said to be "lovely as a dream"[14] in the Oakland section of Pittsburgh and a summer home in Southampton, Long Island.

Porter's public service was not limited to his brief foray into politics. He sought to put his Christian ideals into practice as one of the founders of the Young Men's Christian Association, serving as YMCA president in Pittsburgh and on the international committee of the YMCA from 1875 to 1921. He also held a position on the board of directors for the Western Pennsylvania Institute for the Blind in 1904. Porter had a certain luster in the academic world as well, having met with considerable success as a student at Brown University, where he was elected to Phi Beta Kappa. He was appointed one of the original trustees of the Carnegie Institute (1890–1921) and served as a trustee of his alma mater from 1899 to 1921.

The Porters came to Jekyll Island almost every year from the time they built their cottage until Henry Porter's death in 1921. It was their practice to arrive in mid to late February and enjoy the very height of the club season. They were common figures there for more than twenty years, greeting

Annie Porter, seated, *center,* was well known as an intelligent woman and a genial hostess. Here she entertains with a lawn party at Mistletoe. (Lanier Book, 1911)

people at the dock and seeing them off and entertaining frequently with delightful teas at Mistletoe. In rare seasons when they did not come to Jekyll, they permitted Superintendent Grob to offer their cottage for rental, as he did to Sen. Nelson W. Aldrich in 1912. "I am indeed very glad that you have joined the club, and hope that you will pass some of the winter here. . . . Mr. H. K. Porter and his family are abroad for the winter, [and] I thought their house would be just about right for you. It is one of the most comfortable places on the island, and near enough to the Club so that you could have your meals brought over, in case of inclement weather, no [or?] if you were indisposed."[15] Aldrich's first trip to Jekyll Island had been in November 1910, when he had organized there a secret meeting of bankers and politicians disguised as duck hunters to put together the so-called Aldrich plan, which became a forerunner of the nation's Federal Reserve System. He had been so taken with the place that he decided not long thereafter to become a member.

Most winters, however, the Porters used the cottage themselves. They registered as usual on February 2, 1921, with her daughter for their annual Jekyll vacation, but upon their return to their home in Washington, D.C., Henry Porter was taken ill and died on April 10. With his death, his wife, Annie, never returned to Jekyll Island, and the cottage was held by the Porter estate until it was sold in 1924 to John Claflin from Brooklyn, New York. Annie Porter outlived her husband by only four years, dying at her home at 1600 I Street, Washington, D.C., on February 12, 1925.

The Claflin Years

John Claflin, who bought the Porter cottage for $6,000 in February 1924, was one of the original members of the Jekyll Island Club.[16] In fact, his association with Jekyll went back even further, for when John Eugene du Bignon decided to purchase the various parcels of Jekyll Island that had been sold off during the Civil War and resell the entire island at a profit, John Claflin was one of those who considered buying it (see du Bignon Cottage chapter). He came down to look over the island and do a little hunting with his partner, Edward E. Eames, in 1885. Claflin apparently had hesitations from the beginning about acquiring the island for himself, however, and when the idea of founding the Jekyll Island Club was broached, he readily released du Bignon from the sale and agreed to become a member of the club instead.[17] In fact, it was he who lent the money to du Bignon to make the initial purchase. He would be joined in the club by his younger brother, Arthur Brigham Claflin, a banker who was also a member from 1889 to 1904.

Claflin, born in Brooklyn, New York, on July 24, 1850, the son of Horace Brigham Claflin and his wife, Agnes Phipps Sanger, was a relatively young man of thirty-five and still a bachelor at the time he first came to Jekyll. Described as "short, slender, gentle-mannered but energetic," Claflin had established a reputation for himself as a noted adventurer and, according to the New York Times, "would have been an explorer had he followed his real inclinations."[18] In fact, he had been a world traveler in his youth, not only to Europe and Asia when he was only nineteen and just after his graduation with honors from the College of the City of New York, but also to the jungles of South America where, in 1877, he "penetrated . . . into the wild places of the world, in desert lands and among savages."[19] Trekking across Peru in 1877, he had made his way to the mouth of the Amazon, "travelling the most of the way by mule or canoe. The route he followed has seldom been traversed in its entirety by a white man, and many efforts were made to dissuade him from tempting its perils, . . . but he was not to be stopped." When he could not go to more exotic places, he would spend his two months' vacation hunting grizzly bears in the Rockies.[20]

The more practical world of business won out over other considerations, however, and after his first year of travel in 1869 he entered his father's wholesale dry goods business, H. B. Claflin & Company, which had grown from a rural general store in Milford, Massachusetts, to a multimillion-dollar corporation by the time of the Civil War. John's two older brothers, Horace Jr. and William, had barely survived the war, both dying at age twenty-six in 1866 and 1871 respectively. Thus the pressures on their brother John to take over the family business were increased, a fact he makes clear in a published letter to his children on July 24, 1918: "When I entered college I intended to study law but the death of my older brothers before my graduation made it seem my duty to enter my father's business and to help him as much as I could." [21] Claflin had been a good student, educated in the public schools and at the City College of New York, and he, like Porter, was elected to Phi Beta Kappa.

Prior to the Civil War, the Claflin firm had done a brisk trade in the South, and it was considerably hurt by the loss of that trade during the war. Nevertheless, it was for many years the largest firm of its kind in the world, with annual sales at $100 million. John Claflin was made a partner in the firm in 1873 when he was only twenty-two years old. He was described by financial analyst R. G. Dun at the time as "an honest young man" with "only slight experience in bus[iness]." The firm itself Dun assessed as a "lively good active house doing a very large business, the largest in the city," and "worth about ten million dollars." [22]

In November 1885, just before the founding of the Jekyll Island Club, H. B. Claflin died, and his son John was catapulted to the position of leadership.[23] In 1890 he undertook the major step of reorganizing the firm as the H. B. Claflin Company, but that was only the beginning of his efforts to establish a mercantile empire in the United States. After the panic of 1893 and the years of depression that followed, Claflin took advantage of the upturn in the economy in 1899 and 1900 to establish the Associated Merchants Company in May 1900. To consolidate his other mercantile holdings, in 1909 he incorporated the United Dry Goods Companies,

The young John Claflin considered buying Jekyll Island for himself before it was purchased for a club, in which he participated as a founding member. (Brooklyn Historical Society)

with the establishment of some thirty retail subsidiaries.[24] He would serve as president of all three corporations until his retirement in 1914.

Although considered "easy, affable, and sociable in manner, and an exceedingly interesting conversationalist," [25] Claflin was also noted for his fiery oratory. At a rally for Theodore Roosevelt on October 28, 1898, for example, he "delivered a rousing, thoroughly partisan, not to say demagogic speech on behalf of Theodore Roosevelt for governor [of New York]." [26]

Claflin finally married on June 27, 1890, when he was almost forty. His bride was Elizabeth Hopkins Stewart Dunn, an attractive widow nine years younger than he and the great-granddaughter of Gen. Samuel Hopkins, George Washington's aide-

Elizabeth Claflin stood by her husband through his financial crisis, and her investments were instrumental to his recovery. (Everett Collection, Coastal Georgia Historical Society)

de-camp and a member of Congress from 1813 to 1815. Born in Rock Haven, Kentucky, on September 8, 1859, Elizabeth Dunn was the widow of William Dunn and had one daughter from their marriage, Wilhelmine, whom Claflin adopted. The wedding took place at Monterey, California, and as a wedding gift John Claflin gave his wife $100,000.[27] Over the years he would add to that amount considerably. Three daughters were born from their union: Elizabeth Stewart (June 20, 1891), Agnes Sanger (birthdate unknown), and Mary Stewart (August 26, 1899).

By the Jekyll Island Club season that followed their marriage, however, the new couple were back in the east, and they checked in for their first stay at the club together, accompanied by Mrs. Edward E. Eames, on January 31, 1891. Except for a hiatus in their membership between 1914 and 1921, they were thereafter regular faces at the club, staying almost always in their favorite rooms 33 and 36 in the club house, whenever they could get them, and inviting guests who added sparkle to the club's season. For example, in 1898, they arrived on February 5 with the famous stained-glass artisan Louis Comfort Tiffany, his wife, and daughter. Tiffany would in later years be commissioned to provide a window in memory of club president Frederick Gilbert Bourne for Faith Chapel.[28]

After the 1907 season, however, the Claflins' visits to Jekyll became less frequent. In response to a letter from Charlotte Maurice to his wife, John Claflin wrote to club member and friend Charles Stewart Maurice on January 27, 1908: "We have had a bit of a hospital. Bessie [his daughter Elizabeth] developed grippe on her Xmas vacation, and she is still at home convalescing. Her mother draped herself too closely to her, pending the coming of a trained nurse, and we had two patients instead of one. Bessie is almost well, but Mrs. Claflin is barely able to be out of bed and could not safely travel earlier than a week hence." But that was not Claflin's only concern at the moment. He went on to tell Maurice something of the personal financial problems he had faced during the national fiscal crisis of 1907. "Never before in my experience was trade so paralyzed as during November and December 1907 and in consequence orders were canceled and stocks piled up on every side." For the moment, however, the worst seemed to be over. "January is showing some improvement all around but we look for a very quiet spring trade. As for Jekyl I don't know. We may go down ten days hence for a fortnight or we may not. Much will depend on Mrs. Claflin's health."[29] She was evidently not sufficiently improved to withstand the trip, for the Claflins did not make it for their winter vacation at Jekyll.

The financial problems of that season were but a hint of future calamity. The Claflin firm had seemed rock solid for many decades, and despite considerable losses had survived the panic of 1893 and three major depressions when many smaller establishments had failed. During the panic of 1893 John Claflin had used "my personal fortune to make good to The H. B. Claflin Company insolvent accounts" and reduced his own salary to $18,000 a year.[30] In the summer of 1914, however, on the eve of World War I, the business world was shocked to learn that the H. B. Claflin Company had filed for bankruptcy. Once again John Claflin sacrificed his entire personal fortune in an effort to save his investors, many of whom were company employees, and did everything he could to pay off his creditors. As he began to perceive some of the problems that eventually led to the collapse of his company and in an effort to stave off the inevitable financial disaster, he drew no salary or compensation of any kind from 1912 on, and in that same year, he gave up his membership in the costly Jekyll Island Club. In addition, Elizabeth Claflin, at her husband's request, during the panic of 1907 had used her own accruing fortune to buy up endorsements of the H. B. Claflin Company, thereby becoming one of the company's now-unsecured creditors. Claflin did everything possible to weather the financial shortfall and reorganize the company, but the banks, though they were favorably inclined toward Claflin, failed to act promptly on his requests for a temporary loan similar to one that had tided him over in 1907. His reorganization plans were not accepted by the courts, with the consequence that Claflin's mercantile empire began to crumble. "I could do nothing more than turn over to the creditors all my property of every kind, including my houses and lands, in order to help them to the limit of my ability."[31] Many of these assets would have been fully protected under law, but Claflin was a man of honor, as his father had been before him, and was determined to pay back all his creditors insofar as he possibly could, presumably including the debts the company owed to Elizabeth Claflin. With the fall of the H. B. Claflin Company, Claflin lost as well his holdings in United Dry Goods Companies and the Associated Merchants Company.

John Claflin had always been a "sound money" Republican who embraced the gold standard, and he was also a strong proponent of the founding of the Federal Reserve System. The collapse of the large firm of this fiscally conservative man stunned the nation. Some blamed his financial failure on the new low tariff enacted in 1913 at the urging of Woodrow Wilson. Others, however, contended that the company had over-expanded on the basis of insufficient capital. Still others argued that the company's demise resulted from "an over-extension of credit incurred in financing its retail subsidiaries and payment of dividends in excess of earnings."[32] The official company explanation blamed the "unprecedented shifting of trade centers in New York." In all probability, a combination of these factors toppled the firm that had seemed from the outside impervious to the national financial vicissitudes.

Presumably at least some of the money the H. B. Claflin Company owed Elizabeth Claflin was repaid. And it was this capital that provided the Claflins a means of starting over. In his *Letter to His Children,* Claflin states, "When I had completely divested myself of my own property and was relieved of further responsibility in mercantile matters, I was free to look after your mother's investments, and my recent work under favorable conditions has produced results that are pleasing to her and to me."[33] He had been able to buy back their Morristown home and their camp in the Adirondacks by 1918, and in 1921 he rejoined the Jekyll Island Club.

Jekyll Islanders were delighted to have the Claflins back. Enticed to return by club president Walter James and his friend Stewart Maurice, the Claflins arrived for the first time after rejoining the club on January 26, 1921. President James expressed his pleasure, for both were, he contended "charming people."[34] For the next several years they stayed in rooms 70 and 71 of the club house, as they continued to recoup their losses.

Coincidentally, the year of their return coincided with the year of H. K. Porter's death; however, Annie Porter did not at once sell the cottage, then owned officially by the Porter estate. Only shortly before her own death was the cottage finally put up for sale. When the opportunity arose to purchase Mistletoe, John and Elizabeth Claflin had sufficiently recovered from their financial misfortunes to make a modest offer, which the estate executor readily accepted.

On January 18, 1925, the Claflins registered for the first time in their new Mistletoe Cottage. They spent almost every winter there from 1925 until 1934, coming down regularly from their home in Morristown, New Jersey, until Mr. Claflin, at eighty-three, could no longer make the trip. After 1934 their names conspicuously disappear from the guest register. John Claflin lived to within a month of his eighty-eighth birthday before he finally died at Lindenwold, his Morristown home, on June 12, 1938. His passing marked the end of an era for the Jekyll Island Club, for he had been at the time of his death its only surviving original member. Elizabeth Claflin owned the cottage until 1940, when it was turned over to the Jekyll Island Club.[35]

The State Era

After the state takeover in 1947, Mistletoe Cottage was leased on May 1, 1955, to the colorful and controversial state senator and former mayor of Cochran, Georgia, Jimmy Dykes, who eventually reopened the club house, which he ran as a hotel from 1956 until 1971. A review of leases by the Jekyll Island Authority on April 15, 1957, showed the cottage to be officially leased to the Acme Construction Company, one of Dykes's many operations on the island.[36] From the 1970s until 1996, the Jekyll Island Authority used a portion of the cottage to house the executive directors of the Jekyll Island Museum. Mistletoe has undergone two restorations during the state era, the first under the supervision of Roger Beedle. During the restoration of Indian Mound, Mistletoe housed the museum collection; approximately 75 percent of the "pre-plumbing pottery" that had been collected by the museum's first curator, Tallu Fish, was destroyed when a ceiling collapsed.[37] The most recent restoration to its 1912–15 appearance was completed in 1994, under the supervision of Warren Murphey. The cottage is now open to the public.

Owners: George Frederick Shrady, 1904–7; Hester E. Shrady, 1907–25; Walter B. James, 1925–27; Helen Jennings James, 1927–41; Jekyll Island Club, 1941–47

Constructed: 1904

Architecture: Italian Renaissance

Architect: Unknown

The Shrady Years

Edwin Gould, the son-in-law of the first owners of the cottage known today as Cherokee, was in large measure responsible for the building of this Italian Renaissance residence. He purchased lot 32 from the estate of Walter Gurnee and submitted plans to build a two-story house on it for his in-laws, Dr. George F. Shrady and his wife, Hester.[1] The cottage, which contains twenty rooms and six baths, was constructed in 1904 and appears on the tax rolls for the first time in 1905, valued at $15,000. It

Cherokee Cottage was constructed in 1904 by Dr. George Shrady. (Lanier Book, 1911)

reflects the popularity of the Italian Renaissance architectural style that had been revived by McKim, Mead and White in the early 1880s and had its heyday from the 1890s until the 1930s. Its symmetrical facade, its low-pitched hipped roof covered with ceramic tiles and broad overlapping eaves, and the arches above its doors were typical of the style.[2] Like many such houses, the upstairs windows were smaller than those on the first floor. All in all, it had a clean, uncluttered look that stood in contrast to the Queen Anne and shingle-style houses built on the island in earlier years.

Edwin Gould proposed his father-in-law for membership in the summer of 1904. By the following season, Dr. Shrady was a duly elected member of the club, and the house had been completed. The Shrady cottage is mentioned for the first time in the guest register on February 24, 1905. As the original map of the club compound was drawn, the road that runs in front of the cottage would have passed behind the house; however, a later map shows that the layout was completely redone to provide for a new road that ran between the lots of Edwin Gould and what was to be the Shrady house. At one time, members of the Gould-Shrady family owned five contiguous lots, all used for a veritable complex of buildings that Edwin constructed for his family's enjoyment. (See Chichota chapter.)

The Shradys were welcome additions to the club roster, which was always happy to have distinguished members of the medical profession. And Dr. Shrady fit the bill. Born January 14, 1837, to Margaret Beinhauer and John Shrady, a descendent of Johan Schrade, who came from Württemberg, Germany, to America about 1715. Long before he became a member of the Jekyll Island Club, George

Cherokee Cottage under construction in 1904. (Courtesy of Georgia Department of Archives and History, original in Jekyll Island Museum)

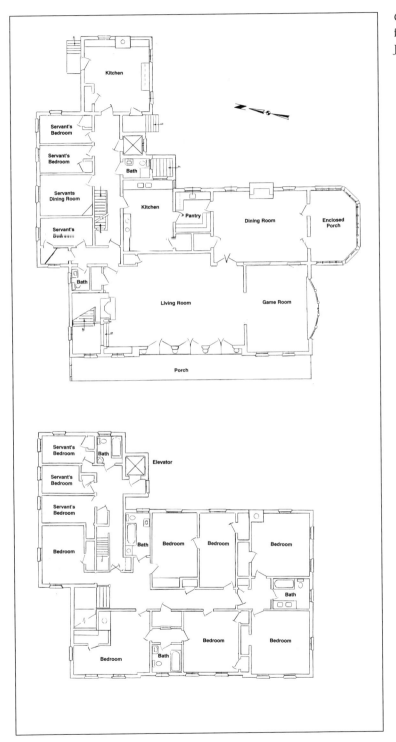

Cherokee, first-floor and second-floor plans. (Based on plans in the Jekyll Island Museum)

Frederick Shrady had risen to national fame as the physician who attended ex-President Grant in his final illness, during which the nation awaited his daily reports on his patient's condition. As a consequence, he was consulted in the case of President Garfield at the time of the assassination, and after Garfield's death he also took part in the autopsy of the assassin Charles Guiteau. In later years, when Emperor Frederick III of Germany was suffering from a malady similar to Grant's, his attendant physician, Sir Morrell Mackenzie, consulted regularly about the case with Dr. Shrady. One of the doctor's least pleasant tasks, but one that nevertheless carried with it a certain notoriety, had come as a result of his selection in 1890 as one of the chief medical experts to attend the execution of William Kemmler, the first man to be electrocuted in the United States. Dr. Shrady "condemned the method in unqualified terms."[3]

Having graduated in 1858 from the College of Physicians and Surgeons in New York, he served as assistant surgeon in the United States Army during the Civil War, first at the Central Park Hospital in New York and then in field duty as part of the operating corps. He returned to private practice after the war, serving as resident surgeon of New York Hospital, surgeon to St. Francis's Hospital, and consulting surgeon to the New York Cancer Hospital, among others.[4]

Recognized as preeminent in his field, he was selected as chief editor of the *Medical Record* when it was founded in 1866 and served in that capacity until 1904. Even before that he had served as editor of the *American Medical Times* and contributed regularly to a variety of medical journals. His contributions to the medical profession were recognized in 1869 by Yale University, which gave him an honorary master of arts degree. He campaigned during his lengthy career against medical charlatans and for reform of medical education and public health.

Dr. Shrady has been variously described as "simple, unaffected, courteous, and with a heart brimming over with kindness, [and] he won the warm affection of all with whom he came in contact."[5] He was widely viewed as "a calm, agreeable person, with an unusual gift for mimicry and a kindly sense of humor."[6] He had married a woman named Mary Lewis in 1860, and before her death in 1883, she had given him three sons, George Jr., Henry Merwyn, and Charles Douglas, and a daughter, Minnie, who became the wife of John Fremont Ambrose, while her brother George married Ambrose's sister, Katherine.[7] Shrady's second marriage, on December 19, 1888, was to Hester Ellen Cantine, a lively widow who for several seasons held subscription dances interspersed with theater parties to train young New Yorkers in the social graces.[8] It was her second marriage as well as his, and she had one daughter, Sarah, whom Dr. Shrady adopted as his own and who would become the wife of Edwin Gould.

Dr. and Mrs. Shrady entertained a variety of guests in their cottage during the club seasons from 1905 through 1907, when Mrs. Shrady's grandchildren and a variety of other relatives were frequently present. Unfortunately, however, the Shradys would not enjoy their island home together for very long, for Dr. Shrady suffered in November 1907 from an attack of gallstones. As a result, sepsis, a bacterial infection, set in, and his beloved medical profession could do nothing to save him. He died a difficult death on November 30, 1907.[9]

Hester Shrady bravely returned to Jekyll Island on her own the following year, where she surrounded herself with her grandchildren, Frank and Eddie Gould, and with friends. She took over her husband's membership in the club from his estate in 1908 and held it through 1916. Tragedy struck her life once more in 1917 when her oldest grandson, Edwin Jr., died a tragic death in a hunting accident during a holiday at Jekyll. (See Chichota chapter.)

Hester Shrady, among her activities, conducted subscription classes and theater parties for society youth in New York. (Courtesy of Gould Foundation for Children)

Dr. George Shrady at Jekyll Island, March 1907, the year of his death. Shrady, the builder of Cherokee Cottage, attended Pres. Ulysses S. Grant during his final illness and served as surgical pathologist when Pres. James A. Garfield was shot in 1881. (Courtesy of Florence H. Hughes)

TWENTIETH-CENTURY COTTAGES :: 214

Hester Shrady sits beside the Chichota pool, with her son-in-law standing behind her. (Courtesy of Edwin J. Gould family)

The incident dimmed Hester Shrady's enthusiasm for continuing in the club. As a consequence, she did not renew her membership that year, nor any year thereafter, though she would continue to own her cottage until 1925.

For several years, neither Mrs. Shrady nor the Goulds came to Jekyll. Their happy times there had been replaced by a memory too painful to contemplate, and they needed time to heal. However, four years later, in 1921, it was Mrs. Shrady who led the way for their return. She registered at the club on February 16, arriving with her grandson Frank, by now a college graduate whose fondness for Jekyll, unlike that of the rest of his family, remained unabated. With them were Mrs. Shrady's maid and several guests. The entire party stayed at the Goulds' cottage, Chichota, rather than her own Jekyll home. Prior to Eddie's death, she had often come to the island with her grandchildren when their parents had remained in New York. More often than not in the years after her husband's death, it was Edwin Jr. who would accompany her to the island. Thus his death there must have been particularly hard for her. Nevertheless, most likely for the sake of Frank

Miller, who still wanted to come to the island, she put aside her own feelings of grief and returned.

On March 16, following his mother-in-law's lead, Edwin Gould also found the courage to return to the island for the first time since his son's death. With him were several business associates, Nelson Burr from New York and Gates Hubbard and Jack Corliss from Tarrytown, New York. But Sally Gould, his wife, adamantly refused ever to return to the island.

Edwin Gould admired his mother-in-law, Hester Shrady, and had followed her lead in other respects as well. Her concern for disadvantaged children, which had led her to work unstintingly for the Messiah Home for Children in New York, giving not only her money but her time and energy to the orphanage, was no doubt one of the factors that led Edwin Gould to establish the Edwin Gould Foundation for Children not long after the death of his son. Undoubtedly at his instigation, Hester Shrady was elected as its first president, while he himself would serve as treasurer.[10]

Sally Gould's opposition eventually took its toll on the Jekyll vacations both for Edwin Gould and Hester Shrady, who confessed to finding it "rather sad" to be there. Her last recorded visit to the island was in 1924 when she arrived on February 11 with her niece Lydia French, who was her frequent companion at Jekyll, "to remain until the close of the season." One can understand the conflict Mrs. Shrady must have felt there, despite the "warm welcome" she had been given by club members and employees. Her niece reported the situation in a letter to Marian Maurice: "Mr. Gould brought us down on the 'Dixie'—but did not come over. . . . Mrs. Gould is quite well, after her summer's long illness. However, she will never come to Jekyl, I fear, and does not even like us to be here."[11]

Following this visit, Hester Shrady acceded to her daughter's wishes and never returned to the island again. Lydia French had noted that she was "very thin [but] otherwise is in better health than for some years—excepting that she has very little strength—only in spurts." Despite the fact that, ac-

Hester Shrady, *right, front,* at Chichota. Her grandson, Edwin Gould Jr., is to her right. (Courtesy of Edwin J. Gould family)

cording to French, "The life here . . . is diverting for her—and much better than life in New York or at a Southern Hotel—which we tried last year—at St. Augustine," Hester Shrady gave up her life at Jekyll and eventually her cottage as well. The following year, she sold it to Walter Belknap James, then president of the Jekyll Island Club, who dubbed it "Cherokee."

The James Years

As a New York physician and a professor of medicine at Columbia University, Walter James had no doubt known the Shradys in New York medical circles even before he encountered them at the Jekyll Island Club. Unlike Dr. Shrady, Walter James was not a surgeon. He had begun his career as a general practitioner before he began to specialize in the treatment of the heart and lungs. Born in 1857, the son and the fourth of twelve children of Henry and Amelia Cate James, in Baltimore, Maryland, James had graduated from Yale in 1879. He received his medical degree in 1883 from the College of Physicians and Surgeons, which was the medical school of Columbia University.

For many years he was head of Medical Services at both Presbyterian and Roosevelt Hospitals and from 1889 until 1918 was a staff member of the College of Physicians and Surgeons, rising from the position of lecturer to the rank of full professor of clinical medicine, a post he held for about fifteen years. For his distinguished teaching at that institution, Columbia University awarded him an honorary LL.D. degree in 1904. At the time he joined the club he was serving as president of the New York Academy of Medicine, a post he held from 1915 to 1918.

Dr. James was elected to club membership on February 19, 1917, just one week before the death of Edwin Gould Jr. The following year, he suffered a hemorrhage in one of his eyes caused by high blood pressure, which prevented him from doing any reading at all for a period of several years. As a consequence, he retired from active medical practice, even though otherwise he was healthy, filled with constructive energy, and endowed with a keen and vigorous mind. Undoubtedly, it was his retirement that allowed him the time to devote to the Jekyll Island Club.

"Retirement," however, was for Dr. James anything but quiet and restful. In 1918 alone, he was elected a trustee for life of Columbia University and became a member of the medical committee of the American Red Cross Hospital in Paris. Gov. Charles S. Whitman of New York appointed him chairman of the State Hospital Development Commission, which over the next few years brought about a complete reorganization of the state hospital system in New York, and Harvard University awarded him a second honorary LL.D. degree in 1922 for his work in this area. He also became president of the Adirondack Cottage Sanitarium for tubercular patients at Saranac Lake, New York. In addition, he served as a trustee of the Natural History Museum and the American Geographical Society.[12]

Nevertheless, he found sufficient time and abundant energy to devote to the affairs of the Jekyll Island Club and was clearly an excellent choice for its president. Known to be a man of culture, well read in both German and English, he also had a good mind for business and an excellent capacity for administration. His greatest attribute as club president was his extremely likable nature that made for him many friends, among whom he counted three presidents, Theodore Roosevelt, William Howard Taft, and Woodrow Wilson, as well as several prominent Jekyll Islanders, including William Rockefeller and J. P. Morgan. Fondly described by his son Oliver as "tall, light haired with curly hair and a twinkle in his eye and one of the best looking men around," he was apparently well liked and admired by all who knew him.[13] By the time of his election, he had become a familiar and extremely popular figure in club circles, recognized not only as "a skilled physician, an upright and public-spirited citizen" but also as "a gentleman of old school courtesy and charm."[14]

At the time Walter James purchased the Shrady house, he already owned apartment 3 in the annex, which he had purchased from John J. Albright in 1917, the same year he joined the club. However, after Dr. James's election as president, the couple spent increasing amounts of time at Jekyll and needed more room to entertain their guests. Thus when Mrs. Shrady decided to sell, the Jameses were eager buyers. Their new name for the cottage, Cherokee, appears for the first time in the guest register on February 19, 1927.

Dr. James was without question the most beloved president in the club's history, for he was enthusiastic about every aspect of island life and spent a couple of months there each winter. He and his wife had both become avid golfers, and he corresponded regularly with Charles Stewart Maurice, with whom he often took "charming drives" around the island, concerning matters relating to Jekyll's natural environment. As the two of them tried to identify the various plants on the island, Dr. James commented: "I suspect that one of our troubles on Jekyl, as far as botany is concerned, is going to be the fact that we do not visit the Island at the right season. We go there for pleasure and not for science, and in order to identify and study and really understand the flora of that beautiful spot, perhaps we ought to take a trip there during the hot summer months when everything is in full bloom and when the plants and trees are doing their very best."[15]

Walter James was an extremely cultured man who had done postgraduate medical study in Germany. He enjoyed music and theater and was also something of a bibliophile. In the same letter to Maurice, he invites him to his home in New York to see his edition of Michaux in French, "the Paris edition of

Dr. Walter B. James was president of the Jekyll Island Club during its most successful years, from 1919 to 1927. (Everett Collection, Coastal Georgia Historical Society)

1805, with copper plate illustrations colored by hand, together with the most beautiful tree illustrations that I know in literature." He confesses to having rescued the volume "from the dump pile of a friend of mine just before they were to be sold for old paper." With his typical good humor, Dr. James commented wryly, "you will wonder that I can still reckon among my friends that man who was going to throw them away."

The Jekyll Island Club swimming pool, built in 1927 under Dr. James's administration as club president, with the completed James Memorial Wall. (Courtesy of Jekyll Island Museum)

Dr. James, *right,* with his nephew Oliver Jennings relaxing at Jekyll Island. (Everett Collection, Coastal Georgia Historical Society)

In another letter to Maurice he recounts Mrs. James's reading to him aloud from Chesterton's history of America.[16] In yet another, he queries Maurice about the relationship between pigs and snakes on the island. Jekyll, he told Maurice with typical humor, seemed to be having a problem with increasing numbers of snakes "which seem to have struck terror to the hearts of certain golfers and to have made their drives wild and their putts tremulous."[17] One can easily understand why Dr. James was admired for both his personality and his intellect.

At the time of his election as club president in 1919, only two years after his selection for membership and following the death of former president Frederick Gilbert Bourne, the Jekyll Island Club was struggling. Dr. James, who would serve as president for the next eight years, set for himself the goal of reviving the flagging membership and shoring up club members' enthusiasm, lending his personal charm to the task. His efforts were well rewarded. Members flocked in, and even the John Claflins, who had long since given up their membership, rejoined. James's leadership style had a personal touch, and his own enthusiasm for Jekyll seemed to be contagious. He understood what was needed to make Jekyll appeal to the younger set in the wake of World War I. Under his leadership the existing golf courses were improved and an excellent new Dunes Course was begun. In addition, the club drew up plans to replace the round pool in front of the club house with a modern new swimming pool. During his tenure as president, the Jekyll Island Club unquestionably enjoyed its greatest popularity.

He pursued lagging members with a gracious touch, repeatedly encouraging people like Cyrus McCormick to make more use of Jekyll. Somehow he made it seem a personal delight to him when members began to take a greater interest. For example, he wrote to McCormick on February 23,

1923, "I cannot tell you what a pleasure it is to us all to have you begin to resume your visits to Jekyl and we are trusting that you will come down next winter for a good long stay."[18] He recruited his vast network of family members who were also involved in the club to help him in his efforts—Jenningses, Brewsters, Coes, Auchinclosses, Rockefellers, and the Norman Jameses, many of whom served as officers or held important committee posts in the club.

Dr. James served as president of the Jekyll Island Club until 1927. Then in his seventieth year and just after the close of the club season, Walter James died in New York of heart failure. One obituary suggests that he had shown in his early fifties the first symptoms of the heart disease that finally claimed his life.[19] According to the account in the *New York Times*, Dr. James became "seriously ill from heart disease . . . at the Jekyl Island Club" three weeks prior to his death. "His relatives were summoned to the club but he improved sufficiently to be removed to his home" in New York.[20] Nevertheless his death seemed a genuine shock to other members of the club.

Upon hearing of it, the club's board of governors approved a statement that underscored Dr. James's value to the Jekyll Island Club. They had, the minutes affirmed, "suffered the loss of a wise leader and the members of the Club have lost a greatly loved companion and friend."[21] No one better than they realized that Dr. James had been elected president at a critical time in the club's history when members seemed to be deserting Jekyll for other fashionable resorts. James, however, had found the right combination of enthusiasm, improvements, and atmosphere of amiability to lure them back, and under his leadership, for the only time in the club's history, demand was so great that the club reached a full membership of a hundred members and developed a waiting list. The executive committee's minutes summed it up in a single sentence: "His grace of manner and the charm of his personality spread throughout the Club and an atmosphere of hospitality and kindliness which will always be treasured and which it is hoped will always be preserved."[22]

Likewise, members of the medical profession grieved his passing. His friend Joseph Collins may have put his finger on Dr. James's primary attribute when he wrote: "He would have gone to the top in any walk of life, for he had ability, insight, imagination, energy and charm; and he loved his fellowmen. He loved them theoretically, practically, individually, collectively."[23]

Club members recognized that Walter James gave so much care and thought to the club's interest "that he re-created it," as R. T. Crane expressed it.[24] As a consequence, club members cast about for a fitting memorial and decided that since "the welfare of the caddies was always very close to Doctor James' heart," a much-needed new dormitory "to give them healthy living conditions" would be appropriate, and they set out to raise $10,000 for this purpose and to build an outdoor memorial. They would later build as well a memorial wall in his memory at the north end of the swimming pool.

Grief was not new to Helen James. She had lost her first child, Walter Jr., many years before when he was only eighteen months old. She had gone on to have three more children: another son, Oliver Burr, named for Helen's father (1896), Helen (1898), and Eunice (1900). She was the daughter of Oliver Burr Jennings, who had gone to California during the gold rush to open a general mercantile business in San Francisco in 1849. He had married Esther Judson Goodsell (1828–1908) of Fairfield, Connecticut, the sister of William Rockefeller's wife. As a consequence of this connection as Rockefeller's brother-in-law, Oliver Burr Jennings became one of the original stockholders in the Standard Oil Company, a director of Standard Oil of Ohio, and a trustee of the Standard Oil Trust that resulted from the company's reorganization in 1882. It was in this endeavor that he made his fortune.

His daughter, Helen James, was described by her son Oliver as one who was "dominated by the people around her, except as to matters of fundamental principle. She was an old fashioned dutiful wife and although in some ways her tastes diverged from those of my father's, she was scrupulously conscientious in subordinating her own ideas, pleasures and interests to his own."[25] Her tastes ran more to the social life of Newport, while her husband's embraced less formal environments where he could hunt and fish. As a consequence they built a camp at Upper Saint Regis Lake, New York, in the Adirondacks. Clearly the camp was not to her liking, and, after Dr. James's death in 1927, Helen James gave it to her daughter Helen and bought herself instead a summer home in Newport.

The house at Jekyll Island was quite another matter. Evidently the club had appealed to both Dr. and Mrs. James. There he could indulge his favorite pastimes, for there were ample opportunities for hunting, fishing, and his new passion, golf, while she clearly found it more than tolerable and enjoyed the physical comforts and the social stimulation it provided and even the golf. Thus after her husband's death, Helen James kept her Jekyll home, continuing to make annual visits to the island well into the 1930s and maintaining her membership in the club until its closing in 1942.

Her enthusiasm for Jekyll is reflected in the fact that, even before her husband's death, she became a member of the Jekyll Island Club in her own right. Proposed for membership by George Brewster on November 15, 1926, a nomination seconded by her brother Walter, she purchased the club share of E. Stanley Gary, a cotton manufacturer from Baltimore who had been postmaster general in President McKinley's cabinet. Her pleasure in Jekyll was no doubt enhanced because many other members of her close-knit family had also chosen it for their winter retreat. Among club members, we find Helen's brother, Walter Jennings, who was elected president of the club in the wake of his brother-in-law's death; her sister, Annie Burr Jennings, who would later be elected as one of only two female vice presidents the club ever had; her uncle William Rockefeller; another sister, Emma Burr Jennings Auchincloss (Mrs. Hugh Dudley Auchincloss); and her son-in-law Henry Edward Coe.

Mrs. James was a vigorous and healthy woman for the most part who prided herself on not having consulted a doctor since the birth of her youngest child, Eunice (Mrs. Henry Edward Coe). However, when she was diagnosed with high blood pressure in the mid-1930s, she chose thereafter to live the life of a semi-invalid. Fortunately, she was "an excellent needle woman and did fine knitting and crocheting."[26] Reading and letter writing were also activities she enjoyed and in which she could still engage until she suffered an apoplectic stroke in 1940. During the last few seasons of the club era, Helen's sister Emma and her family used the cottage. Mrs. James lived on until August 16, 1946, a life of much reduced activity, finally succumbing to death at the age of eighty-six.

The State Era

During the state era, Cherokee was refurbished in the mid-1950s to be used as the "Little Executive Mansion" by the governor during the administration of Marvin Griffin.[27] The use of the cottage by

Cherokee Cottage was refurbished during the early state era as a "Little Executive Mansion" under the administration of Marvin Griffin, but it proved to be so politically controversial that Griffin disavowed that either he or his wife had authorized the expense. (Courtesy of Georgia Department of Archives and History, original in Jekyll Island Museum)

the governor proved to be so politically controversial that Griffin disavowed any authorization given by either himself or his wife for the refurbishing of the house for their purposes, and he never used it as a consequence. However, former governor Herman Talmadge and the Game and Fish Commission did use the cottage for a meeting on May 11–13, 1953. Although several people sought to lease the cottage, no one ever succeeded in doing so. Today Cherokee houses the offices of the Jekyll Island Museum. In 1998 the cottage is scheduled for yet another renovation. It is to be converted into a bed-and-breakfast and will serve as part of the Jekyll Island Club Hotel facilities.

GOODYEAR COTTAGE

Owners: Frank Henry Goodyear, 1906–7; Goodyear Estate, 1907–9; Josephine Looney Goodyear, 1909–15; Frank Henry Goodyear Jr., 1916–30; Dorothy Knox Goodyear (Rogers), 1930–c. 1942; Jekyll Island Club: c. 1942–47

Constructed: 1906

Architecture: Mediterranean Revival

Architects: Carrère and Hastings

Frank Henry Goodyear, who in 1903 contracted with well-known architects Carrère and Hastings to design his Jekyll Island cottage, was a man of self-made wealth. The family of his mother, Esther Permelia Kinne, had been among the nation's early settlers, and her first American ancestor was born in this country in 1623. Goodyear was descended through his father from an early New Englander named Stephen Goodyear, who founded New Haven, Connecticut, in 1638. Despite his ancestry

The Goodyear Cottage, shown here about 1912, was designed by the well-known architects Carrère and Hastings and was built in 1906. (Everett Collection, Coastal Georgia Historical Society)

among the nation's founders, his wealth was not primarily inherited, for his father, Bradley Goodyear, was a country doctor from Groton, New York. Young Frank, a second son born to the Goodyears on March 7, 1849, was, in fact, descended from a line of prolific churchmen, farmers, and doctors, who had never accumulated vast wealth.[1]

Thus the Goodyear boys did not attend the private schools dear to the hearts of the northern elite. Instead educated in public schools, young Frank began his professional life as a teacher. He soon realized that he was not cut out to be a schoolmaster and took a $35-a-month job as a bookkeeper for Robert Looney, a sawmill operator in the town that bore his name, Looneyville (later changed to Wende), New York.[2] These were rather inauspicious beginnings for one who would rise to great wealth and prominence. The bookkeeping job was only the beginning, but it was an important step for Frank Goodyear. On September 13, 1871, he married the boss's daughter, twenty-year-old Josephine, who was born in Looneyville on May 25, 1851, to Robert and Josephine Kidder Looney. Over the course of their married life, she would bear him four children, Grace Esther (born 1872), Josephine (1874), Florence (1884), and Frank Henry Jr. (1891).[3]

Observation of his future father-in-law's sawmill operation during the 1860s taught him a great deal. Thus when Mr. Looney died shortly after Frank and Josephine's marriage, Frank began to purchase timberlands that were part of his father-in-law's estate to add to the eighty-five acres adjacent to the Looney land that he had already bought.[4] These timberlands, coupled with financial help from Elbridge Gerry Spaulding, were the beginning of Goodyear's lumbering business in which his great fortune would be achieved. The Goodyears moved at once to Buffalo, New York, where Frank set up a small coal and lumber company. Before long he branched out into Pennsylvania, where he soon had mills in four counties.

Goodyear would prove to be something of a visionary as far as the lumbering business was concerned, and it was his farsightedness and drive to succeed that made him a wealthy man. Lumbermen had for years passed up many fine stands of timber in the northeast and elsewhere because they were not close enough to a viable waterway to provide transportation for harvested logs. Goodyear, on the other hand, saw it as an important opportunity and conceived the idea of building mills where the timber was located rather than sending it downstream for milling. In December 1884 he bought for an excellent price almost fourteen thousand acres of prime timberland in Potter County, Pennsylvania, and proceeded to contract with a business association to construct a sizable saw mill nearby. According to one source, he was "probably the first large lumberman to contract with others to build and operate mills cutting his timber."[5] He was also one of the first to conceive the notion of using railroads instead of waterways to transport timber, a means that gave him a considerable advantage in that he could harvest timber wherever he chose and was not dependent upon the weather to produce adequate freshets for shipping his logs. It was only natural, therefore, that his business interests turned as well to the building of railways. In that same year, 1885, he began construction on a the line that was first known as the Sinnemahoning Valley Railroad, later absorbed into the Buffalo & Susquehanna, which would tie into the Western New York & Pennsylvania Line.[6]

Two years later, having demonstrated the success of his enterprise but having also driven himself to a state of nervous exhaustion, he persuaded his older brother, Charles Waterhouse Goodyear, to join him in the business and take over some of its responsibilities while he himself took a rest cure in Europe.[7] Charles Goodyear agreed to give up an established law practice in the firm where he had become a senior partner, replacing Grover Cleveland with whom he had worked for a time, to enter into partnership with his brother in a firm known as the F. H. and C. W. Goodyear Company.[8]

Of the two brothers, Frank was the hard-driving

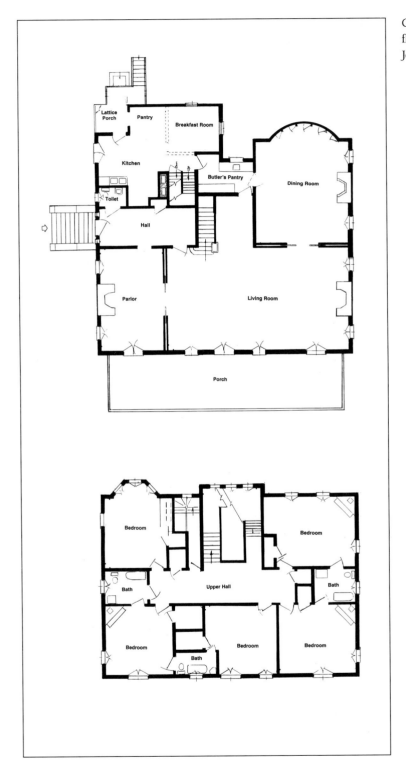

Goodyear, first-floor and second-floor plans. (Based on plan in the Jekyll Island Museum)

Frank Henry Goodyear as a successful lumber baron. Unlike many Jekyll Islanders, he was not born to wealth but was instead self-made. (Courtesy of George F. Goodyear)

one, relentlessly determined to increase his already vast fortune, to the extent that he pushed himself constantly. His brother, Charles, much like Frank in some ways, was nevertheless steadier and less driven by an insatiable desire for wealth. He had begun life as a professional man who was attracted to politics. When Frank Goodyear returned from another trip to Europe in 1904, he found his brother Charles to be a popular contender for the Republican nomination for governor of New York. Charles seemed undecided about seeking the nomination despite the groundswell of support he had received. Grover Cleveland had written a letter to potential

supporters claiming Goodyear as "one of my best and most intimate friends" and indicating that his nomination would not only be "wisest and best" but "a great personal satisfaction to me."[9] However, upon Frank Goodyear's return and following a private meeting between the two brothers, in which Frank allegedly underscored his own poor health and his increasing dependence upon his brother, Charles Goodyear withdrew his name from contention, a decision he would later regret.

As Frank Goodyear's star ascended and his wealth grew, Edmund Hayes proposed him for membership in the Jekyll Island Club on March 2, 1902, and he was duly elected three days later. It was a membership of which Goodyear would take utmost advantage. His brother, Charles, writing to a business associate in 1905, with a certain amount of pride, clearly demonstrated its worth:

My brother, Frank, writes from his winter home on Jekyll Island, where he is making his annual visit to get away from the wretched weather which we have up here at this time of year, that he was fortunate in meeting James J. Hill, who with George F. Baker, J. P. Morgan and other financiers were wont to gather in the clubhouse in the late afternoons for their customary drinks of Scotch and soda. Apparently Mr. Hill was very much interested in our plans for building a railroad from Lake Ponchartrain to Jackson, Mississippi. Advice from an empire builder like James J. Hill, who has achieved such outstanding success in developing the Northwest, did not go unheeded, with the result that we have decided to construct our railroad with long tangents straight up the Pearl River Valley through the heart of our timberlands.[10]

With their Pennsylvania timberlands nearing exhaustion, the Goodyears had turned their sights to the virgin yellow pine of the Deep South. The projects that resulted from this new interest in the South and that Goodyear had no doubt discussed with James J. Hill centered on the Great Southern Lumber Company and the New Orleans and Great

Northern Railroad Company. He and his brother, Charles, would involve themselves not only in the building of railroads, but also in constructing what would prove to be the largest sawmill in the world and in the founding of the town of Bogalusa, Louisiana. Frank was clearly working harder than ever, using even his vacation paradise as a place of business. Nevertheless, aside from the obvious business advantages that Jekyll provided, he also saw it as a place to spend time with his family and get some much-needed rest.

It was obvious to Frank and Josephine Goodyear from the outset that they would need more spacious quarters for their family than the club house provided. During their first full season as club members, the Goodyears rented an apartment in the Sans Souci when they registered on February 20, 1903, with their twelve-year-old son, Frank Jr., a maid, and a valet. In April of that year Goodyear bought lot 6 from William Struthers, and on March 13, 1903, the eminent architect Thomas Hastings from the firm of Carrère and Hastings arrived on the island to look over the site where Frank Goodyear had decided to construct a cottage. At the end of April 1903 the architect and his partner submitted the resulting plans to the executive committee for a sixteen-room cottage, perhaps the first ever approved by the executive committee, which had, only at its meeting on April 10, passed a resolution that "plans for any buildings and location of the same must be submitted to the executive committee and duly approved by said committee."[11] The plans were for a cottage with a facade similar in some respects to that of the home they had designed for the Goodyears in Buffalo that same year. A series of French doors graced the front of the house rather than a clearly defined main entrance. The design also gave a subtle nod with its red-tiled roof toward the Mediterranean influence that was becoming popular in Florida resorts. It would be the only cottage south of the club house that did not have wall cladding of wood shingles. Instead, it was to be

Josephine Looney Goodyear, the boss's daughter, whom Frank Henry Goodyear married. She would succeed her husband as a member of the Jekyll Island Club. (Courtesy of George F. Goodyear)

stucco on frame. At its next meeting on April 29 the executive board approved the plans for the Goodyear cottage, and the architectural firm was notified the following day.

The architects, John Merven Carrère and Thomas Hastings, had met as students at the Ecole des Beaux-Arts in Paris in the early 1880s and had done apprenticeships as draftsmen in the offices of McKim, Mead and White. In fact, Thomas Hastings was the firm's chief designer, while Carrère tended to deal with the clients and business matters. French Renaissance designs were their trademark, though the style of the Goodyear Cottage is perhaps better described as Mediterranean Revival, adapted for the environment and still retaining some of the French flavor. According to one source, "there is no other American architect or firm of architects who have united so much excellence in their plans with so much beauty and distinction of design."[12] Indeed, of all the Jekyll Cottages, that of the Goodyears has perhaps the most pleasing interior. During their years of working together, the firm designed the House and Senate Office Buildings in Washington, D.C., in 1906, the administration building of the Carnegie Institute in 1909, the New York Central Public Library, St. Ambrose Chapel at the Cathedral of St. John the Divine, Henry Flager's Whitehall at Palm Beach, Florida, the Henry C. Frick House in New York, and the Murray Guggenheim mansion in Elberton, New Jersery, to mention only a few of their accomplishments. They also designed for Edwin Gould in 1900 a Fifth Avenue house, described as a "Florentine Renaissance" design, with estimated construction costs at $178,000.[13]

Because the Jekyll cottage was not completed for the 1904 season, the Goodyears were allowed the rare privilege of renting the Maurice cottage, Hollybourne, for the season, while the Maurices stayed in the club house. Nor evidently was it ready for the next two seasons, for the Goodyear family stayed in the club cottage during their visits in 1905 and 1906. The fact that the cottage is listed on a 1906 map but that taxes were not assessed on it until 1907 suggests that it was probably completed after the close of the 1906 season or, at least, too late during that season for the Goodyears to move in.[14]

These years while their Jekyll house was under construction were difficult for the Goodyears. Their oldest daughter, Grace, was recovering from a bout with tuberculosis in St. Moritz, Switzerland, where she and her husband, Ganson Depew, had lived since 1902. In addition, the Goodyears' youngest daughter, thirty-four-year-old Josephine, had contracted typhoid fever in 1904, and on September 7, as her parents were steaming home from Europe to be at her bedside, she died. She left behind not only her husband, George Sicard, but also a three-year-old son and a new baby girl. Relations between Frank Goodyear and Sicard had never been good. In fact, the Goodyears so disapproved of the marriage that it was announced only three months after it took place. Sicard severed all relations with the Goodyear family and Goodyear enterprises, possibly forced out by Josephine's father. Nevertheless, he allowed his in-laws to adopt his two young children, who turned them over to be raised by a couple named Carl and Anna Friedman.[15]

To make matters more difficult, at the same time the Goodyears' Jekyll house was under construction, they were in the process of building a mansion, also designed by Carrère and Hastings, on a far more grandiose scale, at 762 Delaware Avenue in Buffalo. It was ostensibly modeled on a house on the Champs-Elysée in Paris and reputed to be the largest house in Buffalo.[16] The Goodyears moved into the new Buffalo house not long before they moved into the Jekyll house. But Frank Goodyear benefited only briefly from both construction efforts.

In fact, Frank and Josephine Goodyear would spend only one season together in their Jekyll cottage, that of 1907, when they arrived on February 27. Unfortunately, their first stay in their cottage coincided with the year of the national panic of 1907, which brought new strain to Frank Goodyear, already suffering from Bright's disease. His mother lay "desperately ill" at the same time. According to a family account, as a woman of staunch Puritan stock, "she left her bed, was driven to Frank's house, brought in a wheel chair to his bedroom door, got on her feet and walked to his bedside to comfort him. Then she went back home and died."[17] That was on April 19, 1907. The following May 13 Frank Goodyear also died, at the age of fifty-eight, ravaged by disease and "worn out with ceaseless activity and worry."[18] Nevertheless, by the time of his death, Goodyear had achieved his dream of a "coal-iron-lumber-railroad empire."[19]

Following his death, his estate held his club share and membership for two years, until February 23,

Florence Goodyear Wagner Daniels, with her two daughters, Grace, *left,* and Florence. (Courtesy of George F. Goodyear)

The fiery-haired Grace Goodyear, the wife of Ganson Depew, was considered a beauty. She would later become the wife of Howard Ashton Potter. (Courtesy of George F. Goodyear)

Josephine Goodyear, married to George Sicard, died in 1904 at age thirty-four, while the Goodyear Cottage was still in the planning stages. (Courtesy of George F. Goodyear)

1909, when Josephine Looney Goodyear was elected to membership under article II, section V, of the 1901 Jekyll Island Club constitution that provided that the "husband, widow or child of a deceased member may acquire the share of such member, and on transfer of same may become a member of the Club, without the payment of entrance fee."

Unlike many widows who lost interest in the club after their husbands' deaths, Josephine Goodyear was an active club member who would come to Jekyll Island every year, with the exception of 1913, until her own death on October 17, 1915. On February 26, 1908, registering for her first year back at the club after her husband's death, she was joined by her son Frank Jr., who had turned sixteen the week before, and her daughter Florence, who had been recently divorced in Paris from her first husband, George Olds Wagner, but who would remarry the following year Charles Meldrum Daniels, who became in 1924 a member of the Jekyll Island Club.

The family seemed plagued by early death and divorce. Josephine's other surviving daughter, the fiery-haired beauty Grace, was just back from Switzerland, where she and her husband had spent five years as she recovered from her tuberculosis. She had focused less on her health and more on the gala social whirl, it seems, and had given "some indication of straying off the matrimonial reservation."[20] Her husband, upset by the state of affairs, brought her home to Buffalo, where they lived for a time with her mother. They were divorced in 1909, and the following year she married Capt. Howard Ashton Potter, the son of Bishop Henry C. Potter of New York.

Josephine Goodyear had her hands full, recovering from grief herself, coping with a teenage son and her daughters' marital strife, and perhaps overseeing the care of her Sicard grandchildren, George and his sister, Josephine. Certainly wealth did not insulate the family against such problems. Another blow came in September 1914, when Grace, whose tuberculosis had returned with a vengeance, died from the disease. Nevertheless, Josephine Good-

year's strength and courage kept her going until 1915, when her heart finally gave out.

On October 17, she had spent the afternoon with her grandchildren and entertained friends for dinner, and, "in the best of spirits," she, her son, Frank, and her maid had set out for Central Station in Buffalo to board the "Beaver Express" for New York to meet her sister-in-law, Ellen Conger Goodyear (by now a widow as well), when she suffered a massive heart attack.[21] Frank and the maid were with her and immediately paged for a physician. However, no doctor could be found at the station, and the unconscious Mrs. Goodyear was taken by ambulance to her home, where she was dead upon arrival.[22]

Waiting for them on the train was a young lady named Dorothy Virginia Knox, who was already settled in her stateroom, unaware of what was going on outside. She was the fiancee of Frank Goodyear and was accompanying the Goodyears to New York where she was to meet her mother. The porter notified her of Mrs. Goodyear's attack only after the train had departed, and she was obliged to leave the train at Rochester to return to Buffalo.[23] She was no doubt a great comfort to Frank throughout the funeral of his mother, to whom he was quite attached. They invited club superintendent Ernest Grob as well as the Goodyears' closest friend in the club, Edmund Hayes, to serve as pallbearers at Mrs. Goodyear's funeral.

Not long after his mother's death in 1915, Frank Henry Goodyear Jr. married Dorothy Knox, the eldest daughter of Seymour Horace Knox and Grace Millard. It was an auspicious marriage and one that Frank's father would no doubt have approved, for it joined two of the most prominent families in Buffalo. Frank Jr., a member of the Yale class of 1916, left the university without graduating though still in good academic standing. Only a few days after the United States declared war on Germany on April 6, 1917, he enlisted in the Naval Aviation Service with a unit formed by his nephew, Ganson Goodyear Depew. He trained in Buffalo but was eventually stationed in Pensacola, Florida.[24] After the armistice, Frank assumed control of many of the family's business interests and became associated with his cousins Charles and Conger Goodyear in the Southern Lumber Company and the New Orleans and Great Northern Railway, rising to the position of vice president in both. In 1921 he organized a company that acquired exclusive rights to distribute Texaco products in western New York. It would become in 1927 the Goodyear-Wende Oil Company, of which he would serve as chairman of the board, among his many business interests.

Frank Goodyear Jr. and his bride-to-be had come to Jekyll Island together for the first time before their marriage, registering on March 19, 1915, during Josephine Goodyear's final season there. After Mrs. Goodyear's death, Frank inherited the cottage, and Frank and Dot, as she was called, along with his sisters and their families, continued to use the Jekyll cottage. When they were there, they were completely involved in the texture of island life, entertaining fellow club members and club employees as well. On February 20, 1926, for example, the wife of assistant superintendent J. C. Etter recorded in her diary a dance sponsored by Dorothy Goodyear, at which the dancers were entertained by an orchestra brought in from Brunswick and had abundant food in the form of "sandwiches, cake and ice cream, and punch." [25]

While his wife looked after the social aspects of their Jekyll life, Frank Goodyear recognized the need for both workers and members to have better health care on the island. As a tribute to his mother, in 1930 he purchased the Furness cottage from John J. Albright and donated it to the Jekyll Island Club as the Josephine Goodyear Memorial Infirmary. [See Furness Cottage chapter.]

In addition to inheriting his parents' Jekyll cottage, Frank was also heir to their mansion on Delaware Avenue in Buffalo. The couple moved for a time into the splendid structure, making modifications to suit their tastes and life style. They remodeled the stables behind the house as indoor tennis and squash courts, reserving a large upstairs room

Frank Henry Goodyear Jr. inherited his parents' cottage at Jekyll Island in 1915 and enjoyed it with his wife, Dorothy Knox, until his own untimely death in 1930. (Courtesy of George F. Goodyear)

to entertain their guests. In 1920 they built a large country house in East Aurora, on land that had belonged to Dot Goodyear's father, who had also died in 1915. Frank's sporting proclivities were also reflected in the fact that he was an avid yachtsman and had several yachts built, all named *Poule d'Eau* (Water Hen). He brought his newest yacht to the Jekyll Island Club in 1929, but while it was anchored offshore in Miami later in the year, an explosion completely demolished the $300,000 yacht and killed its engineer. [26]

In 1930 the Goodyears were in the process of constructing a splendid new country house designed by John Russell Pope, Crag Burn, on North

Davis Road in Buffalo when on October 13 thirty-eight-year-old Frank, en route to a dinner party, lost control of the Rolls Royce he was driving and slammed into a tree. Among those with him in the car was Bernon Prentice, future president of the Jekyll Island Club, whose foot was pinned in the wreckage, though he was not seriously injured. None of the other passengers, including Dorothy Goodyear and the Clement Despards, who were in the back seat, had more than minor cuts and bruises. However, when the car crashed into the tree on the driver's side, Goodyear suffered a broken neck and leg and a crushed chest. He was rushed to the hospital but died in the emergency room.[27]

At age thirty-four, Dorothy Goodyear was thrust into the role of a widow with four children, the oldest of whom was thirteen and the youngest of whom was only five. They were Dorothy Knox (born in 1917), Frank III (1918), Marjorie Knox (1920), and Robert Millard (1925). During the Goodyears' final season together on Jekyll, their next-door neighbor in the Macy cottage had been an attractive widower, Edmund P. Rogers, a wealthy New York banker with two sons, who also had a house in Westbury, Long Island. An avid sportsman, he rented the Macy cottage for two consecutive seasons, in 1930 and 1931, as the guest of John Sloane. He and the widow Goodyear obviously enjoyed one another's company, for on September 30, 1931, eleven months after Frank Goodyear's death, Dorothy Goodyear married Edmund Rogers.

The following year Rogers became a member of the Jekyll Island Club and would retain that membership until 1941. He and his wife came to the island on a fairly regular basis, usually not arriving until the height of the season sometime in March. They were frequently accompanied by Rogers's two sons, Edmund Jr. and Elliott, and some of Dorothy's children. Those who came varied from year to year.

Only in 1934 did they all arrive together, along with several other guests, for a stay in the cottage, now designated in the club's guest register as the Rogers Cottage.

The family divided its time between New York City, Long Island, Aiken, South Carolina, and Jekyll. Their last trip to Jekyll Island was in March 1937, when they were joined by Elliot and Edmund Jr., Frank, and finally Dorothy, who was to be married in June to Clinton Randolph Wyckoff Jr. Edmund and Dorothy Rogers lived together until his death in 1966, when she was once again left alone, this time an aging widow. No evidence has been found to indicate that she officially transferred her cottage to the Jekyll Island Club; however, she must have done so at the club's closing, for the cottage is listed among the club holdings in their 1944 inventories.

In 1935 the 762 Delaware Street house, built by Frank Goodyear at the same time his Jekyll cottage was under construction, was torn down, although the tennis court remained for family use until about 1950, when the Red Cross took it over and converted it into office space. The Jekyll house remains today as a modest reminder of the splendid work that Carrère and Hastings did for the Goodyear family.

The State Era

During the state era, the cottage was leased in the 1950s to the Oxford Construction Company.[28] At its meeting on December 17, 1973, the Jekyll Island Authority authorized a lease of the Goodyear Cottage to the Jekyll Island Art Association, and on February 11, 1974, the cottage was declared "ready for occupancy."[29] The association has used it for exhibits and activities from 1974 to the present. It is open in this capacity on a limited basis to the public.

Owners: Richard Teller Crane Jr., 1917–19; Florence Higinbotham Crane, 1920–41; Jekyll Island Club, 1941–47

Constructed: 1917

Architecture: Italian Renaissance

Architects: David Adler and Henry C. Dangler

The Crane Years

Richard Teller Crane Jr., the man who built Crane Cottage, by far the most elaborate and expensive house ever constructed during the club era, was born in Chicago on November 7, 1873. He was the youngest surviving son (a younger brother having died in infancy) of Richard Teller Crane and his wife, Mary Josephine Prentice. His father, Richard T. Crane, a man with no formal education who worked in mills and machine shops from the age of nine, was a great enemy of university learning. He insisted that "college graduates were ill-equipped for earning a living," contending that "many of them could not command the salary of a skilled mechanic" and that, furthermore, drunkenness and de-

Facade of the Crane Cottage. Constructed in 1917, this was the most expensive and elegant winter home ever built at Jekyll. (*Architectural Record* [November 1924], copyright [1924] by the McGraw Hill Companies. All rights reserved. Reproduced with the permission of the publisher.)

Richard Teller Crane Jr. was president of the Crane Company, well-known for manufacturing bathroom fixtures. (Courtesy of Tatiana Bezamat)

At the time Richard Jr. joined the Crane Company in 1896, it was already a booming business. Founded in Chicago in 1854, it produced elevators, plumbing fixtures, steam engines, pumps, safety valves, drain and pipe fittings, and air brake equipment, and by the mid 1880s it was employing approximately fifteen hundred workers.

Young Crane moved up rapidly in the company, working first in the iron and brass foundries and then a year in the city sales department "to learn the business."[4] He became a second vice president in 1898 and first vice president in 1912 when his father died and his elder brother, Charles Richard Crane, moved up to president of the company. Charles resigned the position of president in 1914, however, ostensibly because of ill health resulting from malaria that he had contracted in earlier years. He would devote the rest of his life to political and diplomatic affairs, while his younger brother, Richard, took control of the family company, in 1914 assuming its presidency, a post he held until his death in 1931.[5] Under his leadership the Crane Company enjoyed its "greatest expansion in history," to include twenty thousand employees and offices, factories, and exhibition rooms in two hundred cities around the world.[6] During the 1920s the company sold America on the idea that the bathroom could be decorative and luxurious as well as functional and began successfully manufacturing and selling attractive matching bathroom ensembles that found their way into such places as King Hussein's palace in Mecca, Cecil B. DeMille's movie sets, and the Imperial Hotel in Tokyo, as well as the average home.[7]

As Crane gained success in the business world, becoming the second wealthiest man in Chicago, after Julius Rosenwald, president of Sears, Roebuck & Company, he climbed in the social world as well. His name appeared in the Chicago Blue Book, a directory of Chicago's elite, as early as 1891, and like most of his wealthy associates he was active in a variety of exclusive clubs including the prestigious Chicago Club, which boasted among its early mem-

bauchery were rampant at such bastions of higher learning as Yale, Harvard, and Columbia.[1] His eldest son, no doubt influenced by his father, received only a public school education before joining his father's firm, the Crane Company, at age fourteen.[2] Although he was willing to contribute to manual training schools in Chicago, the elder Crane denounced Carnegie Tech as an expensive "blunder."[3] One can only assume that in allowing his son, Richard Jr., to attend Yale, the scientific aspect of his education persuaded the old man and not any promise of culture, which he saw as useless. Thus in 1895 Richard Teller Crane Jr. graduated from the Sheffield Scientific School of Yale University.

bers Marshall Field, N. K. Fairbank, George Pullman, and Robert Todd Lincoln.[8] Crane was viewed by his peers as an affable man of noble character who despised "anything savoring of sharp practice or unfair dealing." He was said to be "devoid of greed for money or power" and one who "found his greatest pleasure in doing good to others."[9]

On June 4, 1904, when he was thirty years old, he married Florence Higinbotham, the daughter of Rachel Debora Davison and Harlow Niles Higinbotham, a partner of Marshall Field and president of the World's Columbian Exposition. A year after the marriage, on June 29, 1905, the Cranes had a son, Cornelius, and less than four years later, a daughter, Florence, born February 25, 1909. Both children would eventually make interesting and rather exotic marriages, Cornelius to Mine Sawahara from Hiroshima, Japan, and Florence to Prince Serge Belosselsky, son of a Russian émigré who came to the United States in the wake of the Russian Revolution.

Crane received a feeler to join the Jekyll Island Club in February 1911, just as his business career was about to burgeon with new responsibilities. "When you are looking around for a charming place for a visit in the winter or spring," wrote Cyrus Hall McCormick, a Chicago member of the club since 1891, "I shall be glad to have you consider the Jekyl Island Club, and I will give you a card if you and Mrs. Crane would like to visit it at any time." He indicated as well that he was "sending you a pamphlet about the Club, thinking you might like to become a member."[10]

Crane responded on February 22 that "I have heard so much of the place that I should like very much to see it." Like many other wealthy businessmen of the era, however, he was not above asking about the cost of fees and dues and was informed that shares were going at $2,000 in 1911 and dues at that time were $500 per year.[11]

When Crane was finally able to decide on a date to visit the island, McCormick took special pains to

Florence Higinbotham married Richard Teller Crane in 1904. She is shown here in a ball gown, circa 1895. (Courtesy of Tatiana Bezamat)

see that his friend was well received, personally contacting club superintendent Ernest Grob to help arrange accommodations to include rooms for the Cranes, their children, and two nurses. He also instructed his private secretary to "write to Grob asking him to introduce Mr. Crane to some of the men there."[12]

Grob, who could always be counted on to do his duty, reported during the visit that "Mr. Crane is getting on very well. I think he has been introduced to about everyone here."[13] And indeed Crane was clearly happy with his reception and accommodations. "We arrived here Monday morning," he informed McCormick, "and found very comfortable rooms awaiting us. The Manager has taken good care of us and we are enjoying the island immensely. It is just the place we needed and I am sure it will do us a great deal of good."[14]

Before leaving the island Crane had decided he would join the club and was officially nominated for membership on March 2, 1911. "We are all delighted with the place," he reiterated to McCormick, "and I want to thank you again for the use of your name in putting me up for membership. Mr. [Robert] Goelet was here and seconded it and I am now a full-fledged member. It is just the kind of place that suits me and I hope we can get here every spring."[15]

Crane would remain a member until his death in 1931, and his widow, who was elected a member in her own right in 1919, remained in the club until 1940. Crane's brother, Charles Richard Crane, would become a club member a few years later in 1916 and would remain in the club until 1924, although his diplomatic missions to Russia, Turkey, and various Asian and African countries did not allow him to use it as frequently as his brother did. After their first year in the club house with the children and their nurses, clearly not an entirely convenient situation, the Richard Teller Cranes returned the following year and leased the Ferguson cottage, which they occupied during the 1914 season as well, later indicating that, had it been for sale at the time, they would have given serious consideration to buying it.[16] But the Ferguson cottage was not for sale, and Crane began to make other arrangements.

On April 6, 1914, club superintendent Ernest G. Grob wrote a letter to club president Commodore Frederick Gilbert Bourne, conveying an offer of $1,500 by Crane to buy club lots 40 and 41, a riverfront lot and the lot across the road in the second row of cottages north of the Maurice cottage. He thought it wise for the executive committee to accept the offer, but pointed out that Crane was concerned that his property would be secured only by a lease and not a deed. The same issue had been raised previously by William Rockefeller, and the Crane attorney questioned whether a lease would "hold good in law." Club president Frederick Gilbert Bourne was prepared to have another attorney look into the matter before going before the board of governors for a final decision, but Robert W. de Forest made a convincing argument that the leases provided to members since the club's inception were indeed legal and valid and served the purpose of allowing the club "to control the use of the land so as to prevent its being used for non-Club purposes." He felt that arrangement had always "been satisfactory to all who built houses" and should continue to be club policy.[17]

While this sticky issue was still under debate, the executive committee deferred its decision in the matter of Crane's offer.[18] The delay was fortuitous for the Cranes, for during the intervening time period, Frederick Baker's widow, who had announced her intention to rebuild immediately following the burning of Solterra on March 9, 1914, changed her mind and decided to sell her lots. It was an opportune moment for Crane, who found these lots closer to the clubhouse and facing the river far more desirable. He made her an offer of an unknown amount for the property, and she accepted.

Crane contracted with Chicago architect Henry C. Dangler, who worked closely with David Adler to draw up plans for an elegant new house. The re-

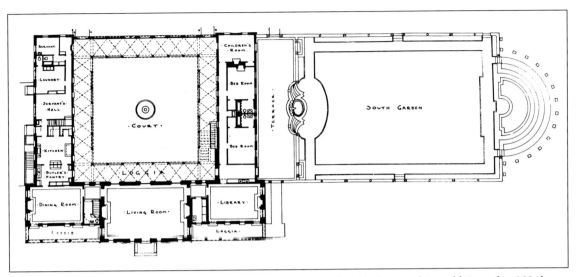

Crane Cottage floor plan, designed by David Adler and Henry Dangler. (*Architectural Record* [November 1924], copyright [1924] by the McGraw Hill Companies. All rights reserved. Reproduced with the permission of the publisher.)

lationship between these two architects is a curious one. They had met in Paris when they were both students at the Ecole des Beaux-Arts. Adler, although he attended classes, failed to submit his *envoi*, a thesis in the form of an architectural design. Nor did he take the final oral and written examinations. He took a similar cavalier attitude toward applying for architectural licenses in the United States. As a consequence, he worked with Dangler, who had completed all the requirements in Paris and who had the necessary licenses. Thus it was Dangler's name that usually appeared on building permits for their jointly done architectural plans. Although the two men never formed a legal partnership, they operated from the same office, divided fees equally, and stressed different interests in their well-orchestrated works. Adler devoted himself to design, while Dangler, who had been more conscientious in his studies, had a knack for the "technical and structural aspects of architecture [that] never interested Adler deeply." [19] Dangler died before the completion of the Crane's Jekyll house, and, even though he was

deeply involved in preparing the original plans and specifications for the villa that Crane and his wife built on the site of the demolished Solterra, it is Adler's name alone that is usually associated with its design. [20] After Dangler's death, Adler was finally compelled to sit for exams as a resident architect, exams that he failed miserably. Following that experience, he formed a partnership with Robert Work that lasted some twelve years, during which time he designed (in 1927) another impressive house for the Cranes, Castle Hill, located in Ipswich, Massachusetts, and called by Adler's biographer "his masterpiece." [21] It was a palatial country house that had "fifty-nine rooms and required an inside staff of nineteen servants." [22] The size and scope of Castle Hill gives one some idea of the perspective that would allow the Cranes to consider their new Georgia villa a "cottage" in the tradition of Jekyll simplicity.

The Jekyll cottage was designed in 1916 and constructed in 1917. Sometime prior to February 14, 1917, Dangler sent the plans and specifications to a

Brunswick contractor, George Cowman, with an offer to bid on the job. Cowman was happy to submit a bid "if it can be arranged for me to do the work on a percentage basis, as I could not handle it as a straight contract job."[23] Apparently Dangler was willing to push forward with Cowman, who gave an estimate of $62,282. However, the figure did not include electrical wiring or heat, and Dangler demanded an estimate for these additional items by March 12. Cowman could not meet the deadline, and differences in timetables and costs could never be worked out to the satisfaction of both parties.[24] Hence the contracting job was turned over to the Chicago firm of Gage and Company, headed by Thomas George Gage, a native of Birmingham, England, who had emigrated to the United States in 1875.[25]

By early August 1917 work on the Crane Cottage was under way. Commenting on the work's progress, Cowman wrote to G. A. Kay, the club's electrical engineer, "they are getting along slow," indicating as well that they brought "everything from Chicago," including the workmen, which evidently added considerably to the cost.[26] The *Brunswick News* reported on "an unusually large force at work," noting that Crane was "anxious to have his winter home already [sic] for occupancy this season. . . . This winter palace is to be one of the handsomest to be found anywhere in the south, and, while it was originally designed to cost $100,000, it is certain that it will go past that amount before it is finished. The cottage will have a total of forty rooms, with sun parlor, large porches, and every possible convenience. It is being constructed of the best material and the work on it is progressing as rapidly as possible."[27]

Progress on the villa did not make such rapid headway as Crane had hoped. Dangler died in 1917 before the house was well begun, and David Adler was required to assume oversight of the building. He visited Jekyll four times between March 24, 1917, and March 25, 1919. The Cranes rented the apartment of Cornelius Bliss in the club annex for the 1917 and 1918 seasons and did not take up full occupancy in the cottage until the beginning of the 1919 season, with Adler showing up one last time to oversee his finished product.[28]

The Crane villa was a beautiful edifice in the Italian Renaissance style. It featured arcaded loggias on both sides of the main entrance, an enclosed courtyard surrounded by additional arcaded loggias, twenty bedrooms, seventeen baths (not unexpected, perhaps, in a Crane home), and to the south of the house a splendid formal garden that was included as part of the original design. Described by Adler's biographer Richard Pratt as an "Italian palazzo," its entrance was said to be influenced by a "small villa on the Brenta River in northern Italy."[29] He goes on to point out that the entrance "opens onto a large living room . . . , the only instance in all Adler's houses where halls and galleries do not form the circulation." The reason for this, he speculates shrewdly, was "that the house was one of an island colony of winter homes where a sort of conscious informality was in vogue."[30]

The Jekyll philosophy of simplicity and informality, certainly "in vogue" during the early years, had not been entirely forgotten, though there had been some elevation in recent years as to what constituted simplicity. But such a deviation was too much for James William Ellsworth, who got wind of the project even before the cottage was constructed. On May 8, 1917, he complained to the executive committee that "the building of pretentious houses on the Island by members" threatened to overshadow the club house, which he considered Jekyll's principal feature, and would tend "to destroy what may be considered the greatest charm, this atmosphere of simplicity."[31] Although he does not mention the Crane cottage by name, there can be little doubt that he was alluding to the Crane "palazzo" that was about to be constructed. The executive committee, headed by George E. Macy, himself the owner of a somewhat simpler cottage,

South side of Crane house, with sunken garden. (Courtesy of Jekyll Island Museum)

Crane courtyard with fountain. (*Architectural Record* [November 1924], copyright [1924] by the McGraw Hill Companies. All rights reserved. Reproduced with the permission of the publisher.)

Crane Cottage loggia. (*Architectural Record* [November 1924], copyright [1924] by the McGraw Hill Companies. All rights reserved. Reproduced with the permission of the publisher.)

discreetly tabled the motion "for future considera-tion." It is never again mentioned in the executive committee minutes.

The Cranes were not totally insensitive to the criticism, although Ellsworth's letter had not men-tioned them by name. According to Nancy Albright Hurd, who recalled the incident, their one gesture toward simplicity was to take up the Italian marble floor of the living room and replace it with a more subtle, though extremely attractive, wooden floor.[32] The house was sufficiently completed in 1917 for the Cranes to be required to pay taxes on it in 1918. It was assessed at $50,000, twice as much as any other cottage on the island.

Their first occupancy of the new cottage began on January 23, 1919, when Mrs. Crane's eighty-one-year-old father, Harlow Niles Higinbotham, who had lived with the Crane family for a decade, arrived with his thirteen-year-old grandson, Cor-nelius. Richard and Florence Crane joined them with young Florence on January 29, and the family enjoyed their first season in the magnificent house, staying until April 2, when they all returned to-gether to New York and checked into the Ritz-Carlton Hotel. The pleasures of their maiden season in their Jekyll house, however, were soon forgotten when tragedy struck on April 18, just two weeks af-ter their return. Despite his advanced age, Higin-

Interior sitting room (designated as a library on the original plans) in Crane Cottage. (Courtesy of Jekyll Island Museum)

A bedroom in Crane Cottage. (Courtesy of Jekyll Island Museum)

botham was still an active man, very much involved in civic and charitable activities. He was on his way to a post–World War I Soldiers' Welcoming Committee meeting to "chat with the boys" when he was struck by an army ambulance, receiving serious head wounds from which he ultimately died, with his son-in-law, Richard Teller Crane Jr., at his bedside. Earlier in the day the family had been summoned and then sent away again, told to return in the late afternoon. Sensing that he needed to be with his father-in-law, Crane returned to the hospital before the others and was there during the brief moments when Higinbotham regained consciousness and at the moment of his death.[33]

It was typical of Crane, whose empathy for others has been well noted by his biographers. He was considered "affable, democratic, approachable, cordial and sympathetic," and, above all, "rigidly honest"[34] and was a noted philanthropist who manifested a deep concern for the welfare of his employees.

As had his father before him, from time to time he gave stock from his own private holdings totaling $10 million to his workers in times of economic hardship. He took his civic responsibilities seriously, for example making an offer to the mayor of New York in 1916 during the infantile paralysis epidemic there to give $25,000 to the individual who could offer a cure within the next year.[35]

Nor did he neglect the needs of the Jekyll Island Club itself. He contributed $2,000 toward a new golf course in 1928 and was appointed chair of the committee to raise money for the James Memorial Wall at the south end of the new swimming pool and for the construction of the James Dormitory for caddies.[36] He and Mrs. Crane also sponsored the Crane Mixed Double Handicap Tennis Tournament, which was held from 1915 to 1940, the winners of which were awarded the R. T. Crane Jr. Cup, engraved with their names.[37] Crane's "genial manner and charming personality," coupled with his business

The Cranes' niece Florence Higinbotham, *right,* and their daughter Florence practice their tennis swings on the club court. (Courtesy of Jekyll Island Club)

acumen, no doubt accounts for his presence and long service on the club's board of directors, as first vice president and member of the executive committee, and on the committees on roads, golf, and finance.[38] Nor was his wife any less congenial. She was a member of the club's welfare committee for years, serving most of the time as chair, and even after her husband's death in 1931, when she had ceased to visit the island, she was still listed as a member of the committee that did its best to raise money to help provide food, hospital services, school upkeep, and a Christmas tree for the club's permanent employees.[39]

Throughout their club membership, the Cranes displayed their friendship and hospitality to club members and employees alike. They had begun entertaining even before their cottage was ready for occupancy. Kate Brown, the young tutor for the Valentine Everit Macy children, was invited to tea in 1917 by the Cranes, staying that season in the club annex. She was greeted at the door "by a perfectly trained man in perfectly fitting plum-colored livery," quite a contrast, she observed, from the way people arrived at her home on Choate Island not far from Ipswich, where people could be seen "taking off their shoes and stockings and wading ashore if the tide is low." [40] A few days later she reported to her family that she "had a long talk with Mr. Crane yesterday, a pleasant, kindly simple soul, and he told me about the golf course he wants to lay out at Castle Neck [his winter abode] with two of the holes on the beach." [41]

Of course the Cranes did not confine themselves to entertaining tutors, though they were democratic enough to do so. They also opened their doors to Rockefellers, Macys, and other islanders of great social standing. During one season in 1927 they chartered a three-masted schooner owned by Cornelius Vanderbilt III and had it brought to Jekyll, where it picked them up along with several of their friends for a cruise in the West Indies.[42]

Evidently, their life style tended to be a bit more formal and elegant than those of many at the Jekyll Island Club, who clung tenaciously to the idea of the simple life. Susan Albright remembered Mrs. Crane as "a gentle lady with an energetic husband" whose children, Cornelius and Florence, were so "shy" and "protected by 'Nurse'" that Nancy and I felt sorry for them." Nevertheless, she had "such happy memories of my friend Florence, whose disagreeable Nanny didn't like me, because Florence was being brought up like a little lady and she didn't approve of our trying to ride the pigs at the Farm, which was up on Plantation Road." [43]

After their usual winter season at Jekyll in 1931, the Cranes returned to Chicago and then departed for their summer home in Ipswich. Crane was suffering from heart disease, and as his health grew worse he was taken to New York for treatment. Concern over the worsening depression and its effect on his employees aggravated his condition. The economic situation that plagued the United States and indeed much of the world had forced retrenchment within the Crane Company, which had been compelled to lay off some of its employees. In addition, worry over his son's asthmatic condition, which was so bad that it had forced the Cranes sometimes to cut short their Jekyll vacations because of the humidity, only exacerbated his own health problems.[44]

On November 7, 1931, his fifty-eighth birthday, Richard Crane died of a heart attack. His will expanded the philanthropy and concerns he had manifested during his lifetime, leaving to veteran employees an additional $1.2 million in stock in the Crane Company, with the stipulation that these gifts should go to only those employees who had retained all the stock he had given them during his lifetime. He also left $50,000 to New York University's centennial fund for the medical college and $30,000 to further the work of the Association Against the Prohibition Amendment.[45]

His death coincided not only with the national depression but also with a decline in the Jekyll Island Club from which it never recovered. As members died or dropped out of the club, fewer were recruited, and the financial condition of the organization was far from sound. Florence Crane deeded her cottage to her children in 1939 and did not visit the island again until March 19, 1940, when she stayed in the club house rather than in the cottage. In 1941 Crane Cottage was turned over to the Jekyll Island Club, and one of the first club functions held there was the Founders' Day luncheon on March 24, 1941, given by the board of governors "on the patio of the Crane villa recently acquired by the club."[46]

The State Era

Just prior to the state takeover of the island in 1947, the furnishings in the Crane Cottage were sold to J. H. Elliott of the Southern Appraisal Company in Atlanta for a total of $11,380. By the early 1950s, members of the Jekyll Island Authority were considering the possibility of leasing Crane Cottage to a hotel association. On January 15, 1954, they received an inquiry from Helen Gould, the widow of Frank Miller Gould, about the possibility of leasing the Crane Cottage. The authority approved a resolution that she be offered a lease at $500 per month, but she evidently declined, for there is no further communication on the matter.[47] In fact, it may have

seemed to her an exorbitant rate, since other cottages were leased for as little as $60 a month. Finally, the matter of what to do with the cottage was settled when the authority leased it, along with the club house and the Sans Souci, to the Jekyll Island Hotel Association, of which state senator Jimmy Dykes from Cochran, Georgia, was the primary stockholder. Crane cottage was refurbished, according to its publicity brochures, "air-conditioned, steam-heated and thoroughly modernized" and opened as the "Crane Hotel" in June 1955, with double rooms available from $6 to $12 a day.[48]

By 1960, however, the Crane Hotel was no more, and the *Brunswick News* announced that the Crane "castle" on Jekyll would be restored once again by Dewey Scarboro, who currently leased the Villa Ospo, and opened to public viewing, though it was not until 1963 that he offered to the Jekyll Island Authority an official proposal to do so.[49] Today the offices of the Jekyll Island Authority are located in Crane Cottage, and its living room and patio are frequently used as sites for official social functions and wedding receptions. Plans are currently in place to refurbish the cottage in 1998 as a bed-and-breakfast addition to the Jekyll Island Club Hotel.

4

THE FINAL
YEARS

Owners: Walter Jennings, 1927–33; Jean Brown Jennings, 1933–42; Jekyll Island Club, 1942–47

Constructed: 1927

Architecture: Elements of Spanish Eclectic and Italian Renaissance

Architect: John Russell Pope

Walter Jennings, brother-in-law of club president Walter B. James, built the cottage he would call Villa Ospo. Jennings was born September 14, 1858, in San Francisco where his father, Oliver Burr Jennings, had assumed a post as senior member of the mercantile firm of Jennings and Brewster. In 1865 the family returned to New York where, as the brother-in-law of William Rockefeller, Oliver Jennings became one of the original stockholders in the Standard Oil Company. There he earned his fortune. His son, Walter Jennings, would continue the family association with the Standard Oil Company. He graduated from Yale University in 1880 and two years later from Columbia University Law School, where he was a classmate of Teddy Roosevelt. He practiced law for only a short time, how-

Villa Ospo, from the scrapbook of Mrs. Walter Jennings, 1930. The cottage was built by Walter Jennings, director of Standard Oil of New Jersey. (Courtesy of Jekyll Island Museum)

ever, before taking a position in the business world with Pratt Manufacturing Company, an affiliate of Standard Oil. He became a director of the Standard Oil Company of New Jersey in 1903 and served as secretary from 1908 until 1911.[1]

Walter Jennings married Jean Pollack Brown, the grandniece of Henry Bergh, founder of the Society for the Prevention of Cruelty to Animals, on November 11, 1891. Three children would be born to the couple, Oliver (born May 2, 1894), Jeannette (May 12, 1898), and Constance (May 16, 1900). Six weeks after the birth of their first child, Jean and Walter Jennings set sail on June 6, leaving their young son behind in the care of nurses, for a three-month trip to Europe. Mrs. Jennings kept a vivid journal of the trip, which lasted until September 14. The Jenningses apparently loved to travel, taking other frequent extended trips abroad, even annually in the early 1920s.

Walter Jennings became a member of the Jekyll Island Club in 1926 while his brother-in-law Walter James was club president. The James and Jennings families were close, sharing adjacent summer estates in Cold Springs Harbor on Long Island.[2] Thus when the Jameses offered their Jekyll cottage to Walter and Jean Jennings for a winter vacation, they accepted with pleasure. Leaving New York in the midst of a blizzard on February 4, 1926, they arrived at Jekyll the following day to "heavenly weather," finding Cherokee Cottage "very attractive, & much pleasanter than their [the Jameses'] apartment, altho' that too is delightful."[3] The Jenningses played golf, admired the camellias blooming in February, and ate grapefruit from the club trees, only to return to snow in New York on February 20 after two weeks on the island. The visit was enough to convince Jennings that he wanted to join the club. The following month he allowed himself to be proposed for membership by Cornelius Lee and seconded by Valentine Everit Macy.

Unfortunately, the James and Jennings families did not long share the pleasures of Jekyll Island, for

Walter B. James died the following year after the close of the club season (see Cherokee chapter) just as Walter and Jean Jennings were making plans for their new Jekyll house. Walter Jennings, although he had been a member of the club only a year, was elected to succeed him. His election to the presidency of the club strengthened Walter Jennings's ties to the island.

On March 4, 1927, Jennings engaged well-known architect John Russell Pope to design a new house for them on lot 40 at Jekyll Island.[4] Pope was a noted architect who had designed the National Gallery of Art and the Jefferson Memorial in Washington, D.C., among important public buildings. The Jennings cottage combines elements of Italian Renaissance architecture (popular between 1890 and 1935) and Spanish Eclectic (popular between 1915 and 1940). Both styles have tiled roofs and arches over the doorways. Like most Italian Renaissance and some Spanish Eclectic houses, it had a low-pitched hipped roof. Arches above the doors and first-story windows, smaller, less decorative upstairs windows, overhanging eaves, and classical pilasters all relate the house to the Italian Renaissance style. However, the asymmetrical facade and the chimney top that resembles a bell tower as well as the covered porch with an arcaded walkway, second-floor balconies, stucco wall surface, and decorative grills reflect elements of the Spanish Eclectic style. In short, the cottage is a pleasing blend of the two. The total cost of the cottage, which was constructed by local contractor George Cowman, was $48,297.[5]

Walter and Jean Jennings decided to name their new cottage Villa Ospo, a name that harkened back to the precolonial era when Jekyll Island was populated by Native Americans who apparently used the island for hunting and fishing. Spanish maps of the sixteenth century label the island, or possibly a Guale Indian town located on the island, Ospo.[6] It may have been Jennings's interest in the island's early history that led the club to request that the

Walter Jennings in 1923. Jennings
was elected president of the Jekyll
Island Club in 1927 to succeed his
brother-in-law, Walter James.
(Courtesy of Day Ravenscroft)

Jean Brown Jennings in 1923.
(Courtesy of Day Ravenscroft)

South terrace of Villa Ospo, from the scrapbook of Mrs. Walter Jennings,
1930. (Courtesy of Jekyll Island Museum)

Courtyard of Villa Ospo, from the scrapbook of Mrs. Walter Jennings, 1930. (Courtesy of Jekyll Island Museum)

Georgia legislature "correct" the spelling of the name of the island from "Jekyl" with a single "l" to "Jekyll," as it had been written by Sir Joseph Jekyll, for whom Oglethorpe had named it. In any case, under the leadership of Walter Jennings, the club lobbied to have the spelling changed. The resolution was approved by the house and senate, and signed by Gov. Lamartine G. Hardman on July 21, 1929.

Unfortunately, the change in the spelling would mark the beginning of the club's decline. With the stock market crash in 1929 and in subsequent years as the Great Depression deepened, club membership began to drop precipitously. That the country's economic situation was a primary factor in the club's declining membership is indisputable, as the

1933 annual report makes clear: "The present stress and upheaval of social and business affairs has been fully reflected in the number of recent resignations and withdrawals of our members. We hope that many of these are of but a temporary nature and that they will mark the end of this difficult phase, throughout which the Club has managed to maintain its activities undiminished in any way."[7] But such was not to be the case. Jennings had become president of the club at its peak. Unfortunately, his administration, through no fault of his own, marked the beginning of the club's decline.

Another contributing factor in the changing fortunes of the Jekyll Island Club was undoubtedly the resignation of its superintendent of forty-two years, Ernest Gilbert Grob. One employee report contends that Grob and Jennings had a falling out over the tipping of employees, with Grob arguing against a new club policy that would prohibit tipping, contending that it would "cause a decline in the quality of service." As the story is recounted, both men stubbornly refused to change their positions, and when "Grob made the statement that as long as he was superintendent tipping would be permitted," Jennings "implied to Grob that he accepted his resignation."[8] Whether the report is true or not, Ernest Grob had reached what most would consider a normal retirement age, and he had already retired from a similar position at the Malvern in Bar Harbor. If there was such a dispute, it merely precipitated an action that was already inevitable in the near future. With Grob's resignation, however, several other long-time employees, among them the Jekyll yacht captain James Clark, also left the club's service, leaving older members to bemoan the changes.

The executive committee hired M. L. DeZutter, a man with more "modern" ideas of how a club should be run. Unfortunately, club members had become accustomed to Grob's old-world, Victorian manner, to a style that reflected a passing era of gentility and charm. More than one island worker, interviewed by staff members of the Jekyll Island

Villa Ospo interior, from the scrapbook of Mrs. Walter Jennings, 1930. (Courtesy of Jekyll Island Museum)

Jean Brown Jennings wrote on the back of this photograph: "From door of Sitting Room from hall, hangings of Fortuny linen, deep crimson—walls grayish white. W's desk at left, mine at right. Room is always full of flowers & growing plants." (Courtesy of Jekyll Island Museum)

Museum, has blamed the club's decline on DeZutter's having "ruined" the island. Certainly some of his policies seemed more appropriate to resort hotels than to the exclusive ambiance of the residential club.

Despite staff changes of such magnitude, Jennings's tenure as club president was generally judged a success by his fellow members. His achievements at Jekyll included the completion of the new golf course that had been planned during President James's administration, as well as indoor tennis courts and general maintenance of the club house and grounds.[9] The 1933 annual report lauded Jennings's experience and qualifications as president and his interest "in all features of the Island" in having taken up "a task entirely congenial to him." He had performed his tasks as president "fully and faithfully" and with "sedulous care."

Certainly he was on hand to take care of club affairs as they arose, for the Jenningses came to the island for virtually the entire club season every year from 1926 until Walter's death in 1933. They usually arrived on the island in December, sometimes even in early December, returning to New York only for Christmas. Mrs. Jennings's diary records one such arrival on December 6, 1929: "12:45 Arr. at Jekyll. Lovely & warm & sunny. Our dear little house lovelier than ever. Gardens have grown wonderfully." Club seasons varied between relaxing days of calm that left time for long walks or drives along the beach and others that were characterized by a busy social whirl. On March 8, 1929, for example, Mrs. Jennings records tea at the Maurices, cocktails with the Coes, and "Loew's picnic on Beach for J.I.C. [Jekyll Island Club]." Tea at the Maurices, the Cranes, or the Claflins was regularly on the agenda.

On March 27, 1930, Jean Jennings recorded in her diary a particular honor that the club had paid to her husband—the renaming of Willow Pond Road as Jennings Road. In fact, the occasion was that of eminent financier George Fisher Baker's nine-

tieth birthday, which he had elected to spend at the Jekyll Island Club, hosting a dinner for sixty people aboard his yacht the *Viking*. As a birthday honor to Baker, the club dedicated Palmetto Road to him. Roads were also renamed for long-standing and honored club members Charles Stewart Maurice (formerly Pine Road) and John Claflin (formerly Oak Road).[10] The following day Jennings wrote Cyrus McCormick to tell him of the event. He had learned that McCormick has been "the arch-conspirator" in having Willow Pond Road renamed in his honor. "It was a great compliment and like-wise a great surprise and my wife and I are over-whelmed with gratitude to you for making the suggestion."[11]

The Jenningses arrived, as usual, on December 29, 1932. The first week of the new year was like any other at Jekyll Island. Mrs. Jennings's diary

The Jenningses entertain Bishop Attwood with a beach picnic in January 1929. *Left to right,* Bishop Attwood, Walter Jennings, Jean Jennings, Claire Jennings. (Everett Collection, Coastal Georgia Historical Society)

records the typical activities of walks and drives and games of golf. The only thing that set that week apart from any other was an automobile accident they had on January 4 when they collided unexpectedly with a truck on Oglethorpe Road. Such events were unheard of at Jekyll, where motorized vehicles had in previous years been discouraged. Mrs. Jennings went through the windshield and suffered two black eyes as a consequence. The following day, Walter Jennings began to complain of stomach pains. A Dr. Avera, called in from Brunswick, diagnosed it as indigestion, though he sent out a nurse for fear of appendicitis.

The following morning Dr. Avera came again to find Mr. Jennings much better. This time he concluded that he must have been bruised by the steering wheel in the accident. That night, however, Jennings began to suffer again, with pain in both back and abdomen. This time Mrs. Jennings sent for Dr. Warfield M. Firor from Johns Hopkins to fly down to attend him. Dr. Firor was a familiar face on the island, for he was frequently in attendance during the club season. Jennings's pains came and went, and he seemed more comfortable after Dr. Firor's arrival. In fact, Mrs. Jennings heard him tell the nurse that "he never felt better." However, at 5:30 the following morning (January 9) Dr. Firor was summoned again. Mrs. Jennings indicated that she "ran in and found him massaging W." But the doctor could do nothing to help him, and by 6 A.M. Walter Jennings was dead of a heart attack.

Mrs. Jennings left Jekyll at 4:30 that afternoon for New York. She wrote in her diary on February 1: "This tragic month has passed like all earthly things. I am grateful for all the kindness shown me. My children are wonderful to me. Isa [her daughter-in-law] walks miles with me in every kind of weather, & they are all better than any other children in the world." On February 26 the club held a memorial service for Jennings at which Alanson B. Houghton spoke, summarizing Jennings's service to Jekyll: "Six years ago he became a member of the Jekyll Island Club. Five years ago he became its President.

And straitway, the interests of every human being connected with the Island became his interests. He knew every nook and corner of it. The birds, the flowers, the trees, the paths were all familiar to him. He knew where the jasmine first bloomed. He knew where the first blue herons could be seen. He knew the woods, and the little creeks, and the marshes, and the multitudinous lives with which they were filled." [12]

Like many men of Jennings's generation and social class, he gave the best of himself to the public but was more reticent to open himself up to his own family. The months following her husband's death were difficult for Jean Jennings. She wrote in her diary on March 1: "Another month gone, & I am still here. It is lonely, even in the midst of loving friends & family. I hope I am not a nuisance to my children. They seem to have me always on their minds & I am never alone." But there had been loneliness within marriage as well, as she had made clear in a rare passage written on November 10, 1926: "Grandchildren sent me orchids last night as today is my 35th anniversary. Think W[alter] must have forgotten as he did not mention it. Knowing him [I] suppose he thought I understood without words, but after so many years when I have tried to make him happy, I wondered whether it was worthwile [sic] after all to put one's self out for another, it does not seem to make much difference in his life. He has so many resources and is so fond of things. People don't make much difference to him." [13]

The summer after her husband's death Jean Jennings sought a change of scenery, making an uncharacteristic trip to Riddle Ranch in Wyoming. Her diary entries of this period are infrequent and seldom introspective, beyond a brief comment like "a sad day" or, in a memorandum at the end of 1933, "This year was not a happy one." But she was a strong and capable woman who rallied and managed to fill her life with a variety of activities just as she had done when her husband was alive.

She had been born in Esopus, New York, on June 21, 1864, and was known to her friends as a

Corridor in Villa Ospo during the Jennings era. It was described by Jean Brown Jennings as "View from Sitting Room door toward Hall door, wh. is an old Spanish 17th Cent. door—lovely carvings. Hall red tiles. Painted doors (old) into 2 bachelor rooms at left & pantry & dining room at right. Stairs in niche at right. Old Spanish lantern." (Courtesy of Georgia Department of Archives and History, original in Jekyll Island Museum)

Corridor in Villa Ospo during the state era, as it was elaborately furnished by Dewey Scarboro. (Courtesy of Jekyll Island Museum)

champion of nature. Described by the *New York Times* as a "well-known horticulturalist," she often opened to visitors her beautiful gardens at Burrwood, her Long Island estate, for charity functions and flower exhibits.[14] Her diaries throughout her mature life reveal a woman who filled her days with social commitments among a wide circle of friends and at family gatherings, interspersed with meetings for charities, civic duties, and church activites. In 1935 she accepted election to the board of Huntingdon Hospital, and for many years she also served as chair of the social service committee of New York Hospital. She was a member of the Colony Club of New York, the Colonial Dames of America, and her beloved North Country Garden Club.

She continued her annual visits to Jekyll, though she came later and stayed for a shorter period of time than she had with Walter. Her son Oliver and his wife, Isa, often came with her. Her daughters, both married now, Jeannette to Henry C. Taylor of New York and Connie to Albert H. Ely of Washington, D.C., had given her grandchildren to enjoy. She continued to own her "dear little house" at Jekyll until the end of the club era. On May 28, 1942, following the close of the club's last season, she deeded the Villa Ospo to the Jekyll Island Club.[15] Jean Jennings lived on at Burrwood, her Long Island estate, until May 2, 1949, when she died at the age of eighty-five.

The State Era

After the state took over the island in 1947 and established in 1950 the Jekyll Island State Park Authority, as it was then called, the Villa Ospo apparently stood empty until it was approved for lease to Dewey Scarboro on May 14, 1955. He furnished the cottage with what the *Brunswick News* described as "the ornate furnishings of France's 'gilded age,'" certainly more ostentatious than any that the Jennings family had ever had in the cottage, and in the spring of 1960 he received permission from the authority to open the cottage "to the public for paid admission."[16] In subsequent years, it was used as a doll museum, and it currently houses the Jekyll Island Museum collection.

Owners: Frank Miller Gould, 1928–45; F. M. Gould Estate, 1945–46; Lawrence R. Condon, 1946–47

Constructed: 1928

Architecture: Spanish Eclectic

Architect: Mogens Tvede

Frank Miller Gould, who in 1928 built the Villa Marianna, had spent many happy winters during his boyhood on Jekyll Island. Born on February 6, 1899, he was the younger son of Edwin Gould and the grandson of financier Jay Gould. His father, Edwin, bought David H. King's house on River Road when Frank was less than two years old, named it Chichota, and proceeded to make Jekyll Island a winter paradise for his young family. (See Chichota chapter.) Thus throughout Frank Gould's boyhood, Jekyll was an idyllic escape from the wintry confinement of New York City.

In 1928 Frank Miller Gould built the Villa Marianna, the last cottage to be constructed in the Jekyll Island Cottage Colony. The cottage was named for Marianne, the daughter of Gould and his wife, Florence Amelia Bacon. Marianne is shown here in front of the cottage. (Everett Collection, Coastal Georgia Historical Society)

Despite the watchful eyes of his parents, Frank and his older brother, Eddie, would sometimes slip away from their tutor to the little island school located just down the lane from his grandmother's island house (see Cherokee chapter) to join the employees' children in play at recess. For the two young boys Jekyll was, in many ways, a dream world where they could roam relatively freely and where nature was an everyday part of their existence. There they encountered children who had grown up on the island and knew it well, children unlike any they knew in their insulated life in New York. On such days they played with Catherine and Freddie Clark, the children of Captain Clark, the skipper of the Jekyll Island steamer, and Ada Thompson and her siblings, children of the Jekyll Island Club fisherman.

Every winter, from the time he was a tot until his seventeenth birthday, Frank Miller Gould and his family spent glorious vacations on the island. From 1912 to 1916, his parents enrolled him at the Browning School in New York in preparation for his entrance into Yale. His older brother, however, was no scholar and had resisted going to college at all. In February 1917 while Frank was away at Yale, the death of his brother, Edwin Jr., during a visit to Jekyll Island ended their dream of an unfettered boyhood. (See Chicota chapter.)

It had happened in a freak accident on his father's hunting preserve at Latham Hammock, a small island in the center of the Marshes of Glynn, clearly visible from the Jekyll Island boat dock. Frank's mother, Sally Gould, was inconsolable and refused ever to return to Jekyll again, nor was she happy when other members of the family vacationed there. But Frank Miller Gould never forgot his delightful boyhood winters at Jekyll, and he was determined not to give up the island. In fact, on more than one occasion, in 1921 and again in March 1924, accompanied only by friends and once by his grandmother, Hester Shrady, he went back to the island.[1]

Frank Gould, who had joined the ROTC program at Yale, was commissioned as a second lieutenant in the U.S. Army in September 1918 and transferred to Camp Zachary Taylor, where he served in the Thirty-ninth Training Battery until

Frank Miller Gould spent a happy boyhood on Jekyll Island. He is shown here with his father, Edwin Gould. (Courtesy of Edwin J. Gould family)

he was discharged less than two months later, after the armistice ending the war was signed on November 11.[2] Following his short-lived active military career, he joined the 212th Artillery of the New York National Guard, where he held the same rank from 1921 until 1922. He graduated from Yale on schedule in 1920 and that same year became assistant secretary of the St. Louis Southwestern Railroad, a restructured version of a railroad that had been originally developed by his grandfather Jay Gould and of which his father had once served as president.[3] Despite his new responsibilities, he was still a young man sowing his wild oats. In November 1922, for example, he was arrested for speeding south on New York's Park Avenue at the unseemly velocity of forty miles an hour. The problem was compounded by the fact that at first he refused to stop and, when he was finally taken into custody nine blocks later, refused to identify himself. According to the account that made the front page of the *New York Times,* he was "fined, fingerprinted and sent to the Tombs handcuffed among thirteen speeders, non-licensed peddlers and other lawbreakers."[4] However, the fair-minded reporter noted that he "took his sentence without comment and submitted cheerfully to be fingerprinted" and that he was "a model prisoner in every respect." It took only four hours for the Gould lawyers to have him released.

The following year, however, he found a reason to think of settling down. At a social function in Dallas where his job often took him, he met a charming young woman selling lemonade for charity. She was none other than Florence Amelia Bacon, the niece of Daniel Upthegrove, president of the St. Louis Southwestern Railroad, for which young Gould worked. Although his prospects were already excellent, a romantic relationship with his boss's niece certainly did not hurt his career, and it is not likely a mere coincidence that in 1924, the year of the couple's marriage, Frank Gould received a rather phenomenal promotion by any standards from as-

sistant secretary to vice president of the railroad, a post he would hold until his death.[5]

The couple became engaged in the summer of 1924, although the families did not formally announce the betrothal until October 17. The marriage of Frank Miller Gould and Florence Amelia Bacon (nicknamed Betsy), both from socially prominent families, was not the society event of the season, as one might have expected. On the contrary, the couple was married quietly on November 17, 1924, at 9 P.M. at the home of the bride's parents, Mr. and Mrs. William Bacon of Highland Park, Dallas. The wedding, which had been planned for December, was unexpectedly hastened, ostensibly because of unspecified business plans of Frank Gould. Evidently, it was a last-minute, rather haphazard affair, because, according to newspaper accounts, "The few who witnessed the ceremony were hastily invited by telephone . . . about an hour before the wedding."[6] Frank Gould's parents were not among those present. Edwin Gould gave a statement to the press indicating that he and his wife "regret very much that we were unable to attend the wedding" because, as he explained the circumstances, he had been "under constant examination as a witness in the Gould accounting suit and it has been impossible for me to absent myself from the city."[7]

The "accounting suit" to which Edwin Gould referred concerned the settlement of the estate of his father, Jay Gould, after a raging battle among the heirs that lasted in its various phases from 1919 until 1927, when the Supreme Court of the state of New York finally settled the matter once and for all.[8] Certainly the newly married couple must have watched with great interest the proceedings which, by all accounts, caused the disintegration of family relations among Jay Gould's children, for Frank Gould had every expectation of being his father's sole heir.[9] The couple would settle in New York, where Frank indulged his interest in horses and racing.

Edwin Gould with his granddaughter Marianne. (Courtesy of Edwin J. Gould family)

One of the first places Frank Miller Gould took his new bride was to Jekyll Island, where they registered together for the first time on January 18, 1925, just two months after their wedding, to spend some time in the Gould family cottage, Chichota.[10] They came again in 1926, but by the following year they had begun to formulate plans to build their own cottage on the island.

By early 1928 Gould had engaged a young Danish architect named Mogens Tvede, who had been a guest of the Jennings family at Jekyll the preced-

ing year, to design a new cottage for him and his family, to which had now been added a little golden-haired girl named Marianne born in 1926.[11] The house, which the Goulds would call Villa Marianna after their daughter, was built during the summer of 1928 in the increasingly popular Spanish Eclectic style which reached its peak in the 1920s and 1930s.[12] With its red-tiled, gabled, and multileveled roof, its arched doorways and stucco wall surfaces, its asymmetrical facade with balconies and a square tower, and its enclosed patio, it typified the architectural style that Addison Mizner was popularizing in Florida resorts during this same period. The cottage contains fifteen rooms and six baths. Its features include a fifteen-foot-square breezeway observatory on the third floor of the tower, a sculptured Italian-style fireplace in the drawing room, a walled courtyard with ceramic tile and fountain, and a reflecting pool in front of the house.

The construction of the cottage was entrusted to Brunswick contractor George Cowman, who had gained a favorable reputation among club members for doing quality work at reasonable cost.[13] As a consequence, he landed most of the contracts among the Jekyll members for work on their houses during the 1920s. The Villa Marianna appears on

the Brunswick tax rolls for the first time in 1929, where it is valued for tax purposes at $29,000.

According to the *Brunswick News* of October 14, 1928, the Goulds were expected to arrive soon to inspect their new house.[14] We may suppose that they spent much of the 1929 season furnishing and putting the finishing touches on the cottage, which would explain the presence of the architect Mogens Tvede on the island in March 1929 as a guest of Frank Miller Gould. But by the beginning of March, it was evidently ready, because Jean Jennings recorded in her diary for March 1: "Dined with Goulds for their house warming. Great fun."[15] The Goulds returned the following season, registering on Valentine's Day, 1930.[16]

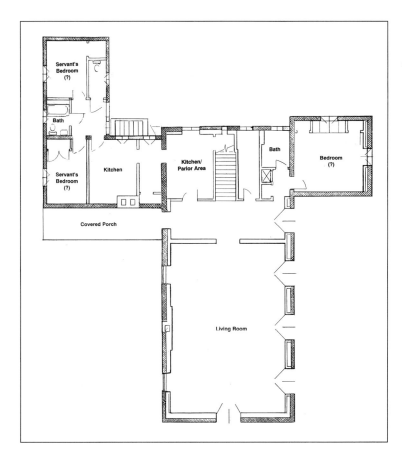

First-floor plan of the Villa Marianna. (Based on plans in the Jekyll Island Museum)

From the opening of their new cottage in 1929 through the 1932 season and from 1939 until the end of the club era in 1942, the Goulds would be staples of the Jekyll Island social life, though they evidently did not come to Jekyll during the mid-thirties. Frank Miller Gould and his growing family, to which a little boy named Edwin Jay would be added by the club season of 1932, were from outward appearances happy enough in the early years. Frank Gould's father, Edwin, had lived long enough to see both his only grandchildren. None of the Goulds came to Jekyll in 1933, and shortly after midnight on July 12, after an uneventful family dinner, Edwin Gould, long a stalwart Jekyll supporter, died.[17]

In 1939 the Frank Goulds resumed their annual visits to Jekyll, where they were very much in the social whirl. They gave a formal dinner dance at the tea house in the dunes at the end of March 1940 as a farewell gesture to close the fifty-fifth club sea-

The Villa Marianna, with Cherokee roses growing on the palm trees. The cottage of Frank Miller Gould in its heyday was typical of the Spanish Eclectic style popularized by Addison Mizner. The cottage contains fifteen rooms and six baths. (Courtesy of Jekyll Island Museum)

son.[18] They held a dinner dance at the Villa Marianna on Saturday, March 22, 1941, as a part of the Founders' Day event to celebrate the fifty-sixth anniversary of the club.[19] In the final season, officially January 28–April 5, 1942, Frank Miller Gould in a gesture of generosity opened Latham Hammock, the private hunting preserve where his brother had died, for wild turkey and quail shooting.[20]

The United States involvement in World War II put an end to the Jekyll Island Club's active history. The club remained open until the end of the 1942 season in April, but because of the U.S. entry into the war in December 1941 after the bombing of Pearl Harbor and the consequent "difficulty of fuel, transportation, labor and supplies," according to club president Bernon Prentice, the club did not open for the following season, nor would it open ever again.[21] Frank Miller Gould, although he was briefly at Jekyll in March 1942, did not see the club's final season to its end. That same month Gould was commissioned an Army Air Corps captain, though even his military service did not keep him away from Georgia. He was assigned duty as an administrative inspector at Cochran Field in Macon, Georgia, where he served until 1944.[22]

Although the strain of the war and his absence from home no doubt undermined his marriage, it had begun to crumble even before the war began. New York columnist Cholly Knickerbocker described it as "one of those off-again, on-again unions with the couple several times on the verge of divorcing, then effecting a reconciliation."[23] The war, however, proved to be its final undoing. Betsy and Frank Gould were divorced in Reno, Nevada, on May 6, 1944. One month later, in Macon, on June 7, 1944, Frank Gould married Helen Roosen Curran, a divorcée with two children—a daughter, Pamela, and a son, William.[24] The couple spent their honeymoon in the Villa Marianna on Jekyll Island.

A letter from Alfred W. (Bill) Jones, president of the Cloister at nearby Sea Island, to the club's last president, Bernon Prentice, on June 22, 1944, com-

Frank Miller Gould as a captain in the U.S. Air Corps during World War II. (Courtesy of the Edwin J. Gould family)

ments on Gould's second marriage: "I wish I had some real information to give you on Frank Gould's new wife. I would say that she was over 35, perhaps 40, a brunette, not beautiful but apparently vivaciously attractive. I have no idea what her name was or where she was from. They were married in Macon a couple of weeks ago and went over to Jekyll for three or four days before going north. Her daughter was along with them and I would guess she was from 18 to 22 years old."[25] In fact, Helen Curran, the former wife of William G. Curran, was said by others to be a "striking brunette." She inherited her beauty from her mother, born Clarita Orizondo, who came from a prominent family in Cuba. He-

The second wife of Frank Miller Gould, Helen Roosen Curran, with her daughter, Pamela, *left.* (Courtesy of Ann C. Felton)

len's father, H. Dudley Roosen, was deceased, and his wife still lived on Fifth Avenue in New York.[26] At the time of the marriage, which took place in Macon at the home of friends, Mr. and Mrs. Ernest Lee, Helen Curran was precisely forty years old. She had lived in Macon for the past year, having accompanied Gould from New York to his earlier post in Albany and then to Macon, where she was renting an estate called Breezy Hill, which has been since demolished.[27]

One wonders in what condition the couple must have found the island, which had not been opened to guests for more than two years. Nevertheless, Frank Gould's continuing fondness for Jekyll is indisputable. He, like several others, wondered what was to become of the Jekyll Island Club when the war ended. Looking toward that eventuality, Gould, Bill Jones, whose Sea Island Company had overseen Jekyll's maintenance during the war years, and Bernon Prentice had by June 1944 begun to look toward salvaging what they could. They made an offer to the few remaining club members, who by that time had dwindled to ten, including one estate, to buy up all the Jekyll Island bonds at ten cents on the dollar and to consider reopening the club after the war as a resort, modeled no doubt on the Cloister on Sea Island.

On June 8, 1944, a letter went out from A. M. Harris, vice president of the National Bank of Brunswick, acting "as agent for Mr. Frank M. Gould and Mr. Alfred W. Jones," making an offer for the Jekyll Island Mortgage Bonds at ten cents on the dollar.[28] As a result they acquired $185,000 worth of the bonds. Gould, encouraged by the response they had received, authorized Bill Jones to have another letter sent out to bondholders "and after waiting a reasonable time for replies" to "send a representative to call on the holders personally." [29] The second letter went out on August 1 extending the offer until September 15, 1944.[30]

All of Frank Gould's brave new projects, his second marriage and his efforts to work with a syndicate to reopen the Jekyll Island Club, came to naught, however. Before the war's end and the scheme to reopen the club on any basis could be realized, Frank Miller Gould died at his breakfast table at his home at Oyster Bay, Long Island, of a ruptured aorta on January 14, 1945.[31] He had been compelled by ill health to retire from the military the preceding July.[32] Nevertheless, his death at age forty-five was sudden and unexpected.

All plans of the Jekyll Island syndicate came to a sudden halt "due to Frank Gould's death" and the uncertainty as to what his estate would do with the

Helen Everett, *left*, and Ann Felton on the second-story balcony beneath the square tower of the Villa Marianna in July 1944. The square tower with its red-tile roof was this cottage's unique architectural feature. (Courtesy of Ann C. Felton)

Attached to the Gould tennis courts was a greenhouse. (Courtesy of Ann C. Felton)

bonds he held.[33] Representatives of the Gould estate and Helen Gould's lawyer, Lawrence Condon, came to Jekyll in mid-August to assess the situation and the value of the property and bonds.[34] On January 11, 1946, Bernon Prentice wrote to Bill Jones that "I had a long conference with Condon today and it now looks as though Helen Gould—perhaps helped by Condon—will buy the bonds from the Gould Estate and assume responsibility of the Gould property at Jekyll. I personally feel that this will be very helpful to us for he is a mighty nice fellow, has ability, and, I understand, has quite a lot of money."[35]

By April the matter had still not been settled, and Bill Jones sent a telegram to L. P. Carmer, vice-president of the Bank of New York and co-executor of Frank Gould's estate, reiterating with a greater sense of urgency an offer similar to one he had made the previous November:

THE JEKYLL ISLAND CLUB SITUATION MUST BE SETTLED ONE WAY OR ANOTHER IN THE IMMEDIATE FUTURE AS CLUB OUT OF OPERATING FUNDS. I NOW OFFER YOU $20,350 AS EXECUTORS OF THE ESTATE OF FRANK M GOULD FOR $101,750 IN BONDS ON JEKYLL ISLAND ONE SHARE OF STOCK IN THE JEKYLL ISLAND CLUB OPEN NOTES SIGNED BY JEKYLL ISLAND CLUB stop IN ADDITION TO THE ABOVE OFFER I WOULD APPRECIATE YOUR SUBMITTING AN OFFER TO MRS GOULD OF $10,000 FOR THE TWO LEASE HOLDS WHICH I UNDERSTAND SHE NOW OWNS ON JEKYLL ISLAND FROM THE FRANK M GOULD ESTATE stop[36]

In fact, the November offer had been slightly more generous, with the initial bid being $25,000 to the executors, an offer now reduced by almost 20 percent.

The problem dragged on until August. In the meantime, Lawrence R. Condon, Mrs. Gould's New York lawyer and a graduate of Columbia Law School, had acquired the Frank Gould properties and interests in the club, was excited about the prospect of the club's reopening, and "had a very definite idea of a plan for opening the Club for the 1947 season."[37] In fact, he believed that he could put together an investment group to raise $200,000, "thought to be the necessary amount to rehabilitate the Club."

In the meantime, maintaining the club property was a perpetual drain on Prentice's and Jones's resources. On August 27, 1946, Prentice sent out a letter to the remaining club members, inviting them to assume a portion of the expense to maintain the property and pay the taxes, expenses which he and Jones had assumed in recent years, or to turn over their stock to himself, Jones, and Condon, who now owned the preponderance of shares and bonds.

Before the matter was finalized, however, just after Labor Day 1946, the state of Georgia became a player in the game of Jekyll Island's fate. Gov. Ellis Arnall sent a letter to Bernon Prentice expressing an interest in taking over Jekyll Island through condemnation proceedings for use as a state park. However, by October Governor Arnall had changed his mind and notified club officials that he was not going to carry through with the proceedings. The is-

sue was reopened on April 2, 1947, by the new governor, Melvin E. Thompson, elected by the General Assembly following a controversial and indecisive general election. Thompson reiterated the intention of his administration to start condemnation proceedings against the island, and with little delay, on June 6, he initiated the necessary court action.[38]

While Prentice and Jones, representing the club, sought to work out the best deal they could, they nonetheless cooperated with the state in the proceedings. On the other hand, Lawrence Condon, the new owner of the Villa Marianna, did everything in his power to block the state's actions. He filed a separate suit, asking to be allowed to keep his property, stating in a letter to the club lawyer: "I really

Left to right, Polly Corn, Florence Domingos, and Ann Felton on the terrace of the Villa Marianna, July 1944. (Courtesy of Ann C. Felton)

love the place and I am sure I would not be troublesome to any neighbors I might have on Jekyll Island." [39] His protests came to naught, however, and his suit was quickly settled when the court refused to hear a separate petition, thereby compelling Condon to be a party to the general condemnation proceedings. The decree that gave the state of Georgia the right to condemn the island was handed down on October 4, and three days later, the state of Georgia took over the property of the Jekyll Island Club and its remaining members for a total compensation of $675,000. [40]

In the settlement Condon received $60,000 for his newly acquired home and all the other Gould property on the island. As one who had never been a member of the club in its active years, he did not have the lifelong attachment to the island that the other dispossessed cottage owners, namely the Maurice sisters, had. Nevertheless, he was unhappy to have his potential paradise, so newly acquired, snatched from his grasp. He returned downcast to his home in New York, where he lived out the rest of his life with his wife Isabel, having to content himself with their summer home on Wyandanch Lane in Southampton, Long Island. He lived until May 11, 1973, when he died at his home in Southampton. [41]

On January 31, 1948, the club corporation was dissolved as a legal entity, and that same year on June 13, Bernon Prentice, its last president, died. The Jekyll Island Club, which had enjoyed its "simple life" and its splendid isolation for sixty-two years, was no more.

The State Era

During the state era the Villa Marianna has continued to be one of the best-maintained houses in the cottage colony, in part because its stucco-on-block construction has sustained fewer moisture problems and is better adapted to the humid climate of the Georgia sea islands than many of the predominantly wooden structures. Its earliest use by the state was to house some of the prisoners brought to work on Jekyll, under the supervision of the earliest state island supervisor, Hoke Smith, not long after the state takeover. When the Jekyll Island State Park Authority was founded in 1950, the cottage became the original authority headquarters, which were later moved to the Jekyll Island shopping center. In late March 1971, however, the Jekyll Island Authority moved its offices for a brief period back into the Villa Marianna. From 1978 until 1995 it was used as the residence for executive directors of the Jekyll Island Authority, Bob Case (1978–80), and George Chambliss (1980–95). [42] Since 1995 it has housed the Jekyll Island Museum Archives.

AFTERWORD

The closing of the Jekyll Island Club not long after the United States' entry into World War II marked the end of an epoch. The class of the social elite that had established the club during the Victorian era was never again so clearly defined after the war's end, and the country witnessed in its wake an extraordinary period of democratization that resulted, in part, from the economic and educational opportunities provided to a wide class of people by the G.I. Bill. Whether rich or poor, young men and women had served their country in the military, had had glimpses of foreign cultures, and had come home to opportunities and experiences that many of them had never known before. In a sense, the takeover of Jekyll Island by the state of Georgia for the founding of a public park for all the people of the state, white and black, wealthy and poor, was symbolic of the new era.[1]

As with any societal shift of such magnitude, both gain and loss were a consequence. As the middle class expanded, the wealthy, social elite seemed to dwindle, and such "elegant leisure" as they had known in places like the Jekyll Island Club began to vanish. The great fortunes that been built by the vision of men like Joseph Pulitzer and William Rockefeller during the industrial and economic expansion of the nineteenth and early twentieth centuries were divided among larger numbers of people, and the enterprises associated with the per-

sonal control of such families as the Morgans, Rockefellers, Pulitzers, Goodyears, and Vanderbilts were being replaced with large, multinational corporations. The new era toppled such wealthy industrialists, already profoundly shaken by the Great Depression, from the exclusive apex of economic control. As a group they had frequently been described as "robber barons." It was an unflattering image that portrayed these businessmen who helped shape modern America as national plunderers, bent only upon enhancing their personal fortunes at public expense.

Few of the Jekyll cottage owners, however, had ever fit the stereotype. They had been, by and large, men and women of substance with a profound sense of social responsibility. Indeed, the stereotype has been called into question by various scholars, and, as one historian has noted, few of the so-called "industrial buccaneers" ever fit the pattern. Most "were actually modelling their lives after a different ideal. They held up for admiration the businessman who was honest in his dealings, bound by domestic ties, and unselfish in his dedication to public causes."[2]

While there is no doubt that Jekyll Islanders accrued or inherited great fortunes and spent a great deal on their own acquisitions and pleasures, they were by and large also concerned with social and cultural philanthropies that left the country as a whole richer and more stable. They lavished both

The Jekyll Island Club, overgrown and unkempt, as it looked during the war years, which would prove to be its final days. (Courtesy of Ann C. Felton)

time and money on such socially conscious organizations as the Children's Aid Society, the New York Association for Improving the Condition of the Poor, the Edwin Gould Foundation for Children, the American Red Cross, the Boy Scouts, the Girl Scouts, and the YMCA, as well as on such issues as the penal system, health care, religion, and education. They dedicated both time and resources to such cultural and educational organizations as the Metropolitan Museum of Art, the American Museum of Natural History, the Albright Art Gallery, the Morgan Library, and various colleges and universities. Not only ivy league schools like Harvard, Princeton, and Yale benefited from their generosity, but also institutions like Berry College in North Georgia, Booker T. Washington's Tuskegee Institute, and the McKay Institute in Kingston, Rhode Island, which was founded by Gordon McKay for the education of young black men. Preservation of our natural resources was another concern of many Jekyll Islanders, which resulted in the founding of a number of public parks and assisted such efforts as the National Audubon Society and the creation of national wildlife preserves. During wartime some, like Frank Miller Gould and Frank Goodyear, served in the military. Others gave their time to raise war funds, serve on diplomatic missions, and aid in relief programs, or donated their personal property, such as their yachts, to be used in the war effort.

In brief, like many other Americans, Jekyll Islanders were willing to give their money, property, time, and energy, even their lives, if the need arose, to further the national interest in a time of conflict. They were not, except in the rarest of cases, merely shallow people, as they have so often been depicted, who collected out of greed or insecurity or who exploited the nation and its resources and gave nothing in return. They were, in the main, cultured people who not only enjoyed their wealth and hoped to preserve it from the tax collector but also felt the noblesse oblige imposed by their class principles to share at least some of it with others. While their own exclusive sphere of existence was decidedly diminished in the wake of World War II, their contributions have left a significant legacy and made an immense impact on the world in which we live today.

The surviving structures in the Jekyll Island Cottage Colony stand today as a reminder of what the island once was—a quiet Southern haven for the wealthy elite—where they sought to find tranquillity and nurture their souls in a natural and simple paradise, away from the icy climes and hurly-burly of the business world in the northern cities they left behind. The club changed considerably over the years, from a hunting club in its earliest days to a quiet retreat that gradually lost its appeal for a new, more modern generation who preferred the livelier resorts of Florida or Europe. In its active years it had lasted from 1888, when the first cottage was built and the club house welcomed its first guests, among them the reigning queen of New York society, Alva Vanderbilt, until 1942, when World War II would close its doors forever. With its closing, one era ended and another began. Today visitors to Jekyll Island can have a glimpse of both worlds.

Thanks to the Jekyll Island Museum's ongoing efforts to preserve the cottages, visitors can still wander through the rooms, once so filled with life, that sheltered such families as those of William Rockefeller and Charles Stewart Maurice. If one pauses for a moment and listens intently with the heart, the echo of children's laughter and the sparkling conversation of society's best from Jekyll's earlier days of splendor may still be heard.

NOTES

Introduction

1. It should be noted that prior to the Civil War, southern states, particularly in the upper South, had attracted the rural gentry to their mineral springs for what they believed to be the health benefits. See Henry W. Lawrence, "Southern Spas: Source of the American Resort Tradition" *Landscape* 27, no. 2 (1983): 1–12. For a discussion of the growth of tourism in the South following the Civil War, see C. Brenden Martin, "Selling the Southern Highlands: Tourism and Community Development in the Mountain South" (Ph.D. diss., University of Tennessee, 1997), 31–60. For a look at Gilded Age resorts, see also Stephen J. Hornsby, "The Gilded Age and the Making of Bar Harbor," *Geographical Review* 83 (1993): 455–68.

2. For addition details on the founding of the Jekyll Island Club, see the du Bignon Cottage chapter in this book and William Barton McCash and June Hall McCash, *The Jekyll Island Club: Southern Haven for America's Millionaires* (Athens: University of Georgia Press, 1989), 1–13.

3. Hornsby, 455.

4. William James to Henry James, April 11, 1882, in *Letters of William James* (Boston, 1920), 1:318. See also William E. Leverette Jr., "Simple Living and the Patrician Academic: The Case of William James," *Journal of American Culture* 6 (1984); David E. Shi, *The Simple Life: Plain Living and High Thinking in American Culture* (New York: Oxford University Press, 1985), 154–74.

5. "Extract from the Report of H. W. S. Cleveland," Prospectus of the Jekyll Island Club, April 1, 1887, 18–20. Hereafter referred to as Club Prospectus.

6. *Brunswick Advertiser and Appeal,* December 1, 1887.

7. Rules and regulations for the government of the game department for the season of 1891–92, carton p-5, Henry B. Hyde Papers, Baker Library, Harvard University Graduate School of Business Administration.

8. Kate Brown to family, [March 17, 1917]. The original letters are in the possession of Katharine Green Owens, Kate Brown's daughter, though copies are in the Jekyll Island Museum. They have been edited by Nanette M. Bahlinger under the title of *It Is a Wonderfully Lovely Place: Jekyll Island as Seen Through Kate Brown's Fresh Eyes, The Letters of Kate Brown, February–March, 1917* (n.p.: Jekyll Island Museum, [1992]). For the sake of consistency, all citations in this volume are to the original letters. The published version does not contain all the letters, and those it does contain are edited.

9. Mrs. Robert Lafayette Reed to Horace Caldwell, April 27, 1971, Jekyll Island Museum.

10. *Atlanta Constitution,* January 13, 1946.

11. See McCash and McCash, 208–12.

12. The Jekyll Island Authority was initially called the Jekyll Island State Park Authority. I have, however, to avoid confusion, referred to it throughout as the Jekyll Island Authority, as it is known today and as it was frequently called even in the 1950s.

13. Jones to Bernon Prentice, May 6, 1948, Sea Island Files.

The Horton House

1. See John Linley, *The Georgia Catalog, Historic American Buildings Survey: A Guide to the Architecture of the State* (Athens: University of Georgia Press, 1982), 22–23.

2. *The Journal of the Earl of Egmont: Abstract of the Trustees Proceedings for Establishing the Colony of Georgia,* ed. Robert G. McPherson (Athens: University of Georgia Press, 1962), 107. Hereafter called *Egmont Journal.* Kenneth Coleman, *Colonial Georgia: A History* (New York: Scribner's, 1976), 122. On the founding of Georgia, see Coleman, 13–38.

3. *Egmont Journal,* 107.

4. Ibid, 107, 109.

5. November 19, 1735, *The Colonial Records of the State of Georgia,* 26 volumes, ed. Allen D. Candler (Atlanta: Franklin Printing, 1904–16), 21:46. Hereafter referred to as *Colonial Records.*

6. *The Journal of the Rev. John Wesley,* edited by Nehemiah Curnock (London: Epworth Press, 1938), 121.

7. Francis Moore, *A Voyage to Georgia, Begun in the Year 1735* (London, 1744), in Collections of the Georgia Historical Society (Savannah: Printed for the Society, 1840), 1:104. Hereafter referred to as Moore, *Voyage.*

8. *General Oglethorpe's Georgia: Colonial Letters 1733–1743,* ed. Mills Lane (Savannah: Beehive Press, 1975), 1:258. Hereafter referred to as *Colonial Letters.*

9. Oglethorpe to Trustees, March 28, 1736, *Colonial Records,* 21:124. See also anonymous letter of April 12, 1736, in *Colonial Letters,* 1:262; Moore, *Voyage,* 122–27.

10. Moore, *Voyage,* 130.

11. Ibid.

12. Ibid., 147.

13. Ibid., 150–51; *Colonial Letters,* 1:271–72.

14. Larry E. Ivers, *British Drums on the Southern Frontier: The Military Colonization of Gerogia: 1733–1749* (Chapel Hill: University of North Carolina Press, 1974), 78; Phinizy Spalding, *Oglethorpe in America* (Chicago: University of Chicago Press, 1977), 100; *Egmont Journal,* 218.

15. *Egmont Journal,* 246.

16. Steven D. Ruple, "Archeology of the Horton House" (master's thesis, University of Florida, 1976), 20; J. Everette Fauber, "Captain Horton's House on Jekyll Island, Georgia: Research Report and a Proposal for Resto-

ration" (prepared for the Jekyll Island State Park Authority, April 10, 1967), 8, 10; copy in Jekyll Island Museum.

17. Ruple, 106.

18. *Colonial Records,* 4:73.

19. *Journal of William Stephens 1737–1740,* December 13, 1737, *Colonial Records,* 4:49, hereafter referred to as *Stephens Journal;* Stephens to Trustees, December 20, 1937, *Colonial Records,* 22, pt. 1:49.

20. *Colonial Records,* 4:72.

21. Ibid., 4, 73; 669.

22. Ibid., 4:75.

23. *Colonial Letters,* 2:344.

24. Ibid., 2:345.

25. Ibid., 2:346.

26. *Colonial Records,* 4:227–28, 247, 249, 327.

27. Coleman, 63–66; *Colonial Letters,* 2:451.

28. For references to Horton's character see *Colonial Records,* 4:50; 5:425.

29. Ibid., 4:535, 538.

30. Ibid., 5:347.

31. Ibid., 5:348, 351, 355.

32. Ibid., 2:388; 5:355, 512, 591; Ivers, 136.

33. *Colonial Letters,* 2:616.

34. Ivers, 151–67.

35. Ibid., 167.

36. *Colonial Letters,* 2:623; Ivers, 170–71.

37. *Stephens Journal,* 226.

38. Ibid., 6.

39. Ruple, 29–50.

40. Ibid., 82, 107–8; Club Prospectus (1887), 27; *New York Times,* April 9, 1892; *Brunswick Journal,* March 16, 1908, p. 3.

41. *Colonial Records,* 25:248–49.

42. *Stephens Journal,* (March 12, 1745), 204–5.

43. *Colonial Records,* 25:97.

44. *Stephens Journal,* 71; Coleman, 116–17.

45. *Colonial Letters,* 2:568.

46. *Colonial Records,* 6:214–15, 219, 224.

47. Ibid., 6:214–15, 219, 224; Pat Bryant, compiler, *Entry of Claims for Georgia Landholders, 1733–1755* (Atlanta: State Printing Office, 1975), 127.

48. *Stephens Journal,* 112, 115, 149.

49. Ibid., 214–15, 217, 232–40, 247.

50. One major dispute that began in 1743 over the salvaging of a French vessel that ran aground on Sapelo Island continued unabated, turning into a veritable feud

that lasted until 1748. The military men had salvaged the ship, but civil authorities, in the form of a salvage court, levied what Horton considered unfair and exorbitant court and clerical fees. In the end, Horton won the dispute. See *Colonial Records,* 24:176, 247–88, 385–411; 25:19–24, 31–35, 108–12, 120–23.

51. Ibid., 25:342. For another favorable view of Horton, see John Martin Bolzus to Trustees, January 16, 1744, ibid., 24:203.

52. Ibid., 25:236, 244.

53. Ibid., 25:365; Hugh McCall, *The History of Georgia* (1811–16; reprint. Atlanta: A. B. Caldwell, 1909), 146.

54. *Colonial Records,* 26:210.

55. Ibid., 9:370.

56. Ibid., 9:402–3.

57. Ibid., 7:265; 16:416. Concerning his property in Savannah, see ibid., 7:175, 347.

58. Ibid., 9:12–13.

59. The will was made on September 9, 1771. A copy of Charles Spalding Wylly's will is in the Jekyll Island Museum.

60. *Revolutionary Records of the State of Georgia,* ed. Allen D. Candler (Atlanta: Franklin-Turner Co., 1908) 1:146, 207, 380; 2:443.

61. See "The Thomas Spalding Family," Georgia Historical Society, Colonial Dames of America Collection 965, box 11, folder 124. E. Merton Coulter quotes the price of Jekyll Island at 34£, 11s. (*Thomas Spalding of Sapelo* [University: University of Louisiana Press, 1940], 13).

62. See Georgia Historical Society, "Plantation Book of Richard Leake," Colonial Dames of America Collection 965, box 11, folder 124.

63. This price is cited in Coulter, 13.

64. Documents relating to his birth and baptism are found in a private collection of Doris Finney Liebrecht under the title "Christophe-Anne Poulain Du Bignon: A Compilation of Information on his life, on his ancestors, the Poulains of Brittany; and on a few of his descendants." The originals of the documents relating to his birth and baptism are located in the *mairie* of Lamballe (Côtes du Nord), France.

65. The company was established by Colbert in 1664 as the Compagnie des Indes Orientales but was reorganized in 1719 as the Compagnie des Indes.

66. A record of du Bignon's career with the Compagnie des Indes is contained in a dossier in Paris, Archives Nationales, cote Marine C^{7}257.

67. She had been previously married to another seaman, Jean Paschal du Jonc de Boisquenay. For Poulain du Bignon's participation in the American Revolution, see Candler, *Revolutionary Records.*

68. See Liberty County Court House, Hinesville, Georgia, Superior Court, Office of the Clerk, Deed Book C (1793–95), 25. This document records the agreement between Poulain du Bignon and Dumoussay signed at Saint Brieuc, France, on October 5, 1790, and recorded in Liberty County on March 29, 1793. The sale of the island from John McQueen to Dumoussay is recorded in the same office, book B, 170–71.

69. Martha L. Turner, "Christophe Poulain du Bignon: The Making of an Emigré" (lecture sponsored by Jekyll Island Museum, May 20, 1989).

70. The other original investors in the Sapelo property were Charles Pierre César Picot de Boisfeuillet, Nicholas François Magon (sometimes given as Mazon) de la Villehuchet, and Grand Clos Meslé, with Chappedelaine purchasing one of the shares of Sapelo in 1792. See Burnette Vanstory, *Georgia's Land of the Golden Isles* (Athens: University of Georgia Press, 1956), 56–57.

71. Thomas Dechenaux would be a good and loyal friend to du Bignon, handling many business matters for him in Savannah and witnessing various agreements, from the reestablishment of the lost agreement concerning land transfers to the baptism of his granddaughter, Maria Louisa, for whom Dechenaux's wife stood as godmother. Evidence of the infant boy's early death is in Liebrecht, unnumbered pages, found in the section of the collection entitled "The Du Bignons of Jekyll Island, Georgia."

72. Curiously, his vessel's arrival is not listed in the *Georgia Gazette* until June 28, 1792, p. 3, col. 1, "Marine List. Entered Inward . . . Sapelo Packet, Dubignon from St. Malo." The vessel had departed from France on or about March 5 and clearly should have arrived much earlier in Georgia. It is possible that du Bignon made a stop in the barrier islands before bringing his vessel north to Savannah, or else there was a delay in recording the vessel's arrival.

73. Quoted from "Act to Relieve the Heirs of Francis Maria Loys Dumoussay de la Vauve, the heirs of Hyacinth

de Chadelane [*sic*] and Christophe Poulain DuBignon," General Assembly of the State of Georgia, February 19, 1796. The act authorized the Superior Court of Glynn County to summon, hear, and examine witnesses before a grand jury.

74. Dumoussay tried almost immediately to unload du Bignon's share, advertising in the *Georgia Gazette* on June 19, 1794, p. 2, col. 2, "one divided Fifth Part of Sapelo Island, containing two thousand two or three hundred acres, formerly the property of M. Poulain Dubignon at the Hermitage Plantation upon Tea Kettle Creek." See Liberty County Court House, Office of the Clerk, Deed Book C (1793–95), 25. The other one-fourth of Jekyll belonged jointly to Villehuchet and Grand-Clos.

75. *Georgia Gazette,* September 25, 1794. Picot de Boisteuillet had sent his nephew Chappedelaine to the island ahead of him to prepare his Sapelo estate, which, as a royalist, he called "Bourbon." But nothing had been done to his satisfaction. Family tradition has it that Picot de Boisfeuillet, aged fifty at the time (he was born May 21, 1744), ordered him to leave but that Chappedelaine refused because of his love for Picot's daughter, Jeanne Marie Melanie. (See "Skeletons in the history of the Jemison and Boisfeuillet Families," compiled by Mamie Jemison Chestney, 1964, Georgia Historical Society, 3–4.) This story seems unlikely since she was born in 1785 and would have been only about nine years old at the time. The men had initially quarreled over the sale of wild cattle on Sapelo Island, a squabble that is recorded in the *Georgia Gazette* on July 14, 1794. That quarrel may have accelerated into the duel in which Chappedelaine was killed. Du Bignon, whose estate in France had neighbored Picot's, went his bond. Picot de Boisfeuillet was tried, but thanks to the eloquence of his attorney, Joseph Clay, he was acquitted. Picot died of fever in 1801. Cathedral of Saint John the Baptist records, Savannah, August 13, 1801.

76. Turner lecture.

77. Georgia Superior Court Deeds and Mortgages 1765–1800, Glynn County (Georgia) 82, box 33, 300–301. See also 199–201. Hereafter cited as Glynn County Deeds.

78. This sale apparently was never officially recorded, but the document attesting to it remains in the hands of the du Bignon family.

79. See *Republican and Savannah Evening Ledger,* May 21, 1812, p. 3.

80. Quoted in Turner lecture.

81. The ad suggested that interested parties could apply to "Poulain Dubignon, Esq. at his residence on the island, or in Savannah to Richard Leake." *Daily Georgian,* November 16, 1819, p. 3.

82. Their marriage license, dated October 27, 1819, is recorded in Chatham County Marriage Records, 1805–52, compiled by Mabel F. LaFar, 1939, no. 654. Clémence's name is given in this typewritten record as "Clemence D. Borgrias," an apparent misreading of Clémence de Boisquenay. Joseph died by 1830 and is no longer listed in the 1830 census record, which gives only "Mrs. Joseph DuBignon." However, it is not until April 20, 1831 (*Daily Georgian,* p. 2), that his brother Henri applies for letters of administration on Joseph's estate. Now that Christophe is dead, Clémence is, by this time, living on Jekyll Island.

83. The original of this document is in the Glynn County Courthouse, Brunswick. Glynn Wills and Appraisals, D 153.

84. War of 1812, Claims under Treaty of Ghent, December 24, 1814, contained in National Archives, Record Groups 76, E 190, Claim #137.

85. See Glynn County Wills and Appraisals, D 153. The values were appraised on December 31, 1825.

86. I shall continue to use the French spelling, however, to distinguish him clearly from his son Henry.

87. Aaron Burr, *Memoirs of Aaron Burr with Miscellaneous Selections from His Correspondence,* ed. Matthew L. Davis, 2 (1836; reprint, Freeport, N.Y.: Books for Libraries Press, 1970), 334. This printed source gives her name as "Mademoiselle Nicholson." The letter is dated August 31, 1804.

88. *Jekyl Island: Some Historic Notes and Legends,* collected by Charlotte Marshall Maurice, and *Brief Outline of the Early Days of the Jekyl Island Club Made by Charles Stewart Maurice,* privately printed, n.d. [between 1923 and 1929], 7, hereafter referred to as Maurice book. Maurice, whose account is based on personal recollections from members of the du Bignon family several generations removed from the incident, says she was staying with the James Hamilton Coopers [*sic*], but the Burr letter makes it clear that it was John Couper who was her host.

89. The civil marriage may have taken place shortly after the signing of the prenuptial agreement, but the Catholic priest made his rounds infrequently, and it was

not uncommon for the religious marriage to be performed somewhat later than the civil marriage. The prenuptial agreement, dated April 30, 1807, is in Glynn County, Georgia, Book F, folio 37–39. See also the records in the Roman Catholic Diocese of Savannah, where the agreement is dated April 13, 1807.

90. Documents relating to the marriage and birth are located in the Glynn County Court House, Ordinary's Office, drawer D, which contains a collection of loose miscellaneous du Bignon papers. These documents are located in folder 352.

91. Du Bignon also owned Central Railroad and Banking stock.

92. Baptisms, Marriages, Deaths, 1816–38, MSS, Cathedral of Saint John the Baptist, Savannah, Georgia. See also Wylly, *These Memories;* Julia Floyd Smith, *Slavery and Rice Culture in the Low Country Georgia 1750–1860* (Knoxville: University of Tennessee Press, 1985), 158.

93. Maurice book, 7–8.

94. On April 19, 1857, Sarah Aust married a man named Willis Reddick. Henri du Bignon paid Sarah Reddick the final insult by leaving her the sum total of $50 in his will. Similarly, he left each of the children she had born him $50. His will left nothing to Ann Amelia Nicolau's children, who had already claimed their inheritance. See Glynn County Court of Ordinary Wills, Inventories, and Appraisals, vol. G, p. 353. Mary Aust du Bignon turned over to her stepson Henry Charles du Bignon the right of administration of her husband's estate on April 1, 1867. See Glynn County Court House, Ordinary's Office, Drawer D (a collection of miscellaneous du Bignon papers), folder 351 D. Subsequent squabbles between Mary du Bignon and her stepson, whom she accused of "very careless and improvident" management of the estate, are recorded in the Ordinary Court Records of Glynn County. See court records of February 5 and 6, 1873.

95. Glynn County Deeds, vol. C, 1859–69, 437–38.

96. Tom Henderson Wells, *The Slave Ship Wanderer* (Athens: University of Georgia Press, 1968), 24. Unless otherwise indicated, information contained herein is based on Wells's excellent account of the incident.

97. Ibid., 28.

98. Ibid., 41.

99. Ibid., 45, 58–59. See also Minutes of the Sixth Circuit Court, Savannah, Federal Record Center, East Point, Georgia.

100. U.S. Navy War Records Office, *Official Records of the Union and Confederate Navies in the War of the Rebellion* (Washington: U.S. Government Printing Office, 1894–1922), ser. 1, vol. 12, p. 592.

101. Jacob Solis Cohen diary in possession of Charles L. Rosenthal, copy in possession of Mrs. L. C. Liebrecht.

102. Maurice book, 9. Maurice notes that after John Couper du Bignon's death, the shack "was torn down."

103. Grob Letter Book 1, May 2, 1898.

Du Bignon Cottage

1. There he entertained friends such as a group from Savannah who stopped over in July 1875 after a "little pleasure cruise" in their yacht *Sunshine.* See *Brunswick Advertiser and Appeal,* July 21, 1875, p. 4.

2. Abstracts of Titles to Jekyll Island Georgia written by J. E. du Bignon, Everett Collection, Museum of Coastal History, Saint Simons Island, Georgia.

3. *Brunswick Advertiser and Appeal,* August 22, 1885, p. 6.

4. Unidentified printed source from John Eugene du Bignon file, Jekyll Island Museum.

5. Marriage records, Superior Court, Glynn County, p. 108.

6. See *Brunswick News,* January 8, 1902 (marriage), and May 13, 1965 (obituary).

7. Clark Howell, *History of Georgia* (Chicago/Atlanta: S. J. Clarke, 1926), 2:246–47.

8. Du Bignon was also a member of the Finance and Auditing Committee and the Light and Water Committee. See *The Evening Call,* January 9, 1901, p. 1. *The Mercantile and Industrial Review,* 1909, issued by the Traffic Department, Atlanta, Birmingham & Atlantic Railroad, p. 27.

9. N. S. Finney to Hon. F. S. Bartow, March 15, 1861; N. S. Finney to Jefferson Davis, March 14, 1861, M 331, compiled service records of Confederate General and staff officers and non-regimental enlisted men (R.G. 109), U.S. National Archives.

10. Information courtesy of Doris Liebrecht.

11. *Brunswick Advertiser and Appeal,* April 25, 1885, p. 6.

12. On the various transactions by which du Bignon reacquired the island, see Glynn County Deeds, vol. 4,

1885, pp. 302–6. There is reason to believe that du Bignon never paid the $100 to his aunt Eliza, who noted the unpaid debt in her will.

13. See Club Prospectus, p. 29, "Extract from Macon Telegraph."

14. *Brunswick Advertiser and Appeal,* June 20, 1885, p. 3, and July 11, 1885, p. 6.

15. Finney to members, November 21, 1887, Hyde Papers.

16. *Brunswick Advertiser and Appeal,* December 2, 1887.

17. See Executive Committee Minutes, 1886, Jekyll Island Museum, pp. 1–9. One of their first orders of business was to rid the island of its feral cattle, horses, and hogs. Du Bignon hired a local man to round them up, and the cattle and mares were delivered to Cumberland Island, where Thomas Carnegie had his estate Dungeness. The stallions were a greater problem, but C. W. Lamb, under contract to do the roundup, agreed to take them himself for $45 a head. The wild hogs, wily as they were, proved to be the greatest problem. Despite the efforts of Lamb with his dogs, and the use of "pens, traps, and every device known," the hogs remained elusive. Ogden "was importuned to permit the enthusiastic sporting members of the Club to exercise their skill in the cause," but to no avail. The hogs continued to be a problem throughout club history. See "Report of R. L. Ogden, Supt., May 1, 1888," Maurice Family Papers, Southern Historical Collection, University of North Carolina Library, Chapel Hill, N.C.

18. See Hyde to Baker, February 5, 1895, Hyde Papers.

19. Finney's bankruptcy petition had been filed on August 29, 1878. See *New York Times,* August 30, 1878, 3:1. Nevertheless, he had started over and recouped his losses.

20. The *Dauntless* story was followed for many weeks in the *Brunswick Times-Advertiser.* See 1896 editions for August 14, 19, 31, September 2–4, 6–11, 14–15, 25, 28, October 6–7, 11, 13, November 3, 5, 8, 9.

21. *Brunswick Times-Advertiser,* August 10, 1896.

22. See Baker to Hyde, July 28, 1896, Hyde Papers.

23. Grob to John G. Moore, February 9, 1898, Grob Letter Book 1. All Grob Letter Books are located in the Jekyll Island Museum.

24. Grob to Ballentine, February 10, 1898, Grob Letter Book 1.

25. Grob to Claflin, October 24, 1899, Grob Letter Book 2.

26. Hyde to du Bignon, December 12, 1896, and December 24, 1896, Hyde Papers.

27. Grob to Hyde, May 22, 1897, Hyde Papers.

28. Du Bignon to Hyde, Baker file, Hyde Papers.

29. See du Bignon to Hyde, July 23, 1898, and McIntyre to du Bignon, July 26, 1898, Hyde Papers.

30. Grob to Mrs. John E. du Bignon, June 28, 1899, Grob Letter Book 2.

31. *Brunswick News,* February 2, 1930.

Brown Cottage

1. *New York Times,* April 9, 1926.

2. Maury Klein, *The Great Richmond Terminal* (Charlottesville: University Press of Virginia, 1970), 98; based on Terminal Directors' Minutes, April 10, 1883, and Annual Meeting Minutes, December 14, 1882; *Chronicle* 35 (1882): 405, 457; *Railroad Gazette* 14 (1882): 654; Henry V. Poor, *Manual of the Railroads of the United States for 1882* (New York: H. V. and H. W. Poor, 1882), 385, and *Manual for 1883,* 955.

3. Klein, 98.

4. *New York Times,* March 31, 1911, p. 20; for clubs see *New York Daily Tribune,* August 28, 1894.

5. *New York Times,* April 9, 1926.

6. Thomas C. Clarke to C. S. Maurice, February 22, 1888, Maurice Papers.

7. It was reevaluated along with all other property in 1925 at $4,250.

8. *Dictionary of American Biography* (New York, Charles Scribner's Sons, 1936), 10:73.

9. W. B. Tuthill, *The Suburban Cottage: Its Design and Construction* (New York: William T. Comstock, 1885), 9.

10. Ibid., 19.

11. *New York Times,* September 26, 1926.

12. Ibid., April 10, 1926.

13. According to one crewman quoted in the *Essex County Telegraph,* April 17, 1926, Brown left in 1887, but subtracting a two-year voyage from thirty-six years at Brightlingsea would make it 1888.

14. *New York Daily Tribune,* August 28, 1894.

15. *New York Times,* March 3, 1911; see also *London Times,* April 9, 1926; *New York Times,* April 9, 1926; the *New York Daily Tribune* of August 28, 1894, contends that he sold it to Grand-duke Michael of Russia.

16. Erik Hofman, *The Steam Yachts* (Lymington, Hampshire, England: Nautical Publishing Company, 1970), 60. The *New York Sun,* August 27, 1894, claims that Brown purchased the vessel in 1889.

17. *New York Times,* April 9, 1926.

18. *New York Daily Tribune,* August 28, 1894.

19. *New York Times,* September 26, 1926.

20. *Essex County Telegraph,* April 20, 1926.

21. Ibid.

22. *New York Sun,* August 27, 1894.

23. *New York Times,* March 31, 1911.

24. Ibid., April 9, 1926.

25. Ibid.

26. *New York Sun,* August 27, 1894.

27. "Memorandum in regard to the Debenture Bonds Issued by the Jekyl Island Club July 1, 1893," Hyde Papers.

28. Grob to Lyman Rhoades, January 18, 1899, Grob Letter Book 1.

29. *New York Times,* March 31, 1911.

30. Ibid.

31. Ibid., April 9, 1926.

32. Ibid.

33. Grob to Lyman Rhoades, January 18, 1900, Grob Letter Book 2.

34. Grob to Lyman Rhoades, January 8, 1900, Grob Letter Book 2

35. Grob to Hugo Richards Johnstone, October 6, 1899, Grob Letter Book 2.

36. Grob to Lyman Rhoades, November 13, 1899, Grob Letter Book 2.

37. "Jekyll Native Returns," interview with E. P. Courier, *Jekyll's Golden Islander,* November 6, 1975.

38. Hofman, *Steam Yachts,* 17. Hofman contends that the vessel was drydocked for only a year and then returned to its "old anchorage of Brightlingsea." For other accounts, see *New York Times,* April 9, 1926; *London Times,* September 27, 1926.

39. *New York Times,* April 9, 1926.

40. *Essex County Telegraph,* April 24, 1926.

41. *New York Times,* May 2, 1926, May 5, 1926.

42. Ibid., April 9, 1926.

43. Ibid., April 10, 1926.

44. *Essex County Telegraph,* April 17, 1926.

45. *New York Times,* April 25, 1926.

46. Source for British holdings, *London Times,* September 27, 1926; source for American estate, *New York Times,* September 26, 1926.

47. Hofman, *Steam Yachts,* 60–61; *New York Times,* December 26, 1926.

48. Marian Maurice Diary, March 1, 1942, Maurice Papers. The cottage was apparently still standing in 1944 and is listed in a December 9, 1944, inventory of all island property from the office of the Commissioners of Roads and Revenue of Glynn County to Hon. Frank M. Sutherland, et al. (Sea Island Files).

Solterra

1. Information based on New York City Directories, 1879–99, R. G. Dun Collection, vol. 383: 646, Baker Library, Harvard University; telephone interview with Audrey Lake (widow of Henri Lake, grandson of Frederic Baker), March 27, 1989.

2. Dun *Collection,* vol. 383:646.

3. Executive Committee Minutes, March 14, 1889.

4. Baker names the contractor in Baker to Hyde, August 3, 1896, Hyde Papers. The architectural firm that designed Mrs. Baker's house in Southampton, Long Island, in 1915 was Hiss & Weeks.

5. Hiss and Weeks might also be considered as candidates for the architects of Solterra, though no records substantiate their involvement. *Brunswick Times,* March 10, 1914.

6. *New York Times,* February 17, 1893.

7. Baker to Hyde, April 10, 1995, Hyde Papers.

8. Evidence of the location of Union Chapel is found in Baker to Hyde, March 17, 1898, Hyde Papers, when he attests that Mrs. Wirt Dexter "owns a lot a little to the rear, and south of, the lot upon which the Chapel is situated." Hers was lot 36, located to the rear and a little south of lot 38, which according to the lot records was the one that contained the orginal chapel. Faith Chapel was constructed on lot 29.

9. Subscription list of February 25, 1897, Hyde Papers.

10. Hyde to Baker, March 15, 1897, Hyde Papers.

11. Baker to Hyde and Scrymser, September 1, 1897, Hyde Papers.

12. Grob to Baker, April 22, 1900, Grob Letter Book 2.

13. De Forest to William D. Foulke, William D. Foulke Papers, Library of Congress.

14. Grob to Bradley & Hubbard Mfg. Co., May 2, 1898. Hyde as well was drawing back from his obsession with running every detail of Jekyll Island affairs. His health was in a rapid state of decline. He, too, failed to come to Jekyll for the 1899 season, and on May 2 he died at his New York home.

15. Marian to Auntie, March 19, 1899, Maurice Papers.

16. *Brunswick Call,* March 22, 1899.

17. Mary C. Hoffman to Charlotte Maurice, September 7, [1901], Maurice Papers.

18. Grob to H. H. Raymond, December 29, 1900, Grob Letter Book 2.

19. Charles F. Maurice to Mamma, May 30, 1901, Maurice Papers.

20. Charles F. Maurice to Mamma, June 7, 1901, Maurice Papers.

21. Mama [Charlotte Maurice] to Arch [Archibald Maurice], January 22, [1908], Maurice Papers. It should be noted that Mrs. Baker's name does not appear in the guest register for the 1908 season. Although occasionally guests failed to sign the register, it is also possible that the letter may be misdated.

22. *Brunswick Journal,* February 17, 1908, p. 1.

23. Ada Thompson Bruand memoir, Jekyll Island Museum.

24. *Southampton Press,* June 19, 1913.

25. See George Cowman papers, Jekyll Island Museum. Cowman gave an $82.50 estimate, n.d.

26. *Brunswick News,* March 10, 1914.

27. Freddie Clark memoir, Jekyll Island Museum.

28. *Brunswick News,* March 15, 1914, p. 5.

Fairbank Cottage

1. Paul Thomas Gilbert and Charles Lee Bryson, *Chicago and its Makers* (Chicago: F. Mendelsohn, 1929), 703.

2. Quoted in Helen de Freitas, *Nathaniel Kellogg Fairbank* (Privately printed, 1980), 14. Lady Helen de Freitas, the granddaughter of Nathaniel Kellogg Fairbank and the daughter of Nathalie Fairbank Bell, has written an interesting and objective biography of Fairbank, based largely on family correspondence and Fairbank's diaries, which are not available to nonfamily researchers. Her book, therefore, has been extremely helpful in writing this chapter.

3. Ibid., 24.

4. Ibid.

5. Ibid., 33.

6. Advertisement for sale of cottage circulated about 1921 by Ralph Beaver Strassburger, Cyrus Hall McCormick Jr. Papers, State Historical Society of Wisconsin, Madison, Wisconsin.

7. Based on description in the Strassburger ad; also E. G. Grob to Mrs. E. H. Hubbard, January 6, 1900, Grob Letter Book 2.

8. De Freitas, 76.

9. On earlier efforts to construct a new church on the island, see McCash and McCash, 82–83.

10. De Freitas, 56.

11. Ibid., 76.

12. Ibid.

13. *Brunswick Times-Advertiser,* March 22, 1895.

14. Henry B. Hyde to Frederic Baker, June 16, 1986, Hyde Papers.

15. See McCash and McCash, 98–99. See also Glynn County Deeds, Book TT, 302, 322.

16. De Freitas, 66.

17. Ibid., 73.

18. On the Swing controversy, see A. T. Andreas, *History of Chicago from the Earliest Period to the Present Time* (1866; reprint, New York: Arno Press, 1975), 3: 827; Bessie Louise Pierce, *A History of Chicago* (Chicago: University of Chicago Press, 1975), 3:428–31.

19. *New York Times,* May 23, 1889.

20. Quoted in de Freitas, 81.

21. *New York Times,* June 26, 1896.

22. Craig Timberlake, *The Life and Works of David Belasco: The Bishop of Broadway* (New York: Library Publishers, 1954), 188.

23. *New York Times,* June 26, 1896.

24. Ibid., June 18, 1896.

25. Quoted in Timberlake, 190.

26. Nathalie Fairbank to Helen Graham Fairbank

Carpenter, n.d. 1900, quoted in de Freitas, 85.

27. De Freitas, 85–86.

28. Glynn County Deeds, 3-L, 519.

29. Grob to Walton Ferguson Jr., January 29, 1899, Grob Letter Book 1.

30. Grob to Walton Ferguson Jr., February 25, 1899, Grob Letter Book 2.

31. Grob to Fairbank, January 29, 1900, Grob Letter Book 2.

32. The letter is dated February 2, 1899, but it could have been written only in 1900. Fairbank used his own cottage in 1899, arriving on the same day as the Walton Fergusons, February 25. In 1900, however, Ferguson arrived, as the letter indicates, on February 15.

33. The cottage was sold to Ferguson on March 20, 1904. See Glynn County Deeds, 3-L, 519.

34. The information on the births of the Ferguson children is based on a letter from Lois R. Dater to June Hall McCash, April 25, 1990.

35. Henry F. Sherwood, *The Story of Stamford* (New York: The States History Company, n.d.), 254.

36. William W. Barton, "Exhaust Fumes," *Stamford Power Squadron Inc.*, April and May 1965.

37. Ibid.

38. Cowman to Walton Ferguson, March 27, 1916, Cowman Papers.

39. The series of delightful, though undated, letters written from Jekyll Island was provided by Mrs. Philip Dater, who indicates that they were written to her husband during his childhood "when he was an invalid."

40. *Stamford Advocate*, April 8, 1922, p. 1.

41. Concerning Bourne's years as president of the Jekyll Island Club, see McCash and McCash, 132–55.

42. See Glynn County Deeds, 3-L, 519.

43. Ralph Beaver Strassburger, *The Strassburger Family and Allied Families of Pennsylvania, Being the Ancestry of Jacob Andrew Strassburger, Esquire of Montgomery County, Pennsylvania* (Gwynedd Valley, Pa.: printed for private circulation, 1922), 171.

44. "Mike" to "Bridget," January 31, 1920, courtesy of Florence H. Hughes, who notes that "the whole Bourne family had nicknames." Florence H. Hughes to June Hall McCash, February 1, 1995.

45. Strassburger, 172.

46. Letters provided courtesy of Florence H. Hughes.

47. The Faith Chapel window was entitled "David Set Singers Before the Lord," according to the March 27, 1921, *Brunswick News* account of the window's installation. The title of the window, which serves to explain its assorted images, was primarily a tribute to Bourne's love of choral music. Not only did he himself have a fine baritone voice, which caught the attention of his benefactor, Alfred Corning Clark, and launched his career in what was then the Singer Manufacturing Company, but he also supported choral music with his great fortune. For example, he gave $500,000 in 1914 to the Cathedral of Saint John the Divine for the maintenance of the choir school of the cathedral. See *New York Sun*, April 19, 1914, p. 6.

48. Almira Rockefeller to Emma McAlpin, Emma Rockefeller McAlpin Correspondence, Rockefeller Family Archives, Tarrytown, New York.

49. A copy of this brochure is in the McCormick Papers.

50. Ralph Beaver Stassburger to Cyrus Hall McCormick, July 16, 1920, McCormick Papers.

51. A. V. Whitson to Ralph Beaver Strassburger, McCormick Papers.

52. Florence H. Hughes (daughter of Florence Bourne Thayer and niece of Marjorie Bourne) to June Hall McCash, February 1, 1995.

53. *Philadelphia Evening Public Ledger*, September 28, 1926.

54. Florence H. Hughes to June Hall McCash [n.d. April 1996].

55. *New York Times*, December 26, 1913.

56. *Philadelphia Bulletin*, October 27, 1926.

57. *New York World*, June 4, 1908.

58. *Philadelphia Record*, December 4, 1926; see also *New York Times*, December 4, 1926; *Philadelphia Inquirer*, December 4, 1926.

59. *Philadelphia Public Ledger*, November 30, 1926.

60. His obituary in the *Philadelphia Inquirer*, January 17, 1968, lists him as "a socialite and former insurance and investment broker."

61. Glynn County Deeds, Book 5-L, 444. The survey, ordered by Henry J. Fisher, who is listed as the president of the Sans Souci Association, was done by W. N. Gramling, Glynn County surveyor, on January 25, 1944.

62. *Philadelphia Inquirer*, January 17, 1968. Florence and Anson Hard had been divorced more than two decades earlier. Alexander Dallas Thayer died on January 16, 1968.

Furness Cottage

1. Owen Wister, "Horace Howard Furness: A Short Memoir," *Harvard Graduates' Magazine* (December 1912), 201.

2. James F. O'Gorman, *The Architecture of Frank Furness* (Philadelphia: Philadelphia Museum of Art, 1973), 16.

3. Walter Rogers Furness to Helen Key Bullitt, February 12, 1886, private collection of Wirt Thompson Jr. All subsequent Furness letters are in this collection.

4. Furness to Bullitt, February 12, 1886.

5. *Philadelphia Inquirer,* June 5, 1886.

6. Furness to Bullitt, February 12, 1886.

7. Memoir of Fairman Rogers Furness, private collection of Wirt Thompson Jr.

8. See O'Gorman's list, "Documented Works" of Frank Furness, p. 200, no. 15; p. 201, no. 32; p. 208, no. 260.

9. Vincent J. Scully, *The Shingle Style and the Stick Style: Architectural Theory and Design from Downing to the Origins of Wright* (New Haven: Yale University Press, 1970), xx.

10. Memoir of Fairman Rogers Furness.

11. Club game book, March 3, 1893, Jekyll Island Museum.

12. Even though Furness seems to have had no active role in the architectural firm after 1898, he continued to use the firm's address at 1001 Provident Building, Philadelphia.

13. Grob to Furness, January 21, 1899, Grob Letter Book 1.

14. Grob to Furness, January 28, 1901, Grob Letter Book 2.

15. Minutes of joint meeting, April 8, 1901, Jekyll Island Museum.

16. Jekyll Island Club Share Book, Jekyll Island Museum.

17. Helen Kate Furness to Fairman Furness.

18. Included in the "Specification" for the construction of the new cottage, Pulitzer Papers, Columbia University.

19. Cowman to J. J. Albright, April 1, 1915, Cowman Papers.

20. See Glynn County Deeds, 4-E, 298–301.

21. *Atlanta Constitution,* July 26, 1956. McMath was appointed construction superintendent on April 11, 1955, but, according to this article in the *Atlanta Constitution,* resigned his post shortly after Gov. Marvin Griffin issued an executive order that prohibited sales to the state by state employees.

Hollybourne

1. Margaret Stewart Maurice is listed in tax records as the legal owner of the house. However, in truth, she owned it in conjunction with her sisters, Marian Maurice, Cornelia Wilkinson, Emily Dall, and, until his death in 1928, with her brother, Archibald Maurice.

2. Box 1, Folder 1, Maurice Papers.

3. Publication of the American Society of Civil Engineers, Memoirs of Deceased Members, prepared by George H. Maurice, 1924, Maurice Papers.

4. *Memorial of Charlotte Marshall Holbrooke Maurice, Regent and Founder of Tioga Chapter, D.A.R.,* Athens, Pa., 1909, copy in Maurice Papers.

5. Articles of Agreement, July 1, 1871, between Charles Kellogg of Athens, Pa., and C. Stewart Maurice of the town of Ossining, N.Y., Maurice Papers.

6. Articles of agreement, March 1, 1884, between Charles Kellogg of Athens, Pa., Charles S. Maurice of Athens, George S. Field of Buffalo, Edmund Hayes of Buffalo, Charles MacDonald of New York, and Thomas C. Clarke of Seabright, N.J., Maurice Papers.

7. "Our dear baby died yesterday," wrote Charlotte Maurice to Auntie from her home in Athens on October 11, 1881, Maurice Papers.

8. Healsy C. deBaud to Charlotte M. Maurice, January 12, 1882, Maurice Papers.

9. See "Members of the Jekyl Island Club, 1886–1947," McCash and McCash, 217–26. The original receipt, dated April 2, 1886, and signed by N. S. Finney, for two shares of stock in the Jekyll Island Club is in the Maurice Papers.

10. T. C. Clarke to Maurice, February 33, 1888, Maurice Papers.

11. A. E. Touzalin to Stewart [C. S. Maurice], July 25, 1888. Maurice Papers. Touzalin did not sell his share of Jekyll stock. He died the following year.

12. The collection was published as *Jekyl Island: Some Historic Notes and Some Legends Collected by Charlotte Marshall Maurice, and a Brief Outline of the Early Days of*

the Jekyl Island Club Made by Charles Stewart Maurice (n.d. [between 1923 and 1929], privately printed), Maurice Papers.

13. Mama [Charlotte Maurice] to Arch [Archibald Maurice], May 15, 1889, Maurice Papers.

14. The name "Hollybourne" first appears in the club's guest register on January 24, 1900.

15. The original plans for the Maurice cottage, signed by architect William H. Day, are in the Maurice Papers, along with copies of the Jekyl Island Club charter, constitution, and by-laws of 1887. Memorandum dated Brunswick, March 9, 1892, on Crovatt and Whitfield letterhead, Maurice Papers. Burr Winston did an additional amount of work [unspecified] in 1892. Receipt signed by Burr Winston, April 11, 1892, Maurice Papers.

16. J. G. Holbrooke to Marion and George, December 17, 1890, Maurice Papers.

17. E. G. Grob to Maurice, August 25, 1893, Maurice Papers.

18. Mama to Arch, November 17, 1893, Maurice Papers.

19. The Pulitzer rental is attested by the *Brunswick Times-Advertiser* of 13 December, 1894, as well as the guest register. The detailed inventory is in the Maurice Papers.

20. Marian to Aunty, December 29, [1901], Maurice Papers.

21. Emily to Grandma, January 28, 1898 [1899?], from Jekyll Island, Maurice Papers. For the 1896 letter, Emily to Grandma, December 31, 1896, Maurice Papers.

22. Albert to Grandmother, January 5, 1899, Maurice Papers.

23. Marian to Aunty, December 29, [1901], Maurice Papers. The spelling of "Auntie" and "Aunty" varies among the letters.

24. Grandma to Arch, February 26, 1893, Maurice papers; the Charlotte Maurice Diary, 1899–1909, Daily Record of Menus and Guests through March each year, is found in the Maurice Papers.

25. Marian to Grandmama [Mrs. J. G. Holbrooke], January 30, 1898, Maurice Papers.

26. Nina recorded such a swim in March 1899. For other pleasures, see, for example, Margaret to Uncle George, February 11, 1897, Maurice Papers.

27. Marian to Auntie, March 16, 1898, Maurice Papers.

28. Marian to Auntie, March 19, 1899, Maurice Papers.

29. Marian to Auntie, March 16, 1898, Maurice Papers.

30. Nina to Grandmama [Mrs. J. G. Holbrooke], February 27, [1898], Maurice Papers.

31. Marian to Aunty, March 19, [1900], Maurice Papers.

32. Information on their thoughts on selling the plantation come from a letter from Emily Maurice to her sister Marian, [November 5, 1910], Maurice Papers.

33. C[harles] S[tewart] M[aurice] to Marian, November 5, [1910], Maurice Papers.

34. Nina to Grandmama, January 15, 1899, Maurice Papers.

35. E. G. Grob to C. S. Maurice, May 2, 1898, Maurice Papers. Also receipt from W. H. Bowen for the work in the amount of $95 plus $35 for building the wall (presumably around the du Bignon cemetery), folder 139, Maurice Papers. The amount of $230 was subscribed for the purpose, with Mr. and Mrs. Maurice each contributing $25. Maurice Papers.

36. J. G. Holbrooke to Marion Maurice, 20 February 1893, Maurice Papers.

37. Bishop of Georgia to Mrs. Maurice, March 23, 1900, Maurice Papers.

38. Bishop of Georgia to Mrs. C. S. Maurice, March 23, 1893, Maurice Papers.

39. Bishop of Georgia to Mrs. Maurice, March 16, 1899, Maurice Papers.

40. Marian to Aunty, March 19, [1900], Maurice Papers.

41. Nina to Grandma, February 1, 1889, Maurice Papers. She mentions that Mr. Perry "is a very good worker as you will see from the fact that he has more than 150 negro children coming daily to his school in which he teaches, and both church and school are more prosperous than anything else in Brunswick so far as we can see."

42. P. J. Luckie to Mrs. Charles Stewart Maurice, March 7, 1899, Maurice Papers.

43. P. J. Luckie, S.M., written from Iglesia de San Lorenzo, Mexico, n.d., Maurice Papers.

44. *Memorial of Charlotte Marshall Holbrooke Maurice,* Maurice Papers.

45. Executive Committee Minutes, April 12, 1900. See also Falk to Frederic Baker, April 26, 1900, Grob Letter Book 2. The surveyor was E. A. Penniman. The survey was mailed to Maurice on May 12 by Capt. James A.

Clark, who had taken over as summer superintendent in the absence of Ernest Grob. Clark, evidently taking into consideration the number of horses and carriages that Maurice kept on the island, informed him: "I had the surveyor measure off a plot 125 × 100 thinking you would require a little more than Mr. Baker whose plot is 100 × 100." James A. Clark to C. S. Maurice, May 12, 1900, Maurice Papers.

46. Frederic Baker to Mr. Maurice, October 17, 1903, Maurice Papers. "My lot is about one half the size of yours but better located. . . . For his stable lot Gould paid $200 I think. His lot is worth more than yours."

47. F. Baker to C. S. Maurice, April 20, 1904, Maurice Papers.

48. For example, he did repairs on May 7, 1913, Cowman Time Book, George Cowman Papers, Jekyll Island Museum. Cowman also sent Maurice a later estimate (undated but written before March 11, 1914) for additional stable repairs. He wanted the roof replaced on the stable, the carriage house, and the house he provided for his coachman, Charlie Hill, as well as new floors in the stable, but he thought Cowman's estimate of $770 too high. Cowman Papers. Cowman also bid $114.50 to re-roof the verandah on the south side of the cottage (Cowman to Maurice, September 3, 1914), but by the following August Maurice had still not authorized him to begin. Cowman wrote to tell him that it had rained hard "and the water came through all over the Roof." Cowman to C. S. Maurice, August 4, 1915.

49. John Claflin to Mr. Maurice, n.d., Maurice Papers.

50. Gratz Dent to Mrs. Maurice, September 2, 1909, Maurice Papers.

51. E. G. Grob to Marian Maurice, September 9, 1909, Maurice Papers.

52. W. H. Merrill to Miss Maurice, April 28, 1909, Maurice Papers. Evidently some member of the Gould family had also had typhoid, for Edwin Gould agreed to have members of his family tested when Dr. Merrill suggested that the only way to detect a carrier was "by examining bacteriologically each person particularly those families that had had the disease."

53. On the typhoid problem, see McCash and McCash, 119–22.

54. Marian to Uncle George, December 30, [1909], Maurice Papers.

55. Emmy to Mamie, December 31, 1912, Maurice Papers.

56. *Brunswick News,* December 19, 1911, p. 6.

57. Emmy to Maurice, October 15, 1913, Maurice Papers.

58. Al to Mamie [Marian Maurice], February 28, 1910, Maurice Papers.

59. *Brunswick Daily News,* December 28, 1911, p. 6.

60. Telegram from C. W. Dall to Miss Maurice, March 21, 1913, Maurice Papers.

61. Memo written in Maurice's hand, dated January 20, 1918, Maurice Papers; Cowman to Grob, January 22, 1919, Cowman Papers. The damage was estimated by Cowman at $239.60.

62. Howard Elliott to Miss Maurice, March 5, 1924, Maurice Papers.

63. Sayre, Pa., February 23, 1924.

64. C[harles] to Molly [Marian?], Friday, [February 8, 1924], Maurice Papers.

65. Ibid.

66. Al to Mamie, February 17, 1924. Maurice Papers.

67. File February–March, 1924, Maurice Papers.

68. Ibid.

69. Deed and attestation of the value of the property sworn by E. G. Grob and club lawyer A. J. Crovatt are in the Maurice Papers.

70. Emmy to Mamie [Marian], [March 13, 1924], Maurice Papers.

71. Both the voucher for the $2,500 and John S. Sheppard to Archibald Stewart Maurice, June 24, 1925, are in the Maurice Papers.

72. Marian Maurice diary, Maurice Papers.

73. Susan Albright to Marian, January 19, 1927; Gratz Dent to Marian, November 20, 1926, Maurice Papers.

74. E. G. Grob to Marian Maurice, March 14, 1931, Maurice Papers.

75. Marian Maurice diary, January 28–February 7, April 5, 1930.

76. Marian Maurice diary, February 16–21, 1931.

77. See Marian Maurice diary, January 3–April 3, 1936, January 4, 1937.

78. See Marian Maurice diary, March 30–April 3, 1940.

79. See Marian Maurice diary, March 15–29, 1942.

80. Bill W. [William B. S. Winans] to Mamie [Marian

Maurice], April 23, 1945, Maurice Papers.

81. John J. Gilbert to George W. Palmer, June 27, 1947, Sea Island Files.

82. John J. Gilbert to Bernon Prentice, July 3, 1947, Sea Island Files.

83. J. D. Compton to Margaret S. Maurice, October 13, 1947, Sea Island Files.

84. Margaret Stewart Maurice to J. D. Compton, October 18, 1947, Sea Island Files.

85. Marian B. Maurice to Mr. Compton, November 19, 1947, Sea Island Files.

Indian Mound

1. Linley, 223.

2. McKay's early life is sketched in *Biographical Dictionary of American Business Leaders,* ed. John N. Ingham (Westport, Conn.: Greenwood Press, 1983), 2:907–8; *Dictionary of American Biography* 2:73–74; *National Cyclopaedia,* 10:397. See letter from C. D. Makepeace, treasurer of Williams College, to M. Victor McKay, November 8, 1949, copy in Gordon McKay File, Jekyll Island Museum.

3. Waldemar Kaempffert, ed., *A Popular History of American Invention,* vol. 2 (New York: Charles Scribner's Sons, 1924), 412.

4. Kaempffert, 2:415.

5. *Biographical Dictionary,* 2:907–8

6. *Springfield (Massachusetts) Republican,* July 8, 1945.

7. *New York Times,* October 20, 1903.

8. Papers of Gordon McKay, Harvard University Archives, Cambridge, Mass.

9. An 1888 photograph of Victor McKay, in the possession of Amy McKay Kahler, is labeled "Victor Fabbricotti," thereby lending credence to the rumor that he was the natural son of an Italian, Arturo Fabbricotti.

10. Letter from John MacKay to Auguste MacKay, October 1, 1889, copy in Gordon McKay file, Jekyll Island Museum, original owned by Marion Virginia McKay.

11. See the will and codicils of Gordon McKay in the Harvard Archives.

12. Codicil of June 6, 1892, 22.

13. Glynn County Deeds, Book WW, 547, April 1, 1891. McKay's cousin Wirt Dexter died suddenly in Chi-

cago on May 17, 1890.

14. Contrary to the usual practice of making payment in the year following a cottage's completion, property taxes were not paid until 1894. The discrepancy can be explained, most likely, by the fact that the club was officially closed in 1893 because of a yellow fever epidemic in Brunswick where the entire city was under quarantine and in general disarray. Thus it is possible that no taxes were collected on his cottage that year. See Glynn County Tax Digest, 1893, 1894.

15. Linley, 223.

16. See *New York Times,* October 20, 1903.

17. E. G. Grob and A. J. Crovatt gave a sworn affidavit on March 24, 1924 (Maurice Papers), in which they estimated the original cost of the "Rockefeller" cottage, "including fixtures, furniture and appurtenances," to have been "more than $40,000." Certainly this estimate seems high for the McKay Cottage at the time it was built, though it may well have reached such an amount when one considers the various improvements and additions made by Rockefeller.

18. *Newport Herald,* October 20, 1903.

19. Florence Treat diary, in private collection of Amy McKay Kahler, November 7, 1895.

20. Marion Treat to Mother, August, 18, [1898?], letter in possession of Amy McKay Kahler.

21. *Newport Herald,* October, 20, 1903.

22. *Springfield (Massachusettes) Republican,* July 8, 1945.

23. Treat diary, December 29, 1894, January 30, 1896. The diary also contains a newspaper clipping of uncertain origin and date, recording "another of the Saturday teas."

24. Treat diary, March 29, March 30, 1895.

25. Hyde to Baker, October 12, 1897, Hyde Papers.

26. Hyde to Baker, March 11, 1898, Hyde Papers.

27. McKay will and codicils, McKay Papers, Harvard.

28. N. S. Shaler, *The Autobiography of Nathaniel Southgate Shaler,* with a Supplementary Memoir by his wife (Boston: Houghton Mifflin, 1909), 387–88.

29. See "The Legal Aspects and Educational Results of the Harvard-Technology Decision," *Harvard Graduates' Magazine* 26 (1918): 391–403.

30. Ruling in 1917 in the case of *President and Fellows of Harvard College v. Attorney General et al.,* Justice De-

Courcy presiding, Harvard University Archives.

31. William Bentinck-Smith and Elizabeth Stouffer, *Harvard University History of Named Chairs: Sketches of Donors and Donations: University Professorships and Those of the Faculty of Arts and Sciences 1721–1991.* (Cambridge, Mass.: Secretary to the University, 1991).

32. Hennin Jennings, *The Gordon McKay Bequest* (privately printed: n.d.), 5. A copy may be found in the McKay Papers, Harvard.

33. Shaler, 328.

34. Ibid., 399–400.

35. Glynn County Deeds, WW-548.

36. Peter Collier and David Horowitz, *The Rockefellers: An American Dynasty* (New York: Holt, Rinehart and Winston, 1976), 9.

37. Thomas W. Lawson, *Frenzied Finance, I, The Crime of Amalgamated* (New York: Ridgway-Thayer Company, 1905), 21.

38. Allan Nevins, *John D. Rockefeller: The Heroic Age of American Enterprise* (New York: Charles Scribner's Sons, 1940), 1:6–7, 16, 110, 233.

39. Anna to Emma McAlpin (ca. September 1922), McAlpin Correspondence, Rockefeller Archives; Collier and Horowitz, 7–10; Nevins, 1:50–53; *Harper's Weekly* 33, no. 1710.

40. Lawson, 22.

41. Nevins, 1:88–89, 121–23; *New York Times,* June 27, 1922, p. 15.

42. Quoted in Collier and Horowitz, 37.

43. On the issue of "elite" religion in America, see Kit and Frederica Konolige, *The Power of their Glory: America's Ruling Class: The Episcopalians* (New York: Wyden Books, 1978).

44. See Nevins, 1:69, 78–79, 107, 129, 139, 196; *Dictionary of American Biography* 8:65–66; *National Cyclopaedia* 2:63.

45. Nevins, 1:198.

46. For these organizational and business developments see Nevins, 1:196–98, 288–93, 449, 540–41, 614–15, 676; *Biographical Dictionary* 2:1182–96.

47. *New York Times,* November 19, 1907, p. 4, November 2, 1911, p. 1.

48. *New York Daily Tribune,* July 6, 1899, p. 6.

49. *New York Times,* September 27, 1903, p. 22. For litigation in this case see ibid., June 29, 1902, p. 2; July 2, 1903, p. 8; July 3, 1903, p. 1; July 23, 1903, p. 3;

December 17 1903, p. 1; December 18, 1903, p. 2; December 28, 1903, p. 7; July 6, 1907, p. 1; *New York Daily Tribune,* July 2, 3, 1903, p. 9; September 19, 1903, p. 5.

50. Anna to Emma McAlpin, 1922, McAlpin Correspondence.

51. *New York Daily Tribune,* January 3, 1900, p. 1; Grob to Hyde, September 8, 1897, Hyde Papers.

52. *New York Times,* September 21, 1908, p. 7.

53. Almira Rockefeller to Emma McAlpin, January [?], 1920, McAlpin Correspondence.

54. Anna to Emma McAlpin, [1922], McAlpin Correspondence; Kate Brown to Family, February 20, 1917, Brown letters.

55. Record of Shares, Jekyll Island Museum; Subscriptions List, 1886, copy in Jekyll Island Museum.

56. Club Register, March 12, 1888, Jekyll Island Museum; *Brunswick Daily Advertiser-Appeal,* March 16, 1888.

57. Rockefeller to Pearsall, April 17, 1888, James J. Hill Papers, James J. Hill Reference Library, Saint Paul, Minnesota, hereafter referred to as Hill Papers.

58. Hyde to Baker, July 29, 1896, McIntyre to W. Rockefeller, December 29, 1896, Hyde Papers.

59. Hyde to Stickney, March 7, 1898; Hyde to Rockefeller, October 8, 1897, Hyde Papers.

60. Baker to Hyde, July 11, 1896, Hyde Papers; list of pledges, February 25, 1897, Hyde Papers; Grob to W. Rockefeller, April 9, 1898, Grob Letter Book 1; Executive Committee Minutes, May 13, 1901; Grob to Pulitzer, March 12, 1903, Pulitzer Papers.

61. Record of Shares, Jekyll Island Museum; Glynn County Tax Digest, 1905.

62. Quoted in Nevins, 2:526.

63. Nevins, 2:603–4; *Biographical Dictionary,* 2:1182–96.

64. *New York Times,* February 18, 1911, p. 11; August 7, 1911, p. 7; October 15, 1911, 2:1.

65. Almira G. Rockefeller to Emma Rockefeller, February 28, 1895, William Rockefeller Family Papers. *New York Times,* June 25, 1906, 1: 5; October 14, 1911, p. 1; October 15, 1911, p. 1; January 8, 1913, p. 1; *New York Daily Tribune,* July 25, 1906, p. 9.

66. *New York Times,* October 20, 1912, p. 1.

67. Ibid., December 28, 1912, p. 3; December 30, 1912, p. 18; December 31, 1912, p. 1; January 1, 1913, p. 1; January 3, 1913, p. 3.

68. Emmy to sisters, January 6, 1913, Maurice Papers.

69. *New York Times,* January 16, 1913, p. 1; January 23, 1913, p. 3.

70. *New York Times,* February 8, 1913, p. 1. All quotations concerning this incident are from this source.

71. Ibid., February 20, 1913, p. 6; Grob to Hon. Joseph E. Willard, February 12, 1913, Willard Family Papers, Library of Congress.

72. Cowman to Grob, April 22, 26, 1912, Cowman Papers.

73. *Brunswick News,* August 15, 1913, p. 1; Cowman Weekly Time Books, March–November, 1913, Cowman Papers.

74. Cowman to Grob, January 2, 1914; Cowman to Rockefeller, February 9, March 17, August 19, 1915, January 19, April 18, 1916, February 24, March 7, 16, 1917, Cowman Papers.

75. See notes, "Restoration of the Rockefeller House," Jekyll Island Museum, which states that the mixture was supposed to give the shingles "an attractive color" but further indicates that "none of the shingles . . . removed during restoration showed any evidence of having been dipped in buttermilk and creosote. . . ." See also Cowman to Rockefeller, April 26, June 21, August 19, 1915, Cowman Papers.

76. Clermont Lee's data, used in formulating the redevelopment plan, are based largely on memories of club employees.

77. *Brunswick News,* January 30, 1917, p. 1.

78. See interview with Charlie Hill, June 4, 1970, in Research Data Used in Planning the Redevelopment of the McKay-Rockefeller-Jenkins Cottage Grounds, January 1970, Clermont Lee, Landscape Architect, Jekyll Island Museum.

79. *Brunswick News,* January 3, 1917, p. 1.

80. *New York Times,* May 15, 1909, p. 6; October 22, 1909, p. 1; December 28, 1912, p. 3; *New York Daily Tribune,* July 30, 1902, p. 1, July 26, 1906, p. 9.

81. *Brunswick News,* March 6, 1915, p. 1; February 6, 1916, p. 1; April 1, 1916, p. 1.

82. Emma McAlpin diary, entry February 15, 1921, Rockefeller Archives.

83. McAlpin diary, March 10, 1922.

84. Executive Committee Minutes, February 10, 1917.

85. Mira Rockefeller to Emma McAlpin, January 14, 1920, McAlpin Correspondence.

86. *New York Times,* May 31, 1900, p. 1.

87. *Brunswick News,* January 18, 1920, p. 1; McAlpin diary, January 19, 1920.

88. McAlpin diary, entries February 10–March 6, 1921.

89. *New York Times,* June 27, 1922, p. 15.

90. Elizabeth Claflin to Emma McAlpin, [June 1922], McAlpin Correspondence.

91. Glynn County Deeds, WW-548, recorded April 17, 1924; reiterated in Deed Book 4-R, 736.

92. *New York Times,* April 25, 1934, p. 22.

93. This information comes from Helen M. Platt, the granddaughter of Helen Hartley Jenkins, in a letter to June H. McCash, February 7, 1989.

94. See *New York Times,* October 13, 1915, 15:1.

95. Charles A. Frumd (secretary to Helen Hartley Jenkins) to Elizabeth Sanders, March 14, 1973, in Charles A. Frumd file, Jekyll Island Museum; Helen M. Platt to June H. McCash, January 1989.

96. Glynn County Tax Digest, 1924; Helen M. Platt to June H. McCash, January 31, 1989.

97. *New York Times,* April 25, 1934, p. 22. Subsequent information and quotations concerning her philanthropic activities come from this article unless otherwise indicated.

98. Concerning Professor Thorndike, see his biography by Geraldine M. Joncich, *The Sane Positivist: A Biography of Edward L. Thorndike* (Middletown, Conn.: Wesleyan University Press, [1968]).

99. *Savannah Morning News,* January 17, 1963.

100. Virginia Crocheron Gildersleeve, *Many a Good Crusade: Memoirs* (New York: Macmillan, 1954), 210.

101. Gildersleeve, 210. All subsequent reminiscences of Dean Gildersleeve are to this source and are found in pages 210–12, unless otherwise indicated.

102. Platt to McCash, January 1989. Her recollection is borne out by an inventory of the house taken in 1947, which mentions red velvet carpet in these rooms. Subsequent information concerning furnishings is taken from this inventory.

103. Gildersleeve, 211; Platt to McCash, January 31, 1989.

104. Bessie Randall to Mama, February 23 [1922], Blanchard Randall Papers, Maryland Historical Society, Baltimore, Md.

105. Mrs. Randall to Bessie, 1926, Randall Papers; Gildersleeve, 213.

106. Em to Bess, February 6, 1926, Randall Papers.

107. Gildersleeve, 213.

108. *New York Times,* February 20, 1928, p. 21.

109. *New York Times,* September 1, 1930; unidentified clippings found in Emma Rockefeller McAlpin diary.

110. McAlpin diary, August 30, 1930; *New York Times,* April 25, 1934, p. 22. As did most Jekyll Islanders, Mrs. Jenkins owned several homes. Besides her New York City, Morristown, and Jekyll properties, she owned a home in Norfolk, Connecticut.

111. *New York Times,* August 1931. p. 17.

112. See Glynn County Deeds 4-S, 282; 4-R, 736.

113. J. D. Compton to Alfred W. Jones, March 29, 1946, Sea Island Files.

114. C. W. Wannop to J. D. Compton, March 24, 1946, Sea Island Files.

115. Jekyll Island Authority Minutes, May 26, 1951, 201.

116. Jekyll Island Authority Minutes, November 22, 1954. The idea of converting Indian Mound into a museum was discussed as early as 1948. *Savannah Morning News,* March 3, 1948.

117. Jekyll Island Authority Minutes, September 27, 1954.

118. Ibid., November 4, 1950, August 31, 1951, November 17, 1951, January 16, 1967, August 11, 1968; "Restoration of the Rockefeller House," Jekyll Island Museum. See also Roger Beedle's address to the National Society of Interior Decorators, April 1970, in Beedle File, Jekyll Island Museum.

119. "Restoration of the Rockefeller House."

120. Research Data Used in Planning the Redevelopment of the McKay-Rockefeller-Jenkins Cottage Grounds, January 1970.

Moss Cottage

1. J. Thomas Scharf and Thompson Westcott, *History of Philadelphia, 1609–1884* (Philadelphia: L. H. Everts, 1884), pp. 2293–94.

2. See Joseph Jackson, *Market Street, Philadelphia: The Most Historic Highway in America: Its Merchants and Its Story* (Philadelphia: Press of Patterson & White Co., 1918), 154.

3. Scharf and Westcott, pp. 2293–94.

4. Dun Collection, vol. 137, p. 568.

5. The various names of the firm are taken from the letterhead on correspondence from the Historical Society of Pennsylvania and from William Struthers's obituary in the *Philadelphia Press,* December 14, 1911.

6. Dun Collection, vol. 137, p. 568. In fact, his marriage certificate gives his occupation as banker. City of Philadelphia Archives, Department of Records.

7. The detail concerning the blue ribbon was supplied by her great-granddaughter, Jean O'Donnell.

8. *Philadelphia Press,* December 14, 1911, gives "grief over the death of his wife" as the reason for Struthers's death. Information on the early years of Struthers and Savannah Durborrow are from a letter from John W. Sears to June Hall McCash, March 1989, and from an interview with Jean O'Donnell in February 1989. Family sources contend that Savannah Durborrow was born in Griffin, Georgia; however, it should be noted that her marriage license gives her birthplace as Philadelphia and her age as twenty-one.

9. *Philadelphia Press,* December 14, 1911.

10. At various times during his membership he purchased lots 1, 6, and 25.

11. J. A. Falk to William Struthers, October 3, 1898, Grob Letter Book 1.

12. The Jekyll Island Museum is currently considering the possibility of restoring the south end conservatory. The presence of electricity is indicated by the repair of the electric bell system in 1899. See Grob to J. A. Montgomery, February 21, 1899, Grob Letter Book 1.

13. See *Philadelphia Inquirer,* November 22, 1876, p. 2.

14. In addition to the evidence in the guest register, the *Brunswick Call* recorded their arrival on December 18, 1899. See the edition for December 19, 1899, p. 1.

15. *Brunswick Times Advertiser,* March 25, 1897, March 27, 1897. See also Grob to McIntyre, March 26, 1897, Hyde Papers.

16. Jean Struthers to Joseph Pulitzer, January 1904, [Monday] February 1904, Pulitzer Papers.

17. Oral interview with Jean O'Donnell, February 1989.

18. Faith Chapel Records.

19. Mama [Charlotte Maurice] to Arch [Archibald Maurice], December 30, [1908], Maurice Papers.

20. See Glynn County Deeds, Book 3-D, 382.

21. See *New York Times,* January 19, 1918.

22. Kate Brown to Mother, February 21, 1917.

23. Brown letters, February 21, 1917.

24. Brown letters, March 24, 1917.

25. Ibid.

26. Lucy W. Hall to June Hall McCash, April 13, 1989.

27. Brown letters, March 28, 1917.

28. Helen Macy Hall to Mr. and Mrs. Ridgeway M. Hall, [n.d.], 1976; copy of letter provided by Mrs. Ridgeway M. Hall.

29. Macy to Members, January 29, 1913, McCormick Papers.

30. Robert Todd Lincoln to Cyrus McCormick, February 14, 1911, McCormick Papers.

31. See Macy to McCormick, March 11, 1909, McCormick Papers.

32. Macy to Pruyn, January 18, 1910, McCormick Papers.

33. Macy to McCormick, March 10, 1909, McCormick Papers.

34. Macy to McCormack [*sic*], November 10, 1909, McCormick Papers.

35. Macy to McCormick, January 21, 1910, McCormick Papers.

36. McCormick to Lanier, November 8, 1910, McCormick Papers.

37. Brown letters, March 2, 1917. This long letter has been much edited in the Bahlinger edition.

38. Brown letters, March 14, 1917.

39. Brown letters, February 23, 1917, and Monday 11 P.M. [n.d., March 5?].

40. Brown letters, March 14, 1917.

41. Brown letters, March 17, 1917.

42. Brown letters, March 26, 1917.

43. Glynn County Deeds, 3-O, 50.

44. His birthdate is given as 1889 in such official biographies as the *National Cyclopaedia;* however, his obituary says 1890, whereas a family-generated pedigree of Fletcher Garrison Hall gives 1891.

45. *New York Times,* July 16, 1961.

46. Details of Kingsland Macy's life can be found in *National Cyclopaedia of American Biography* (New York: James T. White & Co., 1930) 47:200; *New York Times,* July 16, 1961.

47. Kingsland Macy to P. Chauncey Anderson, January 29, 1919. Courtesy of Kingsland Macy Jr.

48. See P. Chauncey Anderson to W. Kingsland Macy, September 16, 1919; WKM to P. Chauncey Anderson, September 18, 1919, W. Kingsland Macy Papers, New York State Library, Albany, N.Y.

49. Jekyll Island Authority minutes, February 20, 1957, Jekyll Island Authority Records. Telephone interview with Peter Asher, October 13, 1997.

Chichota

1. Contract between Richard Butler, American Executive Committee for the Statue of Liberty, and D. H. King Jr., Mumford Moore Collection, Statue of Liberty Committee, copy provided by Carole Perrault.

2. *Engineering News and American Contract Journal,* November 1886, 323.

3. Dun Collection, vol. 385:1300 A/19, A/85.

4. The last two references, which are less well known, are taken from the *New York Daily Tribune,* February 18, 1895, p. 1.

5. *Newport Daily News,* January 17, 1894. King owned the Newport property until 1903.

6. Hyde to Baker, May 22, 1895, Hyde Papers.

7. *New York Daily Tribune,* February 17, 1895.

8. Ibid., February 18, 1895.

9. *New York Times,* September 24, 1895, p. 8.

10. The address for the Hotel Renaissance is alternatively given as 512 Fifth Avenue and 10 West Forty Third Street. Presumably it stood on the corner of these two streets.

11. See *New York Daily Tribune,* January 25, 1896.

12. Henry Hyde to David H. King, April 3, 1895, Hyde Papers.

13. See G. Whyte Smith to John Hill, December 25, 1895, and King to Hyde, December 29, 1895, Hyde Papers; Executive Committee Minutes, April 21, 1896; Hyde to Grob, December 15, 1896, Hyde Papers; Hyde to King, December 28, 29, 1896, Hyde Papers.

14. Hyde to King, February 10, 1897, Hyde Papers.

15. Hyde to King, May 4, 1897, Hyde Papers.

16. King to Grob, June 2, 1897, Hyde Papers.

17. Hyde to King, June 15, 1897, Hyde Papers.

18. Ma to Caleb; no date given, but it must about been written between June 10 and 12, 1897, or thereabout; Hyde Papers.

19. Hyde to Gifford, July 2, 1897, Hyde Papers.

20. King to Hyde, July 14, 1897, Hyde Papers.

21. Hyde to W. H. McIntyre, July 24, 1897, Hyde Papers.

22. These lots had once belonged to Joseph Pulitzer, who had conveyed them to Hyde. See F. M. Scarlett to Alfred W. Jones, December 9, 1944, Sea Island Files.

23. Hyde to Baker, August 8, 1897, Hyde Papers.

24. Baker to Hyde, August 10, 1897, Hyde Papers.

25. Grob to Hyde, September 8, 1897, Hyde Papers

26. Grob to Hyde, December 27, 1897, Hyde Papers. On the artesian well, see Grob to Hyde, October 16, 1897, Hyde Papers; and Grob to King, September 11, 1897, Grob Letter Book 1.

27. Hyde to Baker, January 10, 1898, Hyde Papers.

28. See Grob to J. C. Carter, between May 22 and 26, 1898; Grob Letter Book 1; Falk to D. H. King Jr., September 15, 1898, Grob Letter Book 1.

29. Hyde to Baker, January 10, 1898, Hyde Papers.

30. Baker and King to Gillette, April 9, 1898, Grob Letter Book 1.

31. Hyde to Baker, July 7, 1897, Hyde Papers.

32. Grob to Baker, April 14, 1898, Grob Letter Book 1. The rapprochement of Struthers and King is also suggested by the fact that Struthers had taken care of ordering citrus trees for King. See Grob to J. C. Carter, April 13, 1898, Grob Letter Book 1.

33. Falk to King, October 3, 1898, Grob Letter Book 1.

34. Grob to King, May 1, 1899, Grob Letter Book 2.

35. Grob to Lanier, October 8, 1899; Grob to Ferguson, October 22, 1899; Grob to W. H. Kay, November 18, 1899, Grob Letter Book 2.

36. See Falk to Struthers, December 4, 1899, and Grob to King, December 9, 1899, Grob Letter Book 2.

37. *Brunswick Times-Call,* March 13, 1901.

38. See *National Cyclopaedia,* 24:274; *Men and Women of America: A Biographical Dictionary of Contemporaries* (New York: L. R. Hamersly & Co., 1910), 723.

39. See Grob to Gould, December 20, 1900; Gould to Grob; Grob to Gifford, December 26, 1900, all in Grob Letter Book 2.

40. See Grob to Gifford, December 26, 1900, Grob Letter Book 2.

41. Edwin P. Hoyt, *The Goulds: A Social History* (New York: Weybright and Talley, 1969), 222–23.

42. See *New York Times,* October 27, 1892, p. 5; Hoyt, 122.

43. For Count Boni's comment's, see *How I Discovered America: Confessions of the Marquis Boni de Castellane* (New York: Alfred A. Knopf, 1924), 30, 114.

44. Ernest Stires to Richard Everett, no date [c. 1966], courtesy of Liesel Boettcher. Although Stires's name does not appear in the guest register for the date in question, it was not unusual for guests arriving before the official season to fail to register.

45. Grob to Cornelius Bliss, March 25, 1900, Grob Letter Book 2.

46. *Brunswick Times-Call,* April 30, 1901.

47. Reminiscences of Freddie Clark, Jekyll Island Museum.

48. *Brunswick Times-Call,* January 21, 1901.

49. Grob to Lanier, March 29, 1901, Grob Letter Book 2.

50. See Grob to W. S. Gurnee, March 30, 1901, Grob Letter Book 2, and Record of Shares. At the closing of the club in 1942, Lawrence R. Condon, who would acquire all the property of the Gould estate, owned lots 33, 34, 35, and 38. Lot 32 had been used for the Shrady house. Lot 44, which did not adjoin his property, had evidently been sold prior to the death of Gould's son, Frank Miller Gould.

51. See Walter Blair to George Cowman, July 15, 1913, Cowman Papers; *Brunswick News,* March 16, 1915.

52. *Brunswick Times,* October 12, 1906.

53. *Brunswick News,* January 7, 1912.

54. *Edwin Gould: The Man and His Legacy* (New York: Edwin Gould Foundation for Children, 1986), 13.; see also *New York Times,* December 20, 1914, *Brunswick News,* January 17, 1914.

55. Club circular, December 11, 1913, McCormick Papers.

56. *Brunswick News,* January 7, 1914.

57. Ibid., January 7, 1913.

58. Ibid., January 11, 13, 1914.

59. *New York Times,* February 26, 1917; Hoyt, 271.

60. See Club Game Book, vol. 1, Jekyll Island Museum, entries for December 27, 29, 1916, and January 2, 5, and 13, 1917.

61. Brown letters, March 2, 1917.

62. All quotations concerning the incident, unless

otherwise indicated, are from *New York Times,* February 26, 1917, and *Brunswick News,* February 27, 1917.

63. Kate Brown to family, February 25, 1917, Brown letters. Her other comments on the incident are from this letter.

64. He came in 1921, 1924, 1926, and 1929.

65. Almira Rockefeller to Emma Rockefeller McAlpin, January 14, 1920, William Rockefeller Family Papers.

66. Cornelius Lee to Aldrich, February 29, 1928. Winthrop W. Aldrich Papers, Baker Library, Harvard.

67. Marian Maurice diary, January 5, 1941, Maurice Papers.

Pulitzer Cottage

1. Details of Pulitzer's early life are taken from *Biographical Dictionary,* 1123–28, *Men and Women of America,* 1356; *National Cyclopaedia,* 1:375; *Dictionary of American Biography,* 8: 260–63. See also Don C. Seitz, ed., *Joseph Pulitzer: His Life and Letters* (New York: AMS Press, [1970]); W. A. Swanberg, *Pulitzer* (New York: Charles Scribner's Sons, 1967); James Wyman Barrett, *Joseph Pulitzer and his World* (New York: Vanguard Press [c. 1941]); George Juergens, *Joseph Pulitzer and the New York World* (Princeton, N.J.: Princeton University Press, 1966).

2. *Dictionary of American Biography,* 8:261.

3. Quoted in Swanberg, 309.

4. Joseph to Lucille, January 31, 1892, Pulitzer Papers, Box 1889–1898.

5. See *Saint Louis Republican,* September 22, 1895; *Brunswick Times-Advertiser,* September 24, 1895.

6. Alfred Butes to H. Edward [*sic*] Ficken, October 10, 1895, Pulitzer Papers. The total check remitted was for $586.25, which also included similar services at Bar Harbor.

7. See statement of February 1898 in Pulitzer Papers. The total commission and expenses paid to Charles A. Gifford for the design and overseeing the completion of the residence totaled $1,260.40.

8. Hyde to Pulitzer, June 16, 1897, Hyde Papers.

9. "Specifications—Entire Work for Winter Residence of Joseph Pulitzer at Jekyl Island, Ga. Charles Alling Gifford, Architect," Pulitzer Papers.

10. Hyde to Caleb, January 26, 1898, Hyde Papers.

11. Charles A. Gifford to Alfred Butes, September 26, 1899, Pulitzer Papers.

12. E. G. Grob to C. A. Clifford [Gifford], November 21, 1899, Grob Letter Book 2.

13. E. G. Grob to Charles A. Gifford, December 27, 1899, Grob Letter Book 2.

14. Rose McManus to Mrs. Pulitzer, February 10, 1901, Pulitzer Papers.

15. Arthur H. Billing to Pulitzer, February 22, 1903, Pulitzer Papers.

16. Kate to J. P., March 1, 1904, Pulitzer Papers.

17. Bowen & Thomas to Joseph Pulitzer, February 21, 1903, Pulitzer Papers. The specifications for the addition to the house are in folder March 5–8, 1904, Pulitzer Papers. The cost of the new addition is specified to be $11,500, including materials and labor.

18. Kate to Joseph, March 19, 1906, Pulitzer Papers.

19. Jean Struthers to Joseph Pulitzer, February 1904 (Monday), Pulitzer Papers.

20. Kate to Joseph, March 19, 1906, Pulitzer Papers.

21. Kate to Joseph, March 23, 1906, Pulitzer Papers.

22. Frederic Baker to Hyde, March 25, 1898, Hyde Papers.

23. William H. McIntyre to Joseph Pulitzer, June 14, 1898, Pulitzer Papers; McIntyre to Grob, March 9, 1899, Hyde Papers; Grob to Joseph Stickney, April 3, 1899, Grob Letter Book 2; McIntyre to Stickney, April 7, 1899, Hyde Papers.

24. Kate to Joseph, April 16, 1908, Pulitzer Papers.

25. Joseph Pulitzer to Miss Emma, March 4, 1911, Pulitzer Papers.

26. See Tusby to Pulitzer, February 12, 1910; William Romain Paterson to Mr. Tusby, March 4, 1910, Pulitzer Papers.

27. *Brunswick News,* October 31, 1911, p. 1:4.

28. The price is included in a sworn affidavit by E. G. Grob and A. J. Crovatt, notarized on March 26, 1924, used to estimate the value of the Maurice house in settling C. S. Maurice's estate. Maurice Papers.

29. See Glynn County Deeds, 3–6, p. 205. Ralph Pulitzer resigned on February 16, 1914, but the leasehold is not assigned to Albright until February 25.

30. His partner was Judge William Henry. See Birge Albright, "John Joseph Albright (1848–1931): His Con-

tribution to the Industry and Culture of the Niagara Frontier" (Honors essay, Harvard College, 1957), 70. Birge Albright is the son of Dr. Fuller Albright and the grandson of John J. Albright.

31. Information on Albright's life is found in the Birge Albright thesis and *National Cyclopaedia,* 51:550–51.

32. Albright, 71.

33. *National Cyclopaedia,* 3:183; Albright, 72. Barber was also president of the Trinidad Asphalt Company, incorporated in 1888.

34. See J. N. Larned, *A History of Buffalo* (New York: Progress of the Empire State Company, 1911), 1:238.

35. Albright, 71.

36. Ibid., 72, 98.

37. Prospectus of the Niagara Falls Hydraulic Company, 1853, quoted in Albright, 93.

38. Albright, part 3, 94.

39. Larned, 1:279–80.

40. The family contends that this is the case, and the story is recounted in Birge Albright's thesis, though the Smith College archives failed to turn up any documentation to confirm this story. It is true, however, that Susan Gertrude Fuller, a Smith College graduate in 1891, became the tutor of the Albright children. Ruth Albright, her primary charge, graduated from Smith College in 1900. In addition, two of her own daughters, Elizabeth and Susan, graduated from Smith in 1921 and 1930, respectively.

41. "In Memoriam, Susan Fuller Albright 1891, died June 19, 1928," Smith College Archives.

42. Susan F. Albright to Mrs. Maurice, November 19, 1900, Maurice Papers.

43. Albright, part 3, 101.

44. Ibid.

45. Ibid.

46. Susan Albright Reed to June McCash [n.d., 1989].

47. Susan Albright Reed to June McCash, January 1, 1989.

48. *Buffalo Evening News,* June 5, 1934.

49. See "In Memoriam"; Annual Reports of the President of Smith College, 1899–1900, 1900–1901; Catalogue of Smith College, 1925–26, November 1926, Northampton, Mass.; Albright, part 3, 94.

50. Albright, part 3, 95.

51. Ibid., part 3, 96.

52. Ibid., part 3, 97.

53. Ibid.

54. Alfred Noyes, *Two Worlds for Memory* (Philadelphia: Lippincott, 1953), 217.

55. Albright, part 3, 97.

56. Susan Albright Reed to June Hall McCash [n.d. 1989].

57. Albright, part 3, 102.

58. E. G. Grob to Miss Marian, August 2, 1928, Maurice Papers.

59. Conveyance from sheriff of Glynn County to Jekyll Island Club conveying Albright property, taxes levied, Glynn County Deed Book 4-L, 689.

60. Susan Albright Reed to June McCash, December 13, 1988. See also Susan Albright Reed to Joseph Pulitzer Jr., [n.d.] Jekyll Island Museum. The mansion in Buffalo, located on a circle known as Queen Anne's Gate, was modeled on St. Catherine's Court in England and was built in 1907 to replace an earlier house that had burned in 1901.

61. See Jekyll Island Authority minutes, June 23, 1951.

Mistletoe

1. A summary of Porter's life and achievements can be found in the *National Cyclopaedia,* 29:503, and the *Dictionary of American Biography,* 3:228.

2. Information on Annie de Camp Hegeman Porter is based on family genealogical information. See the Hegeman Bible, printed in Dutch and donated by Mrs. Porter to the New York Historical Society.

3. Adelaide Mellier Nevin, *The Social Mirror: A Character Sketch of the Women of Pittsburgh and Vicinity During the First Century of the County's Existence* (Pittsburgh: T. W. Nevin, 1888), 88–89.

4. Nevin, 89.

5. Grob to Julia W. Anderson, August 23, 1898, Grob Letter Book 1.

6. *Brunswick Call,* April 6, 1899, p. 1.

7. Grob to H. K. Porter, January 20, 1900, Grob Letter Book 2.

8. See Grob to George Bleistein, April 2, 1900, and April 12, 1900, Grob Letter Book 2. This lot is also referred to as the Samuel Thorne lot.

9. See Grob to Charles A. Gifford, June 30, 1900, Grob Letter Book 2.

10. Grob to Porter, November 16, 1900, Grob Letter Book 2.

11. The estimated cost of the Porter house is taken from a sworn affidavit by E. G. Grob and club lawyer A. J. Crovatt, notarized on March 26, 1924; Maurice Papers.

12. Grob to Porter, January 20, 1901, Grob Letter Book 2.

13. Grob to H. K. Porter, November 26, 1900; also Grob to Porter, December 22, 1900, Grob Letter Book 2.

14. Nevin, 88.

15. Grob to Nelson W. Aldrich, December 9, 1912, Winthrop W. Aldrich Papers.

16. The price of the cottage is taken from the sworn affidavit of E. G. Grob and A. J. Crovatt on March 26, 1924; Maurice Papers.

17. See McCash and McCash, 6–7.

18. *Dictionary of American Biography* Supplement 2, 105; *New York Times,* June 12, 1938.

19. *New York Times,* June 12, 1938. On his graduation with honors, see *Harper's Weekly* 32 (October 26, 1889): 859–60.

20. Concerning his trip across Peru and his bear hunts in the Rockies, see *Harper's Weekly* 32: 859–60.

21. John Claflin, *A Letter of John Claflin to His Children,* July 24, 1918 (New York: Privately printed, 1925), 11.

22. Dun Collection, vol. 397:201c.

23. *New York Daily Tribune,* November 15, 1885, p. 7.

24. *New York Times,* June 12, 1938.

25. *Harper's Weekly* 32:859–60.

26. *New York Daily Tribune,* October 29, 1898, p. 1. On Claflin's fiscal stance, see *New York Daily Tribune,* October 31, 1898, p. 3.

27. Claflin, 19.

28. See McCash and McCash, 157.

29. Claflin to Maurice, January 27, 1908, Maurice Papers.

30. Claflin, 14.

31. Ibid., 18.

32. *Biographical Dictionary,* 1:162.

33. Claflin, 23.

34. James to Maurice, November 3, 1920, Maurice Papers.

35. In June 1947, prior to the state of Georgia's condemnation proceedings against the island, she made a de-tailed inventory and valuation of the cottage's contents, perhaps for tax purposes. Inventory in Sea Island Files.

36. *Atlanta Constitution,* July 22, 1956, Jekyll Island Authority Minutes, April 15, 1957.

37. Jekyll Island staff meeting notes, March 2, 1977, Jekyll Island Museum.

Cherokee

1. Executive Committee Minutes, 1904, Jekyll Island Museum.

2. For a description of this architectural style, see Virginia and Lee McAlester, *A Field Guide to American Houses* (New York: Alfred A. Knopf, 1986), 397–407.

3. *National Cyclopaedia,* 7:271.

4. *New York Times,* December 1, 1907, 11.

5. George Frederick Shrady, *General Grant's Last Days. With a Short Biographical Sketch of Dr. Shrady* (New York: Privately printed [De Vinne Press], 1908), 5.

6. *Dictionary of American Biography,* 9, pt. 1:132.

7. George F. Shrady Jr., a physician like his father, was for a time coroner of New York City. His brother, Henry, was a sculptor. See *New York Times,* December 25, 1914, p. 17.

8. *New York Times,* January 8, 1892, p. 8, December 14, 1892, p. 10; February 8, 1893, p. 9.

9. *New York Times,* June 10, 1922, 13.

10. *Edwin Gould,* 25. It should be noted that Edwin Gould's wife, Sally, worked with her mother at the Messiah Home, and both women were serving on its board at the time of Edwin Jr.'s death (33).

11. Lydia French to Marian Maurice, February 16, 1924, Maurice Papers.

12. Details of Dr. James's career and public service are from an excerpt from the *National Cyclopaedia,* 21: 26–27, and from Oliver Burr James, April 15, 1952; private collection of Henry H. Anderson Jr.

13. Memoir of Oliver Burr James, April 15, 1952.

14. *New York Times,* April 9, 1927, p. 18.

15. Walter B. James to C. S. Maurice, April 16, 1918, Maurice Papers.

16. Walter B. James to C. S. Maurice, April 1, 1920, Maurice Papers.

17. Walter B. James to C. S. Maurice, April 12, 1920, Maurice Papers.

18. Walter B. James to Cyrus McCormick, February 23, 1923, McCormick Papers.

19. Joseph Collins, obituary notice in the *New York Academy of Medicine* 3 (1927): 444.

20. *New York Times,* April 7, 1827, p. 25. There is little reason to doubt this account of his having taken ill while at Jekyll, in light of the fact that Dr. James and his wife customarily spent their winters there. It should be noted, however, that the guest register does not include his name for this season.

21. Included in a letter from A. L. Berthet to Cyrus H. McCormick, May 19, 1927, McCormick Papers.

22. Berthet to McCormick, May 19, 1927, McCormick Papers.

23. *New York Academy of Medicine* 3 (1927): 444.

24. R. T. Crane Jr. to Winthrop W. Aldrich, March 8, 1929, Winthrop W. Aldrich Papers.

25. Memoir of Oliver Burr James, Anderson Collection.

26. Ibid.

27. See *Atlanta Constitution,* July 24, 1956.

Goodyear Cottage

1. *National Cyclopaedia,* 47:454. George F. Goodyear, *Goodyear Family History,* part 3 (Buffalo, privately printed, 1976), 1–23.

2. C. W. Goodyear, *The Bogalusa Story* (New York: Privately printed, 1950), 47–50. In G. F. Goodyear, *Family History,* part 3, 48, the salary is given as $10 per week. See also Thomas T. Taber III, *The Goodyears: An Empire in the Hemlocks,* Logging Railroad Era of Lumbering in Pennsylvania, book 5 (n.p.: 1971), 501–2.

3. C. W. Goodyear, *Bogalusa Story,* 47–50. G. F. Goodyear, *Family History,* part 4, 247–65.

4. Taber, 502.

5. Taber, 505.

6. H. W. Hall, ed., *Municipality of Buffalo, N.Y.,* 2:765; also Defebaugh, *History of the Lumber Industry in America,* quoted in Hall but worth looking at in the original; see also Taber, 505.

7. See G. F. Goodyear, *Family History,* part 3, 50.

8. It had been largely through his efforts that Cleveland was nominated for governor of New York in 1882, a post which ultimately led to his presidency three years later. See *New York Times,* April 17, 1911, p. 11.

9. C. W. Goodyear, *Bogalusa Story,* 52.

10. C. W. Goodyear to J. D. Lacey, March 8, 1905. Entire letter cited in C. W. Goodyear, *Bogalusa Story,* 37. The result of these plans was the construction of the largest sawmill in the world and the founding of Bogalusa, Louisiana. Neither of the Goodyear brothers would live to see these grandiose plans come to full fruition.

11. Executive Committee Minutes, April 10, 1903.

12. "The Work of Mssrs. Carrère & Hastings," *Architectural Record* 27, no. 1 (January 1910): 98.

13. *New York Times,* September 1, 1909, p. 9.

14. See the E. A. Penniman Map # 4, drawn up on December 6, 1906, Jekyll Island Museum.

15. G. F. Goodyear, *Family History,* part 4, 255–56.

16. See "The Work of Mssrs. Carrère & Hastings," 78–79. According to this article, the house was designed in 1903, the same year as the Jekyll Island cottage. The Buffalo mansion was torn down in 1938, and the indoor tennis courts were converted into office space for the local branch of the Red Cross. G. F. Goodyear, *Family History,* part 4, 51. Carrère and Hastings also did work in New York for Walter Jennings and Edwin Gould. See Curtis Channing Blake, "The Architecture of Carrère and Hastings" (Ph.D. diss., Columbia University, 1976).

17. G. F. Goodyear, *Family History,* part 3, 22.

18. Ibid, 52.

19. Taber, 511.

20. G. F. Goodyear, *Family History,* part 4, 247.

21. Charles Henry Goodyear died on April 16, 1911.

22. *Buffalo Courier,* October 18, 1915; *Buffalo Commercial,* October 18, 1915.

23. *Buffalo Commercial,* October 18, 1915.

24. G. F. Goodyear, *Family History,* part 4, 252, 263. Details of Frank Goodyear's life after the war are from this source.

25. Diary of Mrs. J. C. Etter, 1926–28, original owned by Howard Etter, copy in Jekyll Island Museum.

26. *New York Times,* October 14, 1930. The *Times* account contends that the explosion occurred at Jekyll Island in early summer; however, George F. Goodyear contends that the yacht blew up in Miami harbor "in late 1929." (*Family History,* part 4, 264.)

27. Accounts of what caused the accident vary. See *Buffalo Courier,* October 14, 1930; *Buffalo Times,* October 14, 1930; *Boston Transcript,* October 17, 1930.

28. See Jekyll Island Authority minutes, April 15, 1957.

29. Jekyll Island Authority minutes, December 17, 1973; February 11, 1974.

Crane Cottage

1. *New York Times,* January 9, 1913, p. 4.

2. *Dictionary of American Biography* 11, supplement 2: 128–30; *National Cyclopaedia,* 30:221–22.

3. *New York Times,* January 9, 1913, p. 3.

4. Ibid., November 8, 1931.

5. Details of Crane's life, unless otherwise indicated, are taken from *National Cyclopaedia,* 26:450–51; *Biographical Dictionary,* 1:209–10.

6. *National Cyclopaedia* 26:450–51.

7. Crane Company pamphlet, Jekyll Island Museum.

8. He also belonged to the Chicago Golf Club, the Chicago Yacht Club, and the South Shore Country Club. See John W. Leonard, ed., *The Book of Chicagoans: A Biographical Directory of Leading Living Men of the City of Chicago* (Chicago: Marquis, 1905), 163.

9. *National Cyclopaedia,* 26:450–51.

10. McCormick to Crane, February 7, 1911, McCormick Papers.

11. Crane to McCormick, February 22, 1911, McCormick Papers.

12. Telegram from McCormick to Grob, February 27, 1912; McCormick to F. A. Steuert, March 3, 1912, McCormick Papers.

13. Grob to Steuert, March 8, 1912, McCormick Papers.

14. Crane to McCormick, March 5, 1912, McCormick Papers.

15. Crane to McCormick, March 14, 1912, McCormick Papers.

16. R. B. Strassburger to McCormick, July 16, 1921, McCormick Papers.

17. Memo from Grob to Bourne, April 6, 1914, and April 11, 1914, Jekyll Island Museum; de Forest to Macy, April 17, 1914, and Bourne to Macy, April 15, 1914, Everett Collection, Museum of Coastal History.

18. See memo from Grob to E. G. Bourne, April 6, 1914, Jekyll Island Museum.

19. Richard Pratt, *David Adler: The Architect and His Work* (Philadelphia: M. Evans and Company, distributed

in association with J. B. Lippincott Company, 1970), 7.

20. In fact, when the house was showcased in *Architectural Record* in November 1924, it was listed as having been designed by Adler and Work. The partner's name was essential, since Adler remained unlicensed.

21. Pratt, 122. Concerning the relationship with Dangler, see also pp. 6–11.

22. Ibid., 22.

23. Cowman to Dangler, February 14, 1917, Cowman Papers.

24. F. Beeman to Henry C. Dangler, March 8, 1917; Cowman to Dangler, [March 3–12, 1917]; Cowman to the Wire and Tram Works, Louisville, Ky. March 26, 1917, Cowman Papers.

25. Edie Lewellyn to Mr. and Mrs. William B. McCash, July 22, 1986. Ms. Lewellyn is the granddaughter of Thomas Gage.

26. Cowman to Kay, August 4, 1917, Cowman Papers.

27. *Brunswick News,* August 28, 1917, p. 1.

28. See club register and Pratt, 7.

29. Pratt, 11.

30. Ibid., 7.

31. Executive Committee Minutes, March 8, 1917.

32. Based on "The Jekyll Island Club: Memories of a Lost Time," a television interview with Nancy Albright Hurd by Jim Darby, Brunswick Public Library.

33. All information about Higinbotham's death is from the *New York Times,* April 19, 1919, p. 1., col. 3.

34. *National Cyclopaedia,* 26:450–51.

35. *New York Times,* November 8, 1931.

36. March 8, 1929, Nelson W. Aldrich Papers, Library of Congress.

37. J. D. Compton to Bernon S. Prentice, October 23, 1947, Sea Island Files.

38. Report of Executive Committee, February 23, 1932.

39. See committee list, Jekyll Island Club folder, 1933, Aldrich Papers.

40. Brown letters, March 6, 1917.

41. Ibid., March 9, 1917.

42. *New York Times,* February 11, 1927, p. 19.

43. Susan Albright Reed to June McCash, December 13, 1988.

44. Interview with Aleathia Parland, June 3, 1970, Jekyll Island Museum.

45. *New York Times,* November 8, 1931.

46. *New York Herald Tribune,* March 24, 1941.

47. See Jekyll Island Authority minutes, January 15 and 16, 1954.

48. See *Atlanta Journal,* July 2, 1955. Brochures are located in the Jekyll Island Museum.

49. *Brunswick News,* December 15, 1960; *Atlanta Journal-Constitution,* May 28, 1961. See Jekyll Island Authority minutes, July 8, 1963.

Villa Ospo

1. *New York Times,* January 10, 1933.

2. Ibid., July 7, 1932, p. 5.

3. Jean Brown Jennings diary, February 4 and 6, 1926, courtesy of her granddaughter, Mrs. Jackson P. (Day Ely) Ravenscroft.

4. See Glynn County Deeds, 5-K, 232.

5. The cost of the cottage is based on a series of vouchers from the office of John Russell Pope to George Cowman. Cowman Papers, Jekyll Island Museum.

6. See letter from the director of the Smithsonian Institution's Bureau of American Ethnology, Frank H. H. Roberts Jr., to Theodosia Hotch, director of the Brunswick Public Library, Jekyll Island Museum.

7. Report of the annual meeting of the members, February 24, 1933, Jekyll Island Museum.

8. Ken deBellis to Mrs. L. L. Hurd, July 18, 1978, Jekyll Island Museum. DeBellis reports that Earl Hill, a black employee of long standing, told him the story of the "no tipping" incident.

9. Report of the annual meeting, February 24, 1933. The indoor tennis courts are, presumably, those referred to today as the Morgan Tennis Courts, although I have found no record of their particular association with J. P. Morgan or J. P. Morgan Jr. While the latter would succeed Mr. Jennings as president, this annual report seems to make it clear that the courts were completed under the Jennings administration.

10. Jennings diary, March 27, 1930.

11. Walter Jennings to Cyrus H. McCormick, March 28, 1930, file 195, McCormick Papers.

12. Houghton's remarks are attached to "Report of the Annual Meeting of the Members," February 1933.

13. Jennings diary, November 10, 1926.

14. *New York Times,* May 3, 1949, 25:1.

15. Glynn County Deeds 5-K, 231. Walter Jennings had also owned lots 25 and 26 at one time, but these he conveyed to the Jekyll Island Club on March 13, 1930. See Glynn County Deeds 4-E, 528. See also F. M. Scarlett to Alfred W. Jones, December 9, 1944, Sea Island Files.

16. *Brunswick News,* March 1, 1960; *Atlanta Journal-Constitution,* May 28, 1961.

Villa Marianna

1. The Club Register shows that he arrived on December 28, 1921, with Norman C, Lee, M. Gilmore and Kimball L. Finkenstaedt.

2. *History of the [Yale] Class of Nineteen Hundred Twenty,* ed. Morehead Patterson, class secretary (New Haven: Tuttle, Morehouse, and Taylor Company, [n.d.]), 193–94.

3. *New York Times,* January 14, 1945, p. 40, September 14, 1911, 14.

4. Ibid., November 16, 1922, p. 1.

5. Ibid., January 14, 1945, p. 40.

6. Ibid., November 18, 1924, p. 25.

7. Ibid.

8. See Richard O'Connor, *Gould's Millions* (Garden City, New York: Doubleday, 1962), 317–18. Jay Gould died on December 2, 1892, leaving his four oldest children as executors of his estate. In fact, it was George Gould, the oldest son, who almost single-handedly managed the estate, which was reduced considerably in value under his supervision. His death in 1922 sparked a series of legal battles that lasted until 1927. Even before his death, however, in 1919, his two youngest siblings, Frank and Anna, both of whom had been minor children at the time of their father's death, had already brought suit against the executors of the estate.

9. In fact, the estate would be split between Frank Miller Gould and his father's favorite charities, not least of which was the Edwin Gould Foundation for Children of which Frank was briefly president after his father's death. He resigned three months later to become chairman of the board, a post he held until his death. According to the biography published by the foundation, "he was never an active trustee and seldom attended." See

Edwin Gould, 18 n.

10. Jekyll Island Club Register, January 18, 1925.

11. Mogens Tvede was the guest of Walter Jennings in 1927 and signed the guest register on February 14, giving his home as Copenhagen. In all probability he is a relative of the well-known Danish architect Gotfred Tvede. He returned on February 28, 1929, as the guest of Frank Miller Gould. Marianne Gould, for whom the cottage was named, eventually married John W. McDonough, whom she would later divorce. She died at age thirty-one on January 21, 1957, leaving a young son, Jay Gould McDonough. See *New York Times,* January 22, 1957, p. 29.

12. For a description of this style, see McAlester, 417–29.

13. See Mogens Tvede to George Cowman, April 30, 1928, Cowman Papers, Jekyll Island Museum.

14. In point of fact, the article says "Mr. and Mrs. Edwin Gould," but it clearly intends to refer to the Frank Miller Goulds. The name is merely an error on the part of the reporter. *Brunswick News,* October 14, 1928.

15. Jennings diary, March 1, 1929.

16. The first time the cottage is mentioned by name is on February 14, 1930; however, the Goulds also registered on January 7, with no indication of where they stayed. It is possible that they stayed in the cottage but had not decided on the its name at that point.

17. See *Edwin Gould,* 18–19.

18. *New York Herald Tribune,* April 1, 1940.

19. Ibid., March 24, 1941.

20. Club brochure for 1942 season, Jekyll Island Museum.

21. Bernon Prentice to Jones, September 23, 1942, Sea Island Files.

22. *New York Times,* January 14, 1945, p. 40.

23. *New York Journal-American,* June 9, 1944.

24. *New York Times,* March 3, 1945; 26. The marriage, performed by Judge Walter C. Stevens, is recorded in the Bibb County marriage records, Book U, 472. Frank's first wife, Betsy Gould, would eventually remarry John Sturgeon III of Bluffton, South Carolina, and live until 1966.

25. A. W. Jones to Bernon Prentice, June 22, 1944, Sea Island Files. In fact, Helen Roosen Curran was forty at the time of her marriage to Frank Miller Gould. Pamela, who was evidently younger than she looked, was estimated to be only twelve by Ann Felton. She indicated that

Bill was the older of the two and was "very handsome." See note 31.

26. *New York Journal-American,* June 9, 1944.

27. Breezy Hill was the Macon estate of North Winship. It was demolished and now houses a subdivision known, curiously, as Winship North.

28. A. M. Harris to John Sloane, June 8, 1944, Sea Island Files.

29. Frank M. Gould to Alfred W. Jones, July 11, 1944, Sea Island Files.

30. A. M. Harris to Dear Sir [sample of letter sent to all remaining bondholders], August 1, 1944, Sea Island Files.

31. This information concerning his death comes from a telephone interview on July 12, 1996, with Ann Corn Felton, the daughter of Frank Miller Gould's Macon physician and a friend of both Frank and Helen Gould. According to Ann Felton, Helen Gould took up residence with the Corn family in Macon for a brief time after Gould's death.

32. *New York Times,* January 14, 1945, p. 40. According to this same account Gould was a sportsman who owned a stable of steeplechase horses and "was well known in hunting circles." In addition to the Jekyll Island Club, he belonged to the New York Yacht Club, the Racquet and Tennis Club, the Turf and Field Club, the Seminole Golf Club, and the Seawanhaka-Corinthian Yacht Club, memberships that reflect his wide sporting interests. According to this account, his two children Marianne (nineteen) and Edwin Jay (fifteen) became the primary heirs of his estate, although it was his new wife, Helen Gould, who inherited the Jekyll Island property.

33. [Alfred W. Jones] to A. B. Hossack, May 21, 1945, Sea Island Files.

34. [Alfred W. Jones] to Bernon S. Prentice, August 18, 1945, Sea Island Files.

35. Bernon Prentice to Alfred W. Jones, January 11, 1946, Sea Island Files.

36. Alfred W. Jones to L. P. Carmer, April 9, 1946, Sea Island Files.

37. "Circumstances leading up the condemnation proceedings of Jekyll Island, and of the taking over of the property by the State of Georgia," November 14, 1947, Sea Island Files.

38. Concerning the state of Georgia's efforts to take

over the island through condemnation proceedings, see McCash and McCash, 209–12.

39. Lawrence Condon to John J. Gilbert, 23 June 1947. Sea Island Files.

40. See the chapter on Hollybourne for additional details on the proceedings. See also "Circumstances leading up the condemnation proceedings of Jekyll Island," Sea Island Files.

41. *New York Times,* May 14, 1973, p. 34; *Southampton Press,* May 17, 1973, p. 2.

42. Information based on interviews with Etienne Elfer Jr. and Yank Moore, May 2, 1996, Jekyll Island Authority minutes, and the diary of Roger Beedle, Jekyll Island Museum.

Afterword

1. The facilities at Jekyll Island were, of course, segregated in 1947, with the south end of the island set aside for African Americans and the north end designated for whites.

2. Helen Lefkowitz Horowitz, *Culture and the City: Cultural Philanthropy in Chicago from the 1880s to 1917* (Lexington: University Press of Kentucky, 1976).

WORKS CITED

Manuscript Collections

Aldrich Papers. Nelson W. Aldrich Papers. Library of Congress, Manuscripts Division, Washington, D.C.

W. Aldrich Papers. Winthrop W. Aldrich Papers. Baker Library, Harvard University Graduate School of Business Administration. Boston, Mass.

Brown Letters. Kate Brown Letters. Originals in possession of Katharine Green Owens. Copies in the Jekyll Island Museum. Jekyll Island, Ga.

Cohen Diary. Jacob Solis Cohen Diary. In possession of Charles L. Rosenthal.

Colonial Dames of American Collection, 965. "The Plantation Book of Richard Leake." "The Thomas Spalding Family." Georgia Historical Society. Savannah, Ga.

Cowman Papers. George Cowman Papers. Jekyll Island Museum. Jekyll Island, Ga.

Dun Collection. R. C. Dun Collection. Baker Library, Harvard University Graduate School of Business Administration. Boston, Mass.

Etter Diary. Ray Etter Diary. In possession of Howard Etter. Copy in Jekyll Island Museum. Jekyll Island, Ga.

Everett Collection. Richard Everett Collection. Museum of Coastal History. Saint Simons, Ga.

Foulke Papers. William D. Foulke Papers. Library of Congress Manuscripts Division. Washington, D.C.

Glynn County Official Records. Brunswick, Ga.
> Deeds and Mortgages
> Tax Digests, 1886–1948
> Wills and Appraisals
> Du Bignon Papers, Ordinary's Office

Grob Letter Books. Ernest Grob Letter Books. Jekyll Island Museum. Jekyll Island, Ga.

Hegeman Family Bible. New York Historical Society. New York, N.Y.

Hill Papers. James J. Hill Papers. James Jerome Hill Reference Library. Saint Paul, Minn.

Hyde Papers. Henry B. Hyde Papers. Baker Library, Harvard University Graduate School of Business Administration. Boston, Mass.

Jekyll Island Authority Minutes. Jekyll Authority Office. Jekyll Island, Ga.

Jekyll Island Club Records. Jekyll Island Museum. Jekyll Island, Ga.
> Executive Committee Meetings 1886–1919, Minutes
> Record of Shares
> Club Register, 1888–1942
> Game Books
> Faith Chapel Records
> Prospectus of the Jekyl Island Club, April 1, 1887
> Subscriptions List
> Constitution and By-Laws
> Report of the Executive Committee to the Annual Meeting of Stockholders, February 1930
> Report of the Annual Meeting of the Members, February 1933

Jekyll Island Museum Files. The museum maintains files on all Jekyll members and on various others associated in some way with Jekyll Island's history. The following files are cited in the notes:
> Roger Beedle File
> James A. Clark Family File

Charles A. Frumd File
Gordon McKay File
Staff Notes

Jennings Diary. Diary of Jean Brown Jennings. In possession of Mrs. Jackson P. Ravenscroft.

Liberty County. Superior Court Records, Deed Books. Hinesville, Ga.

Liebrecht Collection. Papers (copies) relating to the history of the du Bignon family on Jekyll Island and their descendants through the line of Josephine du Bignon Finney. In possession of Mrs. Lawrence Liebrecht.

McAlpin Correspondence and Diary. Emma Rockefeller McAlpin Correspondence and Diary. Rockefeller Archive Center. North Tarrytown, N.Y.

McCormick Papers. Cyrus Hall McCormick Jr. Papers. State Historical Society of Wisconsin. Madison, Wis.

McKay Papers. Gordon McKay Papers. Harvard University Library. Cambridge, Mass.

Macy Papers. W. Kingsland Macy Papers. New York State Library. Albany, N.Y.

Maurice Papers. Maurice Family Papers. Southern Historical Collection, Library of the University of North Carolina. Chapel Hill, N.C.

Pulitzer Papers. Joseph Pulitzer Papers. Rare Book and Manuscripts Library, Columbia University. New York, N.Y.

Randall Papers. Blanchard Randall Papers. Brune-Randall Collection. Maryland Historical Society Library. Baltimore, Md.

Rockefeller Papers. William Rockefeller Family Papers. Rockefeller Archive Center. North Tarrytown, N.Y.

Sea Island Company Files. Jekyll Island Files. Sea Island, Ga.

Struthers Collection. Struthers Family Papers. Photographs and other memorabilia. In possession of Jean O'Donnell.

Thompson Collection. Letters, photographs, and memoirs relating to Walter Rogers Furness Family. In possession of Wirt Thompson Jr.

Treat Diary. Florence Treat Diary. In possession of Amy McKay Kahler.

Willard Papers. Joseph E. Willard Papers. Library of Congress Manuscripts Division. Washington, D.C.

Newspapers

Atlanta Constitution
Atlanta Journal-Constitution
Boston Transcript
Brunswick Advertiser and Appeal
Brunswick Call
Brunswick Daily News
Brunswick Evening Call
Brunswick Journal
Brunswick News
Brunswick Times
Brunswick Times-Advertiser
Brunswick Times-Call
Buffalo Commercial
Buffalo Courier
Buffalo Evening News
Buffalo Times
Chicago Herald
Daily Georgian
Essex County Telegraph
Georgia Gazette
Jekyll's Golden Islander
London Times
Macon Telegraph
Newport Daily News
Newport Herald
New York Daily Tribune
New York Herald Tribune
New York Sun
New York Times
Norristown Herald
Philadelphia Bulletin
Philadelphia Evening Public Ledger
Philadelphia Inquirer
Philadelphia Press
Philadelphia Record
Republican and Savannah Evening Ledger
Saint Louis Republican
Savannah Morning News
Southampton Press
Springfield Republican
Stamford Advocate

Secondary Sources

Albright, Birge. "John Joseph Albright (1848–1931): His Contribution to the Industry and Culture of the Niagara Frontier." Honors essay, Harvard College, 1957.

Andreas, A. T. *History of Chicago from the Earliest Period to the Present Time.* 3 vols. 1884–86. Reprint, New York: Arno Press, 1975.

[Barber, Amy Louise]. "In Memoriam, Susan Fuller Albright 1981, died June 19, 1928." *Smith Alumnae Quarterly,* November 1928, 41.

Barrett, James Wyman. *Joseph Pulitzer and His World.* New York: Vanguard Press, 1941.

Barton, William. "Exhaust Fumes." *Stamford Power Squadron Inc.* April, May 1965.

Beedle, Roger. "Restoration of the Rockefeller House." See Beedle File, Jekyll Island Museum.

Biographical Dictionary of American Business Leaders. Edited by John H. Ingham. 3 vols. Westport, Conn.: Greenwood Press, 1983.

Blake, Curtis Channing. "The Architecture of Carrère and Hastings." Ph.D. diss., Columbia University, 1976.

Brown, Kate. *It's a Wonderfully Lovely Place: Jekyll Island as Seen Through Kate Brown's Fresh Eyes, The Letters of Kate Brown, February–March 1917.* Edited by Nanette Bahlinger. Jekyll Island: Jekyll Island Museum, 1992.

Burr, Aaron. *Memoirs of Aaron Burr with Miscellaneous Selections from His Correspondence.* Vol. 2. Edited by Matthew L. Davis. 1836. Reprint, Freeport, N.Y.: Books for Libraries Press, 1970.

Castellane, Marquis Boni de. *How I Discovered America: Confessions of the Marquis Boni de Castellane.* New York: Alfred A. Knopf, 1924.

Chestney, Mamie Jemison, comp. "Skeletons in the History of the Jemison and Boisfeuillet Families." Georgia Historical Society, Savannah, Ga.

"Christophe-Anne Poulain Du Bignon: A Compilation of Information on his life, on his ancestors, the Poulains of Brittainy; and on a few of his descendents." Copies of documents to Christophe Poulain du Bignon's life. In the private collection of Doris Finney Liebrecht.

Claflin, John. *A Letter of John Claflin to His Children, July 24, 1918.* New York: Privately printed, 1925.

Coleman, Kenneth. *Colonial Georgia: A History.* New York: Scribner's, 1976.

Collier, Peter, and David Horowitz. *The Rockefellers: An American Dynasty.* New York: Holt, Rinehart and Winston, 1976.

Collins, Joseph. "Walter James" [obituary tribute]. *New York Academy of Medicine* 3 (1927): 444.

Colonial Letters. See *General Oglethorpe's Georgia.*

Colonial Records of the State of Georgia. Edited by Allen D. Candler. 26 vols. Atlanta: Franklin Printing, 1904–16.

Coulter, E. Merton. *Thomas Spalding of Sapelo.* University, La.: University of Louisiana Press, 1940.

Defebaugh, James Elliott. *History of the Lumber Industry in America.* Chicago: American Lumber Man, 1906.

De Freitas, Elaine. *Nathaniel Kellogg Fairbank.* Privately printed, 1980.

Dictionary of American Biography. 22 vols. New York: Charles Scribner's Sons, 1928–58.

Edwin Gould: The Man and His Legacy. New York: Edwin Gould Foundation for Children, 1986.

Egmont Journal. See *Journal of the Earl of Egmont.*

Entry of Claims for Georgia Landholders, 1733–1755. Compiled by Pat Bryant. Atlanta: State Printing Office, 1975.

Fauber, J. Everette. "Captain Horton's House on Jekyll Island Georgia: Research Report and a Proposal for Restoration." Prepared for the Jekyll Island State Park Authority, April 10, 1967. Copy in Jekyll Island Museum.

Furness, Fairman Rogers. "Memoir." See Thompson Collection.

General Oglethorpe's Georgia: Colonial Letters 1733–1743. Edited by Mills Lane. Savannah: Beehive Press, 1975.

Gilbert, Paul Thomas, and Charles Lee Bryson. *Chicago and Its Makers.* Chicago: F. Mendelsohn, 1929.

Gildersleeve, Virginia Crocheron. *Many a Good Crusade: Memoirs.* New York: Macmillan, 1954.

Goodyear, C. W. *The Bogalusa Story.* New York: Privately printed, 1950.

Goodyear, G. F. *Goodyear Family History.* 4 vols. Buffalo, N.Y.: Privately printed, 1976.

Hall, Henry Wayland, ed. *Municipality of Buffalo, N.Y.* Vol. 2. New York: Lewis Historical Publishing Co., 1923.

History of the [Yale] Class of Nineteen Hundred Twenty. Edited by Morehead Patterson, class secretary. New Haven: Tuttle, Morehouse, and Taylor Company, n.d.

Hofman, Eric. *Steam Yachts.* Lymington, Hampshire, U.K.: Nautical Publishing Company, 1970.

Hornsby, Stephen J. "The Gilded Age and the Making of Bar Harbor." *Geographic Review* 83 (1993): 455–68.

Howell, Clark. *History of Georgia.* Vol. 2. Chicago and Atlanta: S. J. Clarke, 1926.

Hoyt, Edwin P. *The Goulds: A Social History.* New York: Weybright and Talley, 1969.

Ivers, Larry E. *British Drums on the Southern Frontier: The Military Colonization of Georgia: 1733–1749.* Chapel Hill: University of North Carolina Press, 1974.

James, Oliver Burr. Unpublished memoir. In private collection of Henry H. Anderson.

James, William. *Letters of William James.* 2 vols. Edited by his son, Henry James. Boston: Atlantic Monthly Press, 1920.

"Jekyll Native Returns." Interview with E. P. Courier. *Jekyll's Golden Islander,* November 6, 1975.

Jennings, Hennen. *The Gordon McKay Bequest.* N.p.: privately printed, n.d. A copy may be found in the McKay Papers.

Johcich, Geraldine M. *The Sane Positivist: A Biography of Edward L. Thorndike.* Middletown, Conn.: Wesleyan University Press, [1968].

Journal of the Earl of Egmont: Abstract of the Trustees Proceedings for Establishing the Colony of Georgia. Edited by Robert G. McPherson. Athens: University of Georgia Press, 1962.

Journal of William Stephens 1737–1740. See Colonial Records, vol. 4.

Juergens, George. *Joseph Pulitzer and the* New York World. Princeton, N.J.: Princeton University Press, 1966.

Kaempffert, Waldemar, ed. *A Popular History of American Invention.* 2 vols. New York: Charles Scribner's Sons, 1924.

Klein, Maury. *The Great Richmond Terminal: A Study in Businessmen and Business Strategy.* Charlottesville: University Press of Virginia, 1970.

Konolige, Kit and Frederica. *The Power of Their Glory: America's Ruling Class: The Episcopalians.* New York: Wyden Books, 1978.

Larned, J. N. *A History of Buffalo.* New York: Progress of the Empire State Company, 1911.

Lawrence, Henry W. "Southern Spas: Source of the American Resort Tradition." *Landscape* 27:2 (1983): 1–12.

Lawson, Thomas W. *Frenzied Finance.* Vol. 1, *The Crime of Amalgamated.* New York: Ridgway-Thayer Company, 1905.

Lee, Clermont, "Research Data Used in Planning the Redevelopment of the McKay-Rockefeller-Jenkins Cottage Grounds." January 1970. Jekyll Island Museum.

"Legal Aspects and Educational Results in the Harvard-Technology Decision." *Harvard Graduates' Magazine* 26 (1918): 391–403.

Leonard, John W., ed. *The Book of Chicagoans: A Biographical Dictionary of Leading Living Men of the City of Chicago.* Chicago: Marquis, 1905.

Leverette, William E. Jr. "Simple Living and the Patrician Academic: The Case of William James." *Journal of American Culture* 6 (1983): 36–43.

Linley, John. *The Georgia Catalog, Historic American Buildings Survey: A Guide to the Architecture of the State.* Athens: University of Georgia Press, 1982.

McAlester, Virginia and Lee. *A Field Guide to American Houses.* New York: Alfred A. Knopf, 1986.

McCall, Hugh. *The History of Georgia.* 1811–16. Reprint. Atlanta: A. B. Caldwell, 1909.

McCash, William Barton, and June Hall McCash. *The Jekyll Island Club: Southern Haven for America's Millionaires.* Athens: University of Georgia Press, 1989.

Martin, C. Brenden. "Selling the Southern Highlands: Tourism and Community Development in the Mountain South." Ph.D. diss., University of Tennessee, 1997.

Maurice, Charlotte Marshall, and Charles Stewart Maurice. *Jekyl Island: Some Historic Notes and Some Legends, Collected by Charlotte Marshall Maurice, and a Brief Outline of the Early Days of the Jekyl Island Club Made by Charles Stewart Maurice.* Privately printed, n.d.

Memorial of Charlotte Marshall Holbrooke Maurice, Regent and Founder of Tioga Chapter, D.A.R. Athens, Pa.: Privately printed, 1909.

Men and Women of America: A Biographical Dictionary of Contemporaries. New York: L. R. Hamersley & Co., 1910.

Mercantile and Industrial Review. Issued by the Traffic Department. Atlanta: Birmingham & Atlanta Railroad, 1909.

Moore, Francis. *A Voyage to Georgia Begun in the Year 1735*. London, 1744. Reprinted in *Collections of the Georgia Historical Society*, vol. 1. Savannah: Printed for the Society, 1840.

National Cyclopaedia of American Biography. 63 vols. Clifton, N.J.: James T. White & Co., 1898–1984.

Nevin, Adelaide Mellier. *The Social Mirror: A Character Sketch of the Women of Pittsburgh and Vicinity During the First Century of the County's Existence*. Pittsburgh: T. W. Nevin, 1888.

Nevins, Allan. *John D. Rockefeller: The Heroic Age of American Enterprise*. New York: Charles Scribner's Sons, 1940.

Noyes, Alfred. *Two Worlds for Memories*. Philadelphia: Lippincott, 1953.

O'Connor, Richard. *Gould's Millions*. Garden City, N.Y.: Doubleday, 1962.

Official Records of the Union and Confederate Navies of the War of the Rebellion. Washington: Government Printing Office, 1894–1922.

O'Gorman, James F. *The Architecture of Frank Furness*. Philadelphia: Philadelphia Museum of Art, 1973.

Pierce, Bessie Louise. *A History of Chicago*. Chicago: University of Chicago Press, 1975.

"Plantation Book of Richard Leake." See Colonial Dames of America Collection 965, box 11, folder 124.

Poor, Henry V. *Manual of the Railroads of the United States for 1882*. New York: H. V. and H. W. Poor, 1882.

———. *Manual of the Railroads of the United States for 1883*. New York: H. V. and H. W. Poor, 1883.

Pratt, Richard. *David Adler: The Architect and His Work*. Philadelphia: M. Evans and Company, 1970.

Revolutionary Records of the State of Georgia. Edited by Allen D. Candler. Atlanta: Franklin-Turner Company, 1908.

Ruple, Steven D. "Archeology of the Horton House." Master's thesis, University of Florida, 1976.

Scharf, J. Thomas, and Thompson Wescott. *History of Philadelphia, 1609–1884*. Philadelphia: L. H. Everts, 1884.

Scully, Vincent J. *The Shingle Style and the Stick Style: Architectural Theory and Design from Downing to the Origins of Wright*. New Haven: Yale University Press, 1970.

Seitz, Don C., ed. *Joseph Pulitzer: His Life and Letters*.

New York: AMS Press, 1970.

Shaler, N. S. *The Autobiography of Nathaniel Southgate Shaler, With a Supplementary Memoir by his Wife*. Boston and New York: Houghton Mifflin, 1909.

Sherwood, Henry F. *The Story of Stamford*. New York: States History Company, n.d.

Shi, David E. *The Simple Life: Plain Living and High Thinking in American Culture*. New York: Oxford University Press, 1985.

Shrady, George Frederick. *General Grant's Last Days, With a Short Biographical Sketch of Dr. Shrady*. New York: Privately printed [De Vinne Press], 1908.

"Skeletons in the history of the Jemison and Boisfeuillet Families." Compiled by Mamie Jemison Chestney, 1964. Georgia Historical Society.

Smith College Annual Reports. Printed by the college. Smith College Archives, Northampton, Mass.

Smith, Julia Floyd. *Slavery and Rice Culture in the Low Country Georgia, 1750–1860*. Knoxville: University of Tennessee Press, 1985.

Smith, William Beninck, and Elizabeth Stouffer. *Harvard University History of Named Chairs: Sketches of Donors and Donations, University Professorships and Those of the Faculty of Arts and Sciences 1721–1991*. Cambridge, Mass.: Secretary to the University, 1991.

Spalding, Phinizy. *Oglethorpe in America*. Chicago: University of Chicago Press, 1977.

Strassburger, Ralph Beaver. *The Strassburger Family and Allied Families of Pennsylvania, Being the Ancestry of Jacob Andrew Strassburger, Esquire, of Montgomery County, Pennsylvania*. Gwynned Valley, Pa. Printed for private collection, 1922.

Swanberg, W. A. *Pulitzer*. New York: Charles Scribner's Sons, 1967.

Taber, Thomas T., III. *The Goodyears: An Empire in the Hemlocks*. Logging Railroad Era of Lumbering in Pennsylvania, book 5. N.p., 1971.

Taylor, Paul S. *Georgia Plan: 1732–1752*. Berkeley: University of California Press, 1972.

Thomas, Kenneth H., Jr. "The Sapelo Company: Five Frenchmen on the Georgia Coast, 1789–1794." *The Proceedings and Papers of the Georgia Association of Historians* 10. Edited by W. Benjamin Kennedy and S. Fred Roach. Georgia Association of Historians, 1989.

Timberlake, Craig. *The Bishop of Broadway: The Life and*

Works of David Belasco. New York: Library Publishers, 1954.

Turner, Martha. "Christophe Poulain du Bignon: The Making of an Emigré." Lecture sponsored by the Jekyll Island Museum, May 20, 1989.

Tuthill, W. B. *The Suburban Cottage: Its Design and Construction*. New York: William T. Comstock, 1885.

Vanstory, Burnette. *Georgia's Land of the Golden Isles*. Athens: University of Georgia Press, 1956.

Wells, Tom Henderson. *The Slave Ship Wanderer*. Athens: University of Georgia Press, 1968.

Wesley, John. *The Journal of John Wesley*. Edited by Nehemiah Curnock. London: Epworth Press, 1938.

Wister, Owen. "Horace Howard Furness: A Short Memoir." *The Harvard Graduates' Magazine,* December 1912.

"Work of Mssrs Carrère & Hastings." *Architectural Record* 27, no. 1 (January 1910): 4–120.

Wylly, Charles Spalding. *Annals and Memoirs*. Brunswick, 1920.

INDEX

This book is set in 10 on 13 Berkeley Oldstyle Medium
with Rennie Mackintosh display and ornaments.

Berkeley Oldstyle was designed in 1938 by the imminent
American type designer Frederic W. Goudy and revised
by Tony Stan in 1983 for the International Typeface Corporation.
Berkeley is a modern typeface with flat serifs and
slightly inclining italic. It is considered one of Goudy's
finest book faces.

Rennie Mackintosh is based on the hand lettering of Scottish
architect Charles Rennie Mackintosh (1868–1928). The ornaments
are inspired by architectural details and ornamentation
in Mackintosh's work.

The paper in this book meets the guidelines for permanence
and durability of the Committee on Production Guidelines for
Book Longevity of the Council on Library Resources.

Designed by Erin Kirk New
Composition by G&S Typesetters
Printed and bound by
Maple-Vail Book Manufacturing Group